T0240932

Lecture Notes in Computer Science 10844

Commenced Publication in 1973
Founding and Former Series Editors:
Gerhard Goos, Juris Hartmanis, and Jan van Leeuwen

Editorial Board

More information about this series at http://www.springer.com/series/7409

Samir Chatterjee · Kaushik Dutta
Rangaraja P. Sundarraj (Eds.)

Designing for a Digital and Globalized World

13th International Conference, DESRIST 2018
Chennai, India, June 3–6, 2018
Proceedings

 Springer

Editors
Samir Chatterjee
School of Information Systems
and Technology
Claremont Graduate University
Claremont, CA
USA

Rangaraja P. Sundarraj
Department of Management Studies
IIT Madras
Chennai, Tamil Nadu
India

Kaushik Dutta
Muma College of Business
University of South Florida
Tampa, FL
USA

ISSN 0302-9743 ISSN 1611-3349 (electronic)
Lecture Notes in Computer Science
ISBN 978-3-319-91799-3 ISBN 978-3-319-91800-6 (eBook)
https://doi.org/10.1007/978-3-319-91800-6

Library of Congress Control Number: 2018944300

LNCS Sublibrary: SL3 – Information Systems and Applications, incl. Internet/Web, and HCI

Printed on acid-free paper

This Springer imprint is published by the registered company Springer International Publishing AG
part of Springer Nature
The registered company address is: Gewerbestrasse 11, 6330 Cham, Switzerland

Preface

The interest in design science research in information systems continues to grow. The DESRIST conference series has played a pivotal role in building that interest and establishing a solid knowledge foundation for scholars and researchers. This volume contains full papers that were presented at DESRIST 2018 – the 13th International Conference on Design Science Research in Information Systems and Technology – held during June 3–6, 2018, at Chennai, India.

Over the years, DESRIST has brought together researchers and practitioners engaged in all aspects of design science research. As in previous years, scholars and design practitioners from various areas, such as information systems, business and operations research, computer science, and interaction designers, came together to discuss challenges and opportunities ahead. This year's conference was somewhat unique in that it was the first time that DESRIST was held in Asia, particularly in India, one of the rapidly growing economies of the world. It built on the foundation of 12 prior highly successful international conferences held in Claremont, Pasadena, Atlanta, Philadelphia, St. Gallen, Milwaukee, Las Vegas, Helsinki, Miami, Dublin, St. John, and Karlsrhue.

The theme for DESRIST 2018 was "Designing for a Digital and Globalized World." This year's conference acted as a major forum for the presentation of innovative information system ideas, approaches, developments, and research projects in the area of DSR theory and applications. It also served to facilitate the exchange of ideas between researchers and industry professionals. The latest issues and advancements in the area of IT and its applications that affect everyone around the globe were covered during the conference. We expect that the conference and its publications in this volume will be a trigger for further related research and technology improvements in information systems. DESRIST 2018 attracted researchers from Asia to submit their best work and present it at the conference, thereby making it a more globally inclusive community. The conference was organized around several main themes and tracks: DSR in Health Care, DSR in Cyber Security, DSR in Service Science, DSR for HCI, DSR in Data Science and Business Analytics, DSR Foundations, DSR and Emerging Ideas, DSR in Domain-Specific Applications, and DSR for ICT in Developing Countries. Each theme was headed by distinguished track chairs who managed the papers that were submitted in their respective tracks. In total, we received 96 submissions (61 full papers, 11 product and prototypes, and 24 research-in-progress papers). Each research paper was reviewed by a minimum of two referees. This Springer volume contains 24 full research papers with an acceptance rate of 39%. Research-in-progress papers and few papers designated as posters were made available digitally to attendees.

We would like to thank all the authors who submitted papers to the DESRIST 2018 conference. We hope the readers will find the papers as interesting and informative as we did. We would also like to thank all the track chairs, Program Committee members, and reviewers for their invaluable service. We would also like to thank the other members of the Organizing Committee, as well as the volunteers, whose dedication and effort helped bring about a successful DESRIST 2018 conference. Our special thanks go to Dr. Nargis Pervin for managing the submission system and papers for publication and to Anik Mukherjee for his tireless service as web master and with local arrangements. We would also like to thank the Indian Institute of Technology, Chennai for giving us access to their facilities and thank, all the sponsors for their support. We believe the papers in these proceedings provide many interesting and valuable insights into theory and practice of DSR. They open up new and exciting possibilities for future research in the discipline.

May 2018

Samir Chatterjee
Kaushik Dutta
Rangaraja P. Sundraraj

Organization

General Chairs

Alexander Maedche   Karlsruhe Institute of Technology (KIT), Germany
Jan vom Brocke   University of Liechtenstein, Liechtenstein
Alan Hevner   University of South Florida, USA

Program Chairs

Samir Chatterjee   Claremont Graduate University, USA
Kaushik Dutta   University of South Florida, USA
R. P. Sundarraj   Indian Institute of Technology Madras, India

Theme Chairs

DSR in Health Care

Monica Chiarini Tremblay   College of William & Mary, USA
Gondy Leroy   University of Arizona, USA

DSR in Cyber Security

Arunabha Mukhopadhya   Indian Institute of Management, Lucknow, India
Mia Plachkinova   The University of Tampa, USA

DSR in Service Science

Rahul Thakurta   XIMB, India
Jan Marco Leimeister   University of St. Gallen, Switzerland

DSR for Human–Computer Interaction

René Riedl   University of Applied Sciences Upper Austria
    and University of Linz, Austria
Agnis Stibe   ESLSCA Business School Paris, France

DSR in Data Science and Business Analytics

Atreyi Kankanhalli   National University of Singapore
Ozgur Turetken   Ryerson University, Canada

DSR Foundations

Mala Kaul   University of Nevada, Reno, USA
Shirley Gregor   Australian National University, Australia

DSR for Emerging Ideas

Alan Hevner   University of South Florida, USA
Shankar Prawesh   Indian Institute of Technology, Kanpur, India

DSR in Domain Specific Applications

S. Adhikari   University of Morotuwa, Sri Lanka
Paul Johannesson   Stockholm University, Sweden

DSR for ICT in Developing Countries

Yan Li   Claremont Graduate University, USA
Manoj Thomas   Virginia Commonwealth University, USA

Doctoral Consortium Chairs

Matti Rossi   Aalto University, Finland
Marcus Rothenberger   University of Nevada at Las Vegas, USA

Review Coordinators .

Nargis Pervin   Indian Institute of Technology Madras, India
Saji Mathew   Indian Institute of Technology Madras, India

Industry Chairs

Sathyanarayanan   Consulting Partner IBM, Asia Pacific Global
  Venkatraman   Technology Services

Local Arrangements Chairs

Nargis Pervin   Indian Institute of Technology Madras, India
Dixon Prem Daniel   Indian Institute of Technology Madras, India
Anik Mukherjee   Indian Institute of Technology Madras, India

Website

Nargis Pervin   Indian Institute of Technology Madras, India
Anik Mukherjee   Indian Institute of Technology Madras, India
Dixon Prem Daniel   Indian Institute of Technology Madras, India

Program Committee and Reviewers

Abdulaziz Albarrak
Abraham Bernstein
Ahmed Azam
Alan Yang
Albrecht Fritzsche
Ales Popovic
Alexander Herwix
Alexander Maedche
Alexia Athanasopoulou
Amir Haj-Bolouri
Amir Riaz
Amir Sereshki
Amit Deokar
Amy Connolly
Andreas Drechsler
Anik Mukherjee
Anna Rocca
Arash Barfar
Arthur Conklin
Arturo Castellanos
Au Vo
Avijit Sarkar
Avijit Sengupta
Badr Alsamani
Baidynath Biswas
Barbara Dinter
Bergholtz Maria
Bhattacharya Prasanta
Birgit Schenk
Caroline Lancelot-Miltgen
Cathal Doyle
Chakri Deverapali
Chaminda Thilak
Christine Legner
Christopher Jud
Clinton Daniel
Cristian Anastasiu
Deanna House
Dilruk Perera
Dirk S. Hovorka
Duaa Abaoud
Gerald Onwujekwe

Gladys Diaz
Goran Goldkuhl
Greg White
Gregor Shirley
Gunjan Mansingh
Hemant Jain
Henkel Martin
Hoang Nguyen
Iman Taani
Jae Park
Jalali Amin
Jeffrey Parsons
Johannesson Paul
John Effah
Jonas Sjostrom
Juell-Skielse Gustaf
K. Du
Kajanan Sangar
Kang Dae Youp
Kaul Mala
Khalid Alhayyan
Kristijan Mirkovski
Kweku-Muata
   Osei-Bryson
Leimeister Jan Marco
Leona Chandra Kruse
Li Yan
Magnus Hansen
Mahed Maddah
Manas Tripathi
Maram Almufareh
Mario Nadj
Mark De Reuver
Matthias Herterich
Mauli Dalal
Maung Sein
Mayda Alrige
Michael Feldmann
Michel Avital
Mike Seymour
Mohamed Hefny
Mohammad Mehri

Moritz Becker
Morteza Zihayat
Nicolas Prat
Norah Alharbi
Nurul Huda
Oyku Isik
Perera
Perjons
Philip Menard
Punit Ahluwalia
Raju Gottumukkala
Rajul Mehta
Ranbaduge Thilina
Rasmus Pederson
Ray Vaughn
Riad Alharbery
Roman Lukyanenko
Samaa Elnagar
Sangar Kajanan
Sangwook Ha
Sapumal Ahangama
Shahab Bayati
Shounak Pal
Somnath Bhattacharya
Stefan Morana
Stefan Seidel
Supunmali Ahangama
Szymon Furtak
Thanthriwatta Thilina
Thilak Chaminda
Thilina Thanthriwatta
Thilo Böhmann
Thomas Manoj
Thomas Chapman
Tobias Dehling
Tommy Morris
Troy Adams
Turetken Ozgur
Wai Mok
Xiaoying Xu
Ying Wang
Youcef Derbal

Contents

Advances in Data Science and Analytics

ICT for Development

Designing Cybersecurity

Design Applications

HCI and Design

Design Principles for Room-Scale Virtual Reality: A Design Experiment in Three Dimensions

Jonas Schjerlund$^{(\boxtimes)}$, Magnus Rotvit Perlt Hansen, and Josefine Gill Jensen

Department of People and Technology, Informatics, Roskilde University, Roskilde, Denmark
{jonassc,magnuha,gill}@ruc.dk

Abstract. Virtual reality hardware, and software tools that support developing for virtual reality applications, are rapidly maturing. Specifically, room-scale virtual reality hardware that lets users walk around in virtual environments is becoming increasingly easier to purchase and adopt. With this follows a need for researching potential design theories for how to design and evaluate this class of systems. We contribute with a nascent design theory containing a high-level conceptual framework of dimensions and design principles of how to design room-scale virtual reality applications that create engaging user experiences. We identify meta-requirements from kernel theories from the human-computer interaction paradigm and evaluate two different VR artefacts and their applicability. Two central, higher level design principles are derived from the evaluation.

1 Introduction

We live in a very exciting time for the virtual reality (VR) medium. The immense progress of VR technology within the last few years has manifested in the form of the release of high-end consumer-grade VR hardware products such as the Oculus Rift and HTC Vive [1]. Certain facets of modern VR technology provide unique challenges. For instance, recent years have seen the rise of so-called "room-scale" VR, wherein the user calibrates a physical space with the aid of sensors, which track the position of a head-mounted display (HMD) and potentially handheld motion-tracked controllers. This effectively allows the user to move around within a VR application using their physical body motion [2]. An example of room-scale VR technology would be the HTC Vive, which we use for our study.

Original VR applications did not contain this physical motion-tracking and as a result, room-scale VR designs must consider a whole new degree of spatiality. As opposed to more academically established Human-Computer Interaction (HCI) fields, current room-scale VR design paradigms and best practices are for the most part spread across an array of industry talks and lectures given at various development conferences (e.g. [3, 4]). Traditional WIMP-based (Window Icon Menu Pointer) design paradigms from interaction and user experience design will not, in many cases, translate directly, given the nature of the medium as a post-WIMP technology [5].

© Springer International Publishing AG, part of Springer Nature 2018
S. Chatterjee et al. (Eds.): DESRIST 2018, LNCS 10844, pp. 3–17, 2018.
https://doi.org/10.1007/978-3-319-91800-6_1

In the 1990s, researchers often spoke of VR from a perspective of immersion and presence [6–8] as an outcome that was highly for the user experience, pining for high-fidelity resolutions, graphics and tracking. As we have now reached a point where our hardware is powerful enough to allow for this [1], we have to ask: how do we actually use it in our designs? This should be an exciting opportunity for the field of Design Science Research and VR in general.

We explore the following research question: *"What are central design dimensions and design principles for room-scale virtual reality that can be used to design engaging virtual reality experiences?"*

This paper sets out to methodically explore the new opportunities for VR. To uncover how to design for room-scale VR, we need to solve a range of solution objectives, specifically: (1) find useful design choices and possibilities from other similar design areas, such as 2D interface design and 3D applications; (2) identify design possibilities for translating and conceptualizing movement in VR; (3) identify design possibilities for creating believable interactive feedback; (4) identify design possibilities for creating believable visual feedback; (5) identify a high-level framework of design dimensions that can capture the software and hardware elements of room-scale VR to the benefit of the user.

The paper is structured as a design theory contribution as described by Heinrich and Schwabe [9] and a nascent design theory [10, 11]: We first present related work on VR and similar fields and how this work can benefit from a Design Science Research approach. Then we identify central kernel theories that relate to VR to establish the dimensions that a room-scale VR framework can consist of. Then we propose our method that contain four conditions spread out over two VR artefacts. We propose three practical design principles for designing VR artefacts and explain the rationale of the two VR artefacts. We then evaluate and discuss the results and contribute to design theory by deriving two high-level design principles. We then conclude the paper and propose further research opportunities.

2   Related Work

Room-scale VR should be considered different from the more well-established seated VR paradigm, as traditionally VR technology has predominately focused on a stationary and seated experience [1]. Still, as VR research can be considered the super class of room-scale VR, traditional VR research can in many cases be applied to room-scale VR as well. For example, Bowman and Hodges [12] describe interaction techniques in VR in terms of "viewpoint motion control" of the camera and "selection and manipulation" of objects [12] that remain common VR interaction techniques today.

HCI research in general tends toward either "high-determinacy models with limited scope, or broadly scoped theories with low determinacy" [13, p. 5049]. VR research in particular tends toward the former; research articles usually identify a very specific, low-level issue, and document the design of a small-scale experiment that addresses it (e.g. [14–17]). While scientifically sound, typically there is little reflection on the design methodology behind the experiments themselves and how to generalize these into design theories. The gap of research here lay in high-level VR design guidelines that can clarify functionality and process of how to design and what to look out for.

3   Literature Review

In the following, we identify dimensions from existing kernel theories from the HCI domain and extract meta-requirements to solve the solution objectives. A cross-section of the literature relevant to VR and its relevance for the room-scale technology is condensed into three main dimensions: the 3D aspects (where) defined as spatiality [7, 18], the ways to interact with the 3D world (how) of interaction [19, 20], and the reasons and impact of interaction and movement (why) of narrative [7, 21].

3.1   Spatiality

Spatiality is defined as the environment that the user interacts with and explores while navigating and moving; it is very visually oriented and produces perspective emanating from the point of view of the user. An application containing a high level of spatiality will enhance the user's feeling of having a physical presence [2, 22] while experiencing the environment as "a space for action where events can take place" [23, p. 3] and the sensation of being there [23, 24]. Simply by having bodies, we become spatially aware creatures with a sense of direction in 3D space [7, 25]. This is particularly interesting in the context of room-scale VR, which allows the user to have tracking-based references to their head and hands (via the HMD and Vive controllers, respectively).

Taking a concrete example in the HTC Vive used in our study, a user's head is represented through the HMD, and the Vive has handheld controllers that track hand positions. Since physical motion translates directly to application input, a natural limitation in room-scale VR is the amount of calibrated physical space available. The use of an HTC Vive will allow the user to see so-called chaperone bounds: a transparent blue grid when approaching the edge of their calibrated space.

Spatiality is thus present as soon as the user engages in the experience. What is important to determine are such parameters as the user's size in relation to other objects in the interaction space, the location in 3D space and the distance to not only nearby objects, but also to faraway and non-reachable objects called the world space [26].

We identify the following meta-requirement (MR1) in relation to the dimension of spatiality: Spatiality is where the user navigates and moves to. The virtual space around the user will greatly influence the feeling of presence. For room-scale VR applications, the density of information and possibilities for interaction should be increased around the user and gradually decrease radially from the users' immediate interaction space.

3.2   Interaction

Interaction can be explained by addressing the question of how we interact [19] and is bound by user-intent. That is to say, for something to be considered an interaction, the user must have some explicit or implicit desire to achieve a change or response in the virtual space. Methods for interaction can be defined alongside a continuum of incongruent mapping where action and reaction is decoupled (e.g. the use of pressing buttons on a two-handed controller to use or move around) to natural mapping (HMD registering and responding to head and body movements, as well as Vive controllers that follow and map the natural movements of the user's hands) [18]. To support the feeling of spatial presence, controller mapping has been found to be more important than the HMD itself [27]. Mapping can be more concretely quantified with a degree of integration, which signifies the spatial congruence between an input device and its digital representation by comparing the ratio between the degrees of freedom in their movement [18, 28]. Using the HTC Vive of an example, you can move the HMD and controllers with six degrees of freedom in the physical world, which corresponds directly to how their virtual representations move inside the virtual application (this leaves them with a degree of integration of 1).

Interaction resides on a lower level (the specific possible interactions to manipulate data in the interface) and a higher level (the user's relation to the whole information space presented) [20] that focuses on the user's goal to generate understanding [20]. Examples of higher level of interaction include categories such as to select, explore, reconfigure, encode, abstract/elaborate, filter and connect [19].

Another type of interaction in VR is through manipulating and reconfiguring objects by moving and pressing buttons on the controllers denoted as object interaction. Object interaction can consist of picking up an object, throwing it or using it to facilitate interaction, often through a representation of hands [17].

We identify the following meta-requirement (MR2) in relation to the dimension of interaction: Interaction is what the user does within the VR experience, and how the user does so by taking actions. The user will expect consistency between interaction schemes within the physically limited space. For room-scale VR applications, the mapping of object interaction and camera interaction should be designed around the mapping of the natural movements of the user's body.

3.3 Narrative

In a broad sense, narrative has been a factor in human media consumption for many years. When we read novels, view movies, or play games, we engage ourselves in some form of plot or narrative [29–31]. Such narratives can be divided into two high-level categories: linear and interactive [31, 32].

In a linear narrative, we follow "a temporal sequence of events" [30, p. 176] from beginning to end [32]. This is what we experience in e.g. novels or movies [31]. In an interactive narrative, on the contrary, there is a strong emphasis on the sense of user agency [29, 31], which in this context can be construed as "the satisfying power to take meaningful actions" [31, p. 32].

Agency has been linked to both immersion [29] and presence [31]. Given the established connection between these concepts and VR [6–8], it is no surprise that VR research has explored narrative as well. Slater and Wilbur [7] speak of "plot" as a factor in immersion, defined as the degree to which the virtual environment presents a story-line that is distinct from events unfolding in the real world. As such, this is highly related to the notion of interaction and interactivity: in a VR context, this can be construed as the degree to which the participant can influence the unfolding of events and affect changes in the virtual world [7, 33].

There is a correspondingly strong focus on interactive narratives in VR, and a participatory form of narrative works well in the medium [7, 21]. With this high degree of interactivity, however, arises a need to guide the user's attention *to* the interactivity.

The motivation of the user in the narrative becomes key. Even those VR narratives that most closely resemble the traditional linear narrative (e.g. films presented from a VR perspective) face the issue of guiding user attention to focal plot points as the temporal sequence of events elapses, since the user remains determinant of where they look [15].

There are established tools that designers can draw upon to guide user motivation. Drawing upon Norman's perceived affordances [34], we know that the visual appearances of objects will affect the way perceive their purpose and possibilities for interaction. This extends to VR as well. An abstract representation of a bow and arrow might convince the user that the arrow has to be nocked, though the more detail that goes into the effects of the bow (e.g. having the bow string wobble or be easily interacted with by making it move when struck), the more likely it will be that the user also expects the features of the bow to be used. A specific and detailed representation of the bow and arrow and their use together will thus more strongly support an interactive narrative because the amount of detail simply emphasizes that more can be done with the object. In other words, whenever a virtual interaction has a physical world counterpart, we should make sure the virtual matches the physical as closely as possible [24].

We identify the meta-requirement (MR3) in relation to the dimension of narrative: A strong narrative explains why the user interacts and navigates and describes the user-driven purpose in the VR experience. The user will expect a high degree of interactive freedom as the visualization of the narrative elements become more detailed. For room-scale VR applications, the representation of central plot-points, objects, and actors should match their given functionality and have an effect associated to further the overall narrative structure.

4   Method

To solve our problem and solution objectives, we followed the guidelines for performing Design Science Research by Hevner et al. [35], first by identifying a problem or gap in the current knowledge base, then by building artefacts to assess and refine the instantiated solutions through experimental evaluation, and finally contributing the identified knowledge to the knowledge base. Similar to the proposed structure by Heinrich and Schwabe [9], meta-requirements were identified from existing kernel theories and design principles were proposed to solve these meta-requirements. Since no design principles or theories could be identified within the area of VR or room-scale VR, the proposed design principles were applied in the design of two main artefacts that were hereafter evaluated. The activities of evaluation can be categorized as a quick and simple evaluation strategy, characterized as a summative ex post (assessing the quality of finished artefacts in regards to conforming to the usefulness of design principles) [36] experimental design [35]. For the purpose of attempting to isolate the instantiations of the design principles, the two artefacts were constructed differently and with different aspects changed so that aspects could be compared across four different conditions. We are also minding the process, invention, relevance and extensibility of our research, ensuring the validity of our interaction design research contribution [37].

For our conditions, we used a HTC Vive room-scale VR setup in a 2.5 × 1.5 m calibrated space. To run our experiment, we used a PC with an NVIDIA GeForce GTX 1080 GPU, Intel i7-6700K CPU and 32 GB DDR5 RAM.

Our user study involved (N = 12) participants, of which 5 (41.67%) were female. The average age was 34.8, and the median was 26. We collected data in the form of input logging, screen output capture and follow-up interviews for each participant. We started each experiment by documenting the user's age and experience with various input control schemes (such as Vive controllers, console video game controllers, or keyboard and mouse). Each participant tried all four conditions, distributed in a Latin square matrix so that participants experienced the scenes in different orders. Having (N = 12) participants for our four conditions gave us three full sets of distributed data.

Semi-structured follow-up interviews were conducted and sought to allow the participants to express their general impressions of their VR experience. The interview guide was structured after the key dimensions as a practical short-hand checklist, e.g. "Where did you feel you were?", "Please describe what you did?", "How did you do it?", and "Why did you do what you did?". However, we resorted to this list only if users did not naturally touch upon the dimensions. Users gave verbal consent for data logging, and recording HMD output and semi-structured interviews. Each interview was coded using the design principles for quote-extraction and use in the analysis [38].

5   Communication of Design Knowledge

5.1   Solution Objectives, Meta-Requirements and Derived Design Principles

In the introduction, we identified five solution objectives. Four of these objectives will be answered by the meta-requirements presented in the literature review. The final solution objective will be solved through the discussion and by our main contribution. In order to solve the meta-requirements however, we have derived three practical design principles (DPs) based on the meta-requirements, elaborated below Fig. 1:

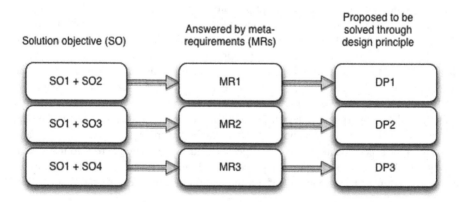

Fig. 1. Solution objectives lead to meta-requirements; from which we derive design principles.

The design principles are as follows: (1) Design for depth of spatiality through inclusion of both interaction and world space; (2) Design for integration of physical and virtual artefacts through camera and object interaction; (3) Design for richness of narrative through representation of concrete visualizations that match functionality and contribute to an interactive plot structure. See Fig. 1 for further clarification on how SOs, MRs are connected to the proposed design principles.

5.2   Representation of Artefact(s)

We designed two artefacts represented as scenes of action (see Fig. 2) with different conditions of the design principles instantiated.

Fig. 2. Left: Scene A, condition 1, wherein the user manipulates the darker object. Right: Scene B, condition 4, wherein the user observes an AI-controlled agent.

Scene A

Scene A consisted of four objects of different shapes and colors placed within reach in the interaction space, and four corresponding targets. The world space was a white field to keep attention on the interaction space. The users were presented with the goal of moving each object to its corresponding target.

The first condition featured a standard room-scale VR setup, with the participant wearing a HMD and holding two Vive controllers. These controllers were used for object interaction; the user could lift an object by touching it with the controller and holding the trigger, and then release it by releasing the trigger.

Condition 2 was designed to play with aspects of interaction and spatiality by disallowing camera translation entirely. The user had no dedicated controllers but moved a circular marker on the ground simply by moving the HMD. When near an object, a radial progress bar would indicate that it was being selected; once selected, the user could then move the object by moving the HMD, until its target.

Notably, both conditions of scene A featured linear, goal-driven narratives; the user had to move all the objects to their targets by different means. However, the room-scale setup featured in condition 1 allowed the user to approach object interaction in a far more interactive way. In condition 2, there was little room for interactive exploration of the narrative; once an object was picked up, it "stuck" to the user's marker until delivered to its goal.

Scene B

Scene B resembled a cartoony forest containing five AI agents following sequential behavior routines. They performed a variety of activities, such as talking to each other, chopping wood, and getting hit by falling apples (which would prompt a laugh from others). The center of the scene (the user's interaction space) contained a tree.

For condition 3, we excluded object interaction and worked exclusively with camera interaction. The user could translate the camera position using an Xbox 360 gamepad controller within a defined interaction space without visualized borders. Rotation was still facilitated by natural movement. For the spatial design, the user could move freely within a designated area of the world space, though no interaction would be possible. The structure of the narrative was linear with no means to impact or change the narrative. The various AI agents would follow their routines at set times, even though the user was still free to explore the narrative through camera interaction.

Condition 4 featured a standard room-scale interaction scheme. We made a conscious design decision to fully distinguish between interaction space and world space. The same characters were used as in condition 3, but here, the user could influence the otherwise linearly sequenced narrative by interacting with and interrupting the AI agents by throwing objects (rocks or apples) at them, prompting a response.

Scene A and its two conditions as well as scene B, condition 3 were purposefully built with aspects of the design principles reversed to evaluate alternative instantiations and their impacts on the users' experiences. Scene B, condition 4 was the only instantiation that adhered fully to the design principles.

Table 1 features a breakdown of the conditions as they were distributed across the two scenes. Scenes were to a substantial extent determined by their visuals and as such many of the aspects of the design principles were bound to each other and not meaningful to change and test. For example, for scene B to work at all, it made little sense to change it to a complete linear narrative structure (although one could argue that condition 3 with limited interaction to a degree makes this possible). Similarly, the lack of visualized world space and the abstract visuals of scene A would not give the user much reason to explore and as such the "full movement" condition of DP1 made little sense to include. Note that users' order of experiencing the scenes and conditions was scrambled due to the Latin square matrix.

Table 1. Four conditions across two scenes, implementing different design principles.

Artefact instantiation	Design principle 1 (Design for spatiality)	Design principle 2 (Design for interaction)	Design principle 3 (Design for narrative)
Scene A: Condition 1	Limited movement. No world space visualization	Controller interaction	Linear. Abstract narrative object elements
Scene A: Condition 2	No movement. No world space visualization	Interaction through camera controller	Linear. Abstract narrative object elements
Scene B: Condition 3	Full movement. World space visualized	No object interaction	Interactive. Concrete narrative object elements
Scene B: Condition 4	Limited movement. World space visualized	Controller interaction	Interactive. Concrete narrative object elements

6 Evaluation of Design Principle Implementation

6.1 DP1: Design for Depth of Spatiality

Throughout the conditions, users expressed a clear distinction between the interaction and world spaces which underlined the importance of visualizing both. In scene A, one user expressed that the grid served as a good indicator: *"I saw that a grid appeared [...] and then sometimes I thought 'Okay, now I'm not going to move further'"* (P8).

Another user expressed the efficacy of the world space design, expressing no desire to move beyond the interaction space due to lack of world space features: *"Yes, it could have been fun to move around, but I could see the whole space, so there was nothing hidden over there"* (P6).

The biggest difference between the users' sense of spatiality in scene A's conditions 1 and 2 came from the lack of the grid in condition 2. As we placed the users on a stationary chair in the center of the interaction space, the grid was, in practice, always invisible. One user expressed that the lack of these borders even led to a decreased sense of spatiality: *"The sense of spatiality was greatest when I stood up. Clearly, it [the grid] gave me a sense of how far the world went. And I knew that when I reached that point, I would have to watch out, or I would risk hitting something."* (P5).

In condition 3, the lack of the visual grid but continued presence of camera translation caused users to express general discontent, noting a clear distinction between interaction and world spaces. In the absence of the grid, users even created arbitrary restrictions for their movement, though this was not implemented. One user felt the tree served as a border for motion, though in reality, the motion space extended beyond the tree: *"I tried getting back, but it felt like I couldn't move any more. It was as though it stopped at the line of the tree."* (P5).

The feeling of spatial discontent was supported by users once again describing the grid as a natural boundary that denoted limitations of their space in condition 4: *"I was placed next to the tree, and the room was limited, so the grid appeared."* (P6).

We found that the various implementations of design principle 1 supported the need for visualizing both interaction and world to attain depth. However, the physical limitations of the room-scale setup should also carefully be considered and designed around to further the feeling of spatiality. Firmware aids such as the HTC Vive's chaperone bounds proved notably influential in how the users experienced the design.

6.2   P2: Design for Integration of Interaction

All of the users discovered the ability to interact with objects, and a lot of the experiences centered around the ability to pick up objects in the interaction space and throw them at the AI agents in the world space in condition 4. Users noted: *"The one where I can throw the apples is the most fun. I could shake the tree. And then more apples fell. Notably more fun, because I get to do stuff. Actually, doing stuff makes me feel the most immersed."* (P2) and *"It was nice to be able to pick up the apples, because I complained that I couldn't before [in condition 3]. I definitely prefer interacting with objects."* (P8).

The positive reactions stood in contrast to conditions 2 and 3. In condition 2, users found the object interaction through camera interaction with the HMD natural but very restrictive, as it imposed a purely linear structure. Similarly, the lack of camera rotation in condition 3, resulted in several users likening the possibilities of movement to that of sitting in a wheelchair: *"It was enormously limiting. I could turn around, but I couldn't do anything. I could just see."* (P6). This passiveness was echoed when users compared condition 4 to the others, with one user saying *"Like I said in the first two [conditions 1 and 2], full body interaction is much more fun in my opinion. In the third one [condition 3] I was completely passive, just looking and seeing what's happening but the fourth one I can actually influence the characters in a way, like even if I just throw a rock at them and then they rub their head, so I prefer the fourth one."* (P11).

We found that the various implementations of design principle 2 supported the need for using both camera and object interaction in order to integrate physical (such as the controllers) with virtual artefacts (such as those represented in the scenes). We also found that the structures and rules that the control mapping imposed influenced the possibilities for exploration.

6.3   DP3: Design for Richness of Narrative

In terms of narrative, users had a strong preference for the interactive exploration of the interaction space of condition 4, regardless of the order they experienced the conditions in: *"It's never been more fun to be allowed to bow down and do things."* (P2). Users notably used more emotional and empathetic expressions to describe their experiences than in the other conditions. One example was feeling sorry for the AI agent scripted to be hit by a falling apple: *"If they are now standing there arguing about that single apple, then I could give them one, and then they wouldn't have to argue."* (P5).

Similarly, users brought their understanding of their natural world into the virtual one and deduced the functionalities of objects based on their real-world equivalents: *"I tried to throw the apples to them, I didn't try to hit them. It might have been a tad too much to throw a rock at the head of one of them."* (P5). Interestingly, despite having identical properties in the physics engine, the users attributed a functional difference between apples and stones that was not there. Another user (P8) picked up two rocks and tried to bash them together, expressing surprise that the design did not create some effect equivalent to doing so in the physical world. When an AI agent laughed at another agent that was hit by an apple, certain users even felt vengeful: *"I tried to hit him after he'd laughed about her getting hit in the head by an apple."* (P10) or: *"They became mad because I threw stuff after them."* (P1).

In general, driven by interactive exploration, the users tried to influence the linear narrative with their actions. They sought a response from the AI agents: *"They were talking to each other, there was a story unfolding. I experienced something happened. That some course of events or a story that I could follow occurred [...] Then I created the story through my interaction, which became about hitting them in the head with the apples because that gave me feedback."* (P6). This can be seen as acknowledgement of the user's own existence in the scene, de-fining themselves through the actions of the AI agents. Users directly linked this sense of presence to a sense of narrative purpose: *"When you are in VR, and you're like a ghost, it doesn't really matter, it gets really boring [...] unless you have some kind of means, some kind of requirement where somebody needs you or you have a job to do."* (P9).

The linearly driven narrative of conditions 1 and 2 with pre-defined goals had a mixed user reaction; when the interaction was forced to be sequential (i.e. condition 2), the users generally disliked it, whereas when the interaction was allowed to be more interactive (i.e. condition 1), the users were more positive. Similarly, the sequential, non-interactive narrative of condition 3 incurred a more negative reaction than the freer condition 4.

We found that the various implementations of design principle 3 supported the need for using concrete visualizations of virtual artefacts that matched their designed functionality (e.g., an apple should behave as an apple would) in order to achieve a richer perception of the narrative structure. The users also expressed a strong preference for the ability to interact with and influence the narrative.

7 Discussion

In relation to DP1, it is worth mentioning that the presence of the firmware "chaperone bounds" that provided an interaction of the calibrated physical space for the VR hardware had a considerable influence on how users experienced the VR application. Naturally, it is possible to disable the chaperone bounds, which is often done for research studies exploring motion in room-scale VR, such as redirected walking (e.g. [8]). However, in more practical situations than a laboratory environment, the chaperone bounds serve an important practical function. As such, chaperone bounds and similar firmware features should be considered in the spatial design in any room-scale application.

In relation to DP2, a few of our users who experienced condition 4 before condition 1 were unfamiliar with room-scale V, and found difficulty in grasping the "standard room-scale" interaction scheme here. In contrast, the inexperienced users who experienced condition 1 before 4 grasped it immediately. This calls back to the importance of mapping interaction [39], and indicates a need for further studies where N > 12 so that the data can be adjusted for experience level, as our data indicates that it might have an impact on the user experience.

In relation to DP3, it became evident that it is not sufficient to consider only the narrative design on an axis of linear to interactive, because users in our study seemed to differentiate between their goals and the means with which they sought to achieve those goals. We found that the ability to influence a narrative has a high impact on the user's experience, which reaffirms the notions held by Aylett and Louchart [21].

From our findings, it became clear that while the dimensions can be thought of as distinct, they are strongly interweaved and design decisions in one dimension will influence others. As such, the narrative dimension of why seemed to highly influence users' perception and reason for moving in the spatial where and interacting with objects through the interactive *what* and *how*. We do acknowledge that many more different combinations could have been made based on the multiple aspects of the design principles. For reasons of scope and to identify the possible high-level principles, we argue that the combinations used were enough. Further research should explore how to exhaust these options more thoroughly.

As our results indicated that the specific dimensions influenced each other, we can furthermore derive two additional design principles. First, designers of room-scale VR applications should be aware that the design dimensions cannot be omitted as this will have a negative impact on the experience. As a result, we derive an additional design principle: *"Design for inclusion of all three dimensions: spatiality (where), interaction (what and how) and narrative (why)"* (DP4). Second, as the design decisions from the dimensions impacted each other, we derive the following second principle: *"Design for balance between dimensions through awareness of interdependent influence"* (DP5). These two high-level design principles can be practically assessed by letting designers consider questions such as:

> "How will the locations of interaction space and world space affect the user's interaction and motivation for acting? How will camera and object interaction affect the space of the user and why the user should or would interact? How will the overall narrative structure affect the user's perception of where to go, what and how to interact?"

The proposed theoretical contribution to the field of room-scale VR design can be characterized as a level 2 exaptation type of design [10], as our nascent design theory extends known solutions from the HCI literature into the new area of room-scale VR design. Further research within this area should include more quantitative and testable hypotheses derived from our dimensions to better assess how to use it for summative evaluation [36]. We furthermore identify a broadening of the applied designs into other areas than the immediate entertainment that contemporary VR technology is currently being marketed to. We thus believe to have expressed the process, invention, relevance and extensibility of our research [37].

8 Conclusion

We have explored and outlined central design dimensions and design principles for room-scale VR that can be used to design engaging VR experiences.

We have proposed a so-called nascent design theory of how to design for room-scale virtual reality through a combination of design principles on lower and higher levels. Through the identification of meta-requirements extracted from related kernel theories and literature from human-computer interaction, we have identified three dimensions of room-scale VR and three corresponding design principles for designing VR artefacts. Two instantiations of the design principles were both evaluated qualitatively through a conditional setup with real users and resulted in the identification of two additional, higher level design principles. The contribution is significant because there is currently a lack of high-level design frameworks for VR, and the identified design dimensions and resulting principles represent new possibilities for designing and evaluating VR experiences.

References

1. Anthes, C., Garcia-Hernandez, R.J., Wiedemann, M., Kranzlmuller, D.: State of the art of virtual reality technology. In: 2016 IEEE Aerospace Conference, pp. 1–19 (2016)
2. Lindeman, R.W., Beckhaus, S.: Crafting memorable VR experiences using experiential fidelity. In: Proceedings of the 16th ACM Symposium on Virtual Reality Software and Technology - VRST 2009, pp. 187–190 (2009)
3. Malaika, Y.: Interaction Design in VR: Valve's Lessons (Valve Corporation). http://www.gdcvault.com/play/1022810/Interaction-Design-in-VR-The
4. Jagnow, R.: Lessons Learned from VR Prototyping (Google Inc.). http://www.gdcvault.com/play/1023926/Lessons-Learned-from-VR
5. Roberts, J., Ritsos, P., Badam, S.K., Brodbeck, D., Kennedy, J., Elmqvist, N.: Visualization beyond the desktop - the next big thing. IEEE Comput. Graph. Appl. 34(6), 26–34 (2014)
6. Pausch, R., Proffitt, D., Williams, G.: Quantifying immersion in virtual reality. In: Proceedings of the 24th Annual Conference on Computer Graphics and Interactive Techniques - SIGGRAPH 1997, pp. 13–18 (1997)
7. Slater, M., Wilbur, S.: A framework for immersive virtual environments (FIVE): speculations on the role of presence in virtual environments. Presence Teleoper. Virtual Environ. 6, 603–616 (1997)
8. Knibbe, J., Schjerlund, J., Petræus, M., Hornbæk, K.: The dream is collapsing: the experience of exiting VR. In: Proceedings 2018 CHI Conference on Human Factors in Computing Systems, CHI 2018 (2018)
9. Heinrich, P., Schwabe, G.: Communicating nascent design theories on innovative information systems through multi-grounded design principles. In: Tremblay, M.C., VanderMeer, D., Rothenberger, M., Gupta, A., Yoon, V. (eds.) DESRIST 2014. LNCS, vol. 8463, pp. 148–163. Springer, Cham (2014). https://doi.org/10.1007/978-3-319-06701-8_10
10. Gregor, S., Hevner, A.R.: Positioning and presenting design science research for maximum impact. MIS Q. 37, 337–355 (2013)
11. Walls, J.G., Widmeyer, G.R., El Sawy, O.A., Sawy, O.A.E.: Building an information system design theory for vigilant EIS. Inf. Syst. Res. 3, 36–59 (1992)

12. Bowman, D.A., Hodges, L.F.: Formalizing the design, evaluation, and application of interaction techniques for immersive virtual environments. J. Vis. Lang. Comput. **10**, 37–53 (1999)
13. Hornbæk, K., Oulasvirta, A.: What is interaction? In: Proceedings of the 2017 CHI Conference on Human Factors in Computing Systems - CHI 2017, pp. 5040–5052 (2017)
14. Eidenberger, H., Mossel, A.: Indoor skydiving in immersive virtual reality with embedded storytelling. In: Proceedings of the 21st ACM Symposium on Virtual Reality Software and Technology - VRST 2015, pp. 9–12. ACM Press, New York (2015)
15. Nielsen, L.T., Møller, M.B., Hartmeyer, S.D., Ljung, T.C.M., Nilsson, N.C., Nordahl, R., Serafin, S.: Missing the point: an exploration of how to guide users' attention during cinematic virtual reality. In: Proceedings of the 22nd ACM Conference Virtual Reality Software and Technology, pp. 229–232 (2016)
16. Lee, M., Kim, K., Daher, S., Raij, A., Schubert, R., Bailenson, J., Welch, G.: The wobbly table: increased social presence via subtle incidental movement of a real-virtual table. In: 2016 IEEE Virtual Reality (VR), pp. 11–17. IEEE (2016)
17. Argelaguet, F., Hoyet, L., Trico, M., Lecuyer, A.: The role of interaction in virtual embodiment: effects of the virtual hand representation. In: 2016 IEEE Virtual Reality (VR), pp. 3–10. IEEE (2016)
18. Sharlin, E., Watson, B., Kitamura, Y., Kishino, F., Itoh, Y.: On tangible user interfaces, humans and spatiality. Pers. Ubiquit. Comput. **8**, 338–346 (2004)
19. Yi, J.S., Kang, Y.A., Stasko, J., Jacko, J.: Toward a deeper understanding of the role of interaction in information visualization. IEEE Trans. Vis. Comput. Graph. **13**, 1224–1231 (2007)
20. Pike, W.A., Stasko, J., Chang, R., O'Connell, T.A.: The Science of Interaction. Inf. Vis. **8**, 263–274 (2009)
21. Aylett, R., Louchart, S.: Towards a narrative theory of virtual reality. Virtual Real. **7**, 2–9 (2003)
22. Rosander, C.: Interactivity and spatiality – experiences of modelling real work places as virtual places in a VR collaborative environment, pp. 1–4 (2000)
23. Brade, J., Lorenz, M., Busch, M., Hammer, N., Tscheligi, M., Klimant, P.: Being there again – presence in real and virtual environments and its relation to usability and user experience using a mobile navigation task. Int. J. Hum. Comput. Stud. **101**, 76–87 (2017)
24. Steuer, J.: Defining virtual reality: dimensions determining telepresence. J. Commun. **42**, 73–93 (1992)
25. Kirsh, D.: The intelligent use of space. Artif. Intell. **73**, 149–173 (1995)
26. Rauhoeft, G., Leyrer, M., Thompson, W.B., Stefanucci, J.K., Klatzky, R.L., Mohler, B.J.: Evoking and assessing vastness in virtual environments. In: Proceedings of the ACM SIGGRAPH Symposium Applied Perception - SAP 2015, pp. 51–54 (2015)
27. Seibert, J., Shafer, D.M.: Control mapping in virtual reality: effects on spatial presence and controller naturalness. Virtual Real. **22**(1), 79–88 (2017)
28. Beaudouin-Lafon, M.: Instrumental interaction: an interaction model for designing post-WIMP user interfaces. In: Proceeding of the 18th International Conference on Human Factors in Computing Systems - CHI 2000, vol. 2, pp. 446–453 (2000)
29. Mason, S.: On games and links: extending the vocabulary of agency and immersion in interactive narratives. In: Koenitz, H., Sezen, T.I., Ferri, G., Haahr, M., Sezen, D., Çatak, G. (eds.) ICIDS 2013. LNCS, vol. 8230, pp. 25–34. Springer, Cham (2013). https://doi.org/10.1007/978-3-319-02756-2_3
30. Eskelinen, M.: Towards computer game studies. Digit. Creat. **12**, 175–183 (2001)

31. Roth, C., Koenitz, H.: Evaluating the user experience of interactive digital narrative. In: Proceedings of the 1st International Workshop Multimedia Alternate Realities - AltMM 2016, pp. 31–36 (2016)
32. Riedl, M.O., Young, R.M.: From linear story generation to branching story graphs. IEEE Comput. Graph. Appl. **26**, 23–31 (2006)
33. Muhanna, M.A.: Virtual reality and the CAVE: taxonomy, interaction challenges and research directions. J. King Saud Univ. – Comput. Inf. Sci. **27**, 344–361 (2015)
34. Norman, D.A.: Affordance, conventions, and design. Interactions **6**, 38–43 (1999)
35. Hevner, A.R., March, S.T., Park, J., Ram, S.: Design science in information systems research. MIS Q. **28**, 75–105 (2004)
36. Venable, J., Pries-Heje, J., Baskerville, R.: FEDS: a framework for evaluation in design science research. Eur. J. Inf. Syst. **25**, 77–89 (2016)
37. Zimmerman, J., Forlizzi, J., Evenson, S.: Research through design as a method for interaction design research in HCI. In: Proceedings of the SIGCHI Conference on Human Factors in Computing Systems, CHI 2007, pp. 493–502 (2007)
38. Lazar, J., Feng, J.H., Hochheiser, H.: Research Methods in Human-Computer Interaction. Wiley, Hoboken (2010)
39. Hornecker, E., Buur, J.: Getting a grip on tangible interaction: a framework on physical space and social interaction. In: Proceeding of the SIGCHI Conference Human Factors in Computing Systems, pp. 437–446 (2006)

Designing Conversational Agents for Energy Feedback

Ulrich Gnewuch[1,2]([⊠]), Stefan Morana[1], Carl Heckmann[2],
and Alexander Maedche[1]

[1] Institute of Information Systems and Marketing (IISM),
Karlsruhe Institute of Technology (KIT), Karlsruhe, Germany
{ulrich.gnewuch,stefan.morana,
alexander.maedche}@kit.edu
[2] hsag Heidelberger Service AG, Heidelberg, Germany
{u.gnewuch,c.heckmann}@hsag.info

Abstract. Reducing and shifting energy consumption could contribute significantly to a more sustainable use of energy in households. Studies have shown that the provision of feedback can encourage consumers to use energy more sustainably. While there is wide variety of energy feedback solutions ranging from in-home displays to mobile applications, there is a lack of research on whether and how conversational agents can provide energy feedback to promote sustainable energy use. As conversational agents, such as chatbots, promise a natural and intuitive user interface, they may have great potential for energy feedback. This paper explores how to design conversational agents for energy feedback and proposes design principles based on existing literature. The design principles are instantiated in a text-based conversational agent and evaluated in a focus group session with industry experts. We contribute with valuable design knowledge that extends previous research on the design of energy feedback solutions.

Keywords: Conversational agent · Chatbot · Energy feedback
Focus group · Design science research

1 Introduction

To combat climate change and reduce greenhouse gas emissions, significant investments are being made in new low-carbon technologies, renewable energy, energy efficiency, and grid infrastructure [1]. To achieve the European Union's (EU) ambitious climate goals of reducing greenhouse gas emissions by 80% by 2050, all sectors are expected to play their part [2]. Since energy consumption of the residential sector still accounts for around 25% of total energy use in the EU [2], sustainable use of energy in households could significantly contribute to reaching the EU's climate goals. Sustainable energy use includes not only reducing energy consumption, but also shifting energy consumption to times when renewable energy sources (e.g., wind or solar power) are abundant [3]. Particularly, non-time critical energy use in households, such as washing machines or dish washers, can be shifted away from peak demand periods [3].

© Springer International Publishing AG, part of Springer Nature 2018
S. Chatterjee et al. (Eds.): DESRIST 2018, LNCS 10844, pp. 18–33, 2018.
https://doi.org/10.1007/978-3-319-91800-6_2

Providing energy feedback to consumers has been found to increase energy use awareness and promote both reducing and shifting energy consumption in households [e.g., 3, 4]. Moreover, reviews of energy feedback research have found that the provision of feedback can result in average energy savings of 10% [5]. In the past, many energy feedback solutions have been developed such as in-home displays, mobile applications, or web portals [5]. Given the large-scale deployment of smart meters that collect high-frequency consumption data and the advances in algorithms for energy disaggregation, these solutions are able to provide direct, real-time feedback on the level of individual appliances [6]. Additionally, they can provide interactive feedback augmented with additional approaches (e.g., personalized recommendations) to provide greater opportunities to engage consumers over time [4]. Although much research has been conducted on their design, recent reviews of energy feedback solutions indicate that no research has been conducted on how conversational agents (CAs) can be used to provide energy feedback [5, 7]. CAs, such as text-based chatbots or voice-based personal assistants like Amazon's Alexa, promise a convenient and intuitive user interface to interact with technology using natural language (i.e., written or spoken) [8]. Because of advances in artificial intelligence and natural language processing, the capabilities of CAs have improved significantly in recent years [9]. While they are limited in their ability to provide visual information on energy consumption (e.g., in the form of graphs or dashboards), they can leverage natural language to answer questions and provide personalized feedback. Given the rising interest in CAs [10], we argue that there is an opportunity to investigate the design of CAs for energy feedback to address the lack of consumer awareness of energy use and facilitate a more sustainable use of energy in households. Although feedback solutions using SMS or email have been developed for related contexts [e.g., 11], research on how to design CAs for energy feedback is scarce. Thus, we aim to fill this gap and explore the following research question:

How to design conversational agents for energy feedback to promote sustainable use of energy in households?

To address this research question, we follow the design science research (DSR) [12] approach to iteratively design and evaluate a text-based CA for energy feedback. Based on a literature review on existing energy feedback solutions, we propose four design principles for CAs for energy feedback. These principles are instantiated in a text-based CA and evaluated in an exploratory focus group session [13] with domain experts from the energy industry. The remainder of this paper is organized as follows. Section two introduces related work on energy feedback and CAs. Section three outlines our DSR project, while section four describes the proposed design of our artifact. In section five, we present and discuss the findings of our evaluation, before we conclude the paper with a short summary and a discussion of limitations in section six.

2 Related Work

2.1 Promoting Sustainable Energy Use Through Feedback

Research in psychology has extensively studied feedback and its impact on behavior change (for an overview, see [14]). Feedback is commonly understood as "the process of giving people information about their behavior that can be used to reinforce and/or modify future actions" [4]. In the context of energy use, feedback has been identified as an effective intervention to promote sustainable use of energy (for a detailed review, see [4, 15]). In general, energy feedback can be provided in different ways. Direct feedback is available in real-time, whereas indirect feedback is provided after the consumption occurs [4]. Moreover, feedback can be aggregated (i.e., a household's total energy consumption) or on appliance-level [4]. Appliance-level feedback contains information about individual devices, such as electronics or water heaters [6]. Furthermore, feedback can be combined with other interventions, such as goal setting or financial incentives, to increase its effectiveness [4]. Reviews of energy feedback research have found that the provision of feedback can result in average energy savings of 10% as well as promote load shifting [5], but its effectiveness depends on the way it is provided [4].

Different technologies have been used to provide energy feedback such as in-home displays, web portals, or mobile applications (for a detailed review of different solutions, see [5]). Many of these energy feedback solutions visualize household energy consumption based on data collected by sensors or smart meters [16], while others focus their feedback on a single device such as a washing machine [e.g., 3]. Moreover, they usually push out information to consumers (e.g., monthly energy reports) or require consumers to pull information from them (e.g., web portal or mobile app) [4, 17]. Modern solutions also frequently include additional features such as community platforms [18] or individual/social level comparisons [17]. However, recent reviews of energy feedback solutions in research and practice indicate that no research has been conducted on how CAs can be used to provide energy feedback [5, 7].

2.2 Conversational Agents

The idea of interacting with computers using natural language has been around for decades [8]. While the literature has used different terms to describe systems with conversational user interfaces (e.g., CA, chatbot, or personal assistant), the underlying concept is always that users "achieve some result by conversing with a machine in a dialogic fashion, using natural language" [9]. In IS research, the most commonly used term is "conversational agent" that refers to both text-based CAs, such as chatbots, and speech-based CAs (e.g., Amazon's Alexa) [19]. Both types of CAs build on the same technology (i.e., natural language processing), but differ in their input/output modality (i.e., voice vs. text). CAs have their roots in the chatbot ELIZA [20] that was primarily developed to simulate human conversation based on pattern-matching algorithms. Since then, the capabilities of CAs have improved enormously and many of them have been implemented on websites and messenger platforms (e.g., for customer service). Moreover, they can be found on many mobile devices as personal assistants to support users in finding information or accomplishing basic tasks (e.g., Apple's Siri) [21].

CAs promise a more convenient and natural user interface than traditional graphical user interfaces since they allow people to interact with computers using natural language, just like engaging in a conversation with another person [8]. Particularly, less IT-savvy users could benefit from this form of interaction because they do not need to learn how to navigate through complex menus and understand detailed dashboards [8]. Moreover, CAs often display human-like characteristics (e.g., human-like appearance or embodiment and communication style) to provide more natural and engaging interactions [22] as well as to build relationships with users [23]. Therefore, CAs might also serve as a natural way to provide energy feedback and promote sustainable energy use.

3   Design Science Research Project

This research project follows the DSR approach [12] to provide design principles (DPs) for CAs for energy feedback promoting sustainable energy use in households. We argue that this research approach is particularly suited to address our research goal because it allows to iteratively design and evaluate our IT artifact in a rigorous fashion [12, 24]. Moreover, this approach enables us to involve experts and real users in the design and evaluation phases to incrementally improve the functionality and relevance of our artifact [12]. The project is conducted in collaboration with experts from an organization in the energy industry. This organization is a medium-sized service provider that offers a range of services, such as consulting, business process outsourcing, and product development, for German energy providers and other companies in the energy industry.

The DSR project is based on the framework proposed by Kuechler and Vaishnavi [24]. In the problem awareness phase, we reviewed extant literature on existing energy feedback solutions to identify potential issues in their design. Based on the results of this review, we proposed four DPs for CAs for energy feedback. These DPs were informed by existing research on the design of energy feedback solutions and feedback theory. Subsequently, we instantiated our DPs in an interactive prototype of a text-based CA (i.e., a chatbot) developed with BotPreview, a platform for building previews of chatbot interactions [25]. This prototype was then evaluated in an explorative focus group session [13] with industry experts from the cooperating company. For the evaluation, we selected the technical risk and efficacy strategy [26] because the implementation and evaluation of a CA for energy feedback in a real setting would be very costly. The evaluation in a real household with real users would require significant investments for setting up the necessary infrastructure (e.g., implementing a smart metering infrastructure, integrating different data sources, and implementing algorithms for the calculation of feedback) and recruiting participants. Therefore, we decided to first evaluate the proposed DPs with a group of industry experts to get feedback and improve our design before conducting a more complex evaluation. In a second design cycle, we will refine our DPs based on the experts' feedback and instantiate the DPs in a fully-functional prototype. This prototype will be implemented using Microsoft's Bot Framework and evaluated with real users in several households that are equipped with smart meters.

4 Designing Conversational Agents for Energy Feedback

4.1 Problem Awareness

Feedback is considered a promising strategy for promoting sustainable energy use and many energy feedback solutions have been developed in recent years [5]. Although much research has been conducted on their design, there is still a need to better understand and validate specific design features and interaction paradigms of these solutions [27]. To inform our design, we conducted a literature review and identified several issues in the design of existing energy feedback solutions, which we summarize below.

Many energy feedback solutions focus on visual feedback including numbers, text, graphics, movement, animation, pictures, icons, colors, or lights [15]. However, these solutions often overload consumers with too much information, dry numbers, and intangible units [18]. In addition, they often lack natural language descriptions of key information and a personal language that is easy to understand for consumers [7, 16]. Moreover, just providing information on energy use may not be sufficient for consumers to draw conclusions for taking effective action (e.g., identifying energy guzzlers) or changing energy use habits [16, 18]. Furthermore, many existing energy feedback solutions either push out information to consumers (e.g., in-home displays positioned in a visible place in the home) or require consumers to pull information (e.g., web portals or mobile apps) [4, 17]. However, researchers argue that effective feedback solutions should combine both push and pull approaches [17]. Furthermore, as energy is a low involvement product [28] and energy feedback is usually optional for consumers [4], there is a need to "design for the least motivated individuals" [17, p. 2]. However, many energy feedback solutions cannot be easily integrated in consumers' life or require a complex system setup and training [6].

In conclusion, we argue that CAs represent a promising technology to address the identified issues in the design of existing energy feedback solutions. While significant progress has been made in the integration of real-time, appliance-level energy consumption data (e.g., from smart meters) and the transformation of data into more comprehensible units (e.g., monetary savings) [e.g., 16], there is a lack of design knowledge on CAs for energy feedback. Therefore, we believe that it is suitable to apply the DSR approach to address this research gap.

4.2 Design Principles for Conversational Agents for Energy Feedback

In this section, we propose four DPs that describe how to design CAs for energy feedback. These DPs focus specifically on the CA and the way it should provide feedback to consumers. In this paper, we do not further consider the underlying technical infrastructure that is necessary to integrate different data sources (e.g., smart meters), nor the algorithms that are necessary to, for example, calculate monetary savings or the best time to start an appliance (e.g., washing machine). Research has made great strides in developing the infrastructure and algorithms [e.g., 6, 16] that are required to implement the technical basis of our DPs. However, since our main goal is to design a CA, we argue that it is suitable to focus our DPs on how this technology can be used to provide energy feedback. Next, we derive and formulate four DPs for CAs for energy feedback.

In general, CAs differ from other technologies in that they do not provide a typical graphical user interface and rely on natural language as the main mode of interaction [8, 9]. While text-based CAs, such as chatbots, are limited to a simple chat window, voice-based CAs usually do not possess a graphical user interfaces at all. Consequently, they are not able to show complex graphs, detailed statistics, or other visual elements about current or past energy use. However, since consumers are able to chat with or talk to them like having a conversation with another human being [8], they might provide a more natural user interface for energy feedback. Consumers should be able to converse with a CA about their current and past energy use, ask specific questions about their energy consumption choices, and receive personal feedback on their energy use. For example, consumers could ask the CA about the current or past energy consumption of a specific device or the best time to start their washing machine. Since this approach might allow consumers to more quickly and effectively obtain answers to questions about energy use (i.e., to pull information), the CA should provide comprehensible feedback that enables them to draw conclusions on how to reduce or shift energy consumption. Therefore, we propose:

DP1: *Provide the CA with reactive energy feedback comprising comprehensible information in natural language in order to help consumers better understand their energy use and enable them to draw conclusions on how to use energy more sustainably.*

However, reactive energy feedback provided by CAs should not be limited to only providing comprehensible information (i.e., informative guidance [29]) but should also include personalized suggestions and advice (i.e., suggestive guidance [29]). Research argues that providing "highly personalized recommendations tailored to the sensed energy usage in the home" influences energy consumption behavior more effectively than the graphical representation of consumption values or the provision of high-level written or verbal messages [17, p. 6]. Therefore, CAs should provide reactive feedback that includes suggestions and advice on how to reduce energy consumption (e.g., by identifying energy guzzlers or "surprise" devices that they are unlikely to monitor [4]) and shift times of consumption (e.g., rescheduling the washing process [3]). Moreover, CAs should be able to support consumers in their decision to buy new energy-efficient devices by performing complex cost/benefit analyses [17]. For example, consumers could ask the CA whether buying a more energy-efficient refrigerator will reduce their energy consumption and save them money in the long term by lowering their future electricity bills. The CA could then support consumers in their purchase decision and even recommend suitable devices. Thus, we propose:

DP2: *Provide the CA with reactive energy feedback comprising personalized suggestions and concrete advice in order to enable consumers to act on it directly and encourage sustainable energy use in the future.*

In many domains, CAs show the promise of enhancing a user's productivity by proactively providing the information the user needs at the right time and at the right place [30]. Similarly, research has demonstrated that energy feedback is much more effective when delivered in the right context [31]. While DP1 and DP2 relate to reactive energy feedback that requires consumers to *pull* information from the agent, CAs can also proactively provide energy feedback to consumers (i.e., *push* information to the consumer). For example, when a water heater is consuming excessive amounts of energy, the CA should be able to promptly alert the consumer and suggest that there is a malfunction so that s/he can take appropriate action. Additionally, the CA could send contact information of a technician or apartment manager. Although solutions, such as mobile apps, can also send proactive feedback using push notifications, we argue that CAs might be more effective as their messages can serve as the starting point for a follow-up conversation and thus, might foster deeper engagement with consumers.

However, while more frequent proactive feedback provides more opportunities to engage consumers' attention, there may also be an upper limit to the amount of time that people are willing to spend on energy feedback [4]. Therefore, the CA should provide proactive feedback only in case of incidents that require the consumers' attention (e.g., device malfunction, anomalies in energy use, or significant money saving opportunities). Thus, we propose:

DP3: *Provide the CA with proactive energy feedback comprising personalized suggestions and concrete advice in order to enable consumers to quickly respond to incidents that require special attention for a more sustainable energy use.*

Finally, there is a rich body of knowledge that explores the design of human-like characteristics for CAs. Following the "Computer are Social Actors" paradigm, many studies have investigated how these social cues (e.g., human-like appearance or use of natural language) enhance a CA's trustworthiness and persuasiveness as well as make the interaction more natural to users [32, 33]. Researchers argue that, to be effective in persuasion, appropriate social cues should be embedded in the design of CAs [32]. Social cues have also been found to increase the effectiveness of energy feedback [34]. For example, social feedback on the energy consumption of a washing machine provided by the social robot iCat was more persuasive than factual feedback provided by an energy meter without any social cues [34]. Therefore, CAs for energy feedback should also display social cues to make the human-CA interaction more natural and their feedback feel more social. Thus, we propose:

DP4: *Provide the CA with appropriate social cues in order to make the interaction with them more natural and their energy feedback more social for consumers.*

4.3   Artifact: Energy Feedback Agent (EFA)

Our proposed DPs were instantiated in an artifact called Energy Feedback Agent (EFA). We decided to design EFA as a text-based CA (i.e., a chatbot) instead of a voice-based CA because of the ubiquity of smartphones and the proliferation of instant messaging applications [35]. More specifically, messaging has become a primary channel for both personal and professional communication across all segments of the population [9, 35]. Furthermore, since energy feedback may also contain sensitive information on personal habits, consumers may not want others to hear the content of the feedback [c.f., 36], which further supports the design as a text-based CA.

To instantiate our DPs, we selected two different scenarios based on examples in existing literature [e.g., 17], which are explained in detail in Sect. 5.1. Figure 1 shows the instantiation of DP1 and DP2 that illustrate how EFA provides reactive feedback based on consumers' questions. The left side of Fig. 2 depicts how EFA provides

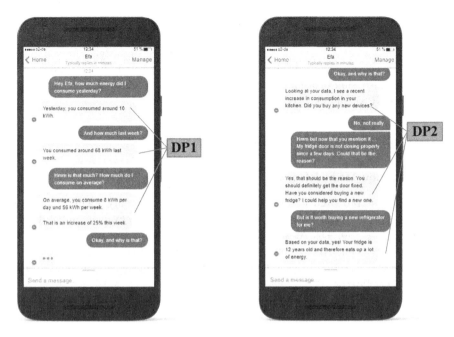

Fig. 1. DP1 and DP2: reactive feedback (information and suggestions)

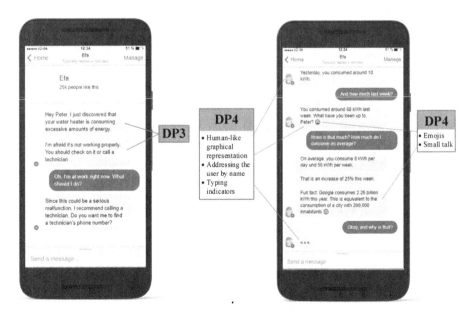

Fig. 2. DP3 (proactive feedback) and DP4 (social cues)

proactive feedback after an incident has been discovered that requires the consumer's attention (DP3). The right side of Fig. 2 shows the instantiation of DP4, that is, the social cues that were implemented in EFA's design. Based on insights from previous studies, we selected several social cues to make the conversation more familiar to the user and the provision of feedback more social, such as a human-like graphical representation [37], small talk [23], and emojis [38].

5   Evaluation

5.1   Evaluation Methodology

To evaluate our proposed design, we conducted an exploratory focus group [39]. Exploratory focus groups have been used regularly in DSR to evaluate initial designs and artifacts [e.g., 40, 41]. As shown in Table 1, the participants of the focus group session were five employees of our partner organization and one employee of a major energy provider. Upon arrival, the participants were asked to read and sign informed consent forms, provide demographic information and answer three questions about their experience with smart metering technology as well as their use of CAs and messaging applications (using a Likert scale from 1 = daily to 6 = never). Our focus group consisted of four males and two females, with an average age of 34 years and an average experience with smart metering technology of 6 years. While most participants stated that they use messaging applications daily (83%), their indicated use of CAs was only a few times a month (50%) or even less (50%). Because of their broad industry experience and familiarity with smart metering technology, we argue that they can be regarded as industry experts and represent an adequate sample for the evaluation as they are "familiar with the application environment for which the artifact is designed so they can adequately inform the refinement and evaluation of the artifact" [39, p. 127].

Table 1. Focus group participants

Participant	Affiliation	Business unit
Expert 1 (EX1)	Service provider	Product management
Expert 2 (EX2)	Service provider	Product management
Expert 3 (EX3)	Service provider	Business development
Expert 4 (EX4)	Service provider	Business development
Expert 5 (EX5)	Service provider	Sales
Expert 6 (EX6)	Major energy provider	Piloting & operations

Two of the authors performed the focus group session, in which one researcher actively moderated the session, while the other one took notes throughout the session. The focus group lasted a total of two hours and was structured as follows. First, the moderator welcomed all participants and briefly explained the procedure of the focus group session. After signing the informed consent forms, we started the audio recording. Next, the participants were given an introduction on energy feedback and CAs. Subsequently, we presented and explained our DPs for CAs for energy feedback and demonstrated how they were instantiated in EFA. We used two scenarios to evaluate the DPs one by one by showing how EFA would work in its intended environment.

The first scenario was used to evaluate EFA's reactive feedback (i.e., DP1 and DP2). In this scenario, participants should imagine that they are watching a news report on the TV showing the consequences of climate change and therefore, wonder if they could also do something to reduce their energy consumption. Realizing that they do not know much about their current energy use, they open a messenger and start a conversation with EFA. During the conversation, EFA answers several questions about current, past, and average energy consumption (DP1). When EFA mentions that energy consumption in the kitchen has been unusually high, they realize that a broken door (i.e., not closing properly) of their refrigerator leads to a waste of energy. In this context, EFA also indicates that the refrigerator is rather old and suggests buying a new, more energy-efficient one to save energy and money in the long term (DP2). After stating their possible interest, EFA calculates the time until the investment pays off and recommends two suitable devices. Next, the same scenario was shown again, however this time, EFA was designed to display social cues (DP4) as described in Sect. 4.3. Apart from these changes, however, the content of scenario was identical.

The second scenario was used to evaluate EFA's proactive feedback (DP3). In this scenario, EFA starts the conversation by alerting the consumers that their water heater has consumed excessive amounts of energy over a long period of time, indicating a technical problem with the device. Then, EFA suggests contacting a technician and provides the phone number of a suitable technician to take care of the malfunction.

During the evaluation, we stopped the demonstration several times to explain how the DPs were implemented. Therefore, participants could provide feedback on EFA and the DPs at any time during the demonstration. After each demonstration, we asked open-ended question about the artifact and the proposed design (e.g., "How did you like the feedback provided by EFA?"). Depending on the course of the discussion, we asked more specific questions about the proposed DPs and the interaction between EFA and the consumer. After the session, we analyzed the participants' feedback using our notes and the audio recording. In the next section, we present the results of the analysis and discuss the feedback of our focus group participants in detail.

5.2   Results and Discussion

In general, the industry experts who participated in our focus group session liked the idea of using CAs to provide energy feedback to consumers in households. They pointed out that EFA would be easier and more comfortable to use than many existing feedback solutions because consumers would not need to install an additional app or buy a new device. Moreover, since consumers frequently use instant messengers to communicate with their friends and family members, EFA would be able to *pick up consumers right where they always communicate* (EX6). The experts further argued that the use of existing communication channels (e.g., Facebook Messenger or WhatsApp) represents a low entry barrier for consumers, *"especially for elderly people or people with low IT affinity who might have difficulties installing an app*" (EX3). In addition, the experts stated that EFA would be of interest for energy providers looking for products based on smart metering technology. Many consumers in Germany seem to be skeptical of this new technology, but energy providers are legally required to implement them on a large scale within the next years. Therefore, solutions like EFA could help to reduce skepticism and facilitate the acceptance of smart meters in private households as "*such feedback can help to provide an added value to the customer*" (EX6).

Besides this general discussion, the experts also provided feedback on each DP. Concerning DP1, one expert mentioned that "*typical consumers have no relation to energy consumption*" (EX5) and their interest in finding out how to reduce or shift energy consumption is rather low. Thus, when EFA provides clear answers to consumers' questions immediately, it would "*address the consumers at the right level*" (EX6) and help them to better understand the abstract and intangible concept of energy [15]. Another expert liked that EFA "*leaves the technical level*" (EX1) of energy feedback by not only using standard energy metrics, such as kilowatt-hours (kWh), but also metrics that are well understood by consumers (e.g., € instead of kWh). Moreover, it was received positively that EFA provided consumers with a reference (e.g., by showing reference consumption values, providing comparisons between devices, and explaining causal relationships). The experts argued that most consumers have difficulties to understand whether a certain amount of energy indicates high or low consumption. Thus, they found EFA's ability to answer specific questions (e.g., "Is the energy consumption of my fridge high?" or "Why is my consumption higher than last week?") and provide tailored feedback to be a great advantage. The experts believed that such feedback would not only increase general energy literacy, but also motivate consumers to use energy more sustainably (e.g., reduce or shift energy consumption) because they would not have to invest the time and effort to look up information about their energy use themselves. They suggested to go even further by identifying the consumer's skill and knowledge level and adapting EFA's reactive feedback based on the consumer's answers to questions such as "*Are you technically/commercially interested? Do you have a technical background? Do you want the information in kWh or in €?*" (EX6). For example, inexperienced consumers would not be confronted with energy metrics at all, while more knowledgeable consumers with a deeper interest in energy should also receive more complex feedback.

During the session, experts also stressed that energy feedback should not be limited to the provision of pure information but should always include a possible explanation: "*With '25% more' [i.e., energy consumption], it should be explained directly why this could be the case, for example: 'It could be the new device'*" (EX5). Consequently, one expert concluded that it is DP2 that makes the energy feedback effective. He argued that when EFA provides personalized suggestions and advice on how to use energy more sustainably, it would make it easier for consumers to respond to this feedback and follow the suggestions rather than draw conclusions themselves. The experts also noted that these suggestions should focus on small changes that can be implemented directly rather than on overly complex or high-level advice. Furthermore, EFA's ability to perform cost/benefit analyses using data from publicly available appliance databases [c. f., 20] was regarded an important aspect of DP2 to help consumers understand the significant energy and cost savings potential of new energy-efficient devices. Again, the reduction of effort for consumers was positively evaluated (e.g., consumers would not need to search for suitable devices themselves).

In general, the experts also liked the fact that EFA "pushes" feedback proactively to consumers (DP3). They argued that EFA should not remain passive because, after some time, consumers naturally begin to disengage with an energy feedback solution [42]. However, one expert argued that proactive feedback should always *"include concrete suggestions and advice so that [one] can rule out possible causes"* (EX2). This point was also addressed by another expert who criticized that a consumer *"[needs] more information in addition to the message to act accordingly"* (EX1). Furthermore, they would not want to receive daily reports on their energy use from EFA, but rather specific messages as a reaction to an important event or incident. However, one expert suggested that EFA should follow up on proactive feedback if consumers do not respond (e.g., *"for less important events, a continuous reminder should come up"* (EX1)). In case of emergencies (e.g., when an oven malfunctions), EFA could even make an automatic phone call to a dedicated emergency number.

The industry experts also believed that appropriate social cues displayed by EFA (DP4) would help to increase consumer engagement and make the energy feedback appear more natural. For example, one expert stated that, by displaying social cues, *"EFA tends to come across as a friend; the flow is more natural and maintains communication. In the second example [i.e., with social cues/DP4], [he] would have asked more questions than in the first example [i.e., without DP4]"* (EX1). Moreover, incorporating social cues, such as emojis, also helps to make the conversation appear more familiar to consumers and thus, might increase feedback effectiveness. However, one expert cautioned that these social cues should be designed carefully to not distract from EFA's main purpose to provide energy feedback: *"The bot should be less cheeky and a little more formal because it's about money"* (EX3). Table 2 summarizes the key findings of our focus group discussion with industry experts.

Table 2. Summary of key findings of the focus group discussion

DP	Key findings
DP1	• Provides easy access to information on energy use in natural language • Facilitates consumers' understanding by quickly giving comprehensible answers • Could be individually adapted to the consumer's skill/knowledge level and preferences
DP2	• Helps consumers to directly respond to feedback by pointing out specific measures • Reduces effort for consumers to find out how to use energy more sustainably
DP3	• Facilitates re-engagement or continued interaction with EFA • Needs to include further information about the potential causes of an incident
DP4	• Encourages consumers to interact with EFA (e.g., ask more questions) • Needs to be designed carefully to not distract from EFA's main purpose

The focus group discussion also brought up some interesting aspects about the modality (i.e., text vs. voice) used by CAs for energy feedback. One expert suggested that consumers should be able to communicate with EFA using text messages (e.g., on the phone when they are not at home) and using voice input (e.g., if they own a device like Amazon Alexa). Moreover, they argued that, in some cases, using a voice-based EFA would further reduce the effort for seeking energy feedback since consumers do not need to enter a text message. One expert mentioned that the modality (text vs. voice) could also be automatically selected based on the consumer's current location. Moreover, EFA's functionality could be extended to be able to turn devices on and off, similar to existing smart home solutions.

In conclusion, the industry experts believed that with CAs, such as EFA, energy feedback could take an important step into consumers' daily life and help them to use energy more sustainably. Moreover, they argued that such a solution would provide energy providers with the opportunity to offer their customers a benefit from smart metering technology, which further indicates the relevance of our proposed design for a real-world context. According to the experts, technological advances within the next years will make it possible to easily extract and integrate the data that is required to provide the basis for the implementation of our design. However, they also noted that EFA needs to possess advanced natural language processing capabilities to provide accurate feedback and ultimately, to ensure adoption and continued use by consumers.

6   Conclusion

This paper presents the findings of our DSR project on how to design CAs for energy feedback to promote sustainable use of energy in households. We identified several issues in the design of existing energy feedback solutions and proposed four DPs to address these issues by designing a CA for energy feedback. We instantiated our DPs in a text-based CA called EFA and evaluated it in an exploratory focus group session with industry experts. Overall, the results of our evaluation indicate that CAs represent a promising technology for energy feedback and designing these CAs based on our DPs could enable consumers to use energy more sustainably. We therefore contribute with valuable design knowledge that extends previous research on energy feedback solutions and serves as a starting point for future research on designing CAs for energy feedback.

Although our research follows established guidelines for conducting DSR [12, 24], there are some limitations that need to be discussed. First, we instantiated our DPs in a text-based CA (i.e., chatbot). However, as also illustrated in the feedback by industry experts, voice-based CAs seem to be a promising medium for energy feedback as well, possibly even in combination with a text-based CA. Therefore, future research could instantiate and evaluate our DPs in a voice-based CA such as Amazon's Alexa. Moreover, the evaluation was conducted with industry experts who might be biased because of their familiarity with energy feedback solutions. Thus, another focus group session with real, non-expert users could provide an important complementary perspective on our DPs. Finally, we used an interactive prototype without real data or algorithms to demonstrate EFA's capabilities in two scenarios. Although we argue that this approach is appropriate for a first evaluation of EFA, further research implementing a full infrastructure is needed. Therefore, we plan to implement a fully functional prototype in several households and perform a field-based evaluation study in our future research.

References

1. International Energy Agency: World Energy Investment (2017). https://www.iea.org/publications/wei2017/. Accessed 28 Jan 2018
2. European Commission: 2050 Low-Carbon Economy Roadmap (2017). https://ec.europa.eu/clima/policies/strategies/2050_en. Accessed 15 Jan 2018
3. Kobus, C.B.A., Mugge, R., Schoormans, J.P.L.: Washing when the sun is shining! How users interact with a household energy management system. Ergonomics **56**, 451–462 (2013)
4. Karlin, B., Zinger, J.F., Ford, R.: The effects of feedback on energy conservation: a meta-analysis. Psychol. Bull. **141**, 1205–1227 (2015)
5. Karlin, B., Ford, R., Squiers, C.: Energy feedback technology: a review and taxonomy of products and platforms. Energy Effi. **7**, 377–399 (2014)
6. Weiss, M., Helfenstein, A., Mattern, F., Staake, T.: Leveraging smart meter data to recognize home appliances. In: 2012 IEEE International Conference on Pervasive Computing and Communications, pp. 190–197. IEEE (2012)
7. Pullinger, M., Lovell, H., Webb, J.: Influencing household energy practices: a critical review of UK smart metering standards and commercial feedback devices. Technol. Anal. Strateg. Manag. **26**, 1144–1162 (2014)
8. McTear, M., Callejas, Z., Griol, D.: The Conversational Interface: Talking to Smart Devices. Springer, Heidelberg (2016). https://doi.org/10.1007/978-3-319-32967-3
9. Dale, R.: The return of the chatbots. Nat. Lang. Eng. **22**, 811–817 (2016)
10. Gartner: Top Trends in the Gartner Hype Cycle for Emerging Technologies (2017). https://www.gartner.com/smarterwithgartner/top-trends-in-the-gartner-hype-cycle-for-emerging-technologies-2017/. Accessed 20 Dec 2017
11. Bourgeois, J., Van Der Linden, J., Kortuem, G., Price, B.A., Rimmer, C.: Conversations with my washing machine: an in-the-wild study of demand-shifting with self-generated energy. In: Proceedings of the 2014 ACM International Joint Conference on Pervasive and Ubiquitous Computing, pp. 459–470 (2014)
12. Hevner, A.R., March, S.T., Park, J., Ram, S.: Design science in information systems research. MIS Q. **28**, 75–105 (2004)
13. Tremblay, M.C., Hevner, A.R., Berndt, D.J.: Focus groups for artifact refinement and evaluation in design research. Commun. Assoc. Inf. Syst. **26**, 599–618 (2010)
14. Kluger, A.N., DeNisi, A.: The effects of feedback interventions on performance: a historical review, a meta-analysis, and a preliminary feedback intervention theory. Psychol. Bull. **119**, 254–284 (1996)
15. Sanguinetti, A., Dombrovski, K., Sikand, S.: Information, timing, and display: a design-behavior framework for improving the effectiveness of eco-feedback. Energy Res. Soc. Sci. **39**, 55–68 (2018)
16. Dalén, A., Krämer, J.: Towards a user-centered feedback design for smart meter interfaces to support efficient energy-use choices. Bus. Inf. Syst. Eng. **59**, 361–373 (2017)
17. Froehlich, J.: Promoting energy efficient behaviors in the home through feedback: the role of human-computer interaction. In: Proceedings of the HCIC Workshop (2009)
18. Weiss, M., Staake, T., Mattern, F., Fleisch, E.: Powerpedia - changing energy usage with the help of a smartphone application. Pers. Ubiquit. Comput. **16**, 655–664 (2012)
19. Gnewuch, U., Morana, S., Maedche, A.: Towards designing cooperative and social conversational agents for customer service. In: Proceedings of the 38th International Conference on Information Systems (ICIS), Seoul, South Korea (2017)
20. Weizenbaum, J.: ELIZA - a computer program for the study of natural language communication between man and machine. Commun. ACM **9**, 36–45 (1966)

21. Maedche, A., Morana, S., Schacht, S., Werth, D., Krumeich, J.: Advanced user assistance systems. Bus. Inf. Syst. Eng. **58**, 367–370 (2016)
22. Beale, R., Creed, C.: Affective interaction: how emotional agents affect users. Int. J. Hum. Comput. Stud. **67**, 755–776 (2009)
23. Bickmore, T., Cassell, J.: Relational agents: a model and implementation of building user trust. In: Proceedings of the 2001 SIGCHI Conference on Human Factors in Computing Systems (2001)
24. Kuechler, B., Vaishnavi, V.: Theory development in design science research: anatomy of a research project. Eur. J. Inf. Syst. **17**, 489–504 (2008)
25. Gall, M.: BotPreview.com (2018). https://botpreview.com/. Accessed 28 Jan 2018
26. Venable, J., Pries-Heje, J., Baskerville, R.: FEDS: a framework for evaluation in design science research. Eur. J. Inf. Syst. **25**, 77–89 (2016)
27. Miller, W., Senadeera, M.: Social transition from energy consumers to prosumers: rethinking the purpose and functionality of eco-feedback technologies. Sustain. Cities Soc. **35**, 615–625 (2017)
28. Watson, A., Viney, H., Schomaker, P.: Consumer attitudes to utility products: a consumer behaviour perspective. Mark. Intell. Plan. **20**, 394–404 (2002)
29. Morana, S., Schacht, S., Scherp, A., Maedche, A.: A review of the nature and effects of guidance design features. Decis. Support Syst. **97**, 31–42 (2017)
30. Sarikaya, R.: The technology behind personal digital assistants: an overview of the system architecture and key components. IEEE Sig. Process. Mag. **34**, 67–81 (2017)
31. Tiefenbeck, V., Goette, L., Degen, K., Tasic, V., Fleisch, E., Lalive, R., Staake, T.: Overcoming salience bias: how real-time feedback fosters resource conservation. Manage. Sci. **64**(3), 1458–1476 (2018). https://doi.org/10.1287/mnsc.2016.2646
32. Fogg, B.J.: Computers as persuasive social actors. In: Persuasive Technology: Using Computers to Change What We Think and Do, pp. 89–120. Morgan Kaufmann Publishers, San Francisco (2002)
33. Nass, C., Steuer, J., Tauber, E.R.: Computers are social actors. In: Proceedings of the SIGCHI Conference on Human Factors in Computing Systems, Boston, MA, USA, pp. 72–78 (1994)
34. Ham, J., Midden, C.J.H.: A persuasive robot to stimulate energy conservation: the influence of positive and negative social feedback and task similarity on energy-consumption behavior. Int. J. Soc. Robot. **6**, 163–171 (2014)
35. Statista Number of mobile phone messaging app users worldwide from 2016 to 2021 (2018). https://www.statista.com/statistics/483255/number-of-mobile-messaging-users-worldwide/. Accessed 28 Jan 2018
36. Easwara Moorthy, A., Vu, K.P.L.: Privacy concerns for use of voice activated personal assistant in the public space. Int. J. Hum. Comput. Interact. **31**, 307–335 (2015)
37. Appel, J., von der Pütten, A., Krämer, N.C., Gratch, J.: Does humanity matter? Analyzing the importance of social cues and perceived agency of a computer system for the emergence of social reactions during human-computer interaction. Adv. Hum.-Comput. Interact. **2012**, 1–10 (2012)
38. Klopfenstein, L.C., Delpriori, S., Malatini, S., Bogliolo, A.: The rise of bots: a survey of conversational interfaces, patterns, and paradigms. In: Proceedings of the 2017 Conference on Designing Interactive Systems, pp. 555–565 (2017)
39. Tremblay, M.C., Hevner, A.R., Berndt, D.J.: The use of focus groups in design science research. In: Hevner, A., Chatterjee, S. (eds.) Integrated Series in Information Systems. Design Research in Information Systems, pp. 121–143. Springer, Boston (2010). https://doi.org/10.1007/978-1-4419-5653-8_10

40. Morana, S., Schacht, S., Scherp, A., Maedche, A.: Designing a process guidance system to support user's business process compliance. In: ICIS 2014 Proceedings, pp. 1–19 (2014)
41. Zheng, G., Vaishnavi, V.K.: A multidimensional perceptual map approach to project prioritization and selection. AIS Trans. Hum.-Comput. Interact. **3**, 82–103 (2011)
42. Snow, S., Buys, L., Roe, P., Brereton, M.: Curiosity to cupboard: self reported disengagement with energy use feedback over time. In: Proceedings of the 25th Australian Computer-Human Interaction Conference, pp. 245–254 (2013)

ServiceDesignKIT: A Web Platform of Digital Service Design Techniques

Xuanhui Liu[✉], Erwin Tak-Ming Leung, Peyman Toreini,
and Alexander Maedche

Karlsruhe Institute of Technology (KIT),
Institute of Information Systems and Marketing (IISM), Karlsruhe, Germany
{Xuanhui.liu,peyman.toreini,alexander.maedche}@kit.edu,
erwin.tm.leung@gmail.com

Abstract. A broad spectrum of design techniques is available to support digital service design processes. With the growing number of available design techniques, selecting suitable design techniques becomes increasingly challenging, especially for design novices. In this paper, we present design principles and their instantiation in the Web platform ServiceDesignKIT for supporting design novices in the process of identifying and selecting design techniques. ServiceDesignKIT is a platform that combines an experts' top-down knowledge-based classification with novices' bottom-up suggested tags. With this work, we contribute to the body of design knowledge of Web-based platforms that provides simple and efficient access to design techniques.

Keywords: Digital service design · Design technique · Selection support
Classification · Web platform

1 Introduction

The availability of networked and scalable digital infrastructures enables a shift in the service industry. Digitalized services are more interactive and more flexible in comparing with traditional human-based services [40]. We consider a digital service as "an activity or benefit that one party can give to another, that is, provided through a digital transaction [40]." The design of digital services is not restricted to specific digital service encounters; it covers the whole service process taking service experiences under consideration [24]. Thus, a lot of design activities need to be considered when designing digital services to make sure that consumers get used to enjoying the interaction with digital services [14]. Therefore, an increasing number of design methods, techniques, and tools have been developed for supporting the design process.

In order to scale design processes of digital services, design novices are typically encouraged to learn and apply design techniques. For example, software developers are suggested to apply usability engineering methods in order to deliver components with high usability [4]. In the design process, appropriate design techniques need to be selected based on different design situations to achieve high service experience [26, 42]. With the growing number of design methods, techniques, and tools, and the increasing

© Springer International Publishing AG, part of Springer Nature 2018
S. Chatterjee et al. (Eds.): DESRIST 2018, LNCS 10844, pp. 34–48, 2018.
https://doi.org/10.1007/978-3-319-91800-6_3

involvement of design novices in the design process, the challenge to support design novices in selecting appropriate design techniques is becoming critical [10, 12].

Previous studies have tried to deal with the difficulties of supporting the selection of design techniques in design processes. In the existing literature, we can see that there are studies that focus on proposing experts' knowledge-based classifications of design techniques for supporting design processes, e.g., [2, 33, 34]. Based on the theoretical studies, several Web-based platforms providing classifications and descriptions of design techniques are developed, such as thedesignexchange.org and allaboutux.org. Although these websites include introductions of existing design techniques and classifications, there is a need in the solid grounding of their design principles. Furthermore, the proposed classifications have not yet been evaluated regarding the effectiveness of supporting design novices to select design techniques. Thus, more work is needed explicitly in the context of systematically deriving design principles for Web platforms that can help novices to select suitable design techniques. Hence, this study seeks to answer the following research question:

Which design principles of a Web platform help design novices in better selecting design techniques within digital service design processes?

In order to answer the research question, we follow the design science research paradigm [31]. The applied design science research approach is depicted in Fig. 1. After reviewing related studies, we derive meta-requirements, design principles as well as propose an instantiation in the form of the Web platform – ServiceDesignKIT (servicedesignkit.org). Theoretically, the derived meta-requirements and design principles can be seen as a type V theory [15], which give guidance for researchers to instantiate the theoretical research on classifying design techniques. Practically, this Web platform aims to help design novices to select suitable design techniques by using major, complementary filters; one is based on a classification that is created by experts (i.e., a top-down structured classification), and another is created by novices (i.e., bottom-up suggested tags). In addition, ServiceDesignKIT provides basic descriptions of design techniques. Moreover, users can add new techniques, and bottom-up suggest tags describing design techniques. Users are also enabled to add comments about techniques to exchange knowledge and communicate with other users. The application of the top-down classification and bottom-up tags as a filter and the collection of bottom-up suggested tags and users' comments, which in turn can benefit the research community as a starting point to explore the effects of classifications on the selection support of design techniques.

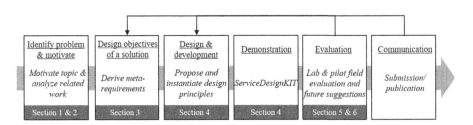

Fig. 1. Design science research approach

The paper is structured in seven sections. In Sect. 2, we introduce conceptual foundations and provide an overview of related works. In Sect. 3, we identify problems and introduce the derived meta-requirements. Section 4 presents design principles and the instantiation of design principles in our Web platform. The evaluation of the Web platform is presented in Sect. 5. Section 6 discusses the contributions, limitations, and suggestions for future works. Finally, in the last section, we provide a conclusion.

2 Foundations and Related Works

2.1 Key Concepts

Before introducing related work, we first explain the following key concepts used in this paper. There are differences between the definitions of tools, techniques, and methods. A tool is a software, a device, a template, etc., which supports a part of the process; a technique is a procedure to achieve the desired outcome, which specifies steps to perform the activity; a method is a problem-solving approach by thinking in a structured way and following principles and rules [3, 20, 35]. However, the usage of these terms is usually mixed, which may cause confusions when identifying and selecting suitable ones in the design process, especially for design novices.

Novices and experts utilize different problem-solving process [36]. When comparing with experts, novices require much effort to access information and find appropriate solutions [36]. Experts incline to solve problems in a top-down manner, while novices tend to use bottom-up procedure [25]. In this study, we focus on providing selection support for design novices. We refer "design novices" to people with little or no formal training in design processes, methods, and tools.

2.2 Related Works

As the purpose of this study is to help design novices in better selecting design techniques, we at first look into the literature that introduces classifications of design techniques. As classification is the beginning of all understanding [39], building classifications can be seen as a first step in supporting the selection process. There are studies classify design methods, techniques, and tools. For example, a taxonomy of design methods and tools with six dimensions is created to guide novices and enhance team collaboration [2]; a framework with three dimensions is suggested to organize design tools and techniques to engage novices to participate in design processes [35]; and a taxonomy with five dimensions is proposed as a basis for selecting design techniques for digital service design processes [23]. An obvious difference among these three studies is: one of them focus on classifying design techniques to benefit the selection process [23], while the other two studies classify two terms together with an emphasis on team collaboration [2, 35]. There are also similarities. The classifications in these three studies are created top-down based on design experts' knowledge. Moreover, the proposed classifications in these three studies lack a systematic evaluation.

Besides the literature that provides classifications, there are Websites build on the theoretical studies of classifying methods, techniques, and tools. For example, thedesignexchange.org is based on the studies of Roschuni et al. [33, 34]; Allaboutux. org is an instantiation of the study of Vermeeren et al. [37]. The theoretical studies behind these two Websites have different purposes of classifying methods. Roschuni et al. aim to provide a standardized way for designers from interdisciplinary backgrounds to communicate design methods by organizing multiple workshops [33, 34]. Vermeeren et al. classify user experience evaluation methods to analyze current states and development needs by conducting surveys with pre-defined categories [37]. The classifications in these studies are foundations when building these two Websites. The Websites provide classifications as filters, which go a step further in the application of the classifications. As the purposes of these two theoretical studies are different, the features of the Websites are also different. In thedesignexchange.org, the provided categories are very complicated. There are five main categories; under each main category, there are at least six sub-categories; under each sub-category, there are more than three sub-sub-categories. However, the large number of categories makes the classification too broad to efficiently help the selection process [27, 29]. On the contrary, allaboutux.org provides limited numbers of pre-defined categories for selecting user experience evaluation methods. There are also similarities between these two Websites. For example, people can leave comments on both Websites. Allaboutux.org enables people to give feedback and ask questions. Comparing with allaboutux.org, the comment feature on thedesignexchange.org is more advanced. Users are also enabled to suggest new design methods, which helps to improve the content on the Web platform. However, the users are only allowed to use the pre-defined categories to suggest the classification, which may not coherent with the categories in the users' mind.

The descriptions and comparisons of related works present that most of the existing studies on classifications are built from a top-down experts' perspective with mixed definitions of tools, techniques, and methods. The instantiations of the theoretical studies visualize classifications as filters to support the selection, but the features still lack the consideration of categorizations from design novices' perspective.

3 Meta-requirements

Based on the literature review, we propose the following meta-requirements which are generalized requirements with a purpose to solve several classes of problems [11].

The first meta-requirement (MR1) refers to providing a filter for narrowing down the choice of design techniques. The currently used categories in existing Web platforms mix the definition of method, technique, and tool, possibly resulting in confusions of terms [3, 20, 35]. Comparing with the term "design method" and "design tool," a "design technique" provides steps of a procedure and can be classified in several ways for support the selection [3, 35]. Also, with a clear explanation of steps, it is convenient for novices to learn and use design techniques in design processes. Thus, it is necessary for the Web platform focusing on design techniques. Although it is impossible for a Web platform to include all design techniques, plenty of design techniques should be included for people to choose. Moreover, for the purpose of supporting the selection process of design techniques, it is necessary to include a classification with a limited number of categories to ensure the categories are useful [27]. Hence, a well-structured classification with useful categories and plenty of design techniques should be included as a basis to support the selection process.

MR1: *Provide a clearly structured classification as a filter to support searching and finding suitable design techniques.*

The second meta-requirement (MR2) refers to enabling co-creation of classifications of design techniques between experts and novices. The key content of the Web platform is the description of design techniques and their categories. It should be possible to extend and improve over time. As it is impossible for the Web platform to contain all complete information of each design technique, users of the Web platform should be enabled to edit the existing techniques on the Web platform. Also, new design techniques are being developed; it should be possible to add new design techniques to the Web platform. So far, the experts' knowledge-based classifications have not yet been evaluated in the field, and the existing categories of design techniques may not be entirely accurate. Moreover, as more and more novices participate in service design processes, people may have different understandings of categorizing design techniques. A bottom-up suggestion of categories and tags should be enabled. Because bottom-up suggested categories and tags can reflect people's understanding of design techniques and provide additional access for filtering and searching design techniques beyond experts' generated categories [7, 13]. The co-creation of the classification can provide better support for the selection of design techniques [29].

MR2: *Enable users of the Web platform to extend and improve the contained design techniques, and bottom-up suggest categories and tags of design techniques.*

The third meta-requirement (MR3) refers to exchanging knowledge of design techniques on the Web platform. As formal training influences the understanding of design techniques, it is necessary to enable people from different backgrounds to communicate and discuss their understandings of different design techniques [12]. Besides, design participants not only need to learn how to use design techniques, but also need to collaborate with others [1]. Moreover, users' comments can further help the optimization of the Web platform to provide better solutions for filtering design techniques. Hence, the Web platform should enable people to share knowledge of design techniques.

MR3: *Enable users of the Web platform to comment and discuss design techniques.*

The fourth meta-requirement (MR4) refers to personalizing the selection of design techniques. Because our target group is novices, they may have different purposes when using the Web platform to filter design techniques and different design situations when using design techniques. It should be possible for the users to save their favorite design techniques to a shortlist which will allow them to retrieve and to have easier access to these design techniques. A personalizing feature should be included to incentivize users' dedication [21], which may also motivate them to contribute to the content of the Web platform.

MR4: *Enable users to save their favorite design techniques to a shortlist.*

4   Design Principles and Implementation of ServiceDesignKIT

In order to address the meta-requirements above, we propose the following design principles (DP). Each design principle may solve multiple meta-requirements, and each meta-requirement may be addressed by multiple design principles.

We identified that novices need selection support for finding appropriate design techniques (MR1). Structured categories of design techniques and plenty of design techniques need to be provided. Because structured categorization can help people's selection process [5], a taxonomy (i.e., classification) with conceptualized categories needs to be used as a basis for the categorization of the design techniques. We use the categories of a top-down taxonomy from Liu et al. on the Web platform [23]. Because the development of the taxonomy follows a widely cited taxonomy development method, which argues that the number of categories should be limited [29], which is consistent with MR1. In addition, as the Web platform should include a sufficient range of design techniques for design participants to select from, many design techniques should be provided. So far, we included 71 design techniques[1]. As the initial content may not be complete, users of the Web platform should be enabled to add new design techniques, edit the content of existing design techniques and bottom-up suggest categories and tags of design techniques, in order to make the Web platform improving and extending (MR2). Ideally, the Web platform will improve over time in this way. Improved content can also support the selection by offering better content that helps users to distinguish and decide between the provided design techniques. A control system should be included in order to allow to check and approve changes to the content [6]. This feature is intertwined with the bottom-up suggestion to make sure the suggested contents are checked before publishing to the public.

DP1: *Include a pre-defined top-down structured classification of design techniques and a controlled knowledge base for people to bottom-up alter the contents.*

A communication capability is needed for fostering discussion (MR3). Professional designers can share their experiences of specific design techniques, which can help others to find suitable design techniques. Novices can ask questions by leaving comments. The knowledge exchange is consistency with the emphasis on collaboration between experts and novices [17]. This feature can further enhance the content of the Web platform (MR2). In order to motivate people to use the Web platform, personalization features should be considered. Users of the Web platform can access a shortlist of favorite design techniques which are suitable for their purposes and design situations (MR4). A benefit of this feature is that recurrent users can save their favorite design techniques and retrieve them on their next visit. Another benefit is that, after saving a shortlist of favorite design techniques, users can filter appropriate ones from a small group of potentially suitable design techniques and further narrow down the selection result.

---

[1] The initial version has 70 design techniques from the literature and websites which provide detail descriptions of design techniques. One of the users suggested a design technique, which makes it become 71. The number will change in the future.

DP2: *Include communication features and personalization features.*

A short summary of the two proposed design principles and associated meta-requirements is presented in Table 1.

Table 1. Design Principles (DP) and Meta-requirements (MR)

DP	MR addressed by DP
DP1: A pre-defined top-down classification and controlled bottom-up suggested tags of design techniques	MR1, MR2
DP2: Communication and personalization features	MR2, MR3, MR4

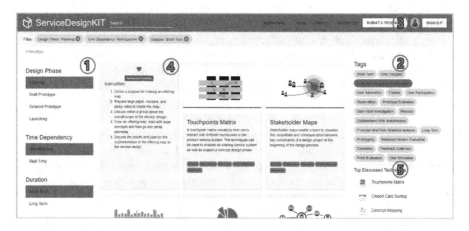

Fig. 2. Homepage of ServiceDesignKIT (Numbers refer to specific features)

On the basis of the proposed design principles, we developed a Web platform – ServiceDesignKIT (servicedesignkit.org). Figure 2 presents the homepage. The filter function is realized by using a taxonomy and a tag cloud (DP1). On the left-hand side, an experts' knowledge-based taxonomy is provided (1 in Fig. 2); on the right-hand side, a bottom-up built tag cloud is included (2 in Fig. 2). A distinct feature of the tag cloud is that the tags are created by users of ServiceDesignKIT. Users are not limited to use only one filter but can mix the two. In order to provide plenty of design techniques for users to select, suggestions of new design techniques are enabled. When clicking on the button for submitting a design technique (3 in Fig. 2), a new design technique can be added, which enables the improvement of the content of the Web platform (DP2). The appearance of each design technique is designed as a flip card (4 in Fig. 2). The use of the flip cards, in which digital objects behave like their counterparts in reality, as shown by the easy transition from front to back. By hovering over a flip card, people can switch from the front to the back. On the back of the flip card, there is a heart symbol which enables people to add the design technique to a favorite list to retrieve (DP2). When clicking on a design technique cards, a subpage that describes detail information of each design technique will appear. Users are enabled to communicate with others by leaving comments, giving feedback and asking questions (DP2). The design techniques that are most discussed are depicted below the tag cloud (5 in Fig. 2). In the subpage of each design technique, users can edit the content, suggest categories and tags of existing design technique. On submission, an edited design technique runs through the content management system that is only accessible to the platform administrator. Pending design techniques are temporarily inaccessible to users of the platform. The administrator can check, approve, edit, and remove the newly added or edited design techniques to ensure the quality of the content (DP1).

5 Evaluation

The evaluation of ServiceDesignKIT is separated into two stages. The first stage is a lab experiment by using eye-tracking and retrospective think-aloud with a specific focus on usability. The second stage represents a small-scale pilot study with the application of ServiceDesignKIT in a Master course for students at our university.

5.1 Lab Evaluation

In the lab evaluation, we sought to know how people use ServiceDesignKIT before they become familiar with it. Eye-tracking and retrospective think-aloud are relevant techniques for the lab evaluation. Eye-tracking can be used to collect people's first impression and cognitive process of websites [8, 30]. Retrospective think-aloud enables experiment participants to work in silence and describe their experience and thoughts afterward [9, 16]. The combination of eye-tracking and retrospective think-aloud can reflect whether the features on ServiceDesignKIT can be recognized by people, which further can be used to analyze whether the implemented design principles caused people's attention when they were using the Web platform.

Six people participated in the lab evaluation. Because three to four participants can yield 80% of the usability findings [22, 38], six participants are sufficient for this usability test. The six participants included four males and two females whose ages ranged from 25 to 34. All of them were pursuing or already had a higher university education (four Ph.D. students and two Master students, with backgrounds related to information, software). None of them was familiar with ServiceDesignKIT. We prepared three tasks for participants: (i) to select up to three design techniques and add them to the favorite list; (ii) to find the top-discussed design techniques and write a comment; (iii) to submit a new design technique with the given attributes. Before giving the three tasks, participants were asked to imagine that they had to create a new service and planned to select design techniques on the Web platform. During the experiment, the participants at first looked at each web page for five seconds and got the first impression. The eye-movement data were recorded by a commercial Web-based eye-tracking application (eyezag.de) [43]. Then, the participants were asked to use ServiceDesignKIT to perform the three tasks. The screen was recorded during the process. After they finished their tasks, they were asked to verbalize their thoughts when using ServiceDesignKIT while watching screen recordings. Their descriptions were recorded for analysis.

The evaluation result shows that all participants could understand the main features of ServiceDesignKIT. They agreed that the categorization of the design techniques was clear, and the function of editing design techniques, adding to the favorites, and giving comments were working well. Overall, ServiceDesignKIT seems to instantiate the proposed design principles successfully. However, there were issues identified in the evaluation, which may need to be considered in the further optimization.

For a detailed analysis of visual activities of participants during the eye-tracking study, we defined different areas of interests (AOIs) on the homepage (Fig. 3). AOIs are defined as areas of a display or a visual environment that are of interest to the research [18]. During the eye-tracking study, we recorded fixations of the participants. Figure 3 (right) presents the heat map of the homepage. In a heat map, cold colors like blue indicate fewer fixations, the warm colors like green, yellow, and red indicate more fixations. Based on collected fixations and the provided heat map, the illustrations of design techniques attracted the attention of the users more than the other parts. In Table 2, the detailed results of the eye-movement data are summarized with the information of hit rate (ratio of participants that were fixed inside the AOI), average fixation duration, and average time to first fixation. The recorded eye-movement data present that design technique cards (AOI2) attracted the most attention (all of the participants with an average duration of 2.81 s) in comparing with the other AOIs. Categories of design techniques (AOI1) also drew a lot of attention (83.33% of the participants with an average duration of 0.84 s) while the top discussed techniques (AOI4) got the least attention. Based on the time to the first fixation, we can see that the first noticed AOI was design technique cards (AOI2) and the last noticed AOI was the

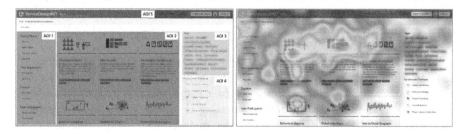

Fig. 3. Left: AOIs of the homepage. AOI1 is the filter function; AOI2 includes design techniques that are presented on flip cards; AOI3 displays the tags; AOI4 includes top discussed design techniques; AOI5 includes functions for submitting a new design technique and viewing favorite design techniques. Right: heat map of the homepage. (Color figure online)

Table 2. Statistics of AOIs

	AOI1	AOI2	AOI3	AOI4	AOI5
Hit rate	83.33%	100%	33.33%	16.67%	16.67%
Average fixation duration	0.78 s (SD = 0.55 s)	2.81 s (SD = 0.64 s)	0.84 s (SD = 0.44 s)	0.13 s (SD = 0 s)	0.77 s (SD = 0 s)
Average time to first fixation	1.39 s (SD = 1.28 s)	0.02 s (SD = 0.02 s)	3.44 s (SD = 0.97 s)	4.44 s (SD = 0 s)	0.33 s (SD = 0 s)

top discussed techniques (AOI4). The submission function (AOI5) was an exception since the location of AOI5 is far from other four AOIs. Only one participant recognized AOI5 (with a fixation duration of 0.77 s and time to the first fixation of 0.33 s).

The combination of the results from eye-tracking with the results from retrospective think-aloud demonstrates that the design features and implemented design principles caused people's attention. For DP1, participants could understand the categories as a filter, as participant3 said: *"That's what I discovered, I could actually draw down and use more than one category."* The feature of bottom-up suggestion of design techniques is also obvious, e.g., *"The next was to submit a technique. It was very nice that I clicked on that directly (Participant4)."* Additionally, the participants were satisfied with the visualization design. For example, flip cards components of design techniques (AOI2), participant1 said: *"I think they are pretty nice the cards getting flip."* For DP2, the comment feature was straightforward to use, as participant5 said *"I clicked on one of the top discussed techniques and I saw the comment box. I added my comment. This step is very easy."* The personalization feature was also well addressed by providing a favorite list, e.g., *"I clicked on the heart and added it to my favorites (Participant2)."* However, some detail features still need optimization. First, the left-side categories can be visualized more like a filter. Although the categories drew participants' attention (AOI1) and can be used to filter design techniques, they are not as self-explaining as we expected, as participant3 told us *"But I didn't know that they are something like a filter."* Second, the top discussed techniques are not easy to be recognized. Eye-tracking result presents top discussed techniques (AOI4) attracted little attention, which is coherent with the participants' feedback in retrospective think-aloud section. Participant3 said *"it was quite difficult to find top discussed techniques because it wasn't highlighted much."* Third, the submission function (AOI5) was not very obvious, but people can find it when they need. The optimization suggestion of the submission function relates to showing the feedback after submitting a design technique.

5.2   Field Evaluation

A first attempt was to use ServiceDesignKIT in the winter semester 2017 within the lecture "Digital Service Design" offered at a Germany university. ServiceDesignKIT was provided as a supplement for students to select and apply design techniques as part of the exercises of an applied capstone project. We introduced the Web platform in the lecture but did not force students to use it to select relevant design techniques. 33 Master students (three to four build up a team, nine teams in total) participated in the capstone project. The capstone project was about a design challenge in the field of financial services given by one of our industry partners. Each student team used several design techniques to address the challenge and delivered a low-fidelity prototype. In the last lecture, we distributed a questionnaire to the students who attended the lecture and collected 13 complete questionnaires. The average age of the students who filled out the survey was 25 years, and five of them were female, eight of them were male. They study industrial engineering as well as information engineering & management. The students can be seen as novices in digital service design, who might be the potential users of ServiceDesignKIT in the future.

The questionnaire for the pilot evaluation was designed based on the design principles. Output quality, user-system relationship, perceived ease of use, perceived usefulness, and intention to use were measured. User-system relationship refers to user's knowledge of the system, involvement, and access to the system [19, 32]. Output quality refers to the relevance, accuracy, precision, and completeness of the output from the system [19, 28]. The output of ServiceDesignKIT is the filter results of design techniques. Besides, it was also important for us to understand the intention to use, perceived ease of use and usefulness of ServiceDesignKIT. Intention to use relates to the extent that people intend to use a system in the future as a routine part of the job at every opportunity [41]. Perceived ease of use and perceived usefulness refer to user-friendly and the enhancement of job performance [41]. Each question was measured on a 7-point Likert type scale (1 = strongly disagree, 7 = strongly agree). We used Excel 2016 to analyze the mean and standard deviation of each item (Cronbach's Alpha = 0.875). The detail result is presented in Fig. 4.

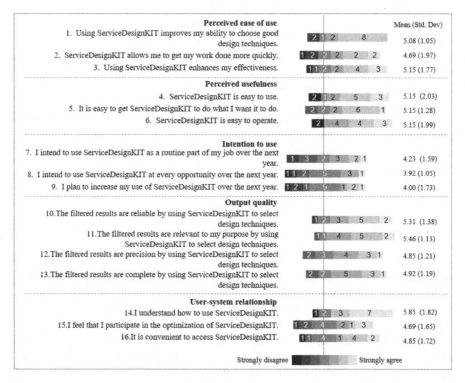

Fig. 4. The result of field evaluation. The number in the stacked bar chart means the number of participants that chose a level of agreement.

The evaluation of perceived ease of use and perceived usefulness presents that the participants agreed that the Web platform could enhance the effectiveness of selecting design techniques and was easy to operate. In Fig. 4. We can see that most of the participants gave positive evaluations to ease of use and usefulness. The output quality also received a high evaluation, which means the filter results by using the Web platform can be considered to be trustworthy by the users. Furthermore, it explains that the implemented top-down classification in the Web platform can provide reliable, relevant and precise filter results and the bottom-up suggested tags can also support the selection process (DP1). If we only look at the means of the questionnaire, the evaluation result of user-system relationship is quite similar to output quality. However, the bar chart presents that there were fewer participants held positive attitude on user-system relationship than output quality. Although the result reflects the easy access of the Web platform, much effort needs to be put into motivating people to participate in the optimization of the Web platform (DP2). Comparing to the mentioned four constructs, the means of items of intention to use are relatively quite low. The stacked bar chart presents that the ratio of participants who gave positive and negative evaluations to intention to use is nearly same. One reason could be that the Web platform needs more features to motivate people to use it in the long run. Another reason may regard to the sample. Some students may only use this tool for the lecture but may not have a further career plan on the domain of digital service.

6   Discussion

6.1   Theoretical Contributions and Application of ServiceDesignKIT

In this study, an artifact is developed based on theoretical studies on classifications of design techniques. The derived meta-requirements and suggest design principles provide guidance for researchers to instantiate theoretical studies on classifications of design techniques to support the selection process of design techniques, which can be seen as a type V theory [15]. The suggested design principles seek to combine the top-down classification from experts' perspective with the bottom-up suggested tags from novices' perspective. This attempt is a starting point to analyze differences and similarities of top-down and bottom-up classifications, which will further generate a theory for analysis (type I theory) [15]. In addition, the attempt of applying different classifications is a basis for the further research on the effects of classifications on the selection support of design techniques.

ServiceDesignKIT offers a practical contribution where it can be used as a filter for the selection of design techniques under different design situations. Besides a top-down classification, ServiceDesignKIT enables people to bottom-up suggest tags of design techniques, which can reflect novices' understandings of design techniques and emphasizes the importance of the involvement of novices in digital service design processes. ServiceDesignKIT enables people to create and improve information about design techniques but also prevents the contribution of inaccurate information. The use of controlled knowledge base and the implementation of communication capabilities in the form of user comments enables the refinement of the categories and extends existing knowledge about design techniques, which further improve the content on ServiceDesignKIT. The combination of a top-down classification and bottom-up tags represents a new approach for filtering design techniques. It can improve novices' performance of deciding suitable design techniques for different design situations.

Additionally, the Web platform enables the exchange of design knowledge and best practices among design experts and novices. Furthermore, ServiceDesignKIT can also be applied to train novices to have an overall understanding of design techniques. The attempt we did in the lecture is an example.

6.2   Limitations and Future Works

There are some limitations of ServiceDesignKIT. The Web platform in its current form contains 71 design techniques with basic information; more time is needed for people to build up a powerful crowd-sourced knowledge base. There are some drawbacks of the evaluation. The results of both lab and pilot field evaluation rely on rather a small sample size. Extensive evaluation with a larger sample size and diverse participants will help to create more accurate and solid results and more in-depth feedback. In the field evaluation, the filter quality received a positive evaluation, but we did not look into how people combined top-down classification and bottom-up tags when filtering design techniques. Further detail research is needed on how different classifications can support the selection process of design techniques. Moreover, people's intention of use needs to be further analyzed and increased. More features are needed to motivate novices to use the Web platform. The differences between novices and experts when using classifications need further research, which will also benefit the collaboration between them. In additions, long-term use may reveal unforeseen issues that require further work to identify and resolve. With the rise in the popularity of machine learning and social media platforms, future research may need to investigate how these concepts can contribute to ServiceDesignKIT. Future research may extend the currently used selection support by recommending bundles of design techniques based on specific design projects and situations.

7   Conclusion

The objective of this study is to derive new design knowledge for Web platforms for supporting novices to select design techniques. To achieve this goal, we analyzed studies on classifications of design techniques and their instantiations, identified meta-requirements and design principles. Based on the identified design principles, ServiceDesignKIT was developed. A lab evaluation and a pilot application were conducted, which shows that ServiceDesignKIT meets the identified design principles. In the future, we will apply further optimizations in the next design cycle.

References

1. Agid, S.: "…It's your project, but it's not necessarily your work…": infrastructuring, situatedness, and designing relational practice. In: Proceedings of the 14th Participatory Design Conference on Full Papers - PDC 2016, Aarhus, Denmark, pp. 81–90 (2016)
2. Alves, R., Jardim Nunes, N.: Towards a taxonomy of service design methods and tools. In: Falcão e Cunha, J., Snene, M., Nóvoa, H. (eds.) IESS 2013. LNBIP, vol. 143, pp. 215–229. Springer, Heidelberg (2013). https://doi.org/10.1007/978-3-642-36356-6_16

3. Brinkkemper, S.: Method engineering: engineering of information systems development methods and tools. Inf. Softw. Technol. **38**, 275–280 (1996)
4. Bruun, A.: Training software developers in usability engineering: a literature review. In: Proceedings: NordiCHI, pp. 82–91 (2010)
5. Bussolon, S.: Card sorting, category validity, and contextual navigation. J. Inf. Archit. **1**(2), 5–29 (2009)
6. Chaturvedi, A.R., Dolk, D.R., Drnevich, P.L.: Design principles for virtual worlds. MIS Q. **35**(3), 673–684 (2011)
7. Choi, Y.: A complete assessment of tagging quality: a consolidated methology. J. Assoc. Inf. Sci. Technol. **66**(4), 798–817 (2015)
8. Duchowski, A.T.: A breadth-first survey of eye-tracking applications. Behav. Res. Methods Instrum. Comput. **34**(4), 455–470 (2002)
9. Fonteyn, M., Kuipers, B., Grobe, S.: A description of think aloud method and protocol analysis. Qual. Health Res. **3**(4), 430–441 (1993)
10. Fuge, M., Peters, B., Agogino, A.: Machine learning algorithms for recommending design methods. J. Mech. Des. **136**(10), 101103 (2014)
11. Walls, J.G., Widmeyer, G.R., El Sawy, O.A.: Assessing information system design theory in perspective: how useful was our 1992 initial rendition? J. Inf. Technol. Theory Appl. **6**(3), 43–58 (2004)
12. Gerrard, V., Sosa, R.: Examining participation. In: Proceedings of the 13th Participatory Design Conference on Research Papers, PDC 2014, Windhoek, Namibia, pp. 111–120 (2014)
13. Golder, S.A., Huberman, B.A.: Usage patterns of collaborative tagging systems. J. Inf. Sci. **32**(2), 198–208 (2006)
14. Goldkuhl, G., Perjons, E.: Focus, goal and roles in e-service design five ideal types of the design process. e-Service J. **9**(2), 24–45 (2014)
15. Gregor, S.: The nature of theory in information systems. MIS Q. **30**(3), 611–642 (2006)
16. Van Den Haak, M.J., De Jong, M.D.T., Schellens, P.J.: Constructive interaction: an analysis of verbal interaction in a usability setting. IEEE Trans. Prof. Commun. **49**(4), 311–324 (2006)
17. Hileman, R.: An introductory lecture for digital designers (1998). http://www.smsys.com/pub/dsgnmeth.pdf
18. Hyrskykari, A., Ovaska, S., Majaranta, P., Räihä, K.-J., Lehtinen, M.: Gaze path stimulation in retrospective think-aloud. J. Eye Mov. Res. **2**(4), 1–18 (2008)
19. Ives, B., Olson, M.H., Baroudi, J.J.: The measurement of user Information satisfaction. Commun. ACM **26**(10), 785–793 (1983)
20. Kettinger, W.J., Teng, J.T.C., Guha, S.: Business process change: a study of methodologies, techniques, and tools. MIS Q. **21**(1), 55–80 (1997)
21. Kim, S.S., Son, J.: Out of dedication or constraint? A dual model of post-adoption phenomena and its empirical test in the context of online services. MIS Q. **33**(1), 49–70 (2009)
22. Lewis, J.R.: Sample sizes for usability studies: additional considerations. Hum. Factors J. **36**(2), 368–378 (1994)
23. Liu, X., Werder, K., Mädche, A.: A taxonomy of digital service design techniques. In: Thirty Seventh International Conference on Information Systems, pp. 1–12 (2016)
24. Lusch, R.F., Vargo, S.L.: Service-dominant logic: reactions, reflections and refinements. Mark. Theory **6**(3), 281–288 (2006)
25. MacKay, J.M., Elam, J.J.: A comparative study of how experts and novices use a decision aid to solve problems in complex knowledge domains. Inf. Syst. Res. **3**(2), 150–172 (1992)

26. Maguire, M.: Methods to support human-centred design. Int. J. Hum Comput Stud. **55**, 587–634 (2001)

27. Miller, G.A.: The magic number seven plus or minus two: some limits on our capacity for processing information. Psychol. Rev. **63**, 91–97 (1956)

28. Mirani, R., King, W.R.: Impacts of end-user and information center characteristics on end-user computing support. J. Manag. Inf. Syst. **11**(1), 141–166 (1994)

29. Nickerson, R.C., Varshney, U., Muntermann, J.: A method for taxonomy development and its application in information systems. Eur. J. Inf. Syst. **22**, 336–359 (2013)

30. Nielsen, J., Pernice, K.: Eyetracking Web Usability. New Riders, Berkeley (2009)

31. Peffers, K., Tuunanen, T., Rothenberger, M.A., Chatterjee, S.: A design science research methodology for information systems research. J. Manag. Inf. Syst. **24**(3), 45–77 (2007)

32. Raymond, L.: Organizational characteristics and MIS success in the context of small business. MIS Q. **9**(1), 37 (1985)

33. Roschuni, C., Kramer, J., Agogino, A.: Design talking: how design practitioners talk about design research methods. In: Proceedings of the 12th International Conference on Design Education DEC 2015, Boston, Massachusetts, USA, pp. 1–8 (2015)

34. Roschuni, C., Kramer, J., Qian, Z., Zakskorn, L., Agogino, A.: Design talking: an ontology of design methods to support a common language of design. In: Proceedings of the 20th International Conference on Engineering Design (ICED 2015), Milan, Italy, pp. 285–294 (2015)

35. Sanders, E.B.-N., Brandt, E., Binder, T.: A framework for organizing the tools and techniques of participatory design. In: Proceedings of the 11th Biennial Participatory Design Conference, PDC 2010, Sydney, Australia, pp. 195–198. ACM (2010)

36. Schenk, K.D., Vitalari, N.P., Davis, K.S., Schenk, K.D.: Differences between novice and expert what do we know analysts: systems and what do we do? J. Manag. Inf. Syst. **15**(1), 9–50 (1998)

37. Vermeeren, A., Law, E., Roto, V.: User experience evaluation methods: current state and development needs. In: Proceedings of the 6th Nordic Conference on Human-Computer Interaction (NordiCHI 2010), Reykjavik, Iceland, pp. 521–530. ACM (2010)

38. Virzi, R.A.: Refining the test phase of usability evaluation: how many subjects is enough? Hum. Factors J. **34**(4), 457–468 (1992)

39. White, H.: Tropics of Discourse: Essays in Cultural Criticism. The Johns Hopkins Press, Baltimore (1978)

40. Williams, K., Chatterjee, S., Rossi, M.: Design of emerging digital services: a taxonomy. Eur. J. Inf. Syst. **17**(5), 505–517 (2008)

41. Wixom, B.H., Todd, P.A.: A theoretical integration of user satisfaction and technology acceptance. Inf. Syst. Res. **16**(1), 85–102 (2005)

42. Zomerdijk, L.G., Voss, C.A.: Service design for experience-centric services. J. Serv. Res. **13**(1), 67–82 (2010)

43. Zugal, S., Pinggera, J.: Low–cost eye–trackers: useful for information systems research? In: Iliadis, L., Papazoglou, M., Pohl, K. (eds.) CAiSE 2014. LNBIP, vol. 178, pp. 159–170. Springer, Cham (2014). https://doi.org/10.1007/978-3-319-07869-4_14

Design Foundations

Making Sense of Design Science in Information Systems Research: Insights from a Systematic Literature Review

Alexander Herwix[(⌧)] and Christoph Rosenkranz

University of Cologne, 50969 Cologne, Germany
{herwix, rosenkranz}@wiso.uni-koeln.de

Abstract. This study presents insights from a systematic literature review of design science in IS. A lack of agreement on how to classify and demarcate design science from behavioral science research led to the iterative development of a theoretically-grounded, encompassing framework of knowledge contributions in the larger context of general scientific inquiry as well as associated coding schemata. The results of the systematic literature review support our framework and the idea that paradigmatic boundaries (e.g., design science versus behavioral science research) are difficult to uphold for contemporary information systems research.

Keywords: Conceptual framework · Coding schema
Systematic literature review · Paradigms · Design science

1 Introduction

Design science research (DSR) as a distinct paradigm of research [1] has been gaining more and more acceptance and interest in the information systems (IS) discipline [2–5]. Despite or maybe due to this general success, however, different perceptions of DSR and its role in the IS discipline exist [1, 6–15]. The situation is so diverse as to prompt some researchers to call the current state a "hodgepodge" [14, 15], and to question the necessity of DSR as a distinct paradigm altogether [11]. In particular, it remains unclear if or how DSR and *behavioral science research (BSR)* should be demarcated and integrated, as design science studies may contribute not only design science outcomes (i.e., innovative artifacts or prescriptive knowledge) but also behavioral science outcomes (i.e., descriptive theory) (e.g., [16]) and, conversely, behavioral science studies may articulate important design knowledge (e.g., [17]). To start resolve this confusion, research efforts have been directed at developing frameworks and perspectives to make sense of this complex entanglement of research methods and contributions [2, 14, 18–21]. For example, elementary frameworks have used descriptive dimensions such as "knowledge goals" (i.e., design and science) and "knowledge scope" (i.e., situational vs. abstract) to map possible knowledge contributions in DSR with the intention of improving its execution and communication [14, 20, 21][1].

---

[1] We group these related frameworks under the label of *dualities of goals and scope frameworks*.

© Springer International Publishing AG, part of Springer Nature 2018
S. Chatterjee et al. (Eds.): DESRIST 2018, LNCS 10844, pp. 51–66, 2018.
https://doi.org/10.1007/978-3-319-91800-6_4

This study contributes to this line of research by investigating the implications that these emerging perspectives on knowledge contributions have for the framing of DSR as a distinct paradigm within IS research. We set out to answer the research question: *What are the implications of the dualities of goals and scope frameworks on DSR as a distinct paradigm of IS research?* Towards this goal, this paper reports the development of an encompassing framework for the classification of knowledge contributions in the larger context of general scientific inquiry. The development is supported by a systematic literature review of DSR-related studies in the AIS senior scholars' basket of journals [22]. The main insight of this work is the recognition that extant research on knowledge contributions in DSR can usefully be extended to traditional BSR, which suggests that the entanglement of design and science runs so deep as to render the often-articulated framing of DSR as a distinct research paradigm for individual studies difficult to hold up. As a way forward we propose to move towards more fine-grained and meta-paradigmatic models of scientific inquiry such as articulated in this article.

2   Theoretical Background

It is common consensus that novel and reliable knowledge contributions are the constituent goal and purpose of any scientific enterprise [23]. However, what exactly constitutes a valid knowledge contribution and how it should be formulated is less clear and has been a topic of debate within the IS discipline [2, 7, 24–26]. Underlying this discussion is the recognition of the different knowledge goals that may come with different kind of scientific inquiries (e.g., BSR vs. DSR) and the divergent knowledge production processes as well as evaluation criteria that come with it [1, 2, 14, 25–27]. For example, it is common sense that the knowledge production processes of typical BSR such as a large scale quantitative study or a small scale qualitative study, and a DSR study are qualitatively different and should therefore be evaluated differently. This phenomenon is particularly pronounced in DSR, where an inherent duality between design and science is presumed [14]. Whereas *design* is a practical, generally creative and hard to structure process concerned with the construction of useful artifacts, *science* is a rigorous, systematic and highly structured endeavor concerned with the discovery of new knowledge about the nature of things – DSR is difficult to grasp because it aims to integrate the two in a mutually supporting whole [14].

To deal with this tension several studies have started to develop means of demarcating DSR studies into related but distinct knowledge production episodes that allow for a more accurate tracing of research processes and the use of appropriate evaluation criteria [14, 20, 21]. For example, Baskerville et al. [14] articulate the genres of inquiry framework which identifies two orthogonal dualities along which to classify knowledge production episodes: (1) the aforementioned design-science duality of knowledge goals and (2) the idiographic-nomothetic duality of knowledge scope. Knowledge scope describes the range of applicability that a specific knowledge contribution has [14]. For example, some knowledge pertains to complete classes of things (e.g., Newtonian gravity applies to all things with mass) whereas other knowledge is specific to a given instance (e.g., practitioners' theories about the adoption of a specific IT system). Consequently, these differences in scope are characterized as a duality of *idiographic* (i.e., pertaining to particular instances) and *nomothetic* (i.e., pertaining to a complete class). These orthogonal dualities lead Baskerville et al. [14] to formulate four distinct genres of inquiry inherent to DSR as summarized in Table 1. Akoka et al. [20] extend this perspective with an existing taxonomy of evaluation methods in DSR [28] by mapping a set of six different knowledge types into the four quadrants and associating appropriate evaluation methods with them.

Table 1. Genres of inquiry of design science knowledge based Table 2 (p. 553) of [14].

		Knowledge Goals	
		Design	Science
Knowledge Scope	Nomothetic	**Nomothetic Design** *Nature*: Knowledge applicable to general classes of design problems, general solution artifacts, and their relationships *Criteria*: utility, inventiveness, innovativeness, originality, applicability, generalizability, external validity, transferability, consistency, reliability	**Nomothetic Science** *Nature*: Generalized knowledge and generalized theories about natural or social settings and how these settings interact with classes of artifacts. *Criteria*: objectivity, internal validity, applicability, generalizability, external validity, consistency, reliability
	Idiographic	**Idiographic Design** *Nature*: Knowledge necessary for the research-and-development of an individual product. The knowledge role of the artifact is one of materializing or embodying this knowledge. *Criteria*: utility, inventiveness, innovativeness, originality, prolonged engagements, persistent observation, triangulation, contextualization, dialogical reasoning, sensitivity to multiple interpretations, suspicion	**Idiographic Science** *Nature*: Knowledge to understand the underlying causes, structures, and generative mechanisms responsible for observed patterns of an individual artifact in a unique environment. *Criteria*: credibility, transferability, dependability, confirmability, prolonged engagements, persistent observation, triangulation, contextualization, dialogical reasoning, sensitivity to multiple interpretations, suspicion

Barquet et al. [21] propose a related but slightly different perspective for the demarcation of knowledge production episodes. They build on (1) Gregor and Hevner's [2] distinction between *prescriptive*[2] vs. *descriptive*[3] knowledge types which together are argued to form the bedrock of DSR and (2) Goldkuhl and Lind's [19] differentiation between *situational* vs. *abstract* knowledge to propose the *Prescriptive Descriptive Situational Abstract (PDSA)* framework. While the differentiation between situational vs. abstract knowledge is portrayed and used very similarly to the idiographic vs.

---

[2] Knowledge concerned with the bringing into being of something based on the ancient greek notion of technê.

[3] Universally discoverable knowledge of how things are based on the ancient greek notion of epistêmê.

nomothetic duality of the genres of inquiry framework, the distinction between two different knowledge types provides a different perspective from the knowledge goals of the genres of inquiry framework. Whereas the PDSA framework necessarily assumes the existence of exactly two different knowledge types, the genres of inquiry framework remains agnostic on this front (e.g., [20] extend the framework by mapping six different knowledge types within the four genres). Moreover, in contrast to the genres of inquiry framework, the PDSA framework aims to integrate a time component by recognizing different phases of DSR projects (see Fig. 1). This allows for the tracing of knowledge contributions over time, which may facilitate theorizing and over time even lead to novel research opportunities on aggregated research data [21].

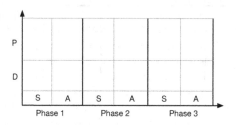

Fig. 1. The PDSA framework based on Fig. 2 (p. 405) in [21].

Taken together, these research efforts demonstrate the necessity and utility of demarcating knowledge production episodes for a complex endeavor such as DSR. While there seems to be no complete consensus about the best way of demarcating knowledge production episodes yet, the similarities of the proposed frameworks are striking. This leads us to group these frameworks under the label of *"dualities of goals and scope" frameworks*.

3   Research Approach

Our research approach is inspired by [18, 19, 29] and visualized in Fig. 2 according to our conceptual framework of scientific inquiry (cf. Sect. 4).

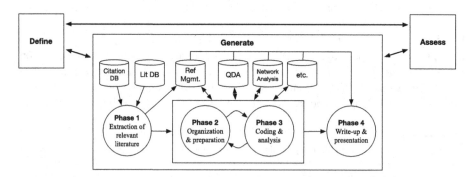

Fig. 2. Research approach based on the tool-support literature review approach by [29].

On the most abstract level, our research inquiry followed a complex and recursive movement pattern through three different generic activities, sic. *definition* of an objective, *generation* of a solution and *assessment* of the objective and/or solution. In particular, the study did not follow a linear path through these generic activities but iterated between them until a satisficing state was achieved. For example, the overarching objective of this inquiry was (after formative assessments, i.e., collegial feedback) refined multiple times, starting from *understanding the current state of DSR as paradigm of IS research,* to the final research question elaborated in this paper: "*What are the implications of the dualities of goals and scope frameworks on DSR as a distinct paradigm of IS research?*" To answer these objectives, we conducted a systematic literature review of DSR-related studies in high quality journals (i.e., the AIS senior scholar basket of eight [22]). This approach is an appropriate research method for this goal as high quality journals have emerged as the outlet of choice for the IS community [30, 31].

Methodologically, the literature review followed a version of the four-phase tool-supported literature review approach proposed by Bandara et al. [29]. The core idea of this approach is to increase the rigor of the literature review with comprehensive tool support. Tools such as reference managers and qualitative data analysis (QDA) tools are used to extend the analyses that can be done based on the literature and associated metadata. After having defined the objective for the review, the relevant literature was extracted from the knowledge base in phase 1. This phase corresponds to a multi-staged search inquiry for journals, databases, and finally literature based on keywords, references or citations [32] utilizing tools such as literature databases or citation analysis tools [29]. Table 2 summarizes the keyword search that this research is based upon.

The literature search was supported by LitSonar.com [33] an online tool which can generate appropriate search queries for a variety of literature databases (i.e., it converts a generic search query as shown in Table 1 into queries tailored for selected databases). The exact queries used for the literature search, the resulting data set and other supplementary data (e.g., complete article classification) can be retrieved from the authors. Based on a search of the IS senior scholar's basket ranging from 1977–2017[4], a sample of 145 records was identified. A reference manager was used to consolidate the literature and associated meta data. Due to intersecting journal names, a handful of articles did not correspond to the selected journals and were consequently removed from the data set. Additionally, errata notes, editorials, and commentaries were also removed.

Afterwards, and extending Bandara et al. [29], the literature *processing* was executed as a multi-instance conceptual analysis cycle with two main phases of *organization & preparation* as well as *coding & analysis*. The general goal of the literature processing was to make sense of the literature and, more specifically, to get an empirically grounded picture of what the actual characteristics of DSR in IS are. To facilitate the processing, the bibliometric metadata (including title, keywords, abstracts) was loaded into the QDA tool MaxQDA.

---

[4] The exact date of the search was the 2nd of November, 2017.

Table 2. Overview of keyword search

Logical Query (title, keywords, abstract)	"design science" OR "design research" OR "design theory" OR DSR OR "science of design" OR "science of the artifical" OR "sciences of the artifical" OR (design AND (artefact OR artifact))			
Journal	Coverage	Database	Records	
JAIS	2000-11/2017	AISeL	33	~23%
MISQ	1977-11/2017	EBSCO BSC	32	~22%
EJIS	1991-11/2017	ProQuest	22	~15%
JMIS	1984-11/2017	EBSCO BSC	22	~15%
JIT	1986-11/2017	ProQuest	11	~8%
ISR	1990-11/2017	EBSCO BSC	10	~7%
ISJ	1998-11/2017	EBSCO BSC	10	~7%
JSIS	1991-11/2017	ScienceDirect	5	~3%
		Total	145	

Next, extant literature was reviewed to find suitable inclusion and exclusion criteria as well as classification schema for DSR-related literature. While this exercise sounds cursory easy, few literature reviews on DSR in IS present a literature selection approach that is able to identify and classify all of the different DSR-related studies effectively [34]. Thus, a sound conceptual basis needed to be developed to underpin the construction of a comprehensive classification schema. Towards this goal, seminal conceptualizations of scientific inquiry [35, 36] were reviewed and integrated with the emerging research around the dualities of goals and scope frameworks in DSR to explicate the interdependent relationships between these aspects and facilitate the development of a comprehensive classification schema.

The development proceeded iteratively via the concurrent construction of a conceptual framework, operationalization in the form of a comprehensive coding schema for the classification of design science related studies, and assessment through coding of random samples of the data set through the first author as well as discussions of the results between the authors of this paper and a further colleague. The final conceptual framework and classification schema, which is presented and demonstrated in Sect. 4, was then used by the first author to assess the complete set of bibliometric metadata. These results are presented in Sect. 5 and provide empirical evidence for the utility of the conceptual framework and classification schema as well as preliminary insights into the current state of DSR-related studies.

4   Scientific Inquiry Framework and Classification Schema

Underlying any serious sense making effort of DSR in IS must be a grounded understanding of the relationship between design and science [1, 2, 6, 14]. While the mainstream of literature on DSR in IS is generally rooted in Herbert Simon's seminal work the *Sciences of the Artificial* [35] and its central idea of establishing a rigorous discipline around the construction of useful artifacts, design has always been recognized as an indispensable part of the natural sciences and the scientific method itself [36]. As Fig. 3 highlights, purposefully designed artifacts are the window through which scientists aim to generate insightful data that allows them to discover the, otherwise hidden, true state of nature (e.g., the Large Hadron Collider at CERN is such a purposeful artifact for the natural sciences). Thus, design must be an important component in any scientific inquiry. Where natural science and a design science as envisioned by Simon differ is the goal to which design is utilized. Whereas design in science is strongly focused on developing artifacts that help to discover the true state of nature, design science has a broader focus on accumulating knowledge about developing artifacts that have utility for solving challenging problems. Thus, on the one hand, science might be viewed as one of the stakeholders of design science but not its sole raison d'être and on the other, design science aims to be a science itself – that is to accumulate a reliable body of knowledge about the true nature of how to effectively and efficiently solve challenging problems with useful artifacts through the application of the fundamental principles of science as articulated in the scientific method (see Fig. 3) [1, 2, 36]. Viewed in this way design science may (controversially) be seen as a scientific framework broader than the natural sciences aimed at employing the principles of the scientific method to increase the utility and effectiveness of artifacts for the achievement of human goals.

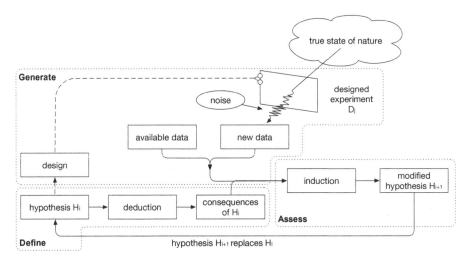

Fig. 3. An overview of the scientific method, based on Gauch [36] (Fig. 12.1, p. 407) who refined Box et al. [37] (Fig. 1.2, p. 4).

Figure 4 introduces the *scientific inquiry framework* (SIF) as a possible starting point for such a broad, integrated design science view on generic scientific inquiries. In general terms, the SIF focuses on a specific scientific inquiry and describes selected relevant relationships between the material artifacts, knowledge, as well as environment relative to it. More detailed, a scientific inquiry is conceptualized as a generic possibly highly iterative, complex and nested process through three generic phases or activities that characterize the scientific method or any other problem solving inquiry: *define* a problem (e.g., not enough knowledge and data to know if a hypothesis is likely to be true), *generate* a solution (e.g., design an experiment and collect empirical data) and *assess* in how far the solution has solved the problem (e.g., analyze the new data to support or refine the hypothesis; see Fig. 3). This generic demarcation of a problem solving inquiry is reminiscent of and inspired by Simon's articulation of the generator-test cycle [35] (pp. 128–130), which views design as the generation of possible alternatives that can be tested in regards to a given goal. However, where Simon's articulation has only an implicit recognition of problem/goal definition within the generator phase, it is explicitly recognized in the SIF as this allows for a cleaner separation of concerns and a recursive application of the framework. For example, execution of an experiment can be defined as a high-level research inquiry with multiple sub-inquiries being defined and conducted within it (e.g., identification of a proper sample population, etc.).

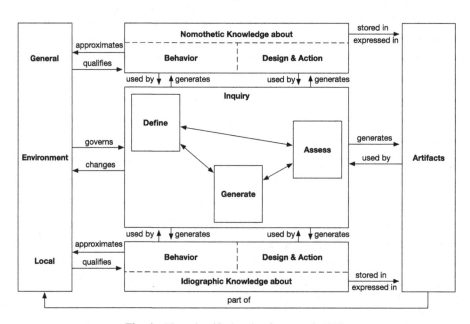

Fig. 4. The scientific inquiry framework (SIF)

Any scientific inquiry is posited to be situated in and *governed* by an *environment,* which is *changed* through the enactment of the inquiry as new *material artifacts* and *knowledge* are *generated*. Following Goldkuhl and Lind [19], a specific inquiry is positioned as the arbiter between abstract or *nomothetic knowledge* on the one hand and situational or *idiographic knowledge* on the other.[5] During the enactment of scientific

---

[5] We decided to use idiographic/nomothetic rather than situational/abstract to describe the different scopes of knowledge as it seems plausible to have abstract representations of situational knowledge, which might lead to unnecessary confusion.

inquiries, general theories or other forms of nomothetic knowledge are applied to solve idiographic problems, which generate new insights that may in turn ground new or support existing nomothetic knowledge. Adapting Baskerville et al. [14], knowledge in general is conceptualized as being focused on understanding *behavior* (i.e., knowledge goals of science) or *design & action* (i.e., knowledge goals of design).[6] In this view, any scientific inquiry – be it focused on developing useful and innovative artifacts for business needs as in mainstream DSR in IS or understanding the true state of nature as in the natural sciences – builds on prior knowledge about the behavior or nature of things as well as effective design or action, and may extend them in turn. For example, the scientific method itself can be characterized as knowledge about the effective design of inquiries for the purpose of generating convergent knowledge about phenomena. Moreover, any well documented scientific inquiry – even in the natural sciences – can be considered to generate a small idiographic (design) knowledge contribution about the tailoring of the scientific method to a specific circumstance (i.e., an illustrative example of an instantiation of the scientific method).

Material artifacts are the visible and intersubjective outcomes that persist and manifest the scientific enterprise over time. Thus, material artifacts must be produced by any rigorous scientific inquiry that aims to contribute to a scientific discipline. However, DSR highlights that material artifacts may not only store but also embody knowledge and generally facilitate the achievement of goals [1, 2, 25]. Consequently, a highly generative cycle may be created when scientific inquiries are focused on iterative self-improvement. For example, material artifacts (e.g., software support for scientific inquiries) support the generation of new knowledge (e.g., improvements for scientific inquiries) which in turn allows the construction of superior material artifacts (e.g., better software support) and new knowledge (e.g., improvements for scientific inquiries). This overt feedback cycle supports the inherent importance and entanglement of design and science articulated in the SIF and highlights the multiplicative value of (meta-)research focused on the improvement of scientific inquiries [38].

Tables 3 and 4 show the classification schemata that were developed in concert with the SIF. The general idea behind the classification of scientific inquiries is the focus on artifacts (constructs, models, methods and instantiations [39]) as communicable outputs of scientific activity (see Table 3). Each relevant research artifact that is communicated within a given article is mapped to a set of criteria (based on [14, 19]) which summarize the underlying scientific inquiry in general terms. This allows for a concise and comparable representation of research methodologies. In addition to the classification schema for scientific inquiries, we also propose a schema for the classification of complete articles to allow for insights regarding the combination of related but not nested scientific inquiries[7], and the traditional distinction between BSR and DSR paradigms.

---

[6] We chose the label *behavior* rather than *science* as we argue that design also applies to science.

[7] Here we build on and extend Iivari's [40] notion of research strategies in DSR. The basic idea is to identify research strategies by examining in what order idiographic or nomothetic inquiries are executed. For example, research developing a nomothetic methodology and then testing it in a case study would be classified as *Top-Down*; design action research engaging in a practical problem and distilling nomothetic insights from it would be classified as *Bottom-Up; Mixed* is used to classify research which exhibits elements of both strategies.

Table 3. Classification schema for scientific inquiries

Criteria	Values			
Artifact	Free text			
Artifact type	Construct (+subcode)	Model (+subcode)	Method (+subcode)	Instantiation (+subcode)
Knowledge focus	Behavior		Design & Action	
Knowledge scope	Idiographic		Nomothetic	
Method	Free text			
Theoretical grounding	Free text		No	
Empirical grounding	Free text		No	
Evaluation	Free text		No	

Table 4. Additional classification schema for complete articles (grey shadowing indicates the exemplary classification of this research article, see Sect. 4.1)

Criteria	Values				
Research strategy	Nomothetic	Top-Down	Mixed	Bottom-Up	Idiographic
Traditional "paradigm"	Behavior			Design & Action	
Meta-DSR	Yes			No	

4.1 Demonstration

This article is used as a running example to illustrate the use of the SIF and the associate classification schemata. Figure 2 in Sect. 3 has already utilized the SIF to visualize the executed literature review approach more accurately than the original source, which only presented an idealized picture of the research approach (cf. [29]). Visual representations of sub-inquiries are also possible but would generally go beyond the scope of a scientific article published as a static text and require a more dynamic medium to become interesting and useful. For example, one could imagine detailed interactive representations of applied research methods with the possibility of drilling-down into specific aspects of the research method.

Table 5 classifies the relevant artifacts (i.e., contributions) and scientific inquiries of this article. In general, five different inquiries can be classified as relevant contributions of this work. For example, the SIF for describing scientific inquiries in context is a model (framework) with a focus of contributing to nomothetic knowledge about the behavior of scientific inquiries. It was conceptualized based on a synthesis of extant literature and empirical grounding through concurrent use for the analysis of literature (a proxy for scientific inquiries). The SIF has been instantiated (see SI3) but not formally evaluated.

Table 5. Classification of relevant artifacts and scientific inquiries

Criteria	SI₁	SI₂	SI₃	SI₄	SI₅
Artifact	SIF for describing scientific inquiries in context	Schemata for classifying scientific inquiries and articles	Demonstration of the SIF and classification schemata	Aggregated results of the systematic literature review	Demonstration of the systematic literature review process
Artifact type	Model (Framework)	Model (Schema)	Instantiation (Example)	Model (Implicit)	Instantiation (Example)
Knowledge focus	Behavior	Behavior	Design & Action	Behavior	Design & Action
Knowledge scope	Nomothetic	Nomothetic	Idiographic	Nomothetic	Idiographic
Method	Conceptualization	Analysis	Analysis	Literature analysis	Sys. lit. review
Theoretical grounding	[14, 19, 35, 36]	SIF + [14, 19]	SIF + Schemata	SIF + Schemata	SIF + Schemata + [29]
Empirical grounding	Literature analysis	Literature analysis	Literature analysis	Literature analysis	Literature analysis
Evaluation	No	No	No	No	No

Table 4 presents the overall classification of this research article as following a mixed research strategy of iteratively combining empirical insights from idiographic application as well as nomothetic kernel theory; being generally affiliated with the behavioral science paradigm as the largest emphasis is set on the description and explanation of scientific inquiries; and contributing explicitly to meta-research about DSR.

5 Results

The aggregated results of the coding of the bibliometric metadata are shown in Tables 6, 7, and 8. Table 6 shows the balanced distribution between articles positioned in the *design/action* and *behavioral science* paradigms in our data set. Articles are classified as *design/action* if they explicitly position their work as action (design) research, DSR, or overtly engage in the development of useful artifacts (e.g., IT artifact or a research method). More traditional observational studies as well as experiments are classified as *behavior*. As would be expected, meta-research about design science is slightly more commonly found to be positioned in the behavioral paradigm. Regarding research strategies, a strong emphasis of top-down focused research is found for the *design/action* paradigm, which indicates that DSR published in high quality IS journals is mostly theory-driven (i.e., strategy 1 of [40]). Interestingly, mixed strategies that combine theory-driven and practice-driven work are also observed (e.g., [41, 42]), which suggests that commonly held views [40] of two different strategies for DSR may need to be refined.

Table 7 shows that almost half of all behavioral articles in the data set contributed nomothetic design knowledge (e.g., design principles or theories). This fact strongly suggests that a simple distinction between two research paradigms is not an adequate way of describing the complex nature of scientific inquiry. Interestingly, articles which do not fall into the design/action paradigm report significantly less evaluations than articles associated with the behavioral paradigm, which might suggest that a recognition of DSR principles in behavioral studies could improve the rigorousness of research contributions. For example, reminiscent of iterative DSR, nascent theories derived from cases could be formally evaluated regarding their utility for practice (e.g., through focus groups of practitioners).

Table 8 highlights that all research, regardless of paradigm, produces artifacts as outputs (e.g., theoretical frameworks, etc.). Moreover, it confirms that even behavioral studies may produce highly design-oriented output such as methods or theories for design and action [25, 26].

Table 6. Overall distribution of articles and distribution of Meta-DSR studies and research strategies per paradigm. Except for the total, percentages are relative to the paradigm.

| | | Total | Meta-DSR | Research Strategies | | | | |
				Nomo-thetic	Top-Down	Mixed	Bottom-Up	Idio-graphic
Paradigm	Design/Action	77 ~53%	14 ~18%	0	61 ~79%	10 ~13%	6 ~9%	0
	BSR	68 ~47%	26 ~38%	11 ~16%	30 ~44%	8 ~12%	17 25%	1 ~1%
	Total	145	40 ~28%	11 ~8%	91 ~63%	18 ~12%	23 ~16%	1 ~1%

Table 7. Distribution of scientific inquiries per paradigm. Counts reflect at least one coding per article. Except for the total, percentages are relative to the paradigm.

| | | Scientific Inquiries | | | | | | |
| | | Behavior | | Design & Action | | Grounding | | Evalua-tion |
		Idio-graphic	Nomo-thetic	Idio-graphic	Nomo-thetic	Theo-retical	Empiri-cal	
Paradigm	Design/Action	53 ~69%	21 ~27%	50 ~65%	73 ~95%	76 ~99%	56 ~73%	64 ~83%
	BSR	44 ~65%	62 ~91%	6 ~9%	34 50%	53 ~78%	52 ~76%	20 ~30%
	Total	97 ~67%	83 ~57%	56 ~39%	107 ~74%	129 ~89%	108 ~75%	84 ~58%

Table 8. Distribution of artifacts per paradigm. Counts reflect at least one coding per article. Except for the total, percentages are relative to the paradigm.

		Artifacts				
		Construct	Model	Method	Instantiation	Design Theory
Paradigm	Design/ Action	9	39	48	70	9
		~12%	~51%	~62%	~91%	~12%
	BSR	15	53	21	28	6
		~22%	~78%	~31%	~41%	~9%
	Total	24	92	69	98	15
		~17%	~63%	~48%	~68%	~10%

6   Discussion

First, it must be noted that the aggregated results of the systematic literature review can only to be taken as a coarse approximation of the true state of research as only abstracts, titles, and keywords were used for this analysis. Nevertheless, the results – even at this level of detail – do strongly suggest that the BSR/DSR paradigm view of IS research is too simplistic, and that more fine-grained approaches for making sense of research are needed. For example, there are clear and explicit cases of behavioral design studies, for example, a field study that is combined with design theorizing to arrive at a design theory without the actual construction and evaluation of an artifact [43]. We classified this study as belonging to the BSR paradigm as it does not conform to the traditional articulation of DSR as put forward by [1], but see it as a clear example for the necessity of moving beyond simple paradigmatic distinctions in IS research. The results of the systematic literature review demonstrate that our more accurate, metaparadigmatic model of scientific inquiry can relieve this situation.

More generally, our results support the existing research stream on knowledge contributions in DSR [14, 20, 21] by providing a first systematic overview of the diversity of knowledge scope and goal in high quality design-oriented IS research. We extend this research stream by being the first to suggest that this perspective is not only applicable to DSR but can also be used to make sense of scientific inquiries in general. Specifically, we argue that knowledge goal and scope are important characteristics of BSR, too. However, as the examined data set only consisted of bibliometric metadata and was biased towards design-oriented research, future research should evaluate the framework with a more comprehensive (i.e., full texts) and less biased data set to strengthen the evidence for the generalizability of the framework. Further, future research could also move beyond a simple aggregated analysis as presented in this article and investigate new ways of analyzing and supporting research via their constituent scientific inquiries. For example, combinations of scientific inquiries could be analyzed and recommendations be made (e.g., using a theory of research utility [44] or based on historical data). Research on scientific diversity [3, 44] could inspire such an effort.

7 Conclusion

This article presents a conceptual framework which reconciles the "dualities of goals and scope" frameworks from DSR in the larger context of general scientific inquiry. The framework as well as the results of a systematic literature review provide strong evidence for the necessity of moving beyond simplistic paradigmatic boundaries in IS research. The adoption of a metaparadigmatic model of scientific inquiry as proposed in this article could be an important step towards successfully integrating design and behavior-oriented IS research into a more cohesive and cumulative discipline.

References

1. Hevner, A.R., March, S.T., Park, J., Ram, S.: Design science in information systems research. MIS Q. **28**, 75–105 (2004)
2. Gregor, S., Hevner, A.R.: Positioning and presenting design science research for maximum impact. MIS Q. **32**, 337–355 (2013)
3. Rai, A.: Diversity of design science research. Manag. Inf. Syst. Q. **41**, iii–xviii (2017)
4. vom Brocke, J., Hevner, A., Maedche, A.: Call for papers, issue 1/2019 - design science research and digital innovation. Bus. Inf. Syst. Eng. **59**, 309–310 (2017)
5. Goes, P.B.: Editor's comments: design science research in top information systems journals. MIS Q. **38**, iii–viii (2014)
6. McKay, J., Marshall, P., Hirschheim, R.: The design construct in information systems design science. J. Inf. Technol. **27**, 125–139 (2012)
7. Fischer, C., Winter, R., Wortmann, F.: Design theory. Bus. Inf. Syst. Eng. **2**, 387–390 (2010)
8. Niederman, F., March, S.T.: Design science and the accumulation of knowledge in the information systems discipline. ACM Trans. Manage. Inf. Syst. **3**, 1–15 (2012)
9. Iivari, J.: A paradigmatic analysis of information systems as a design science. Scand. J. Inf. Syst. **19**, 5 (2007)
10. Baiyere, A., Hevner, A., Gregor, S., Rossi, M.: Artifact and/or theory? Publishing design science research in IS. In: ICIS 2015 Proceedings (2015)
11. Lee, A.S., Chiasson, M., Alter, S., Kremar, H.: Long live design science research! .... and remind me again about whether it is a new research paradigm or a rationale of last resort for worthwhile research that doesn't fit under any other umbrella. In: ICIS 2012 Proceedings (2012)
12. Purao, S., Baldwin, C., Hevner, A.R., Storey, V.C., Pries-Heje, J., Smith, B., Zhu, Y.: The sciences of design: observations on an emerging field. Commun. AIS **23**, 523–546 (2008)
13. Hevner, A.R.: A three cycle view of design science research. Scand. J. Inf. Syst. **19**, 4 (2007)
14. Baskerville, R., Kaul, M., Storey, V.C.: Genres of inquiry in design-science research: justification and evaluation of knowledge production. MIS Q. **39**, 541–564 (2015)
15. Iivari, J.: Information system artefact or information system application: that is the question. Inf. Syst. J. **27**, 753–774 (2017)
16. Qiu, L., Benbasat, I.: Evaluating anthropomorphic product recommendation agents: a social relationship perspective to designing information systems. J. Manag. Inf. Syst. **25**, 145–181 (2009)
17. Germonprez, M., Hovorka, D., Gal, U.: Secondary design: a case of behavioral design science research. J. Assoc. Inf. Syst. **12**, 662 (2011)

18. Goldkuhl, G.: The empirics of design research: activities, outcomes and functions. In: International Conference on Information Systems (ICIS 2013), 15–18 Dec 2013, Milan, Italy. AIS eLibrary (2013)

19. Goldkuhl, G., Lind, M.: A multi-grounded design research process. In: Winter, R., Zhao, J. L., Aier, S. (eds.) DESRIST 2010. LNCS, vol. 6105, pp. 45–60. Springer, Heidelberg (2010). https://doi.org/10.1007/978-3-642-13335-0_4

20. Akoka, J., Comyn-Wattiau, I., Prat, N., Storey, V.C.: Evaluating knowledge types in design science research: an integrated framework. In: Maedche, A., vom Brocke, J., Hevner, A. (eds.) DESRIST 2017. LNCS, vol. 10243, pp. 201–217. Springer, Cham (2017). https://doi.org/10.1007/978-3-319-59144-5_12

21. Barquet, A.P., Wessel, L., Rothe, H.: Knowledge accumulation in design-oriented research. In: Maedche, A., vom Brocke, J., Hevner, A. (eds.) DESRIST 2017. LNCS, vol. 10243, pp. 398–413. Springer, Cham (2017). https://doi.org/10.1007/978-3-319-59144-5_24

22. AIS. http://aisnet.org/?SeniorScholarBasket

23. Popper, K.: The Logic of Scientific Discovery. Routledge, Abingdon (2005)

24. Walls, J.G., Widmeyer, G.R., El Sawy, O.A.: Building an information system design theory for vigilant EIS. Inf. Syst. Res. 3, 36–59 (1992)

25. Gregor, S., Jones, D.: The anatomy of a design theory. J. AIS 8, 312–335 (2007)

26. Gregor, S.: The nature of theory in information systems. MIS Q. 30, 611–642 (2006)

27. Sein, M.K., Henfridsson, O., Purao, S., Rossi, M., Lindgren, R.: Action design research. MIS Q. 35, 37–56 (2011)

28. Prat, N., Comyn-Wattiau, I., Akoka, J.: A taxonomy of evaluation methods for information systems artifacts. J. Manag. Information Syst. 32, 229–267 (2015)

29. Bandara, W., Furtmueller, E., Gorbacheva, E., Miskon, S., Beekhuyzen, J.: Achieving rigor in literature reviews: insights from qualitative data analysis and tool-support. Commun. Assoc. Inf. Syst. 34, 154–204 (2015)

30. Baskerville, R., Lyytinen, K., Sambamurthy, V., Straub, D.: A response to the design-oriented information systems research memorandum. Eur. J. Inf. Syst. 20, 11–15 (2011)

31. Österle, H., Becker, J., Frank, U., Hess, T., Karagiannis, D., Krcmar, H., Loos, P., Mertens, P., Oberweis, A., Sinz, E.J.: Memorandum on design-oriented information systems research. Eur. J. Inf. Syst. 20, 7–10 (2011)

32. vom Brocke, J., Simons, A., Niehaves, B.: Reconstructing the giant: on the importance of rigour in documenting the literature search process, pp. 1–13 (2009)

33. Sturm, B., Schneider, S., Sunyaev, A.: Leave no stone unturned: introducing a revolutionary meta-search tool for rigorous and efficient systematic literature searches. In: ECIS (2015)

34. Fischer, C.: The information systems design science research body of knowledge–a citation analysis in recent top-journal publications. In: PACIS 2011 Proceedings (2011)

35. Simon, H.A.: Sciences of the Artificial. MIT Press, Cambridge (1996)

36. Gauch, H.G.: Scientific Method in Practice. Cambridge University Press, Cambridge (2003)

37. Box, G.E., Hunter, W.G., Hunter, J.S.: Statistics for Experimenters (1978)

38. Venable, J., Baskerville, R.: Eating our own cooking: towards a design science of research methods. In: Proceedings of the 11th European Conference on Research Methods in Business and management, University of Bolton, Bolton, UK, pp. 399–407 (2012)

39. March, S.T., Smith, G.F.: Design and natural science research on information technology. Decis. Supp. Syst. 15, 251–266 (1995)

40. Iivari, J.: Distinguishing and contrasting two strategies for design science research. Eur. J. Inf. Syst. 24, 107–115 (2015)

41. Kolfschoten, G.L., de Vreede, G.-J.: A design approach for collaboration processes: a multimethod design science study in collaboration engineering. J. Manag. Inf. Syst. **26**, 225–256 (2009)
42. Nissen, M.E.: Dynamic knowledge patterns to inform design: a field study of knowledge stocks and flows in an extreme organization. J. Manag. Inf. Syst. **22**, 225–263 (2005)
43. Germonprez, M., Kendall, J.E., Kendall, K.E., Mathiassen, L., Young, B., Warner, B.: A theory of responsive design: a field study of corporate engagement with open source communities. Inf. Syst. Res. **28**, 64–83 (2017)
44. Grover, V., Lyytinen, K.: New state of play in information systems research: the push to the edges. MIS Q. **39**, 271–275 (2015)

Design Science in the Field: Practice Design Research

Göran Goldkuhl[1,2(✉)] and Jonas Sjöström[1]

[1] Department of Informatics and Media, Uppsala University, Uppsala, Sweden
jonas.sjostrom@im.uu.se
[2] Department of Management and Engineering, Linköping University,
Linköping, Sweden
goran.goldkuhl@liu.se

Abstract. There exist different types or genres of design science research (DSR) in information systems, like laboratory-oriented and practice-oriented DSR. This paper investigates arguments for a practice-oriented approach to DSR. It uses the research approach of practice research as a starting point to elaborate on a practice-oriented DSR approach we label Practice Design Research (PDR). In doing so, we address two unresolved issues in IS DSR: Theorizing and evaluation. PDR consists of two inter-related sub-activities: theorizing and situational design inquiry. The conduct of situational design inquiry is described as iterative cycles of (1) pre-evaluate, (2) plan & design, (3) test & intervene and (4) post-evaluate. We justify the foundations of these iterative sub-activities/cycles through a theoretically informed argument based on pragmatist philosophy and practice theory.

Keywords: Design science · Practice research · Epistemology
Practice theory · Evaluation · Theorizing · Pragmatism

1 Introduction

Design science research (DSR) has emerged as a viable research approach in information systems (IS). The interest for this type of research among IS scholars seems to be still growing. We see many applications of DSR, and there are many meta-scientific contributions concerning DSR methodology and epistemology. Despite several years of progress in DSR, there are unresolved issues, controversies and even confusion among IS scholars concerning how to conduct DSR. Gregor and Hevner [11, p. 338] state: "We contend that ongoing confusion and misunderstandings of DSR's central ideas and goals are hindering DSR from having a more striking influence on the IS field. A key problem that underlies this confusion is less than full understanding of how DSR relates to human knowledge". Iivari [15, p. 107] takes a similar position, stating that "the scientific discourse on DSR is still in a state of conceptual confusion", suggesting that one cause of confusion exists due to different types or DSR genres. He has identified two types of DSR genres that are also characterized but not labeled. We have given them the following labels: (1) A *laboratory approach*, in which the DSR scholar addresses a general problem (conceived of as a "class of problems") through

© Springer International Publishing AG, part of Springer Nature 2018
S. Chatterjee et al. (Eds.): DESRIST 2018, LNCS 10844, pp. 67–81, 2018.
https://doi.org/10.1007/978-3-319-91800-6_5

the design of "conceptual artifacts" and possibly materialized instantiations. The laboratory approach does not require specific and real problems in real-life practice contexts. (2) A *practice approach*, in which the DSR scholar solves real-life issues by building and implementing artifacts into practice. Collaboration with practitioners, in this genre of DSR, is essential.

Iivari [15] claims that the laboratory genre seems to be the prevailing approach in the IS DSR community following such bias in the seminal work of Hevner et al. [14]. This can explain the criticism and argumentation of Sein et al. [35] when introducing their intervention-oriented approach to DSR labeled Action Design Research (ADR). They claim that "traditional design science does not fully recognize the role of organizational context in shaping the design as well as shaping the deployed artifact." [ibid, p. 38]. How to take into account specific practice contexts in DSR efforts is thus one critical concern for DSR.

The two identified DSR genres have a close resemblance to a similar discourse within the discipline human-computer interaction (HCI). Zimmerman and Forlizzi [47] label this type of research as "research through design" and they distinguish between the two strategies of (1) *research through design in the lab* and (2) *research through design in the field*. Confer also characterizations in [17].

Interestingly – despite the emerging recognition within the IS community that DSR may benefit from elaborating on the relationships between research and practice – there has not been any substantial efforts to exapt ideas from the field of practice research into the DSR field. Practice research (PR) has emerged as a viable research approach in different social sciences. There exists an active branch within the discipline of social work [28, 32, 40]. Similar approaches, with the same or similar labels, appear in e.g. nursing [38], organizational strategy [45], urban planning [44], education [26] and human-computer interaction [19]. Practice research in IS [7, 8, 23] may arguably encompass action research, design research and evaluation research as special variants. Practice research resonates well with mode 2 knowledge production [6] and engaged scholarship [41].

With this backdrop, we turn to two controversies and not yet fully resolved issues in DSR: *Theorizing* and *evaluation*. First, the role of *theorizing* in DSR. Early dominant publications, e.g. [14, 29], downplayed the role of theory as an outcome from DSR. There have been many objections to this a-theoretical stance; e.g. [10, 12, 18, 20, 42]. It is not only a matter of the nature of a theory outcome (as design theory or design principles), but also how theorizing takes place as an integral part of the DSR process. In some established DSR process models, e.g. [29], theorizing has no distinct place. Second, the role of *evaluation* in DSR. In Hevner et al. [14] DSR is understood, in its essence, as an iterative cycle of build and evaluate activities. However, these authors did not detail how evaluation should inform the design process in different stages. As a response to this, DS researchers proposed several evaluation frameworks, suggesting roles and process points for evaluation, e.g. [37, 43]. In addition, there are alternative approaches, like ADR [35], where evaluation is fully integrated into other activities of building and intervention and thus not seen as separate and distinct activities.

We could add to these two DSR issues the intersection of the two. How is evaluation related to theorizing? Should it be seen as a part of theorizing or should be closely related to the design process of a new artifact?

In this paper, we embrace a practice view of DSR. The main purpose is to elaborate a practice-based DSR approach. When doing this we seek to clarify the meaning of different aspects of DSR, especially theorizing and evaluation by exploring DSR as a mode of practice research. We exapt ideas from practice research as a general topic as a means to conceptualize DSR and its constituents of evaluation and theorizing. The purpose of the paper is thus to describe and explain DSR based on an explicit practice perspective.

2   Research Approach

We use two unresolved DSR issues – evaluation and theorizing – together with the knowledge need for an elaborated practice-based DSR as impetuses for this paper. They form together a problematic situation in this inquiry. The way that we frame DSR, either as a laboratory exercise or a practice improvement effort in the field, has fundamental consequences for DSR conceptualization and performance. Our purpose is to give a contribution to *DSR as research in the field* (i.e., into practices). We define DSR as a practice loop, i.e., moving from problematic situations in a practice through design and back to an artifact-renewed and improved practice (Fig. 1).

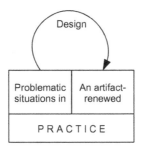

Fig. 1. Design research as a practice loop

It is fundamental to start the process with the practice and its problematic situation and to end the process with a renewed and improved practice. This means that we propose to use design (research) as a way to conduct an inquiry process in its original pragmatic sense [4], i.e. as movement from a problematic situation to a resolved and settled situation.

The way we have conducted this is in itself through an inquiry. The different problems, concerns and issues described above constitute the problematic situation that needs to be resolved through our inquiry of this paper. The resolved situation, as our knowledge contribution, is a practice-oriented conceptualization of design research. We sketch an approach to design research that we have labelled practice design research (PDR). We will in the next Sect. 3 go through some important literature sources that have argued for practice DSR concerns. We do not start our work of developing PDR from scratch. As mentioned, we obtain our main inspiration from the research approach of practice research. We will account for some fundamentals of this research approach in Sect. 4.1. In the remainder of Sect. 4 we will articulate practice design research as a possible DSR approach with the main idea to direct design research as a practice improvement endeavor. In this section we will not only present conceptualizations and models of PRD. We will give theoretical grounding through literature references. The theoretical sources are mainly obtained from pragmatist philosophy and theory since our approach is positioned within this paradigmatic stance [9, 13, 49, 50]. The paper is ended with conclusions in Sect. 5.

3 Practice Orientation in Current Design Science

Several DSR approaches consider practical problems the starting point, e.g. [14, 29]. However, critics state that these approaches pay too little attention to the organizational context of IT artifact design [1, 24, 30, 31, 35]. Hevner [13] defines DSR as consisting of three cycles (relevance, design, and rigor). The separation of relevance cycle from design cycle might, however, be inappropriate for making design sufficiently practice-based. Sein et al. [35, p. 37] criticize established DSR approaches to "value technological rigor at the cost of organizational relevance, and fail to recognize that the artifact emerges from interaction with the organizational context even when its initial design is guided by the researchers' intent." Sein et al. [35] apply an ensemble view of IT artifacts, from [27], describing IT artifacts as carriers of "social structures" and embedded in social practices. Thus, ADR demands a close interaction with practice. Sein et al. [35] object to a separation between building, intervention, and evaluation. Instead, they speak of interweaving these types of activities. Evaluation should be seen as an ongoing and concurrent activity to building and not as they interpret current DSR to "relegate evaluation to a subsequent and separate phase" [ibid, p. 37]. DSR emphasizes organizational intervention as an integral activity of DSR; "current DR methods … consider organizational intervention to be secondary" [ibid, p. 39]. Hevner [13] considers intervention as a matter of technology transfer managed through action research. The fundamental idea of ADR is the opposite; to integrate and fuse DSR and action research into one coherent research approach.

McKay et al. [24, p. 135] demand DSR to be "geared more toward intervening in contexts to make improvements and ensuring that change works well." They argue against a narrow "construction-oriented view" of DSR and claim the importance of a broader human-centered perspective including topics like "how IT … artifacts appear to users, what they mean to users, how they communicate to users, the nature of the user experience with the artifact, the value ascribed to designed artifacts within contexts of use by users." [ibid, p. 137].

Baskerville and Myers [1] put forth an ethnographic approach to design science called Design Ethnography, comprising a traditional ethnographic study of practices as a basis for design and also the use of ethnographic techniques integrated into design. The authors claim "the design task itself can be used as a vehicle to better understand the everyday lives of the people" [ibid, p. 25].

Rohde et al. [30, 31] investigate epistemological foundations of DSR from a social practice perspective. Their stance is to conceive "design as an intervention into social practices" [30]. Such a design practice is seen "as a reflective practice confronted with wicked situations." They claim the importance that evaluation should be conducted in real-world settings. The introduction of new IT artifacts in social practices is always made through an appropriation process. Rohde et al. [30] claim social practices to "evolve together with the appropriation of the IT artifact. In this process, unanticipated opportunities for the design of the artifact may emerge organically within work practices." The consequence of this is that "emergence in the appropriation process cannot be observed before the intervention has occurred" [ibid]. There needs thus to be an intervention before a proper evaluation can be conducted. The appropriation view is far from seeing IT artifact implementation as a matter of technology transfer as claimed by Hevner [13].

Simplistic sequences of DSR activities (like build → evaluate → intervene) should thus be avoided. Epistemologically, a sound action logic is much more complex and nuanced.

Arguments for a more practice-based foundation of DSR can be found in the referenced contributions above. General arguments are presented for adopting a practice approach to DSR [1, 24, 30, 31]. Sein et al. [35] have operationalized a DSR approach in the field: the Action Design Research method. Their arguments against sequencing evaluation after building and before intervention are convincing. However, a DSR scholar is not much helped through their descriptions of interweaving building, evaluation, and intervention. Even if these activities are closely related it is not helpful to claim them as integrated and fused in the way it is done in Sein et al. [35]. It should be possible to analytically differentiate such activities and specify how they can be possibly sequenced in different ways. We will present such attempts in the following section when introducing Practice Design Research.

Even if there are several similarities between ADR and our approach (PDR), there seem to be differences between our starting points. Our interpretation is that Sein et al. [35] have started with DSR and then adapted it and fused it together with action research. Our starting point is practice research. We have then proceeded with this research approach and specified how design research could be one variant (sub-class) of it.

4 Practice Design Research

4.1 Practice Research Foundation

Practice research means research into some practice(s) with the purpose to improve such and similar practices. Fundamentally, we base our practice view on Dewey's idea of inquiry as a theory of knowledge [4]. Through an inquiry into social practice, experiences are gained through activities aiming at improving practice.

The presented PDR approach here takes the practice research approach as presented in [7, 8] as a starting point. Practice research has described as an interplay between the two sub-practices of situational inquiry and theorizing [7]. Practice research is related to three target practices (research community, general practice, local operational practice).

Situational inquiry (SI) means an investigation into one local practice or sometimes into several such local practices. The situational inquiry is driven by conceiving problematic situations in the local (operational) practice. The aim is to understand the practice in order to improve it. A situational inquiry (1) can be just a diagnosis or (2) it can include design proposals or (3) even implementation of change measures and new artifacts [7]. The result from SI in relation to local practice(s) is labelled a local practice contribution. This means that a local practice contribution can be (1) an evaluation or (2) a design/change proposal or (3) implemented change measures. SI will often be conducted collaboratively between researchers and practitioners.

SI will interplay with theorizing during a practice research. Theorizing comprises both furnishing of "theoretical tools" to SI and taking care of empirical data from SI. Theorizing means knowledge production. It produces useful knowledge aimed for "general practice", that is practice communities that are not limited to the local practice studied. This is called general practice contribution. Theorizing as a sub-practice of PR exists also with the purpose of adding to the scientific body of knowledge within the research community.

4.2 The Interplay of Situational Design Inquiry and Theorizing

We have applied the perspective and the anatomy of practice research to elaborate a practice-oriented DSR approach. We label our approach Practice Design Research (PDR). While the ADR originators refer to action research as the fundamental inspiration and a reference model when adapting DSR, we base our DSR adaptation on practice research. What we accomplish in this development is thus the formulation of a form of practice research oriented towards design as the focal kind of inquiry and practice improvement. An analysis of similarities and differences between action research and practice research is presented in [8].

Drawing from the ideas of situational inquiry in PR [7] we use the term "situational design inquiry" in PDR to emphasize the design orientation of our approach. The structuring of theorizing and situational design inquiry has been done in new ways within PDR (Fig. 2) compared with general PR.

Following PR, it is essential to conceive of theorizing as a distinct and separate sub-activity within a DSR study. PR thus addresses the confusion concerning DSR outcomes as local artifacts vs. general knowledge. In [14] the result of DSR is emphasized to be an artifact – a construct, method, model or instantiation. Hevner et al. [14] mention that artifacts may be technology-based (e.g., software), people-based (e.g., incentives that affect people's actions) and organization-based (e.g., process design). Several scholars are demanding DSR outcome to also be of abstract and theoretical character, e.g. [20, 36, 42, 46]. Gregor and Hevner [11] differentiate between contributions on different abstraction levels, from instantiations (level 1), nascent design theory (level 2; constructs, methods, models, design principles, and technological rules), to design theory (level 3; 'mid-range and grand theories'). Our interpretation of this discourse is that IS scholars recognize that theorizing is an insufficiently conceptualized part of DSR. The division in PDR into theorizing and design inquiry emphasizes that theorizing is an explicit part of such an approach aiming for general and abstract knowledge, in addition to contributions made to the local practice. Theorizing in PDR should result in (1) general practice contributions and (2) additions to the scientific body of knowledge following the principles of PR (Fig. 2). Such results can be abstracted descriptions of artifact features and their contributions to practical use values (as a kind of design principles).

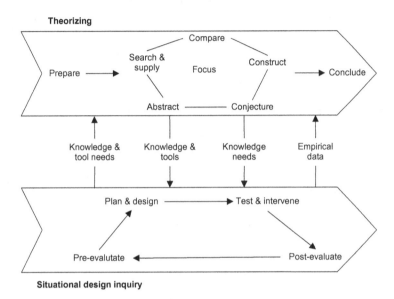

Fig. 2. Theorizing and situational design inquiry in practice design research.

While we separate situational design inquiry from theorizing for the sake of conceptual clarity, we acknowledge the entanglement of the two. Figure 2 illustrates the anticipated value creation in PDR: Through the inquiry process needs for knowledge and cognitive tools are identified. These trigger the theorizing activity, i.e., search for or articulation of knowledge to apply in the situational design inquiry. Through theorizing, different knowledge needs are generated like hypotheses and questions sometimes operationalized in data collection instruments. Situational inquiry feeds empirical data into theorizing as a source for analysis, abstraction, and formulation of theoretical propositions. The remainder of Fig. 2 is discussed in depth in Sects. 4.3–4.5.

4.3 Situational Design Inquiry

PDR recognizes four stages as fundamental in the design inquiry process: (1) Pre-evaluate, (2) plan and design, (3) test and intervene, and (4) post-evaluate. Figure 2 illustrates the four stages on a high level. The stage-division is inspired by the inquiry process as described by Dewey [2, 4] and the principal stage division of the act by Mead [48]. We synthesize Mead's division of four phases (impulse, perception, manipulation, and consummation) with the three-stage model presented in [9], consisting of pre-assessment, intervention (including simultaneous monitoring), and post-assessment. In comparison with [9 and 48], we inserted a second phase of planning between pre-assessment and intervention. PDR thus follows Dewey's concept of inquiry by acknowledging the crucial moments of suggestions and reasoning before taking action. Each stage in the PDR view on situational design inquiry, in turn, consists of activities as elaborated in Fig. 3.

The PDR inquiry process corresponds well with the phases in canonical action research (CAR) as described by Susman and Evered [39]. Pre-evaluate corresponds directly to "diagnosing" in the CAR model [39]. Plan & design corresponds to "action planning," and test & intervene corresponds to "action taking." Post-evaluate includes "evaluation" and parts of "specifying learning." This latter activity is however also included in theorizing; cf. [8].

The **pre-evaluate** phase (of this new SI model) starts with the experience of problematic situations; something "difficult" or "disturbing" following Dewey [2]. The next stage is the generation of data about the problematic situation ("observe"). Data should be recorded and analyzed ("describe & abstract"). PDR advocates an explicit evaluation ("assess") of the situation (according to generated data and conducted descriptions). This initial phase of establishing a problematic situation and its evaluation is part of with an emerging focus and demarcation. Evaluators of the current situation should not only investigate with critical knowledge intent, i.e., a search for "what does not work.", but also with interest for "what works (well)," i.e., different strengths in the situation. Such an analysis is often called an appreciative inquiry [22].

The activities of pre-evaluate should be seen as iterative and continual. The principal epistemic order described above and in Fig. 3 is not only a model of "frozen stages", but also pertains to the overall inquiry structure and the other three inquiry stages.

Plan & design means the generation of proposals and a direct assessment of these. It is necessary to reflect on and articulate values ("desire") as a basis for proposing. Otherwise, there is a risk for an amendment of minor problems, and neglecting serious issues. Value analysis can thus also slightly shift the focus from the pre-evaluate stage in this design stage.

The propose phase covers the generation of new designs of different degrees of realization; spanning from hunches and ideas to visualizations in models and further to instantiated prototypes and full-blown products.

Assessment in plan & design is a desktop evaluation of proposals before any practical test searching for implied consequences of the projected suggestions. The assessment includes a comparison between status quo (problem statements from pre-evaluate) and the proposed solution and anticipated (through reasoning) identified consequences.

Test & intervene means that new actions are taken in relation to the inquired practice. Actions, following the tenets of design science, may include the use of new artifacts. A current practice might be resilient to changes and new ways of working. To get new procedures to work, it is often necessary to appropriate these new procedures to fit the situation [30, 31]. Modifications and adaptations sometimes need to be done. This appropriation is conducted based on experiences, and an "assessment-in-action" following the theories of Schön [33] stated as "reflection-in-action". Typically, this stage of test & intervene iterate until a new (modified) way of working is functioning satisfactorily. What is implemented can thus deviate from the planned intervention.

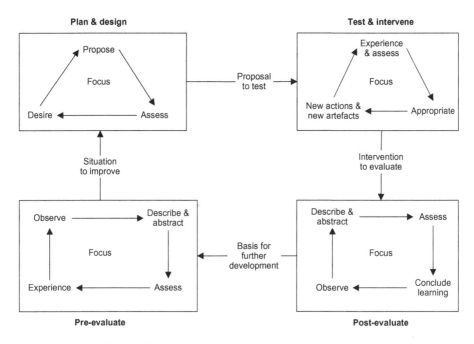

Fig. 3. The situational design inquiry process unfolded.

This new action is, in an inquiry context, seen as a test. And as such, it should be appropriately evaluated, not only through an assessment-in-action. There should be an explicit **post-evaluation**. Such an evaluation includes data collection ("observe"), description, abstraction and explicit assessment. This finalizing post-evaluation should also comprise an overall statement of the learning from the inquiry process; i.e., the transformation of the problematic situation into a satisfactory one. Dewey [4] describes the closure of an inquiry as a resolution of the problematic situation into a settled one.

4.4   Theorizing Activities in PDR

We divide PDR theorizing into three stages (Fig. 2), slightly revised from [7]: Prepare, continual theorizing, and conclude.

The **prepare** stage includes an initial formulation of research interest and research questions, as well as an initial establishment of the knowledge base for the study (i.e., literature review). Further, there is a need to make initial arrangements for the empirical work in situational design inquiry, including the furnishing of cognitive tools – selection and situated adaptation of ideas from the knowledge base – for SI. It is important to emphasize these initial formulations of research interest and establishment of knowledge bases are provisional and open to later refinement. The prepare stage is to give the design study an initial focus and direction.

The **continual theorizing** stage in PDR means a continual interest in conceptualizing and explaining the emerging theoretical focus at hand. A focus emerges through on-going reflection and learning, which may lead to a revised understanding of the problem and its solution, and sometimes to a shift in research interests and theoretical focus. Continual theorizing consists of several generic activities: (i) Abstraction (data analysis and conceptual development), (ii) search and supply of relevant extant knowledge that may be relevant in the PDR process, (iii) compare, i.e., a continual analysis and comparison of (1) different empirical elements, (2) various theoretical elements and (3) consistency between data and theory, (iv) construct/design of cognitive tools for descriptive, explanatory, normative and prescriptive purposes, and (v) conjecture, i.e. articulation of hypotheses and issues to study in the empirical SI. These activities are considered 'generic' in the sense that they exist in some form in all theorizing situations, whether explicitly reflected upon or not. We conceive of theorizing as a continual shift between these activities, aligned with SI events. It is hard to state a precise epistemic order between the activities; therefore there are no arrows in Fig. 2 to indicate any particular order.

The **conclude** stage corresponds to the formalization of learning in ADR and refers to the post-inquiry work to make final reflections and formalize the results of the theorizing process intended for targeted audiences (research community and general practice).

4.5 Evaluation in PDR

At the heart of pragmatism lies an interest to engage with the development of ideas that support human understanding and govern human action. We differentiate between theoretical ideas and situated ideas proposed by designers and researchers in the situational design inquiry. We conceive of an 'idea' in a broad sense. It encompasses any representation of knowledge (instantiations, methods, models, concepts, design principles, design theory, etc.).

Evaluation plays crucial roles in both sub-practices of practice design research. In the design inquiry process, evaluation is vital for understanding the current practice, emergent design ideas and the usefulness of new artifacts put into test and use in practice. Evaluation appears in all four stages of the inquiry process, which is found in Fig. 3 (through the word 'assess'). However, these evaluation activities in the inquiry stages differ in character. Table 1 summarizes the differences.

Activities in situational design inquiry provide empirical data to the theorizing process potentially signaling the applicability and usefulness of the ideas used in an inquiry. Ideas may be either (i) theoretically informed proposals from researchers, (ii) creatively crafted ideas by practitioners and researchers, or a combination of (i) and (ii). For example, a design proposal from the researchers, based on theory X, is rejected by the local practice due to incoherence with the existing technological base. The implication for the situational inquiry is that the proposal is rejected in its current form. The implication for theorizing is that the researcher has new data regarding the applicability of the theory in the particular context of inquiry. When the researcher presents a revised version of theory X to their academic peers, a set of values (e.g., rigor and relevance) different from the values in the local practice (e.g., technological fitness) will be used to determine the goodness of the generic idea.

Table 1. Different types of evaluation in the stages of situational inquiry.

Stage	Temporality	Evaluation object	Character of evaluation
Pre-evaluate	Evaluation-before-design	Current practice	Observation-based explicit evaluation
Plan & design	Evaluation-in-design	Proposals	Evaluation of anticipated consequences
Test & intervene	Evaluation-in-action	Experiences of new action and artifact	Reflection-in-action
Post-evaluate	Evaluation-after-action	Experiences of new action and artifact	Observation-based explicit evaluation

Evaluation of ideas in theorizing thus seeks to (i) draw from the experiences in practice of a situated idea to (ii) phrase a generic idea, and (iii) evaluate the generic idea based on values in the academic community.

Evaluation in PDR theorizing can thus mean learning from experiences of implementing ideas in situational inquiry. Following James' [16] view that ideas also need to be anchored in older truths, ideas may also be assessed through theoretical studies. Evaluation is not a separate and explicit activity in theorizing (Fig. 2) due to its continual presence in the abstraction process. Evaluation occurs both in studying the empirics and in studying theoretical sources. It occurs throughout the abstraction process. The view of evaluation as an integrated part of theorizing calls for attention to how data is collected and documented for research purposes. PDR calls for data collection that allows for a reconstruction of design rationale as well as a transparent empirical justification of generic idea propositions.

To account for evaluation in theorizing, we need to further elaborate on PDR knowledge outcomes. In the PDR context, our primary interest is ideas that support inquiry, either by (i) promoting an enhanced understanding of existing practice (e.g., a business modeling technique) or by (ii) providing prescriptive advice for design (e.g., design principles). That is; PDR does not only focus prescriptive knowledge: Ideas that support description and explanation of practice are considered equally important.

Everything that can be conceived of as a proposal in theorizing can be assessed in different ways. Every proposal can be pre-assessed before any use; to determine if it applies to the situation. Such pre-assessment usually occurs through theoretical scrutiny, but it can also be conducted by the support of naturalistic evaluation through collaboration with practitioners, or through artificial evaluation techniques from the laboratory genre of DSR. It can be post-assessed after use (either in theorizing or situational design inquiry) concerning its usefulness regarding intended purposes or emergent reasons. This conceptualization of evaluation in theorizing follows the inherent nature of evaluation (both pre-assess and post-assess) in actions [9, 48]. It also follows from the importance of reasoning and judgments of ideas as necessary parts of the inquiry process as described by Dewey [2, 4].

What can be seen as proposals to be assessed in theorizing? The answer is everything that is put forth in these processes conceived of having an epistemological value. The articulated research focus directs what is done in PDR and this needs to be assessed. Extant theoretical knowledge is brought into the PDR process to be used for different purposes. What kind of extant knowledge that is selected needs to be assessed. In theorizing, cognitive tools are generated and adapted to be used for further theorizing or situational design inquiry. These tools need to be evaluated. One important task in theorizing is the generation of hypotheses or other conjectures. Such hypotheses need to be assessed to inquire if they are interesting, valuable and applicable in the research process. Empirical data are supplied from situational inquiry to be used for analysis and abstraction in the theorizing process. Such data cannot be taken for granted. They should be assessed to scrutinize their validity, sufficiency, coverage, and usefulness. Theorizing should produce theoretical constructs (such as design principles and design theory) as outcomes directed to the research community and general practice (Fig. 2). The evaluation of such theoretical constructs needs to be conducted following academic standards as well as values from other target groups.

5   Conclusions

We acknowledge that existing DSR approaches recognize the role of practice in design-oriented research in various ways. There is, however, a significant difference between current DSR approaches and our proposed approach to practice design research. Other approaches, on the one hand, do not use practice as a vantage point for conceptualization, resulting in a set of scattered – albeit meaningful and useful – ideas on how to relate to practice in design-oriented research. Practice design research, on the other hand, is an exploration of how to understand design-oriented research, grounded in the ontological and epistemological roots of pragmatism and practice research. Practice design research is a consequent elaboration of practice-oriented DSR as described as one genre of DSR as a contrast to laboratory-oriented DSR; these genres described by [15, 47].

ADR is the only other elaborated approach we have found that builds on an articulated underlying philosophy. ADR relates to interpretivism and interventionism as a measure to position itself against DSR as accounted for by Hevner et al. [14]. ADR, however, puts the idea of an ensemble artifact at the fore and builds their method around it. Second, in contrast to other design-oriented approaches, our approach offers an analytically viable view on theorizing and its relation to design inquiry. Inquiry as a starting point is a contrast to different DSR approaches regarding the idea of knowledge contributions. PDR, coherent with Dewey's inquiry as a theory of knowledge, serves to develop and evaluate ideas in a broad sense, whether they aim at describing, explaining or even predicting phenomena. The idea of contributions beyond prescriptive knowledge and instantiations is a clear distinction from the prevalent DSR discourse. The roots of PDR in pragmatism and Dewey's notion of inquiry give a solid foundation for the creative and possibility-exploring aspect of DSR. Inquiry and knowledge is the basis for change and improvement of the world; Dewey [3] writes "reason has a creative function … which helps to make the world other than it would have been without it".

There is a risk that the approach presented is conceived of as 'yet another model,' thus causes even more confusion about evaluation and theorizing in DSR. Our response to such argumentation is that the approach – while still in its infancy – offers an enhanced conceptual understanding of the role and nature of evaluation in DSR, as well as increased clarity regarding theorizing and its interrelations with situational design inquiry. PDR has a clear difference to ADR since neither theorizing nor evaluation has conceptually clear and distinct positions in ADR. We acknowledge that evaluation should be conducted in close alternation with the build and intervene activities in entangled ways, but we find it essential to analytically clarify the different roles and positions of evaluation in both situational design inquiry and theorizing.

We emphasize that PDR addresses the practice genre of DSR, and in doing so we explore the consequences of addressing design-oriented research drawing from practice theory and pragmatism. There is a contemporary stream of practice theory, e.g. [5, 19, 25], and a related discourse on socio-materiality, e.g. [21, 34], that elaborate more in detail about various aspects of practice. For instance, as the entanglement of technology and the social world, power and politics in organizations, and the emergent characteristics of socio-material practice. The very idea of Dewey's moral inquiry is to be able to identify and improve the social world taking into account such complex aspects. The cohesive ontological and epistemological foundations of PDR support commensurability with contemporary streams of practice theory and socio-materiality.

The purpose and scope of this paper was to describe and present the basic features of the Practice Design Research approach including its philosophical foundation in pragmatism. We have used different parts of PDR in design oriented research projects, so this approach should not be seen as just a methodological idea. There exist an empirical base, although not presented in this paper. Future research will analyze and present findings from such empirical research.

References

1. Baskerville, R., Myers, M.: Design ethnography in information systems. Inf. Syst. J. **25**, 23–46 (2004)
2. Dewey, J.: How We Think. D.C. Heath & Co., Boston (1910)
3. Dewey, J.: The development of American pragmatism. In: Dewey, J. (ed.) Philosophy and Civilization. Minton, Balch & Co., New York (1931)
4. Dewey, J.: Logic: The Theory of Inquiry. Henry Holt, New York (1938)
5. Feldman, M., Orlikowski, W.: Theorizing practice and practicing theory. Organ. Sci. **22**, 1240–1253 (2011)
6. Gibbons, M., Limoges, C., Nowotny, H., Schwartzman, S., Scott, P., Trow, P.: The New Production of Knowledge. The Dynamics of Science and Research in Contemporary Societies. Sage, London (1994)
7. Goldkuhl, G.: The research practice of practice research: theorizing and situational inquiry. Syst. Signs Actions **5**(1), 7–29 (2011)
8. Goldkuhl, G.: From action research to practice research. Australas. J. Inf. Syst. **17**(2), 57–78 (2012)
9. Goldkuhl, G.: Pragmatism vs. interpretivism in qualitative information systems research. Eur. J. Inf. Syst. **21**(2), 135–146 (2012)

10. Goldkuhl, G., Lind, M.: A multi-grounded design research process. In: Winter, R., Zhao, J. L., Aier, S. (eds.) DESRIST 2010. LNCS, vol. 6105, pp. 45–60. Springer, Heidelberg (2010). https://doi.org/10.1007/978-3-642-13335-0_4

11. Gregor, S., Hevner, A.: Positioning and presenting design science research for maximum impact. MIS Q. **37**(2), 337–355 (2013)

12. Gregor, S., Jones, D.: The anatomy of a design theory. J. AIS **8**(5), 312–335 (2007)

13. Hevner, A.R.: A three cycle view of design science research. Scand. J. Inf. Syst. **19**(2), 87–92 (2007)

14. Hevner, A.R., March, S.T., Park, J., Ram, S.: Design science in information systems research. MIS Q. **28**(1), 75–105 (2004)

15. Iivari, J.: Distinguishing and contrasting two strategies for design science research. Eur. J. Inf. Syst. **24**, 107–115 (2015)

16. James, W.: Pragmatism. A New Name for Some Old Ways of Thinking. Longmans, Green & Co., New York (1907)

17. Koskinen, I., Zimmerman, J., Binder, T., Redström, J., Wensween, S.: Design Research Through Practice. From the Lab, Field, and Showroom. Morgan Kaufmann, Amsterdam (2011)

18. Kuechler, B., Vaishnavi, V.: A framework for theory development in design science research: multiple perspectives. J. AIS **13**(6), 395–423 (2012)

19. Kuutti, K., Bannon, L.: The turn to practice in HCI: towards a research agenda. In: Proceedings CHI-2014, Toronto (2014)

20. Lee, J.S., Pries-Heje, J., Baskerville, R.: Theorizing in design science research. In: Jain, H., Sinha, A.P., Vitharana, P. (eds.) DESRIST 2011. LNCS, vol. 6629, pp. 1–16. Springer, Heidelberg (2011). https://doi.org/10.1007/978-3-642-20633-7_1

21. Leonardi, P.: When flexible routines meet flexible technologies: affordance, constraint, and the imbrication of human and material agencies. MIS Q. **35**(1), 147–167 (2011)

22. Ludema, J., Cooperrider, D., Barrett, F.: Appreciative inquiry: the power of the unconditional positive question. In: Reason, P., Bradbury, H. (eds.) Handbook of Action Research. Sage, London (2001)

23. Mathiassen, L.: Collaborative practice research. Inf. Technol. People **15**(4), 321–345 (2002)

24. McKay, J., Marshall, P., Hirschheim, R.: The design construct in information systems design science. J. Inf. Technol. **27**, 125–139 (2012)

25. Nicolini, D.: Practice Theory, Work, & Organization. Oxford University Press, Oxford (2012)

26. Nilsen, P., Nordström, G., Ellström, P.-E.: Integrating research-based and practice-based knowledge through workplace reflection. J. Workplace Learn. **24**(6), 403–415 (2012)

27. Orlikowski, W.J., Iacono, C.S.: Desperately seeking the "IT" in IT research – a call to theorizing the IT artifact. Inf. Syst. Res. **12**(2), 121–134 (2001)

28. Pain, H.: Practice research: what it is and its place in the social work profession. Eur. J. Soc. Work **14**(4), 545–562 (2010)

29. Peffers, K., Tuunanen, T., Rothenberger, M.A., Chatterjee, S.: A design science research methodology for information systems research. J. Manag. Inf. Syst. **24**(3), 45–77 (2007)

30. Rohde, M., Stevens, G., Brödner, P., Wulf, V.: Towards a paradigmatic shift in IS: designing for social practice. In: Proceedings DESRIST-2009, Malvern (2009)

31. Rohde, M., Brödner, P., Stevens, G., Betz, M., Wulf, V.: Grounded design – a praxeological IS research perspective. J. Inf. Technol. **32**, 163–179 (2016)

32. Salisbury Forum Group. The Salisbury Statement. Social Work & Society, vol. 9 (2011)

33. Schön, D.: The Reflective Practitioner - How Professionals Think in Action. Basic Books, New York (1983)

34. Scott, S., Orlikowski, W.: Entanglements in practice: performing anonymity through social media. MIS Q. **38**(3), 873–893 (2014)
35. Sein, M., Henfridsson, O., Purao, S., Rossi, M., Lindgren, R.: Action design research. MIS Q. **35**(1), 37–56 (2011)
36. Sjöström, J., Ågerfalk, P.J.: An analytic framework for design-oriented research concepts. In: Proceedings of AMCIS-2009, San Francisco (2009)
37. Sonnenberg, C., vom Brocke, J.: Evaluation patterns for design science research artefacts. In: Helfert, M., Donnellan, B. (eds.) EDSS 2011. CCIS, vol. 286, pp. 71–83. Springer, Heidelberg (2012). https://doi.org/10.1007/978-3-642-33681-2_7
38. Stevenson, C.: Practical inquiry/theory in nursing. J. Adv. Nurs. **50**(2), 196–203 (2005)
39. Susman, G.I., Evered, R.D.: An assessment of the scientific merits of action research. Adm. Sci. Q. **23**(4), 582–603 (1978)
40. Uggerhøj, L.: What is practice research in social work - definitions, barriers and possibilities. Soc. Work Soc. **9**(1), 45–59 (2011)
41. Van de Ven, A.: Engaged Scholarship: A Guide for Organizational and Social Research. Oxford University Press, Oxford (2007)
42. Venable, J.: The role of theory and theorising in design science research. In: Proceedings of DESRIST 2006, Claremont (2006)
43. Venable, J., Pries-Heje, J., Baskerville, R.: FEDS: a framework for evaluation in design science research. Eur. J. Inf. Syst. **25**, 77–89 (2016)
44. Watson, V.: Do we learn from planning practice?: the contribution of the practice movement to planning theory. J. Plann. Educ. Res. **22**, 178–187 (2002)
45. Whittington, R.: Completing the practice turn in strategy research. Organ. Stud. **27**(5), 613–634 (2006)
46. Winter, R.: Towards a framework for evidence-based and inductive design in information systems research. In: Helfert, M., Donnellan, B., Kenneally, J. (eds.) EDSS 2013. CCIS, vol. 447, pp. 1–20. Springer, Cham (2014). https://doi.org/10.1007/978-3-319-13936-4_1
47. Zimmerman, J., Forlizzi, J.: Research through design in HCI. In: Olson, J., Kellogg, W. (eds.) Ways of Knowing in HCI. Springer, New York (2014). https://doi.org/10.1007/978-1-4939-0378-8_8
48. Mead, G.H.: Philosophy of the Act. University of Chicago Press, Chicago (1938)
49. Lee, A., Nickerson, J.: Theory as a case of design: lessons for design from the philosophy of science. In: Proceedings of the 43rd Hawaii International Conference on System Sciences (2010)
50. Goldkuhl, G.: Design research in search for a paradigm: pragmatism is the answer. In: Helfert, M., Donnellan, B. (eds.) EDSS 2011. CCIS, vol. 286, pp. 84–95. Springer, Heidelberg (2012). https://doi.org/10.1007/978-3-642-33681-2_8

Utilizing, Producing, and Contributing Design Knowledge in DSR Projects

Andreas Drechsler[1]([⌧]) [iD] and Alan R. Hevner[2] [iD]

[1] Victoria University of Wellington, Wellington, New Zealand
andreas.drechsler@vuw.ac.nz
[2] University of South Florida, Tampa, USA
ahevner@usf.edu

Abstract. We distinguish several design knowledge types in IS research and examine different modes of utilizing and contributing design knowledge that can take place during design science research (DSR) projects. DSR projects produce *project design knowledge*, which is project-specific, possibly untested, conjectural, and temporary; thus, distinct from the more stable contributions to the propositional and prescriptive human knowledge bases. We also identify *solution design knowledge* as distinct from solution design entities in the prescriptive knowledge base. Each of the six modes of utilizing or contributing knowledge (i.e. *design theorizing modes*) we examine draws on different knowledge types in a different way to inform the production of project design knowledge (including artifact design) in a DSR project or to grow the human knowledge bases in return. Design science researchers can draw on our design theorizing modes and design knowledge perspectives to utilize the different extant knowledge types more consciously and explicitly to inform their build and evaluation activities, and to better identify and explicate their research's contribution potential to the human knowledge bases.

Keywords: Design knowledge · Design theorizing · Knowledge bases
Knowledge contribution · Knowledge for action
Knowledge for entity realization

1 Introduction

Two major genres of inquiry in the IS discipline contribute to knowledge growth [9, 23]: science-oriented research activities primarily grow propositional knowledge or Ω-knowledge (comprising descriptive and explanatory knowledge), while design-oriented research activities primarily grow applicable (or prescriptive) knowledge or λ-knowledge. Contributions to λ typically comprise knowledge about technological innovations that are or can be useful for individuals, organizations, or society – and also to develop future technological innovations. Contributions to Ω enhance our understanding of the world and the phenomena our technologies harness (or cause). Research projects may combine both genres of inquiry and contribute to both knowledge bases.

S. Chatterjee et al. (Eds.): DESRIST 2018, LNCS 10844, pp. 82–97, 2018.
https://doi.org/10.1007/978-3-319-91800-6_6

Many IS literature sources highlight the importance of utilizing the knowledge in both knowledge bases together in design-oriented IS research projects [12, 23, 39, 42]. However, these sources usually do not cover the particular ways of doing so in greater detail. This not only leads to challenges for the researchers involved in DSR projects to ground their design decisions explicitly on extant knowledge and transparently document the decisions and their justification. It also challenges these researchers to systematically articulate contributions to Ω and λ in ways that allow a cumulative accumulation and evolution in both knowledge bases.

As a first remedy for this issue, we illustrate how researchers in DSR projects can grow and utilize all knowledge types through different modes of design theorizing. We also distinguish two distinct design knowledge types in the process, which allows us to provide a more comprehensive perspective on knowledge utilization, production, and contribution in DSR. We integrate unconnected positions in the IS literature concerning design knowledge and related concepts, as well as approaches to grow both knowledge bases. We employ the term *design theorizing* for all activities utilizing or contributing knowledge in the context of design. In doing so, we follow Weick's [55, 56] distinction between theory and theorizing. He particularly emphasizes the important roles of pre-theoretical knowledge in the process towards developing a more fully articulate (explanatory) theory and we do the same to illustrate how all forms of knowledge can contribute to informing artifact realization processes or vice-versa.

2 Distinguishing Project Design Knowledge and Solution Design Knowledge

The first distinction we wish to make concerns (1) design knowledge that is produced and remains within a single DSR project, and (2) design knowledge that is part of the λ-knowledge base. We call the former *project design knowledge* and the latter *solution design knowledge* in the remainder of the paper.

Within a DSR project, researchers draw on the existing knowledge bases as well as other sources (their own and others' experience or creativity, for instance) to produce a plethora of temporary, tentative, and highly project-specific design knowledge. Such knowledge comprises knowledge regarding the project's problem space (including the specific (class of) contexts, the problem diagnosis, and the related goodness criteria for the resulting artifact) and the solution space (including the (meta-)artifacts or artifact components as the actual solution entities, but also the corresponding search criteria, or the build and evaluation activities) [23, 26, 27]. The search and goodness criteria should not only address the artifacts' immediate goodness of fit (utility), but also the artifacts' potential for evolution in order to stay sustainably useful [20].

Over the course of a project (and possibly several iterations), the involved researchers may produce, test, and discard several instances of the afore-mentioned knowledge entities until they have reached a reasonably accurate understanding of problem and context, and a reasonably well-tested and useful solution. We see only the final results of the project to be candidates for an addition or contribution to the existing human knowledge bases through distinct and rigorous processes or *modes of design theorizing*. In particular, the refined understanding of context and problem primarily contributes to Ω, whereas the artifacts or other solution entities primarily contribute to λ. However, we see also another knowledge type with contribution potential to λ: artifact or entity-independent design knowledge, which we term *solution design knowledge*. Several authors have examined how such artifact-independent design knowledge could bridge Ω- and λ-knowledge [13, 14, 16, 46]. Here, the emphasis has frequently been on linking theory and IS design science research (DSR) artifacts [18, 23, 31]. However, the used terminologies, conceptualizations, representations, roles, and implications vary widely among the sources cited above. In the upcoming sections, we therefore take a closer look to find common ground across solution design knowledge and its roles in design theorizing.

3   Positioning Solution Design Knowledge in Relation to Artifacts and Design Theories

In this and the next section we first lay the foundation for illustrating how separating solution design knowledge from artifacts and design theories on one hand and Ω-knowledge (including theory) on the other hand contributes to a clearer picture on how these knowledge types can enhance artifact design and corresponding knowledge contributions in different design theorizing modes.

Traditionally, IS artifacts as design entities are said to constitute concepts, models, methods, and instantiations [35]. In our conceptualization, it makes sense, however, to understand abstract concepts, models, and methods as components of meta-artifacts, while the corresponding instantiations are components of artifact instances that have a physical existence in the real world [24]. Meta-artifacts are artifacts that lead to the development of other artifacts [28, 30] and constitute more abstract (nomothetic) knowledge about technology. In contrast, knowledge about artifact instances constitutes local (idiographic) knowledge [9]. Drawing on the most recent contributions to the 'artifact debate' [4, 10, 15, 29, 32, 43], we conceptualize IS artifacts as (1) consisting of any number of technical, social and/or informational components, (2) collectively supplying one or more functionalities, and (3) thus fulfilling an (a) information-related or (b) information technology-related purpose. Note that the informational components themselves may actually be comprised of knowledge. Due to space restrictions, we are unable to follow up with this 'recursion', however.

How then does solution design knowledge relate to artifacts within λ? In fact, some authors in the literature do not distinguish further between solution design knowledge (by the name of design propositions) and artifacts as an outcome of IS DSR [14]. Instead, they regard a body of design propositions as design theory that should be built on kernel theories, proposed, tested, and subsequently refined. In contrast, for others, solution design knowledge (by the name of techniques) can be artifacts as well – as long as one can formulate a means-end statement for the artifact – but does not necessarily have to be one [18]. In a third perspective, other authors conceptualize solution design knowledge as being distinctly separate from artifacts and theories – for instance, Kuechler and Vaishnavi's design relevant explanatory and predictive theories [31].

To solve these contradictory conceptualizations, we go back to Simon [50], for whom an artifact exhibits the following key property, among others: An artifact is a human-made entity that constitutes an interface between its inner and an outer environment. As solution design knowledge exists in the knowledge base independently of a specific (class of) immediate application context(s), there is no class of or specific outer environment for solution design knowledge. For this reason, solution design knowledge in our understanding does not fit Simon's artifact definition. Solution design knowledge's nature is more abstract. We therefore argue solution design knowledge to be in a separate realm from knowledge about artifacts, but within λ.

Besides artifacts, design theories are also seen as common outputs of IS DSR [23]. Therefore, it is worthwhile to distinguish these two knowledge contribution types further. Gregor and Jones [24] list eight components of a full-fledged design theory: (1) its purpose and scope, (2) constructs of the entities of interest, (3) principles of form and function, (4) artifact mutability, (5) testable propositions, (6) justificatory knowledge, (7) implementation principles, and (8) an expository instantiation.

In the terminology we have used so far, the principles of form and function closely correspond to the *meta-artifact* design entity and the expository instantiation to the *artifact instance.* The implementation principles highlight the need to consider a complementary *implementation or instantiation 'design'* in addition to an artifact, which transforms a meta-artifact to an instance, and integrates it into a socio-technical system, possibly by means of *interventions* [1, 2]. Likewise, the artifact mutability highlights the need for regular artifact redesigns as part of an *artifact evolution* to retain the artifact's utility over time [20]. The remaining design theory elements provide further guidance during artifact design and evaluation (purpose and scope, testable propositions) or highlight the links to the knowledge bases (constructs, testable propositions, justificatory knowledge).

We therefore conclude that a design theory is more encompassing than a perspective on artifacts alone and provides links to specific knowledge types. For the purposes of this paper, we will, however, take an artifact-centric perspective and highlight more general ways of building on and linking back to knowledge for the different types of artifacts. In keeping with Weick's distinction between theory and theorizing [56], we call these more general ways design theorizing (see Sect. 7 for further elaboration). Nevertheless, design theories remain an established mode of communicating a DSR knowledge contribution in IS research papers.

4   Positioning Solution Design Knowledge in Relation to Propositional Knowledge

Having highlighted the difference between artifacts, design theories, and solution design knowledge, we now distinguish solution design knowledge from existing understandings of propositional knowledge, including theory.

As with artifacts, the precise definition of theory and its distinction from other forms of theoretical knowledge are contended concepts in the IS and neighboring disciplines [5, 6, 22, 33, 51, 54, 56, 57]. As described in the Introduction, we distinguish between two basic knowledge types: applicable human knowledge (λ-knowledge) and the corresponding foundation in descriptive or propositional knowledge (Ω-knowledge). This broad and high-level distinction allows us to side-step most of the debates around theory and be inclusive to different forms of Ω-knowledge. To do so makes particular sense in the context of utilizing knowledge in DSR projects because design is an inherently creative process where the designers can draw on a wide range of possible knowledge sources in Ω and λ, be it to directly inform their designs, to understand their problems and contexts, or only to spark their creativity.

With respect to Ω-knowledge, the consensus in the debates in the literature in the IS and neighboring disciplines is that potentially worthwhile theoretical research contributions can encompass explanatory and predictive theories in a rather focused understanding of what constitutes a theory [54, 57], but also other conceptual forms of knowledge [3, 36, 38, 58] that are produced by generalizing, specializing, or theorizing real-world phenomena or other existing knowledge about real-world phenomena [5, 25, 48, 49, 56]. For the IS discipline, Gregor [21] proposes five theory types: (I) for description, (II) for explanation, (III) for prediction, (IV) for explanation and prediction, (V) for design and action. Only type V belongs to λ-knowledge (already covered in the previous section), whereas the other types belong to Ω-knowledge. Likewise, most other forms of theoretical knowledge discussed in the literature belong to Ω-knowledge. A notable exception is Markus' [36] distinction between theories of the problem and theories of the solution. The latter are also called theories of the intervention in Majchrzak and Markus [34] in the context of policy research. These theories of the solution or intervention belong to λ-knowledge, similarly to type V theories.

5 Solution Design Knowledge Types and Sub-types

In this section, we further refine our understanding of solution design knowledge based on solution design knowledge types that are commonly used in the IS literature. Note that the documentation of the underlying literature review and analysis process lies outside the scope of this paper, due to space restrictions. For the same reason, only a limited number of sources are referenced within each section, and only three major types are distinguished.

5.1 Technological Rules: Solution Design Knowledge for Action

In a philosophy of science perspective, Bunge proposes the technological rule concept to document solution design knowledge for action [13]. Note that Bunge understands technology in a wide interpretation that encompasses all knowledge and means to address practical problems. Technological rules ground instrumental knowledge on scientific knowledge. In particular, Bunge uses the term technological theory for theoretical statements that capture the effect of actions aimed at achieving real-world goals. Niiniluoto highlights that such technological theories – or norms, as he calls them – differ from nomological or law statements (which belong to Ω) in that they are instrumental and encompass an aspect of uncertainty [41]. Hence, they can be expressed as follows: "If you want A, and you believe you are in situation B, then you ought to/it is rational for you/it is profitable for you do X." The assumption is that actions based on technological theories – which, in turn, are based on well-founded hypotheses and reasonably precise data – are superior to actions based on unquestioned traditions [13]. Hypotheses and data can thus be used to justify these technological theories.

The concept of technological rules has been picked up in disciplines such as IS [7, 14], management [16], or sociology [45] to semi-formalize actionable knowledge. For instance, Carlsson proposes to extend the components of a technological rule in IS to a PIMCO format – (P)roblem situation, (I)S initiative, (M)echanism, (C)ontext, (O) utcome. Baskerville and Pries-Heje [8] propose to formalize them in the form "$(\sim Z, \sim Y) \rightarrow \sim X$", meaning "if you want to achieve something like Y in a situation similar to Z, then something like action X will help". Note that each of their three components can, but does not have to be, ambiguous [7]. Their proposal thus highlights the ambiguous nature of technological rules even further than Niiniluoto's version mentioned above [41]. As technological rules present merely options for action and do not constitute a coherent design entity directed at addressing a particular real-world problem or problem class, we understand these rules to be different from IS artifacts as defined in Sect. 3. We discuss ways of utilizing knowledge for action for artifact design in Sect. 7.

5.2 Requirements, Principles, Features: Solution Design Knowledge for Entity Realization

A second common type of solution design knowledge in the IS literature concerns intermediate steps on the path towards (meta-)artifact (or solution entity) designs that address real-world problems (or problem classes). Even Walls et al. in 1992 emphasize the importance of deriving design meta-requirements before moving on to the meta-design [53] and requirements engineering is a well-established practice in software engineering [11]. More recently, Meth et al. propose to consider design requirements, principles, and features in this order before actually designing an artifact [37]. The benefits of doing so include a greater transparency with respect to design decisions and a possibility to re-use (meta-)requirements, (meta-)principles, and (meta-) features for the design of similar (meta-)artifacts to address similar problem (classes) in similar context (classes). In other words, these (meta-)requirements, (meta-)principles, and (meta-)features likewise do not represent IS artifacts, but re-usable solution design knowledge for solution entity realization within λ. Simultaneously, they are distinctly different from technological rules or other knowledge for action and thus represent a second distinct type of solution design knowledge. We will further discuss this type's roles in the design process in Sect. 7.

5.3 Solution Design Knowledge for Design Processes and Systems

Following Walls et al. [53], we also include knowledge for design processes into the realm of solution design knowledge. Further, these design processes often take place in the context of design systems [20]. Our inclusion is based on the rationale that solution design knowledge as actionable knowledge can not only inform the design of solution entities, but also the corresponding design processes and design systems. In research, these design processes largely correspond to the employed research methodologies. The corresponding solution design knowledge is usually presented as methodological contributions. By including design systems, our perspective, however, goes beyond research methodologies and includes, for instance, initiating and retaining engagement with practitioner clients [44] or established techniques such as design thinking [17].

5.4 Other Types and Forms of Solution Design Knowledge

We acknowledge that the solution design knowledge types identified above are not exhaustive and the same applies for the mentioned terminologies and representations. For instance, design patterns are another established type of solution design knowledge for technical artifact design (software [19]), social artifact design (change management [47]), or even for DSR itself [52]. Design patterns can be understood as a particular form of technological rules (representing options for design action) and simultaneously a form of codifying design principles or features as that can be drawn on or applied during artifact design. However, space restrictions prevent us from further exploring other solution design knowledge types that are somewhat less prevalent in the IS literature than the three types discussed in Sects. 5.1 to 5.3.

6   A Unified Knowledge Utilization and Contribution Perspective for IS DSR

Based on the distinctions made in Sects. 2 to 5, we now propose a conceptual framework (Fig. 1) that places the covered realms among and within our two knowledge bases (λ and Ω) and shows six directions to utilize, produce, and contribute knowledge as modes of design theorizing. Figure 1 modifies and extends Fig. 1 in Gregor and Hevner [23]. First, our Fig. 1 separates project design knowledge from the two knowledge bases. The underlying rationale (cf. Sect. 2) is that a DSR project, in addition to drawing on and utilizing existing knowledge, produces untested, conjectural, and temporary knowledge and entities in a potentially unstructured, creative, and heuristic manner. This project design knowledge is shared only among the members (or a subset of them) of a single project. In the end, only selected knowledge may turn out to be suitable to be contributed back into the more widely disseminated human knowledge bases (for instance, in the form of publications). Second, our Fig. 1 shows how we conceptualize solution design knowledge. Solution design knowledge is actionable or technological knowledge, and therefore belongs to the body of λ-knowledge. It differs from artifacts in λ in that solution design knowledge is independent from a particular manifestation in a distinguishable design entity.

Note that we included implementation/intervention/instantiation processes (shortened to *i-processes* in Fig. 1) as a separate solution design entity besides artifacts (cf. Sect. 3). Likewise, we included processes to redesign existing artifacts as part of a necessary artifact evolution to retain their utility [20] as separate design entities. Moreover, we regard design processes and systems as further and distinct entities beyond the solution entities such as artifacts (cf. Sect. 5.3).

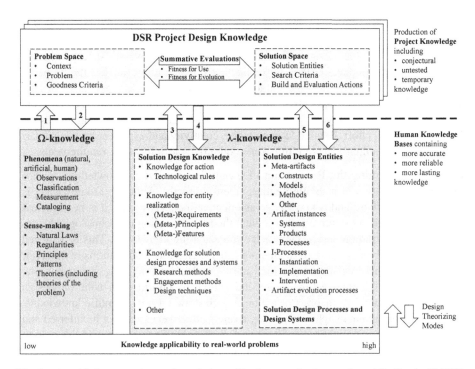

Fig. 1. A unified perspective on knowledge utilization, production, and contribution in IS DSR

7 Modes of Design Theorizing

Figure 1 contains six numbered block arrows that correspond to six design theorizing modes. They all draw on the different knowledge types either to utilize them in a DSR project for the purpose of producing project design knowledge, or to contribute selected knowledge back to a distinct part of the knowledge bases. Note that each mode merely represents an archetype; it is well possible that an actual knowledge contribution draws on more than one mode at a time. Note further that we, for simplicity's sake, focus on the design and evaluation of an IS artifact as solution entity.

7.1 Mode 1: Ω-Knowledge Informs the Understanding of a Problem, Its Context, or the Design of a Solution Entity

The design theorizing mode utilizes propositional or Ω-knowledge (which includes natural laws or behavioral theories that are formulated as law-like statements) to increase and substantiate the understanding of the context and the problem (mode 1A) or to inform the options for entity realization (mode 1B).

Mode 1A: Understanding the Context and Diagnosing the Problem. One way how Ω-knowledge informs a DSR project is the path towards deriving the (meta-)requirements for subsequent (meta-)artifact or entity design. Here, the primary interest is the in-depth understanding of the (class of) context(s) and the diagnosis of the real-world problem (class). Both draw on our existing understanding of the real world (and also add to it in the process), so that the researchers can formulate or reformulate a clear goal statement for the design effort and, subsequently, develop specific (meta-) requirements and goodness criteria for evaluating if the solution satisfies the problem. In other words, mode 1A lays the foundation for and forms a key part in theorizing about the requirements for effective and context-specific solutions to a given problem or means to reach a given goal. This mode of design theorizing anchors and guides the subsequent design effort. Beyond Ω-knowledge, creativity and experience and also past requirements for similar design efforts (cf. mode 3B) can inform the requirements.

Mode 1B: Informing the Realization of a Solution Entity. Ω-knowledge can also inform the realization of a solution entity, albeit indirectly. Although Ω-knowledge is evaluated as true/false and λ-knowledge as effective/ineffective [13], it is nevertheless possible to ground substantive technological theories for action or technological rules (as instances of solution design knowledge) on scientific knowledge. This is achieved by predicting and retrodicting (or abducting [40]) reasonably stable norms of behavior and combining these existing behavioral norms with nomopragmatic statements that capture effects of human action. A second source to inform such solution design knowledge are operative theories of action, which draw on non-scientific knowledge, experience, or intuitive insights. However, a rule's effectiveness cannot be inferred and the whole process is fraught by ambiguity (cf. Sect. 5.1), assumptions, and the need to reduce the complex reality to specific factors that are understood to significantly affect a rule's effectiveness [41]. However, in a DSR project such newly produced tentative solution design knowledge is only a precursor to artifact design to inform and justify specific design decisions. Moreover, further layers of 'obfuscation' are added by having more than one rule informing the design of an artifact that is later used as a coherent entity to affect the real world.

7.2 Mode 2: The Design and Real-World Application of Solution Entities or Knowledge Enhances Our Understanding of the World

During artifact evaluation, the respective findings may confirm, contradict, or extend our original understanding of the real world with respect to the nature of the context or problem (mode 2A) or to the knowledge that that originally informed the formulation of the technological rules underlying artifact design (mode 2B). In a sense, mode 2A corresponds to mode 1A and mode 2B to 1B above.

Mode 2A: Improving the Understanding of the Context and Problem. This design theorizing mode allows improving or extending our general understanding of the real-world context and the addressed problem in particular by uncovering yet un-researched aspects or facets of the context during the artifact evaluation.

Mode 2B: Improving our Understanding of Behavioral Regularities. A separate design theorizing mode may contribute to confirming, challenging, or extending our given understanding of how people, organizations, or societies behave. This can be achieved by comparing the actual effects of an artifact's interaction with its context with the intended ones, and relating the findings to the interim solution design knowledge developed in mode 1B. A prerequisite to design theorize in this mode 2B is a high traceability of the process in the preceding mode 1B from Ω over the developed interim solution design knowledge to the eventual artifact design. Moreover, such design theorizing has to take into account the resulting technological rules' inherent ambiguity, their combination with other rules, their 'embeddedness' within an artifact, and the limitations when design theorizing from more idiographic to more nomothetic knowledge.

7.3   Mode 3: Solution Design Knowledge Informs the Design of a Solution Entity, a Design Process or a Design System

Each of the three types of solution design knowledge distinguished in Sect. 5 corresponds to a sub-type of design theorizing.

Mode 3A: Knowledge for Action Informs Solution Entity Design. As already hinted at in the description of Mode 1B, extant knowledge for action (such as technological rules) can inform artifact design. Technological rules represent possible ways of action to achieve goals, while artifact design principles and features seek ways to implement specified requirements to reach a particular goal to address the real-world problem (class) in question. Relying on existing technological rules to inform design decisions (either more abstract (meta-)principles or less abstract (meta-)features) means selecting particular options for action from the range of possible options to be embedded into the (meta-)artifact later on. Here, the artifact thus serves as a vessel to eventually trigger or change human or systems' behaviors so that the problem is addressed or solved. In this context, this mode of design theorizing makes it explicit how particular design decisions are related to the body of solution design knowledge for action.

Mode 3B: Knowledge for Entity Realization Informs Solution Entity Design. As mentioned in Sect. 5.2 above, one benefit of explicitly documenting (meta-)requirements, principles and features of solution entities is their possible re-use when designing similar entities to address similar problems in similar contexts. A key aspect of this design theorizing mode is to deal with the issue of 'similarity' between problems and contexts and the corresponding 'projectability' of the existing (meta-)requirements, principles and features to different problems, contexts, and – eventually – solution entities [8]. Note that designing specific artifact features that implement more abstract principles to satisfy requirements and that are based on the most suited action options is still a wholly distinct step from actually implementing these features in instances of social or information technologies. Often, there are a multitude of ways how even well-defined features can actually be implemented in a design entity. The same applies for the corresponding implementation/instantiation/intervention to bring about the necessary changes in the social and/or technical system.

Mode 3C: Knowledge for Solution Design Processes and System Informs the Design of the DSR Project System. A third design theorizing mode can inform the design of the design processes and design system. However, as stated above, we focus mainly on the artifact or solution entity design and not the DSR project system design in this paper, due to space restrictions.

7.4 Mode 4: Effective Principles, Features, Actions, or Effects of a Solution Entity or a Design Process or System Are Generalized and Codified in Solution Design Knowledge

There are three sub-types of this design theorizing mode that are counterparts to the three sub-types for mode 3.

Mode 4A: Codifying Effective Actions. During artifact evaluation, it is among the researchers' tasks to evaluate the chosen technological rules that informed the design decisions. In this design theorizing mode, effective technological rules that are new or need to be changed are codified to add/change them in the knowledge base. In additional, the evidence level of extant technological rules that proved to be effective can be raised [18]. Due to the pervasive ambiguities both in the artifact's application context, the preceding 'chain' of design decisions and developed artifact knowledge, and a possible necessity to move from more idiographic to more nomothetic knowledge, such attributions may not be trivial, yet are crucial for this design theorizing mode.

Mode 4B: Codifying Effective Design Principles or Features. In this mode, it is the researchers' task to evaluate how effective facets of the resulting artifact can be isolated with respect to underlying features, principles, and/or requirements that future DSR projects can draw on. The challenges mentioned in mode 4A apply here likewise.

Mode 4C: Codifying Effective Aspects of Design Processes or Design Systems. This mode is the counterpart to mode 3C and largely covers individual methodological knowledge contributions that arise out of a DSR project.

7.5 Mode 5: Previously Effective Solution Entities, Design Processes, or Design Systems Are Re-used for or Inform Future Designs of New Entities, Processes, or Systems

There are two sub-types for this design theorizing mode, one regarding solution entity design and one regarding the design of design processes and systems.

Mode 5A: Re-using Previous Solution Entities. This mode is similar to mode 3B, except that the researchers here draw on previously effective artifacts to either re-use or adapt them in similar contexts for similar problems, or to merely inform their (meta-) principles, features or actual solution entity design. The afore-mentioned issues of similarity and projectability apply likewise.

Mode 5B: Re-using Previous Design Processes and Systems. Similarly to mode 3C, this design theorizing mode is concerned with re-using not mere knowledge about design processes and systems, but a more coherent and extensive set of design processes, methodologies, and systems in a new DSR project.

7.6 Mode 6: Effective Solution Entities, Design Processes, or Design Systems Are Contributed to λ-Knowledge

As with the previous even-numbered design theorizing modes, the number of sub-types correspond to the number of sub-types among the preceding odd-numbered design theorizing mode, and form their counterparts.

Mode 6A: Contribute Effective Solution Entities. This design theorizing mode is probably the most established mode in IS DSR among all the discussed ones in this paper. It essentially concerns documenting the final resulting solution entity (e.g., artifact) and demonstrating its utility to address the initial problem (class) in a (class of) contexts.

Mode 6B: Contribute Effective Design Processes and Systems. Similar to mode 4C – however, the emphasis here is less on individual methodological contributions, but more on contributing a coherent set of design processes, methods, techniques, and systems that effectively work together in a specific context to address a specific problem.

8 Discussion, Conclusion and Outlook

We identified two substantially different forms of design knowledge (project design knowledge and solution design knowledge), developed a comprehensive perspective on knowledge utilization, production, and contribution in DSR, and identified several design theorizing modes that either utilize knowledge to inform entity realization or contribute knowledge to the two knowledge bases Ω and λ.

Separating DSR project design knowledge from the two knowledge bases extends the prevalent perspective on knowledge growth [23] by highlighting the DSR project's role as 'knowledge engine'. DSR projects produce a plethora of – possibly temporary, conjectural, creative, and untested – knowledge and utilizing and contributing well-tested knowledge (including artifacts) to the knowledge bases (=the modes of design theorizing) are separate and distinct actions that researchers need to take, possibly through several iterations. We envision project repositories that maintain this design knowledge for future use and reflection.

Distinguishing solution design knowledge from Ω and design entities such as artifacts contributes to a more refined understanding of artifact-independent techno-logical and actionable knowledge. While – what we have called – solution design knowledge has received its share of attention in the literature so far, there has been a lack of a comprehensive perspective that can unify several different extant research streams that all approach solution design knowledge from different angles (and possibly conflate solution design knowledge with solution entities). Here, our perspective provides a foundation for refining our understanding of further solution design knowledge types and their relation with one another and with Ω-knowledge and artifacts in the future.

We further discussed several design theorizing modes that utilize the different knowledge types within Ω and λ to improve the process and the outcome of DSR projects (including the production of project design knowledge). Our proposed design theorizing modes advances the DSR discourse beyond the debate around artifact-centric or design theory-centric DSR by emphasizing (1) the important roles all the other forms of knowledge can play within all DSR project phases and (2) the different knowledge contributions a DSR project can make to Ω and λ. These contributions may comprise additions to the knowledge base as well as 'subtractions' in the form of challenging or refuting knowledge that was believed to be valid or effective.

We believe that an increased attention to growing all forms of knowledge – in addition to designing artifacts and developing design theories – can play a crucial role for the maturing DSR paradigm within and beyond IS research. We therefore issue a call to all design researchers for bolder and more explicit design theorizing to make increasing and stronger knowledge contributions of all types, including artifact or design theory-independent contributions. Simultaneously, we would like to emphasize that we do not see every design theorizing mode to be mandatory for design science researchers to consider. Instead, we see these as opportunities for knowledge re-use, enhancement, or the stimulation of creativity. Sometimes, a bold leap of imagination or deep intuitive insight may be what a design project requires instead of a rigorous but ultimately more limited by-the-book design theorizing, in order to have a substantial impact on organizations and society and to make substantial knowledge contributions at the end.

Note that our perspective on design knowledge as proposed in this paper is limited in several ways, however. First, space restrictions only allow us to begin exploring the various extant contributions in the literature that cover – what we have called – solution design knowledge and its different roles and representations. The same applies to the corresponding modes of design theorizing. Second, based on our focus on the artifact in design knowledge, we have not proposed a definitive representation of *design theory* in our Fig. 1 framework. As discussed in Sect. 3, we find aspects of design theory throughout the knowledge bases. Finally, our current perspective only remains on the conceptual level and lacks a practical example or application. We therefore see it as a task for further research to develop an even more comprehensive understanding of design knowledge and modes of design theorizing and to demonstrate the corresponding benefits and challenges for design science researchers in actual DSR projects. By doing so, we ultimately believe to improve the utility of the resulting designs and to improve the quantity and quality of contributions to all knowledge bases.

References

1. van Aken, J.E.: Design science and organization development interventions. J. Appl. Behav. Sci. **43**(1), 67–88 (2007)
2. van Aken, J.E.: Management research based on the paradigm of the design sciences: the quest for field-tested and grounded technological rules. J. Manag. Stud. **41**(2), 219–246 (2004)
3. Alter, S.: Nothing is more practical than a good conceptual artifact… which may be a theory, framework, model, metaphor, paradigm or perhaps some other abstraction. Inf. Syst. J. **27** (5), 671–693 (2016)

4. Alter, S.: The concept of 'IT artifact' has outlived its usefulness and should be retired now. Inf. Syst. J. **25**(1), 47–60 (2015)
5. Avison, D., Malaurent, J.: Is theory king?: a rejoinder. J. Inf. Technol. **29**(4), 358–361 (2014)
6. Avison, D., Malaurent, J.: Is theory king?: questioning the theory fetish in information systems. J. Inf. Technol. **29**(4), 327–336 (2014)
7. Baskerville, R., Pries-Heje, J.: Design logic and the ambiguity operator. In: Winter, R., Zhao, J.L., Aier, S. (eds.) DESRIST 2010. LNCS, vol. 6105, pp. 180–193. Springer, Heidelberg (2010). https://doi.org/10.1007/978-3-642-13335-0_13
8. Baskerville, R., Pries-Heje, J.: Design theory projectability. In: Doolin, B., Lamprou, E., Mitev, N., McLeod, L. (eds.) Working Conference on Information Systems and Organizations. Advances in Information and Communication Technology, vol. 446, pp. 219–232. Springer, Heidelberg (2014). https://doi.org/10.1007/978-3-662-45708-5_14
9. Baskerville, R.L., et al.: Genres of inquiry in design-science research: justification and evaluation of knowledge production. MIS Q. **39**(3), 541–564 (2015)
10. Benbasat, I., Zmud, R.W.: The identity crisis within the is discipline: defining and communicating the discipline's core properties. MIS Q. **27**(2), 183–194 (2003)
11. Braun, R., Benedict, M., Wendler, H., Esswein, W.: Proposal for requirements driven design science research. In: Donnellan, B., Helfert, M., Kenneally, J., VanderMeer, D., Rothenberger, M., Winter, R. (eds.) DESRIST 2015. LNCS, vol. 9073, pp. 135–151. Springer, Cham (2015). https://doi.org/10.1007/978-3-319-18714-3_9
12. Briggs, R.O., Schwabe, G.: On expanding the scope of design science in IS research. In: Jain, H., Sinha, A.P., Vitharana, P. (eds.) DESRIST 2011. LNCS, vol. 6629, pp. 92–106. Springer, Heidelberg (2011). https://doi.org/10.1007/978-3-642-20633-7_7
13. Bunge, M.: Scientific Research II: The Search for Truth. Springer, Berlin (1967). https://doi.org/10.1007/978-3-642-48138-3
14. Carlsson, S.A.: Design science research in information systems: a critical realist approach. In: Hevner, A., Chatterjee, S. (eds.) Design Research in Information Systems: Theory and Practice, pp. 209–233. Springer, New York (2010). https://doi.org/10.1007/978-1-4419-5653-8_15
15. Chatterjee, S., et al.: The information systems artifact: a conceptualization based on general systems theory. Presented at the HICSS (2017)
16. Denyer, D., et al.: Developing design propositions through research synthesis. Organ. Stud. **29**(3), 393–413 (2008)
17. Dorst, K.: The core of 'design thinking' and its application. Des. Stud. **32**(6), 521–532 (2011)
18. Fettke, P., et al.: On the relevance of design knowledge for design-oriented business and information systems engineering - conceptual foundations, application example, and implications. Bus. Inf. Syst. Eng. **2**(6), 347–358 (2010)
19. Gamma, E., et al.: Design Patterns. Elements of Reusable Object-Oriented Software. Addison-Wesley Longman, Amsterdam (1994)
20. Gill, T.G., Hevner, A.R.: A fitness-utility model for design science research. ACM Trans. Manag. Inf. Syst. **4**(2), 5:1–5:24 (2013)
21. Gregor, S.: The nature of theory in information systems. MIS Q. **30**(3), 611–642 (2006)
22. Gregor, S.: Theory – still king but needing a revolution! J. Inf. Technol. **29**(4), 337–340 (2014)
23. Gregor, S., Hevner, A.R.: Positioning and presenting design science research for maximum impact. MIS Q. **37**(2), 337–355 (2013)
24. Gregor, S., Jones, D.: The anatomy of a design theory. J. Assoc. Inf. Syst. **8**(5), 312–335 (2007)

25. Hassan, N.R., Lowry, P.B.: Seeking middle-range theories in information systems research. In: ICIS 2012 Proceedings (2015)
26. Hevner, A.: A three cycle view of design science research. Scand. J. Inf. Syst. **19**(2), 87–92 (2007)
27. Hevner, A., et al.: Design science in information systems research. MIS Q. **28**(1), 75–105 (2004)
28. Iivari, J.: Distinguishing and contrasting two strategies for design science research. Eur. J. Inf. Syst. **24**(1), 107–115 (2015)
29. Iivari, J.: Information system artefact or information system application: that is the question. Inf. Syst. J. **27**(6), 753–774 (2016)
30. Iivari, J.: The IS core - VII: towards information systems as a science of meta-artifacts. Commun. Assoc. Inf. Syst. **12**(1), Article 37 (2003)
31. Kuechler, W., Vaishnavi, V.: A framework for theory development in design science research: multiple perspectives. J. Assoc. Inf. Syst. **13**(6), 395–423 (2012)
32. Lee, A.S., et al.: Going back to basics in design science: from the information technology artifact to the information systems artifact. Inf. Syst. J. **25**(1), 5–21 (2015)
33. Lee, A.S.: Theory is king? But first, what is theory? J. Inf. Technol. **29**(4), 350–352 (2014)
34. Majchrzak, A., Markus, M.L.: Methods for Policy Research: Taking Socially Responsible Action. SAGE Publications, Ltd., London (2014)
35. March, S., Smith, G.: Design and natural science research on information technology. Decis. Support Syst. **15**(4), 251–266 (1995)
36. Markus, M.L.: Maybe not the king, but an invaluable subordinate. J. Inf. Technol. **29**(4), 341–345 (2014)
37. Meth, H., et al.: Designing a requirement mining system. J. Assoc. Inf. Syst. **16**, 9 (2015)
38. Miller, D.: Paradigm prison, or in praise of atheoretic research. Strateg. Organ. **5**(2), 177–184 (2007)
39. Niederman, F., March, S.T.: Design science and the accumulation of knowledge in the information systems discipline. ACM Trans. Manag. Inf. Syst. **3**(1), 1:1–1:15 (2012)
40. Niiniluoto, I.: Defending abduction. Philos. Sci. **66**, S436–S451 (1999)
41. Niiniluoto, I.: The aim and structure of applied research. Erkenntnis **38**(1), 1–21 (1993)
42. Nunamaker Jr., J.F., Briggs, R.O.: Toward a broader vision for information systems. ACM Trans. Manag. Inf. Syst. **2**(4), 20:1–20:12 (2012)
43. Orlikowski, W.J., Iacono, C.S.: Research commentary: desperately seeking the "IT" in IT research—a call to theorizing the IT artifact. Inf. Syst. Res. **12**(2), 121–134 (2001)
44. Otto, B., Osterle, H.: Principles for knowledge creation in collaborative design science research. In: ICIS 2012 Proceedings (2012)
45. Pawson, R.: Evidence-Based Policy a Realist Perspective. SAGE, London (2006)
46. Purao, S.: Design Research in the Technology of Information Systems: Truth or Dare (2002). http://purao.ist.psu.edu/working-papers/dare-purao.pdf
47. Rising, L., Manns, M.L.: Fearless Change: Patterns for Introducing New Ideas: Introducing Patterns into Organizations. Addison-Wesley Longman, Amsterdam (2004)
48. Seddon, P.B., Scheepers, R.: Generalization in IS research: a critique of the conflicting positions of Lee & Baskerville and Tsang & Williams. J. Inf. Technol. **30**(1), 30–43 (2015)
49. Seddon, P.B., Scheepers, R.: Towards the improved treatment of generalization of knowledge claims in IS research: drawing general conclusions from samples. Eur. J. Inf. Syst. **21**(1), 6–21 (2012)
50. Simon, H.A.: The Sciences of the Artificial. MIT Press, Cambridge (1996)
51. Sutton, R.I., Staw, B.M.: What Theory is Not. Adm. Sci. Q. **40**(3), 371–384 (1995)
52. Vaishnavi, V., Kuechler, W.: Design Science Research Methods and Patterns. Auerbach, Boca Raton (2008)

53. Walls, J.G., et al.: Building an information system design theory for vigilant EIS. Inf. Syst. Res. **3**(1), 36–59 (1992)
54. Weber, R.: Evaluating and developing theories in the information systems discipline. J. Assoc. Inf. Syst. **13**(1), 1–30 (2012)
55. Weick, K.E.: Theory construction as disciplined imagination. Acad. Manag. Rev. **14**, 516–531 (1989)
56. Weick, K.E.: What theory is not, theorizing is. Adm. Sci. Q. **40**(3), 385–390 (1995)
57. Whetten, D.A.: What constitutes a theoretical contribution? Acad. Manag. Rev. **14**(4), 490–495 (1989)
58. Yadav, M.S.: The decline of conceptual articles and implications for knowledge development. J. Mark. **74**(1), 1–19 (2010)

Design in Healthcare

Designing "Living" Evidence Networks for Health Optimisation: Knowledge Extraction of Patient-Relevant Outcomes in Mental Disorders

Hoang D. Nguyen[1]([⊠]), Øystein Eiring[2],
and Danny Chiang Choon Poo[1]

[1] Department of Information Systems and Analytics, School of Computing,
National University of Singapore, Singapore, Singapore
{hoangnguyen, dpoo}@comp.nus.edu.sg
[2] Norwegian Knowledge Centre for the Health Services, Oslo, Norway
oystein.eiring@fhi.no

Abstract. Over 70 randomised controlled trials (RCTs) are published in MEDLINE every day; in which the volume and velocity of unstructured evidence data have become a great challenge to human manual processing capabilities. There is an emerging need for a dynamic, evolving design of "living" evidence networks as the best source of health optimisation in evidence-based medicine. This study, therefore, investigated the text and layout features of unstructured full-texts in the biomedical literature to design IT artefacts for building high-quality and up-to-date evidence networks of RCTs. As a result, network meta-analyses can be automated for comparative adverse effects of treatments in chronic disorders such as Major Depressive Disorder and Bipolar Disorder. The study outcomes extended the technological boundary of health optimisation technologies, and contributed to the cumulative development of patient-relevant health care and shared decision-making.

Keywords: Evidence networks · Living systematic reviews
Health optimisation · Knowledge extraction · Major depressive disorder
Bipolar disorder

1 Introduction

Health optimisation has become an increasingly important topic in health research. It is promising as a next viable wave of interventions for better patients' health and well-being. The core of health optimisation is about enabling health decisions informed by the best available evidence to ensure patients obtain the best possible outcomes from their treatments [1]. Hence, evidence and their applications in clinical settings are the cornerstone of evidence-based decision-making towards optimal health care for patients.

Randomised controlled trials, or RCTs, have been widely regarded as high-quality evidence, the golden standard for clinical trials to minimise most of systematic biases in

© Springer International Publishing AG, part of Springer Nature 2018
S. Chatterjee et al. (Eds.): DESRIST 2018, LNCS 10844, pp. 101–115, 2018.
https://doi.org/10.1007/978-3-319-91800-6_7

evidence-based practice [2]. An RCT is a type of medical experiment, in which subjects are randomly assigned to different groups to determine the comparative effects of a treatment. Furthermore, systematic reviews are designed to provide a complete, aggregated evidence of multiple scientific studies, which are typically collected in RCTs [3]. They have been broadly used to support clinicians' confidence in decision-making, to promote clinical and patient health education, as well as, to reduce duplication of research work [4]. Nevertheless, over 75 RCTs and 11 systematic reviews are published every day in biomedical journals [5]; in which the volume and velocity of unstructured evidence data have emerged as an ill-structured challenge to human manual processing capabilities [6]. In additions, Shojania and his co-authors reported that 23% of evidence in systematic reviews were outdated within 2 years based on the publication date [7]. This issue may lead to the decay of currency, accuracy, and utility of evidence in optimising health care for patients [8]. Therefore, this study adopted the design science approach to create technological artefacts for harnessing the dynamic, evolving networks of evidence in evidence-based medicine.

We designed several IT artefacts for building "living" evidence networks, which can be continually updated with strings of newly available RCTs, towards high-quality and update-to-date health optimisation and systematic reviews. Such evidence network encompasses computational and visual representations of evidence ranging from experimental settings and reported outcome occurrences to statistical comparative effects of medical treatments. Moreover, we implemented a computational method for extracting effects of patient-relevant outcomes as integral components of shared decision-making. As a result, the developed IT artefacts do not only facilitate health care professionals and patients to discuss the best available evidence, but also enable health optimisation technologies to elicit preferred treatments for patients.

Our study is situated in shared decision-making for patients with mental disorders including major depressive disorder and bipolar disorder. The lifetime prevalence of mental disorders was estimated between 18.1–36.1% worldwide, which have been recognised as seriously impairing to health care in many countries [9]. Hence, the study targeted to extend the technological boundary of health optimisation systems to establish magnitudinal impact for a large number of patients with mental illness.

The evaluation of our artefacts was conducted using biomedical datasets of full-text journal articles in both major depressive disorder and bipolar disorder. The evidence networks, as the study' deliverables, were evidently demonstrated and were embedded in a decision optimisation system. The study, therefore, contributed to the cumulative development of evidence-based decision-making and the advancement of automated technologies in modern medicine.

The structure of the paper is as follows. Firstly, we discussed the background of our study in the next section. Secondly, we identified the key problems of building dynamic, evolving evidence networks. And then, the paper highlighted the design and implementation of our IT artefacts. Fourthly, an experiment was conducted with two data sets in mental disorders to evaluate the performance of the developed artefacts. Lastly, we concluded our paper with findings and contributions of the research in the final section.

2 Background

We employed the systematic reviewing process as the backbone of our study investigation. It is a principled approach of summarising evidence based on a clearly formulated question, relevant search strategies, and explicit use of methodology for extracting and reporting the findings [10]. A manual process of systematic reviewing, however, is highly labour-intensive, and conventionally takes several years to complete, in which evidence extraction constitutes to a long duration of the processing time. This study, thus, reviewed the automated technologies for evidence extraction and highlighted the gap elements of systematic reviews about patient-relevant outcomes for shared decision making.

2.1 Automated Technologies for Evidence Extraction

Systematic reviews, which have been recognised as the foundation of evidence-based medicine, are designed to search, assess, synthesise, and interpret the evidence published in the biomedical literature. The systematic reviewing process consists of several sub-processes, where data extraction from included research studies is one of most time-consuming operations. Hence, many algorithms and tools were developed to assemble knowledge in randomised controlled trials. Recent research work have been devoted to extracting elements of clinical trials which ranged from participants' summary to study design and clinical results [11–13].

The Cochrane Handbook for Systematic Reviews [14], the CONsolidated Standards Of Reporting Trials (CONSORT) [15], and the Standards for Reporting of Diagnostic Accuracy [16] are the primary standards in systematic reviews. They provide the comprehensive coverage of knowledge elements that are usable in evidence-based decision-making. According to a systematic review conducted by Jonnalagadda et al. [17], there are over 50 knowledge elements of clinical trials about participants, method, interventions, outcomes and results; nonetheless, there is no known knowledge extraction algorithm for 27 elements, especially in the category of clinical outcomes. Outcomes and results are necessary evidence for patients to arrive at a right choice; hence, we highlighted patient-important outcomes in the next section.

2.2 Patient-Important Outcomes

In evidence-based health care, the selection of treatment should be consistent with patients' values and preferences, where relative importance of therapy outcomes should be explicitly presented to patients [18]. Evaluations of treatments are subject to the choice of outcomes due to the trade-off between benefits and harms of treatment options. To reach a good decision, comparative effects of multiple treatments on a range of outcomes are required to elicit patients' preferences during consultations.

Eiring et al. proposed a taxonomy of patient-important outcomes, in which avoid the burden of treatment was discussed as the main outcome in the hierarchy of outcomes [19]. Several sub-categorical outcomes were proposed for patients with Bipolar Disorder such avoid side effects (e.g., headache, dry mouth, and insomnia) and avoid bother (e.g., treatment regimen).

Patient-relevant outcomes of pharmaceutical treatments, including adverse drug reactions and other events, are reported in randomised controlled trials and spontaneous reports. Nevertheless, only a small percentage of recent systematic reviews has surveyed comparative effects of patient-relevant outcomes among treatments.

3　Problem Identification

Knowledge extraction has been a key driver of automated technologies for evidence extraction to improve the systematic reviewing process and to enable the "living" evidence networks. Despite the growing number of knowledge extraction methods for biomedical researchers, there were many drawbacks of existing studies according to a recent systematic review [17] as highlighted in Table 1.

Table 1. Existing methods for automated data extraction

Study	Dataset	Output	Extraction					Highest F-score
			P	I	C	O	AE	
de Bruijn et al. [20]	88 RCT full-text papers	Sentence, Concept	Y	Y	N	Y	N	100.0%
Hassanzadeh et al. [21]	1000 abstracts	Sentence	Y	Y	N	Y	N	91.0%
Hsu et al. [22]	42 full-text papers	Sentence	N	Y	N	Y	N	90.0%
Hansen et al. [23]	233 abstracts	Concept	Y	N	N	N	N	86.0%
Kim et al. [24]	1000 abstracts	Sentence	Y	Y	N	Y	N	80.9%
Kiritchenko et al. [13]	50 full-text papers	Concept	Y	Y	N	Y	N	92.0%
Lin et al. [25]	93 full-text papers	Concept	Y	Y	N	N	N	83.0%

P: Population; I: Intervention; C: Comparison; O: Outcome; AE: Adverse Events
Y: Yes, the element was included; N: No, the element was not included.

We identified several roadblocks in designing a dynamic, evolving evidence networks as the following.

Limited Full-Text Support. Evidence elements were automatically extracted from abstracts but not full-texts in several studies [12, 26]. This issue, however, limits the computational capabilities to harvest useful knowledge elements such as detailed clinical results or reported event rates, which are typically included only in full-texts.

Absence of Patient-Important Outcomes. There was no study that was capable of extracting patient-relevant outcomes in the published reports on automated data extraction in randomised controlled trials and systematic reviews [17].

Neglected Document and Layout Features. Rule-based and model-based approaches were applied to identify texts such as sentences or concepts as data elements of clinical trials [11, 22]. There are a number of knowledge elements; which are only available in non-text parts of RCTs; for instance, the adverse reaction events in treatments as shown in Fig. 1. Thus, the document format (e.g., HTML or pdf) and layout features (e.g., figures or tables) should be considered in the data extraction techniques.

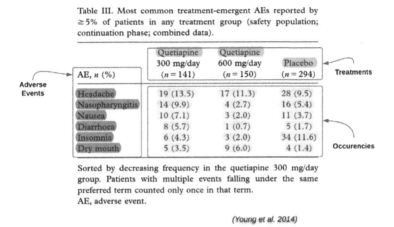

Table III. Most common treatment-emergent AEs reported by ≥5% of patients in any treatment group (safety population; continuation phase; combined data).

AE, n (%)	Quetiapine 300 mg/day (n = 141)	Quetiapine 600 mg/day (n = 150)	Placebo (n = 294)
Headache	19 (13.5)	17 (11.3)	28 (9.5)
Nasopharyngitis	14 (9.9)	4 (2.7)	16 (5.4)
Nausea	10 (7.1)	3 (2.0)	11 (3.7)
Diarrhoea	8 (5.7)	1 (0.7)	5 (1.7)
Insomnia	6 (4.3)	3 (2.0)	34 (11.6)
Dry mouth	5 (3.5)	9 (6.0)	4 (1.4)

Sorted by decreasing frequency in the quetiapine 300 mg/day group. Patients with multiple events falling under the same preferred term counted only once in that term.
AE, adverse event.

(Young et al. 2014)

Fig. 1. Treatment-emergent adverse events reported in treatments of depression

4 Design of IT Artefacts for Building Evidence Networks

Reaching a good, informed decision is always complex for preference-sensitive conditions including major depressive disorder and bipolar disorder, in which there are multiple conflicting factors to consider in the decision-making process [27]. It involves a number of alternatives, and the information available such as efficacy, benefits, harms, or adverse reactions about each alternative are often incomplete [28]. Moreover, in many scenarios, finding a unique and perfect solution is not always possible for decision makers; hence, optimising a decision focuses on the preferred solution, in which trade-off certain factors for others is necessary. The use of structured, explicit methods with mathematical considerations of multiple criteria, as defined as multiple-criteria decision analysis (MCDA) [29], is a viable approach to model preferences and trade-offs for finding the most preferred alternative. MCDA has been explored as an integral part of shared decision-making, where patient-important outcomes have been taken into account as multiple criteria in deriving satisfactory decision optimisation models. This study, therefore, utilised the multi-criteria decision analysis (MCDA) as a kernel theory to design IT artefacts for enabling such model.

In MCDA, a decision matrix can be built to express the expected performance of options against multiple criteria. For example, in the maintenance of bipolar disorder, a number of pharmaceutical treatments can be defined as options in the decision model; while many patient-important outcomes such as avoid manic depression, or avoid sleeping disorders can be specific as criteria. The expected performance can be computed using a simplified formula as the following [29]:

$$Ev(a) = \sum_{i=1}^{m} W_i V_i(a)$$

where

m is the number of criteria
$Ev(a)$ is the expected value of alternative a
W_i is the relative importance of criterion i^{th}
$V_i(a)$ is the score/effect of alternative a on criterion i^{th}

In the context of evidence-based decision-making, W_i refers to relative importance of option characteristics such as the patient's values and preferences; while, $V_i(a)$ represents evidence networks which consists of effect estimates including network meta-analyses or surveys of option outcomes.

To establish "living" evidence networks, there are several computational methods for knowledge extraction, as IT artefacts, were designed as illustrated in Fig. 2.

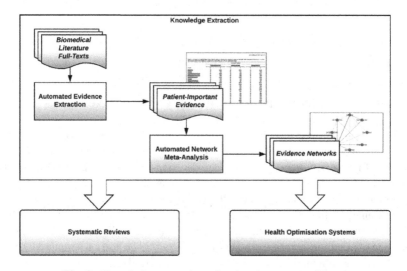

Fig. 2. Knowledge extraction of patient-important evidence

Automated Evidence Extraction. A method for extracting knowledge elements of detailed clinical results and reported event rates from biomedical full-text journals such as publicly available RCT or systematic review articles. As many knowledge elements were embedded in figures and tables, the document and layout features of clinical trial reports were investigated in our design to produce association rules for identifying knowledge elements. Furthermore, patient-relevant outcomes can be extracted as criteria and effect estimates for the MCDA model. In addition, the patient-important evidence can be visualised for clinical experts to inspect and edit if necessary.

Automated Network Meta-Analysis. A method for estimating the comparative effects of multiple treatments using network meta-analysis. A knowledge ontology of evidence can be built based on N-triples to capture the data elements from the automated evidence extraction. These can be fitted into a Generalised Linear Model (GLM) as arm-level network elements. The evidence networks were designed to feed high-quality evidence into decision optimisation models in MCDA.

While systematic reviews are the direct source of evidence for health care professionals; health optimisation systems require both human- and machine- interpretable data to facilitate the optimisation process. As a result, the integration of evidence networks in a health optimisation system for eliciting best possible treatment of bipolar disorders is illustrated in Fig. 3.

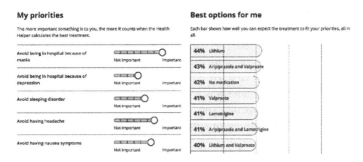

Fig. 3. Integration of evidence networks in a health optimisation system

5   Implementation

This study developed a machine learning approach to extract knowledge elements from full-text journal articles in the biomedical literature. It involved multiple methods for automating evidence extraction and network meta-analyses as described the subsequent sections.

5.1   Automated Evidence Extraction

Knowledge extraction of evidence networks involved multiple steps as shown in Fig. 4 to identify, assess, and learn textual and expository contents of clinical trials. This allowed the development of a classification algorithm to identify data elements of evidence networks in biomedical full-text articles. The computational and visual representations of networks of evidence, then, can be produced for health optimisation. The steps of automated evidence extraction are described in detail as the following.

Pre-processing. Research articles are published in a variety of file formats, and the most commonly used type is the Portable Document Format (PDF). The PDF standards allow researchers to render their content consistently in multiple devices; however,

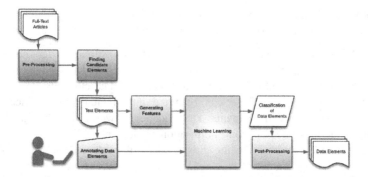

Fig. 4. Multi-step methods for knowledge extraction

structural and layout information are typically missing in existing computational methods. Therefore, the analysis of full-text articles in PDF required the combination and interpretation of textual and layout elements in different levels to produce usable information. In addition, other components such as figures, headers, and trademarks can be distracting to the knowledge extraction process.

The first step of this study was to parse full-text articles in the PDF file format. Then, various elements were extracted based on spacings and alignments to produce information in blocks. A data frame was created from a PDF which provided the types, coordinates, and content of elements. The output of this pre-processing step was critical for high-accuracy machine learning in subsequent steps.

Finding Candidate Elements. Full-text articles of randomised controlled trials are valuable sources of evidence, in which participants' information, intervention details, research design, outcomes, comparisons, and results are reported in accordance to practices of evidence-based medicine. In this study, the key elements for data extraction were the intervention, outcomes, and results of clinical trial reports. In Fig. 1, the patient-important outcomes are psychiatric adverse events which were reported based on three drug treatment groups: Quetiapine 300 mg/day, Quetiapine 600 mg/day, and Placebo. There are several components including event names, treatment groups, and occurrences. This step utilised the SIDER database for finding candidate data elements of drug and side effects [30].

Generating Extraction Features. Several tasks were performed to create features for knowledge extraction based on textual and layout components of full-text research articles. The first task was to determine elements that are vertically and horizontally aligned with the candidate data items in the previous step. The second task was to identify the pages that contained data elements of interest. In our data sets, only pages with relevant data elements were kept for further steps. It is based on the layout rules where outcome elements are horizontally aligned within a delta configuration.

The third task employed a set of 'weak' rules using Regular Expressions (RegEx) to match the data values in the identified contexts. For instance, results could be represented in integer, float, or percentages; moreover, additional notes and symbols were handled by RegEx wildcard operations. Table 2 shows the full range of our data element features which were generated in this step.

Table 2. Data elements features in full-text articles

Variable	Description	Type
Research	The full-text article where the data element was extracted	\<Author > < Year>
Page	The page number where the data element was located in the full-text article	Integer
Element type	The type of data element which can be page, text, or image	Enumeration
Element X1	The x-coordinate of the bottom-left point of the data element	Float
Element Y1	The y-coordinate of the bottom-left point of the data element	Float
Element X2	The x-coordinate of the top-right point of the data element	Float
Element Y2	The y-coordinate of the top-right point of the data element	Float
Element text	The extracted text of the data element	Text
Digits/string	The ratio of numerical digits over the text length	Float
Is whitespace	The data element is empty or a set of white spaces	Boolean
Is HA group	The data element is horizontally aligned with a group	Boolean
Is VA group	The data element is vertically aligned with a group	Boolean
Is HA outcome	The data element is horizontally aligned with an outcome	Boolean
Is VA outcome	The data element is vertically aligned with an outcome	Boolean
DF rules	Matched with hand-crafted data formats	Boolean
Layout rules	Matched with hand-crafted layout formats	Boolean

Machine Learning. The main task of this study was to classify and extract knowledge elements of clinical results using the generated features. The classification problem was to determine whether a text element, extracted in the previous steps, was a relevant data element. A multi-layer feedforward artificial neural network model was trained with stochastic gradient descent. For hidden layers, we adopted the hyperbolic tangent and rectifier linear unit functions as the activation functions; while, the sigmoid function was used as the activation function for the output layer. The cross-entropy was chosen as the loss function for our classification problem and a learning rate was specified to accelerate our training process. The dependent variable is a class whether the data element is a data value of clinical results. For training and evaluation, manual human annotations were rigorously conducted for the above-mentioned supervised learning methods, the procedure for manual annotation is discussed in the data collection section.

Post-processing. A programming script was developed to display the data elements in PDF file formats as highlighted in Fig. 1. This step allowed researchers to inspect the outcomes, treatment groups, and clinical results of randomised controlled trials. While the performance of the classification was evaluated, handling errors were permitted for building evidence networks in next steps. In this post-processing step, data values are obtained and associated with treatment groups and outcomes of clinical trials. An extension of OCRe ontology standards was developed and utilised to capture the detailed results of clinical trials. The knowledge elements, therefore, can be reusable for subsequent analyses in evidence-based medicine.

These steps can be reproducible for new sets of documents to keep the knowledge ontology up-to-date with the dynamic nature of evidence networks.

5.2   Network Meta-Analysis and Evidence-Based Decision-Making

Network Meta-Analysis (NMA) has been gaining attention over recent years as a statistical technique in conducting systematic reviews. The critical focus of NMA is to simultaneously compare multiple treatments on a clinical outcome as high-quality evidence. In this research, NMA was performed programmatically under Bayesian settings. Drawing from the knowledge ontology in the previous section, arm-level network elements was fitted into a Generalised Linear Model (GLM) in the NMA program. This step involved modelling the relative effects of treatments and handling heterogeneity and inconsistency in evidence networks. Then, comparative treatment effects were estimated to display matrices of odds ratios, and to report in different types of plots.

The results of this NMA step plays a critical role in Evidence-Based Decision-Making, especially for patient participation. The findings of this study enabled the process of Preference Elicitation through Multi-Criteria Decision Analysis (MCDA), which was capable of producing relative rankings of treatments based on certain health outcomes for patients towards good decision-making.

6   Evaluation and Applications of Evidence Networks

In recent decades, a large number of evidence-based studies in mental illness has emerged to address the high worldwide prevalence of mental health disorders. Increasingly, patients with mental conditions desire for involvement in shared decision-making [31], which facilitate them to opt for satisfactory treatments. This study, hence, utilised the wealth of scientific biomedical literature of two major preference-sensitive diseases: Major Depression Disorder (MDD) and Bipolar Disorder (BP).

The burden of such mental disorders has been surveyed worldwide, which are often seriously impairing in many countries [9]. Hence, these conditions were examined to evaluate the performance of our proposed artefacts. This study adopted the harmonic mean F-score as an adequate performance measure. The F-score was widely accepted for evaluation of extraction methods in evidence-based health care. Jonnalagadda et al. [17] examined 1190 unique citations in information extraction methods of clinical trials, in which most of them achieved F-scores of 0.70 (70%) and above.

6.1 Data Collection

There are several steps to conduct a systematic review including developing eligibility criteria for including studies, establishing search protocols, and extracting studies' characteristics for further analysis. This study aimed to evaluate the knowledge extraction method; hence, eligible criteria and search strategies were adopted from recent, well-regarded systematic reviews of pharmaceutical treatments in MDD and BP. In our data collection procedure, the systematic review: "Comparative efficacy and acceptability of 12 new-generation antidepressants: a multiple-treatments meta-analysis" by Cipriani et al. [32] was used for MDD; while the systematic review: "Comparative efficacy and tolerability of pharmacological treatments in the maintenance treatment of bipolar disorder: A systematic review and network meta-analysis" was utilised for bipolar disorder by Miura et al. [33].

The training set was collected for MDD which covered 117 randomised controlled trials between 1991 and 2007. It provided comprehensive comparisons of multiple new-generation antidepressants on efficacy and acceptability. The related biomedical citations were examined using a snowball technique to crawl full-text articles. In the final training set, 48 full-text articles were included for knowledge extraction of treatments, outcomes, and results. Besides, Miura et al. [33] reviewed 33 randomised controlled trials of BP treatments between 1970 and 2012. Based on their systematic review, the evaluation set consisted of 16 full-text research articles. Nonetheless, the systematic reviews did not cover the effects of adverse reaction events as the patient-important outcomes, which were extracted as new knowledge in our proposed methods.

Table 3. Summary of data sets for knowledge extraction in MDD and BP

Data set	Disease	No. of articles	N	Positive class
Training set	Major depression disorder	48	7428	1382
Evaluation set	Bipolar disorder	16	2973	517

Table 3 shows a summary of the data sets for knowledge extraction in this study; where N is the number of extracted elements. As the training and evaluation sets were adapted in different domain diseases, this study attempted to establish generalisability of the proposed method to other diseases.

6.2 Results and Discussion

The overall performance of the knowledge extraction method was presented in Table 4. The algorithms provided adequate overall accuracy of 99.31% and 98.69% for the training and evaluation set respectively.

In the training set, the recall was 99.06%, and the precision was at 97.30%, where only 51 data elements were incorrectly classified. The overall F-score was considerably high as 98.17% for the classification task.

In the evaluation set, the evaluated model achieved the F-score of 96.30%, which was usable to minimise the burden of data extraction for systematic reviewers. 39 data elements were incorrectly classified which could be fixed during the post-processing step for further analysis. As two datasets were drawn from a variety of journals in two different domains, overfitting was arguably handled during the evaluation.

Table 4. Overall performance in knowledge extraction

MDD training set		BP test set	
Measure	Value	Measure	Value
Recall	0.9906	*Recall*	0.9826
Precision	0.9730	*Precision*	0.9442
F-score	0.9817	*F-score*	0.9630
Overall accuracy	0.9931	*Overall accuracy*	0.9869

6.3   Evidence Networks of Pharmacological Treatments in the Maintenance of Bipolar Disorder

The worldwide prevalence of Bipolar Disorder has been estimated to be 2.4% [34]. It is a chronic, relapsing, and causes elevated mood disorders, known as mania or hypomania. There is a number of pharmaceutical treatments used in the maintenance phase of Bipolar Disorder [33]; however, such treatment is not without non-serious adverse effects. Based on the knowledge extraction in this study, patient-relevant outcomes of randomised controlled trials for treating drugs for BP were extracted to supplement the existing systematic reviews as new knowledge.

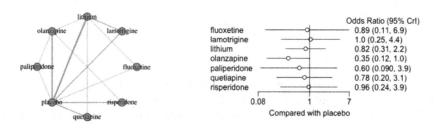

Fig. 5. Network and forest plots for insomnia

For example, insomnia is a sleep disorder that causes difficulty for a patient to fall asleep or to stay asleep. It can sap the energy and mood levels of the patient which affect the work performance and quality of life; therefore, avoiding insomnia while taking drugs for Bipolar Disorder is one the common patient-important outcome. Figure 5 visualises the evidence network of 8 treatment drugs using the network and forest plots in NMA for Insomnia.

The results demonstrated the applicability of our knowledge extraction methods. Such evidence networks including network and forest plots are a digitally-transformed representation of systematic reviews which are ready to use for health care professionals and researchers.

7 Conclusion

Knowledge extraction is the key to mining evidence in randomised controlled trials, thereby fuelling health optimisation for patients. This study presented novel methods of automated extraction and analysis as evidence generating artefacts to enable "living" evidence networks. The evaluation of the study resulted in a F-score of 96.30% which is promising to save time and human resources on one of the most time-consuming tasks in evidence-based paradigm. The design artefacts are capable of transforming decision-support for patients with preference-sensitive diseases towards the more precise and dynamic optimisation in health care. As a result, the evidence networks of pharmaceutical treatments in the maintenance phase of Bipolar Disorder were evidently highlighted to demonstrate the practicality of the proposed knowledge extraction method.

This study is not without some limitations. We did not include a number of the full-text research articles in the original systematic reviews for several reasons where the articles were: (i) not accessible from any biomedical literature database, (ii) paid or restricted access, (iii) published in the scanned format, and (iv) not reporting adverse events or reporting in improper formats. Besides, our study did not cover newly published reports for comparison purposes; nevertheless, the proposed method can be applied to new biomedical articles based on the same search strategies. In additions, we are in progress to evaluate the safety and effectiveness of our health optimisation system in multiple countries including Norway, Singapore, and United States.

References

1. Eiring, Ø., Nytrøen, K., Kienlin, S., Khodambashi, S., Nylenna, M.: The development and feasibility of a personal health-optimization system for people with bipolar disorder. BMC Med. Inform. Decis. Mak. **17**, 1–11 (2017)
2. Burns, P., Rohrich, R., Chong, K.: The levels of evidence and their role in evidence-based medicine. Plast. Reconstr. Surg. **128**, 305–310 (2011)
3. Cochrane, A.L.: 1931–1971: a critical review, with particular reference to the medical profession. Med. year. **1979**, 1 (2000)
4. Nguyen, Hoang D., Poo, D.C.C., Zhang, H., Wang, W.: Analysis and design of an mHealth intervention for community-based health education: an empirical evidence of coronary heart disease prevention program among working adults. In: Maedche, A., vom Brocke, J., Hevner, A. (eds.) DESRIST 2017. LNCS, vol. 10243, pp. 57–72. Springer, Cham (2017). https://doi.org/10.1007/978-3-319-59144-5_4
5. Bastian, H., Glasziou, P., Chalmers, I.: Seventy-five trials and eleven systematic reviews a day: how will we ever keep up? PLoS Med. **7**, e1000326 (2010)

6. Djulbegovic, B., Guyatt, G.H.: Progress in evidence-based medicine: a quarter century on. Lancet **6736**, 1–9 (2017)
7. Shojania, K.G., Sampson, M., Ansari, M.T., Ji, J., Doucette, S., Moher, D.: How quickly do systematic reviews go out of date? A survival analysis. Ann. Intern. Med. **147**, 224–233 (2007)
8. Elliott, J.H., Synnot, A., Turner, T., Simmonds, M., Akl, E.A., McDonald, S., Salanti, G., Meerpohl, J., MacLehose, H., Hilton, J., Tovey, D., Shemilt, I., Thomas, J.: Living systematic review: 1. Introduction—the why, what, when, and how. J. Clin. Epidemiol. **91**, 23–30 (2017)
9. Kessler, R.C., Aguilar-Gaxiola, S., Alonso, J., Chatterji, S., Lee, S., Ormel, J., Ustün, T.B., Wang, P.S.: The global burden of mental disorders: an update from the WHO World Mental Health (WMH) surveys. Epidemiol. Psichiatr. Soc. **18**, 23–33 (2009)
10. Khan, K.S., Kunz, R., Kleijnen, J., Antes, G.: Five steps to conducting a systematic review. J. R. Soc. Med. **96**, 118–121 (2003)
11. Zhao, J., Bysani, P., Kan, M.-Y.: Exploiting classification correlations for the extraction of evidence-based practice information. In: AMIA Annual Symposium Proceedings, vol. 2012, pp. 1070–1078 (2012)
12. Kelly, C., Yang, H.: A system for extracting study design parameters from nutritional genomics abstracts. J. Integr. Bioinform. **10**, 222 (2013)
13. Kiritchenko, S., de Bruijn, B., Carini, S., Martin, J., Sim, I.: ExaCT: automatic extraction of clinical trial characteristics from journal publications. BMC Med. Inform. Decis. Mak. **10**, 56 (2010)
14. Higgins, J.P., Green, S.: Cochrane Handbook for Systematic Reviews of Interventions. Wiley, Chichester (2011)
15. Begg, C.: Improving the quality of reporting of randomized controlled trials: the CONSORT statement. JAMA **276**, 637 (1996)
16. Bossuyt, P.M., Reitsma, J.B., Bruns, D.E., Gatsonis, C.A., Glasziou, P.P., Irwig, L.M., Lijmer, J.G., David Moher, D.R., de Vet, H.C.W.: Towards complete and accurate reporting of studies of diagnostic accuracy: the STARD initiative. Clin. Chem. Lab. Med. **41**, 68–73 (2003)
17. Jonnalagadda, S.R., Goyal, P., Huffman, M.D.: Automating data extraction in systematic reviews: a systematic review. Syst. Rev. **4**, 78 (2015)
18. Gionfriddo, M.R., Leppin, A.L., Brito, J.P., LeBlanc, A., Shah, N.D., Montori, V.M.: Shared decision-making and comparative effectiveness research for patients with chronic conditions: an urgent synergy for better health. J. Comp. Eff. Res. **2**, 595–603 (2013)
19. Eiring, Ø., Nylenna, M., Nytrøen, K.: Patient-important outcomes in the long-term treatment of bipolar disorder: a mixed-methods approach investigating relative preferences and a proposed taxonomy. Patient **9**, 91–102 (2016)
20. de Bruijn, B., Cherry, C., Kiritchenko, S., Martin, J., Zhu, X.: Machine-learned solutions for three stages of clinical information extraction: the state of the art at i2b2 2010. J. Am. Med. Inform. Assoc. **18**, 557–562 (2011)
21. Hassanzadeh, H., Groza, T., Hunter, J.: Identifying scientific artefacts in biomedical literature: the evidence based medicine use case. J. Biomed. Inform. **49**, 159–170 (2014)
22. Hsu, W., Speier, W., Taira, R.K.: Automated extraction of reported statistical analyses: towards a logical representation of clinical trial literature. In: AMIA Annual Symposium Proceedings, vol. 2012, pp. 350–359 (2012)
23. Hansen, M.J., Rasmussen, N.Ø., Chung, G.: A method of extracting the number of trial participants from abstracts describing randomized controlled trials. J. Telemed. Telecare **14**, 354–358 (2008)

24. Kim, S., Martinez, D., Cavedon, L., Yencken, L.: Automatic classification of sentences to support evidence based medicine. BMC Bioinform. **12**, S5 (2011)
25. Lin, S., Ng, J.-P., Pradhan, S., Shah, J., Pietrobon, R., Kan, M.-Y.: Extracting formulaic and free text clinical research articles metadata using conditional random fields. In: Proceedings of the NAACL HLT 2010 Second Louhi Workshop on Text and Data Mining of Health Documents, pp. 90–95 (2010)
26. Wallace, B.C., Trikalinos, T.A., Lau, J., Brodley, C.E., Schmid, C.H.: Semi-automated screening of biomedical citations for systematic reviews. BMC Bioinform. **11**, 55 (2010)
27. Nguyen, H.D., Poo, D.C.C.: Analysis and design of mobile health interventions towards informed shared decision making: an activity theory-driven perspective. J. Decis. Syst. **25**, 397–409 (2016)
28. Thokala, P., Devlin, N., Marsh, K., Baltussen, R., Boysen, M., Kalo, Z., Longrenn, T., Mussen, F., Peacock, S., Watkins, J., Ijzerman, M.: Multiple criteria decision analysis for health care decision making—an introduction: report 1 of the ISPOR MCDA emerging good practices task force. Value Health **19**, 1–13 (2016)
29. Belton, V., Stewart, T.J.: Multiple Criteria Decision Analysis: An Integrated Approach. Springer US, Boston (2002). https://doi.org/10.1007/978-1-4615-1495-4
30. Kuhn, M., Letunic, I., Jensen, L.J., Bork, P.: The SIDER database of drugs and side effects. Nucleic Acids Res. **44**, D1075–D1079 (2016)
31. Patel, S.R., Bakken, S.: Preferences for participation in decision making among ethnically diverse patients with anxiety and depression. Community Ment. Health J. **46**, 466–473 (2010)
32. Cipriani, A., Furukawa, T.A., Salanti, G., Geddes, J.R., Higgins, J.P., Churchill, R., Watanabe, N., Nakagawa, A., Omori, I.M., McGuire, H., Tansella, M., Barbui, C.: Comparative efficacy and acceptability of 12 new-generation antidepressants: a multiple-treatments meta-analysis. Lancet **373**, 746–758 (2009)
33. Miura, T., Noma, H., Furukawa, T.A., Mitsuyasu, H., Tanaka, S., Stockton, S., Salanti, G., Motomura, K., Shimano-Katsuki, S., Leucht, S., Cipriani, A., Geddes, J.R., Kanba, S.: Comparative efficacy and tolerability of pharmacological treatments in the maintenance treatment of bipolar disorder: A systematic review and network meta-analysis. Lancet Psychiatry **1**, 351–359 (2014)
34. Merikangas, K.R., Jin, R., He, J.-P., Kessler, R.C., Lee, S., Sampson, N.A., Viana, M.C., Andrade, L.H., Hu, C., Karam, E.G., Ladea, M., Medina-Mora, M.E., Ono, Y., Posada-Villa, J., Sagar, R., Wells, J.E., Zarkov, Z.: Prevalence and correlates of bipolar spectrum disorder in the world mental health survey initiative. Arch. Gen. Psychiatry **68**, 241–251 (2011)

Assessing Strategic Readiness for Healthcare Analytics: System and Design Theory Implications

Sathyanarayanan Venkatraman[1(✉)], Rangaraja P. Sundarraj[1], and Ravi Seethamraju[2]

[1] Department of Management Studies, IIT Madras, Chennai, Tamil Nadu, India
sathya.venkatraman68@gmail.com,
rpsundarraj@iitm.ac.in
[2] Business School, The University of Sydney, Sydney, Australia
ravi.seethamraju@sydney.edu.au

Abstract. The adoption of analytics solutions in hospitals is a recent trend aimed at fact-based decision making and data-driven performance management. However, the adoption of analytics involves diverse stakeholder perspectives. Currently, there is a paucity of studies that focus on how the practitioners assess their organizational readiness for health analytics (HA) and make informed decisions on technology adoption given a set of alternatives. We fill this gap with our study by designing a strategic assessment framework guided by a DSRM approach that iteratively extends our past artifact. Our approach first entails the use of many in-depth case-studies, as well as embedded experts from the industry to inform the objective setting and design process. These inputs are then supported by two multi-criteria decision-making methods. We also evaluate our framework with healthcare practitioners for both design validity and future iterations of this project. Implications of our work for *theory of design and action* are also highlighted.

Keywords: DSRM · IPA · DEMETAL · Health-Analytics
Theory for design and action

1 Introduction

Healthcare organizations (HCOs) around the world have been investing in emerging information technologies to solve their business issues and challenges related to cost reduction, patient care, and performance management. Examples of this trend include the adoption of Health-Analytics (HA) to enable data-driven decision-making capability [1] and to improve healthcare processes [2, 3]. These adoptions have spread across multiple areas of the hospital (including clinical, operational, administrative and strategic business areas to derive business insights [4]) and have contributed to both long-term and short-term goals [5].

While the business case for HA may appear to be there anecdotally, as with any emerging technology, during the process of adoption, hospitals face many challenges related to cost, financial, business-case, culture, executive support, skills, clarity, and

© Springer International Publishing AG, part of Springer Nature 2018
S. Chatterjee et al. (Eds.): DESRIST 2018, LNCS 10844, pp. 116–131, 2018.
https://doi.org/10.1007/978-3-319-91800-6_8

data availability [6]. As an example, lack of availability of EMR system and data limits hospitals in leveraging HA for their clinical decision support. Some researchers have raised doubts on value creation of information technologies in hospitals [7], and past studies point out that, despite investments in technologies there are increasing evidence of entrenched inefficiencies and suboptimal clinical outcomes [8]. The key to success of HA adoption is the hospital's readiness to adopt the technology. Hence, the HA adoption-decision entails multiple stakeholders at multiple levels and due consideration of factors that impact the success of adoption. Despite the fact that the requirements of the stakeholders from various departments differ, at a foundational level, the hospital needs to be strategically ready and fit to adopt HA. The research question addressed herein is: *how can hospitals strategically assess their readiness for HA technology with a system driven approach and make informed decisions on adoption?* Our objective of this study is to design a framework to support the above.

Past IS management studies have primarily focused on post-adoption. One example of a system for a particular pre-adoption decision can be found in [9], wherein the focus is on technology-related organizational factors. Given this gap, our research considers a strategic-level assessment. While (as in [9]), we follow the Design Science Research Method (DSRM) approach [10], we bring-in: (i) the additional richness of fourteen case-studies; and (ii) also embed industry experts to evaluate and provide inputs based on their real-life experience. These steps of the design process provide the inputs for the instrument that forms part of our system. In addition, since the adoption of HA is a complex decision-making process, we embed suitable multi-criteria decision-making (MCDM) techniques [11, 12]. An example instantiation of a prototype tool of this design framework is by a team of practitioners from a hospital. With many hospitals across the world seriously exploring the feasibility of adoption of HA solutions, our research is timely, and relevant for practitioners.

The paper is organized further as follows: Sect. 2 provides a background to our study; Sect. 3 describes the method and the guidelines of our study; Sect. 4 details the design and development process and the artifact; Sect. 5 details demonstration and evaluation process that we followed; Sect. 6 discusses the design theory construct, learnings, and implications of this study; and Sect. 7 summarizes and concludes.

2 Background

Health-Analytics (HA) is a recent innovation in healthcare IT, which enables the hospitals in making evidence-based decisions in their various process areas on a day to day basis. There are several examples of past studies that highlight how hospitals leverage HA to analyze the clinical data [13], operational data [14], administrative data [15], and strategic data [16]. They derive value through the systematic use of above-said data and the related business insights developed through applied analytical disciplines such as statistical, contextual, quantitative, predictive and cognitive models to drive fact-based decision making for planning, management, measurement and learning [8, 17]. These business insights eventually help transform the business processes in many departments of hospitals [5] which results in increased efficiency of patient care, reduction of healthcare costs and increase in clinical outcomes [3].

Hospitals, today, are also collecting significant amounts of structured and unstructured data [1] and this availability of data offers organizations opportunities for innovations to their business processes and services through the adoption of HA technology.

In line with our research on the development of an artifact to help the adoption of HA, we review the past IT adoption studies towards evaluating the models suitable to be used in pre-adoption stages by practitioners. IT adoption body of knowledge has been made theoretically rich by popular models like TAM [18, 19], UTAUT [20], DeLone & McLean IS Success Model [21]. TAM and UTAUT focus on user level adoption and IS Success Model focuses on post-implementation success. Several studies have used these models in various industry contexts including healthcare domain [22, 23]. Also, few HA-specific models also have been developed such as Brook's BI Maturity assessment model [24] and HOT-Fit model [25]. Brook's model focuses on maturity assessment of HA and HOT-fit model is the extension of the original IS success model.

Practitioners to a large extent, follow the models developed by the industry such as "Healthcare Information and Management Systems Society (HIMSS)" [26] or the "Healthcare Analytics Adoption Model (HAAM)" [27]. HIMSS EMR model has eight stages that track hospital's progress towards a paperless patient record environment, and this integrates closely with HIMSS analytics model which measures organization's analytical maturity across data, enterprise approach, leadership, strategic targets, and analytical staff capabilities. In contrast, the HAAM model is more technical and defines various stages of HA adoption in hospitals in the increasing order of maturity. The above models being developed by the industry, are practitioner-oriented with a focus on maturity assessment of hospitals post adoption of technology. However, neither the academic models nor the practitioner ones cited above can be used for pre-adoption evaluation and decision scenario although they provide insights on the phenomenon of adoption of technology and also methods to measure or evaluate the HA systems. Also, except the Brook's model, rest of the cited ones are more theoretical, trying to understand the phenomena of IT adoption and not meant for practitioners' use in hospitals. Though there is a need in the industry for pre-adoption focused models and techniques, the past studies have not addressed the same.

Secondly, apart from the standard IT adoption studies from the past which model the phenomenon of adoption, we also explore studies [4, 28] that focus on the antecedents of HA adoption and they provide indicators on the factors that a practitioner would consider while adopting HA at a strategic level. On similar lines, the study by Ghosh and Scott [29] highlight the technical catalysts and antecedents to developing analytics competency in healthcare domain.

Myers et al. [30] called for a need for frameworks for IS to assess and justify the investments in IT. Developing either artifacts, systems or instruments focused on assessment of a concept is not new. We have seen similar studies in IS domains [31, 32] although the objective of most of these instruments was to support quantitative survey. Ebner et al. develop an instrument for IT benchmarking which is practitioner-oriented [33], and this was developed over several iterations of interaction with the industry. However, it is not healthcare domain specific. In healthcare IT domain, Venkatraman et al. [9] develop an artifact for the a pre-adoption decision support HA [9]. However, its focus is only on the organizational aspects, and it ignores the environmental and economic aspects which impact HA adoption decisions. Hence, we found a clear need to develop and enhance our past study with more exploratory and qualitative work and also embed practitioners in the process to increase the rigor. Our current study addresses the above need, and we further provide the details of the iterative method that we adopted in our study and the artifact that we developed through that process.

3   Method

As per Hevner et al., the design science contributes to building innovative IT artifacts to solve identified business needs [34]. The identification of the design research problem was triggered by the industry requirements for a tool or framework which executives can use to assess their readiness for adoption of HA technology. As the heart of our study lies in the design science, our emphasis is on the construction-oriented view of IS. Keeping with the above principle, we follow the Design Science Research Process (DSRP) proposed by Peffers et al. [10] to develop an artifact which can be used by practitioners in hospitals while making decisions on adopting HA technology.

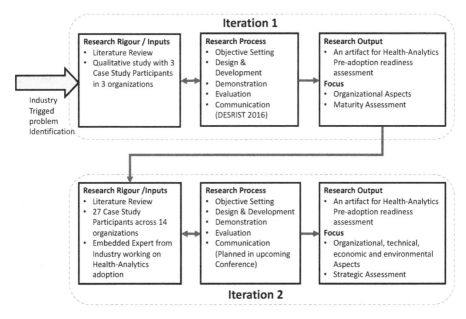

Fig. 1. Iterative design of artifact.

DSRP, the gated methodology with six stages emphasizes on continuous evaluation and feedback to previous steps to refine the design. Past studies [33] have developed instruments (artifacts) with multiple iterations of testing on the field with organizations. Our current study (Ref. Fig. 1) aims to achieve a similar aim with two iterations of the design process but provides additional rigor by the use case study approach and novel methods like embedding experts into the design. The objective of this research is to refine the outcome from iteration one [9] and produce an artifact closer to industry requirements. In doing so, we now explain how our study followed the guidelines of design science research, as codified by Hevner et al. [34]:

1. **Design as an Artifact:** The objective of our research is to produce a tangible artifact in the form of a Strategic Assessment Framework for HA Adoption Decisions.
2. **Problem Relevance:** The problem that we intend to solve is helping executives make informed decisions on HA adoption to minimize risks. The relevance of this problem is high, as the industry, amidst uncertainties of business value from IT investments [7], is on the cusp of adopting HA into their mainstream business towards enhancing the clinical outcomes and streamlining the hospital management processes while optimizing the cost of operations.
3. **Design Evaluation:** The design was carried out in two iterations (Ref. Fig. 1). With our engagements with industry practitioners in the case study organizations, we received a feedback on the initial version of the artifact from the past study [9] which led us to enhance the objective of our study. The new artifact includes strategic assessments of readiness apart from maturity assessment (tactical) in the original artifact. Section 6 has the details of the further evaluation of the enhanced artifact in this study and the feedback from practitioners. We will continue to evolve in our design through further evaluations and refinements.
4. **Research Contributions:** There is a paucity of research in the areas of defining antecedents that can explain the adoption-decisions and artifacts that can be used by the practitioners to assess their readiness to adopt HA technology. Our research intends to fill this gap.
5. **Research Rigor:** We use the qualitative case study approach to explore landscape of HA adoption factors, antecedents and challenges before the development of the artifacts. In our first iteration we had three participants from industry and in the current study we expanded our reach to twenty seven practitioners to understand the aspects of the problem and possible solutions. Apart from this, we also embedded experts from a hospital to support our design process with an intent of constructing an artifact closer to industry requirements.
6. **Design as a Search Process:** We understand the reiterative nature of design science research and hence every artifact (typology, framework, assessment tool) that we produce is planned to be tested & validated in the field and provide for a feedback loop to modify, change the artifacts based on actual usage.
7. **Communication of Research:** We will use conferences and publications as a means to present both the technical and management view of the synthesized information, research data, findings and the artifact.

4   Design and Development of the Artifact

In this stage, the core of our design science research, we started by determining the artifact's functional requirements (Ref. Fig. 2) and then designed the actual artifact by closely engaging with a team of expert practitioners from one of our cases. We built the framework in an iterative approach. Our team regularly met to validate and enhance the technical design and accuracy of the algorithms. Design-science research relies upon the application of rigorous methods in both the construction and evaluation of the design artifact [34], and we relied on past literature and detailed case study analysis to determine the functional requirements. The review of past research [4, 5, 35] gave us insights on the areas where hospitals implement analytics, and we used that as a base to explore and conduct our case study interviews.

Our case study analysis confirmed that, broadly, HA is adopted in: (a) clinical areas to make decisions pertaining to diagnosis and medical interventions; (b) operational areas such as labs, pharmacies, theatres, and all support functions to the core clinical function; (c) the administrative areas such as HR, resources, and facilities; and (d) the strategic areas such as finance, planning, and customer relations. Apart from the validating functional areas of HA, our discussions with the cases in the second iteration provided the following three crucial inputs on the considerations for assessment of the HA adoption readiness:

1. The readiness of hospitals could vary based on the functional area that they want to adopt HA. As an example, many cases in our study were ready for HA adoption in operational and administrative areas, but not on the clinical side.
2. While assessing their readiness for HA, hospitals consider several factors related to economics, technology, organization, and environment. HA adoption is a complex multi-criteria decision.
3. Since the span of applications for HA is vast, the requirements of the stakeholders from various departments differ. More so, the functional responsibility (CIO/CTO/CFO/COO/CEO) of the stakeholder has an impact on how he/she would evaluate the HA and assess their readiness to adopt.

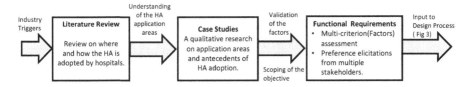

Fig. 2. Determining the core functional requirements of the artifact.

Our expanded case study analysis carried out in the second iteration provided us fifteen antecedents or "factors of considerations" (as compared to basic five factors considered in first iteration) that hospitals should use to assess their readiness to adopt HA. We derived these factors based on the coding of text segments in the interview transcriptions using MAXQDA 2018 software. Initially, *a priori* coding was set up based on past literature and the TOE theoretical framework [36]. We applied axial coding to select core thematic categories present in interview transcripts and discovered common patterns and relations. The codes were grouped under the technological, organizational, environmental themes, and based on further grouping we added economic factors as an additional theme. Out of totally 1232 code segments in the transcripts from interviews of 27 respondents, the codes with high frequency and widely said by the participants as an important factor were short-listed.

The details of the codes, coding frequency, and their definition in the context of the artifact that we plan to develop are given below (Ref. Table 1). The table also has the addition information on the primary focus area (marked as P on the table) of the stakeholders by their functional responsibility. Our CxO level case study participants had a mix of technical, operational and business profiles. In our cases, the technical executives (CIO, CTO) were focused on ensuring the readiness from a HA technology

Table 1. Short-listed factors and stakeholder's focus

Factors, and their definitions in the artifact code frequency (in brackets)	Stakeholders priority			
	CIO	COO	CFO	CEO
Economical				
F1	**Cost** (28): The extent to which the HA cost is affordable			P	
F2	**ROI** (26): The extent to which the HA delivers return on investments			P	
F3	**Benefits** (58):The extent to which the HA provides qualitative benefits	P			
F4	**Economies of scale** (20): The extent to which the HA offer economies of scale				P
Technological				
F5	**IS maturity** (40): The extent of the current maturity of IS (EMR, HIS) which needs to integrate with HA	P			
F6	**IT maturity** (40): The extent of the current maturity of underpinning IT which needs to integrate with HA	P			
F7	**Medical infra maturity** (46): The extent of the current maturity state of the available medical equipment which needs to integrate with HA	P			
F8	**Data quality** (76): The extent to which the current systems produce quality data which are analysable by HA	P			
Organisational				
F9	**Leadership & vision** (56): The extent to which the HA aligns with leadership vision and would gain support for adoption				P
F10	**Competency** (29): The extent of the required skills that we have to develop, use, and sustain HA competency	P			
F11	**Culture** (24): The extent to which the organizational culture supports fact based decision making with HA		P		
F12	**User Adoption** (84): The extent to which the users would accept and adopt HA		P		

(continued)

Table 1. (*continued*)

Factors, and their definitions in the artifact code frequency (in brackets)	Stakeholders priority			
	CIO	COO	CFO	CEO
Environmental				
F13 **Govt. regulation** (38): The extent to which HA helps achieve compliance to govt. regulations				P
F14 **Competition** (16): The extent to which HA helps the hospital operate in an competitive environment				P
F15 **Supply-demand state** (13): The extent to which the current supply-demand state of resources would cause issues in HA adoption		P		

perspective; the operational executives (COO) were concerned about role of HA in enhancing hospital performance; and the business executives (MD, CEO) of the hospitals were focussed on alignment of HA with their long-term vision. Based on the above we derived the two critical functional requirements for the artifact:

- Strategic assessment to include fifteen factors (F1–F15) (Ref. Table 1).
- Preference elicitation methods to be used to seek inputs from the group of stakeholders.

4.1   The Artifact: Strategic Readiness Assessment Framework for HA

We will now describe the details of the artifact development stages (Ref. Fig. 3). The case study data provided the inputs on the factors of consideration for readiness assessment, the functional areas of the hospital, and the types of stakeholders involved in decision making. For us to construct the framework with the desired output, these inputs had to be coded in to mathematical derivations and algorithms. To ensure reliability and accuracy of such algorithms, we depended on the reusable and time-tested techniques from past studies which have been proven in many empirical studies. One of the key benefits of reusable design artifacts is that, they can be instantiated and combined in different ways to produce concrete designs [37, 38]. Also, our objective was to develop an artifact for the practitioners that puts to use the techniques from the academic world. Towards that objective, we embedded IPA [11] and DEMATEL [12] techniques in our artifact, which we will explain now.

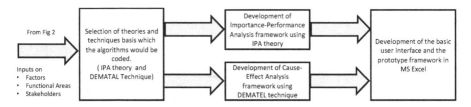

Fig. 3. Artifact development stages.

IPA, a well-known technique was first introduced by Martilla and James [11] as a means to the management diagnosis of new product success in marketing. Due to its simplicity and ease of interpretation with IPA maps, it has been used in many studies including IS [39]. In our study, we use it as a framework to capture the judgments of the stakeholders on their perceived importance ("importance") of the readiness factor (F1–F15) (Ref. Table 1) and about envisaged performance ("performance") of the HA adoption in the context of the factor. We elicit the judgments from multiple stakeholders with a Likert scale of 1–7 and calculate the mean of the responses for each of the fifteen factors. In short, for every readiness factor, there would be a pair of importance and performance mean scores. Based on the scores of importance and performance, we then draw an IPA Graph (Ref. Fig. 4) plotting the factors in four quadrants. The IPA Graph presents the factors segregated in four quadrants, with a logic that: (a) factors with high importance and low performance need more focus; (b) the ones with high importance and high performance need to maintained status quo; (c) for the ones with low importance and high performance, should be defocused because of possible overkill and current undue focus; and (d) the ones with low importance and low scores can be ignored as low priority. IPA graph gives executives a simple interface to understand their overall readiness for HA adoption and areas that they need to focus on getting business value from HA investments.

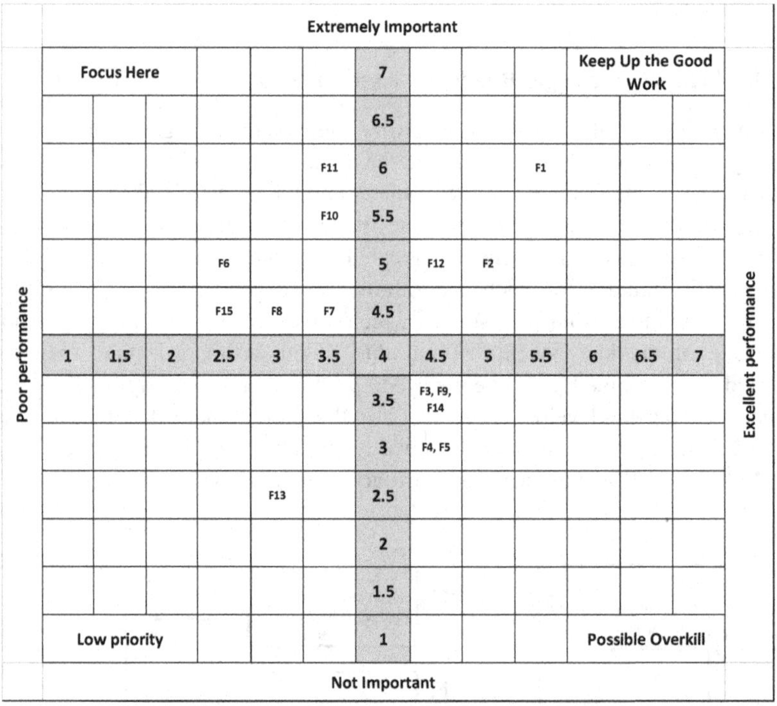

	1	1.5	2	2.5	3	3.5	(imp)	4.5	5	5.5	6	6.5	7
Extremely Important													
Focus Here							**7**			Keep Up the Good Work			
							6.5						
						F11	6			F1			
						F10	5.5						
				F6			5	F12	F2				
				F15	F8	F7	4.5						
	1	1.5	2	2.5	3	3.5	4	4.5	5	5.5	6	6.5	7
							3.5	F3, F9, F14					
							3	F4, F5					
					F13		2.5						
							2						
							1.5						
Low priority							**1**			Possible Overkill			
Not Important													

(Left axis: Poor performance — Right axis: Excellent performance)

Fig. 4. IPA: importance – performance graph.

DEMATEL was originally proposed by Gabus and Fontela [12] to study and resolve the complicated and intertwined problem groups in decision scenario with multiple criterions. DEMETEL has been successfully used in many studies in the past [40, 41] dealing with complex decisions, and HA adoption being a similar one, we embed this technique in our artifact. The advantage of DEMETEL is its ability to investigate the interrelations among criteria and build a Network Relationship Map (NRM) as an outcome (Ref. Fig. 5). Following are the steps (The detailed explanation of mathematics involved in deriving relationships is beyond the scope of this paper) involved in this technique:

- **Step 1:** Multiple stakeholders' input is captured on the impact of a given factor on others through a pairwise comparison, and they are aggregated to arrive at direct relationship matrix (D).
- **Step 2:** The direct relationship matrix is then normalized (N).
- **Step 3:** A total relationship matrix is arrived based on N ($T = N\,(I - N)^{-1}$).
- **Step 4:** From the T, the influence strength of the factors are calculated.
- **Step 5:** Finally the NRMs (causal diagrams) are built based on the influence strengths.

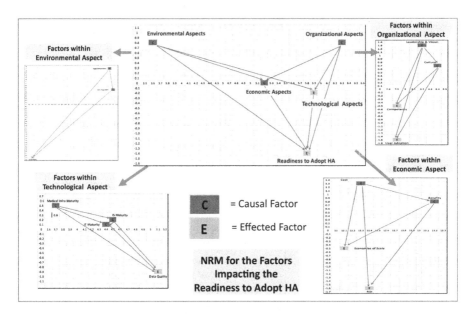

Fig. 5. DEMETAL: network relationship map for the factors impacting HA.

In our artifact, we use the DEMATAL to assess the interrelationship between the HA factors and we do this two hierarchical levels, (a) group level inter-relationships between economic, organizational, technological and environmental aspects and (b) factor level inter-relationships within the aspect. As an output, we get five NRMs which provide insights on the cause-effect relationships of the factors (Ref. Fig. 5). A combination of IPA Graph and a DEMATAL NRMs provide a strategic view of the readiness of the organization to adopt HA.

5 Demonstration and Initial Evaluation

We built the artifact in collaboration with a team of practitioners in one of our cases with whom we carried out a formal demonstration and walk-through of the Strategic Readiness Assessment Framework for HA. Our objective of this initial evaluation was to assess and take feedback on its usefulness and the realistic representation of decision scenarios. The hospital chosen for evaluation is one of the largest eye-care hospitals in India and in the cusp of adopting HA to enhance their clinical outcomes. The evaluation team comprised of the CITO (Chief information and technology Officer) and two IT managers from his team who have been working closely with many HA vendors and piloting their solutions. We carried out an initial presentation of the system, detailing the objectives, and various factors for which the inputs are needed in the framework. Subsequently, we carried out a walk-through of the complete system to the practitioners and demonstrated with test data. The practitioners worked on the prototype hands on and provided their feedback on their perceptions of adopting the framework for making HA adoption decisions. We used the instrument designed by Moore and Benbasat [32] to measure the perceptions of adopting an information technology innovation for our formal evaluation. The details of the constructs used in the evaluation and the expert review feedbacks are summarized (Ref. Table 2) below.

Table 2. Evaluation of strategic readiness adoption framework for HA.

#	Constructs evaluated	Expert review comments (verbatim)
1	**Voluntariness:** Degree to which the use of RAF is perceived being voluntary	*"Use of such assessment framework is voluntary. We already have been doing similar assessments but may not be very structured."*
2	**Relative advantage:** The degree to which the use of RAF enhances the job performance	*"RAF is useful, but more than a strategic assessment, it would be good to have a technical assessment or evaluation tool for HA products. The demands of each of functional departments which includes clinical and administration drives adoption of Analytics and assessments differently."*
3	**Compatibility:** The degree to which the use of RAF is compatible with or requires a change in one's job	*"This tool fits into the kind of strategic work I do on a daily basis. Good for managers who need to make technology investment decisions."*
4	**Ease of Use:** The degree to which RAF is easy to learn and use	*"Currently the interface is very rustic and not intuitive. More automation is needed to improve the tool."*
5	**Result demonstrability:** The degree to which the results from RAF are demonstrable	*"The results reflect my assessments i have done earlier using other informal methods. However, the RAF method seems to be more scientific."*
6	**Trialability:** The degree to which it is possible to try using RAF	*"Need to try out again after the user interfaces are improved."*

Our initial evaluation provided many crucial findings. First, the user interface needs to be improved with more automation to increase the ease of use for the practitioner. This learning validates the past research on impact of "ease of use" [19] in ensuring technology is adopted. Second learning we have is "One size does not fit all." Separate modules of evaluation each for clinical, operational, administrative, strategic functions need to be provided, as the readiness requirements of each of the them in a hospital is different and this was reinforced through a written comment from the practitioner on the evaluation form: "*Having one view of the organization maturity will be quite difficult to develop and implement in view of specific challenges and diverse needs of operations.*" Finally, Technical evaluation for HA products needs to be included as a separate module to be used at the next level once the organizational readiness for HA is determined. The above could also be an independent artifact by itself.

6 Discussions

We have constructed an artifact that can bring in efficiency and effectiveness into the HA adoption decision-making process. In the DSR design contribution framework [42] that maps the application domain maturity and solution maturity, the artifact that we developed falls under quadrant "Extended Known Solutions for New Problems", i.e. adopting solutions from other fields and applying it in new domain. In the process of developing the artifact, we used the known solutions from different domains and applied in our new problem which is "technology adoption in healthcare". The application of IPA techniques is more prevalent in marketing domain and DEMATEL MCDM in social and industrial domains. We applied these techniques in solving our problem of enabling healthcare executives to make informed decisions on HA adoption.

6.1 Artifact as a DSR Knowledge

While communicating the process of the design work it is critical that we also look into how the developed artifact plays a role in theorizing design science [42], in other words, "Artifact as DSR knowledge." Reflecting the iterative DSR process that we went through in designing the artifact, the we map (Ref. Table 3) the process and the output to the eight components of design theory structure proposed by Gregor and Jones [43].

Our artifact aids in a decision making which is scientific, evidence-based and involves relevant stakeholders in the organization. The multi-case study analysis, iterative design, and the "embedded expert" approach to the design process gave us several learnings. First, our involvement with practitioners in evaluation cycle not only enhanced the artifact but also fundamentally changed the objective of the design. The above highlights the importance of evaluation and the constant feedback between stages [10]. Second, our study reiterated importance of user-centric design thinking as many people look at the same given problem in different ways. Hence, it is not just about "what problem", but also the "whose problem" which is equally important.

Table 3. Design theory for strategic readiness adoption framework for HA adoption.

Components	Description
Purpose and scope	• Constructing a strategic framework that can be used by healthcare executives to make informed decisions on HA adoption
Constructs	• Semi-structured case study questionnaire • Interview transcripts • Algorithm for IPA analysis • Algorithm for DEMATEL analysis
Principles of form and function	• Strategic assessment to include economic, organizational, technological and environmental factors • Preference elicitation methods to be used to seek inputs from the multiple stakeholders (CIO/COO/CFO/CEO)

Artifact mutability	• The two iterations that changed/enhanced artifacts provide insights into the mutability:
	  – The semi-structured questionnaire for case study interviews had to be modified for organizational profiles (health service provider, health service eco-system partner such as insurance)
	  – Based on where HA is adopted the assessment focus changes

Testable propositions	• P1: The readiness factors change based on the functional area where HA is adopted • P2: The importance of factors change based on stakeholder profile and responsibility (CIO/CTO/COO/CFO/CEO)
Justificatory knowledge	• The readiness factors/antecedents were derived from past academic literature and further validated with case studies • The case study was based on TOE framework • IPA and DEMATEL techniques formed the basis of the artifact
Principles of implementation	• The artifact designed to be used for group decision making and the assessment to be carried with multiple stake holders to get an organizational view of readiness • Recommended sample size (6–15) to get a reliable output
Expository instantiation	• MS Excel based elicitation tool with built-in functions to calculate the IPA and DEMATEL logic

Third, design that embeds practitioners can produce useful artifacts closer to the industry requirements.

Finally, in our view, a study focused on pre-adoption is as important as post-adoption of technology as rightly put by Sherer [7] that *"traditional IT value research approaches that deal with the outcome of past IT investments through post hoc analysis will be neither timely nor relevant to influence health care practice now, when substantial investment incentives are spurring adoption and industry change"*. Our study is a step towards supporting practitioners who face challenges in demonstrating the business value of IT in healthcare [7] by providing them with a useful framework and tool.

7 Conclusion

Triggered by real-life industry issues in HA adoption and using design science research method, we progressed from identification of the problem to the construction of an artifact for hospitals make an informed decision on HA adoption. We also applied the research rigor in engaging with industry and embedding experts in the design process. Our design would be an ongoing activity with multiple iterations of future enhancements with the industry seriously exploring to adopt HA technology we believe that our study has been valuable. For the academicians, this study opens up the possibility of studies focused on developing artifacts for HA technical maturity assessments and decision support tools. The other possible options are creating web-based benchmarking tools that can assess the industry on technology adoption and provide a comparative view of the organization.

References

1. Groves, P., Kayyali, B., Knott, D., Van Kuiken, S.: The "big data"revolution in healthcare. McKinsey Q. **22** (2013)
2. Ammenwerth, E., Brender, J., Nykänen, P., Prokosch, H.U., Rigby, M., Talmon, J.: Visions and strategies to improve evaluation of health information systems: reflections and lessons based on the HIS-EVAL workshop in Innsbruck. Int. J. Med. Inform. **73**, 479–491 (2004)
3. Raghupathi, W., Tan, J.: Information systems and healthcare: charting a strategic path for health information technology. Commun. Assoc. Inf. Syst. **23**, 501–522 (2008)
4. Venkatraman, S., Sundarraj, R.P., Seethamraju, R.: Healthcare Analytics Adoption-Decision Model: A Case Study. In: 2015 Proceedings of the PACIS (2015)
5. Ward, M.J., Marsolo, K.A., Froehle, C.M.: Applications of business analytics in healthcare. Bus. Horiz. **57**, 571–582 (2014)
6. Lavalle, S., Hopkins, M.S., Lesser, E., Shockley, R., Kruschwitz, N.: Analytics: the new path to value. MIT Sloan Manag. Rev. **52**(1), 1–24 (2010)
7. Sherer, S.A.: Advocating for action design research on IT value creation in healthcare. J. Assoc. Inf. Syst. **15**, 860–878 (2014)
8. Cortada, J.W., Gordon, D., Lenihan, B.: The value of analytics in healthcare. IBM Institute for Business Value Healthcare (2010)
9. Venkatraman, S., Sundarraj, R.P., Mukherjee, A.: Prototype design of a healthcare-analytics pre-adoption readiness assessment (HAPRA) instrument. In: Parsons, J., Tuunanen, T., Venable, J., Donnellan, B., Helfert, M., Kenneally, J. (eds.) DESRIST 2016. LNCS, vol. 9661, pp. 158–174. Springer, Cham (2016). https://doi.org/10.1007/978-3-319-39294-3_11
10. Peffers, K., Tuunanen, T., Rothenberger, M.A., Chatterjee, S.: A design science research methodology for information systems research. J. Manag. Inf. Syst. **24**, 45–77 (2008)
11. Martilla, J.A., James, J.C.: Importance-performance analysis. J. Mark. **41**, 77–79 (1977)
12. Gabus, A., Fontela, E.: The DEMATEL observer - DEMATEL 1976 Report - Battelle Geneva Research Center, Geneva, Switzerland (1976)
13. Shneiderman, B., Plaisant, C., Hesse, B.W.: Improving healthcare with interactive visualization. IEEE Comput. Soc. **46**, 58–66 (2013)

14. Songthung, P., Sripanidkulchai, K., Luangruangrong, P., Sakulbumrungsil, R.C., Udomak-sorn, S., Kessomboon, N., Kanchanaphibool, I.: An innovative decision support service for improving pharmaceutical acquisition capabilities. In: 2012 Annual SRII Global Conference, pp. 628–636 (2012)

15. Peck, J.S., Benneyan, J.C., Nightingale, D.J., Gaehde, S.A.: Characterizing the value of predictive analytics in facilitating hospital patient flow. IIE Trans. Healthc. Syst. Eng. **4**, 135–143 (2014)

16. Aktaş, E., Ülengin, F., Önsel Şahin, Ş.: A decision support system to improve the efficiency of resource allocation in healthcare management. Socio-Econ. Plann. Sci. **41**, 130–146 (2007)

17. Davenport, T.H., Harris, J.G.: Competing on Analytics: The New Science of Winning. Harvard Business Press, Boston (2007)

18. Davis, F.D.: A technology acceptance model for empirically testing new end-user information systems: theory and results (1986)

19. Venkatesh, V., Davis, F.D.: A theoretical extension of the technology acceptance model: four longitudinal field studies. Manage. Sci. **46**, 186–204 (2000)

20. Venkatesh, V., Morris, M.G., Davis, G.B., Davis, F.D.: User acceptance of information technology: toward a unified view. MIS Q. **27**, 425–478 (2003)

21. DeLone, W.H., McLean, E.R.: The DeLone and McLean model of information systems success: a ten-year update. J. Manag. Inf. Syst. **19**, 9–30 (2003)

22. Hikmet, N., Bhattacherjee, A., Menachemi, N., Kayhan, V.O., Brooks, R.G.: The role of organizational factors in the adoption of healthcare information technology in Florida hospitals. Health Care Manag. Sci. **11**, 1–9 (2008)

23. Yu, P.: A multi-method approach to evaluate health information systems. Stud. Health Technol. Inform. **160**, 1231–1235 (2010)

24. Brooks, P., El-Gayar, O., Sarnikar, S.: A framework for developing a domain specific business intelligence maturity model: application to healthcare. Int. J. Inf. Manage. **35**, 337–345 (2015)

25. Yusof, M.M., Kuljis, J., Papazafeiropoulou, A., Stergioulas, L.K.: An evaluation framework for health information systems: human, organization and technology-fit factors (HOT-fit). Int. J. Med. Inform. **77**, 386–398 (2008)

26. Davis, M.W.: The seven stages of EMR adoption: majority of hospitals are in stage 3 and rising. Healthc. Exec. **25**, 18–19 (2010)

27. Sanders, D., Burton, D., Protti, D.: The healthcare analytics adoption model (HAAM): a framework and roadmap. https://www.healthcatalyst.com/white-paper/healthcare-analytics-adoption-model

28. Malladi, S.: Adoption of business intelligence & analytics in organizations – an empirical study of antecedents. In: 2013 Proceedings of the AMCIS, vol. 2016, pp. 1–11 (2013)

29. Ghosh, B., Scott, J.E.: Antecedents and catalysts for developing a healthcare analytic capability. Commun. Assoc. Inf. Syst. **29**, 395–410 (2011)

30. Myers, B.L., Kappelman, L.A., Prybutok, V.R.: A comprehensive model for assessing the quality and productivity of the information systems function. Inf. Resour. Manag. J. **10**, 6–26 (1997)

31. Lee, Y.W., Strong, D.M., Kahn, B.K., Wang, R.Y.: AIMQ: a methodology for information quality assessment. Inf. Manag. **40**, 133–146 (2002)

32. Moore, G.C., Benbasat, I.: Development of an instrument to measure the perceptions of adopting an information technology innovation. Inf. Syst. Res. **2**, 192–222 (1991)

33. Ebner, K., Mueller, B., Urbach, N., Riempp, G., Krcmar, H.: Assessing IT management's performance: a design theory for strategic IT benchmarking. IEEE Trans. Eng. Manag. **63**, 113–126 (2016)

34. Hevner, A.R., March, S.T., Park, J., Ram, S.: Design science in information systems research. MIS Q. **28**, 75–105 (2004)
35. Zhang, N.J., Seblega, B., Wan, T., Unruh, L., Agiro, A., Miao, L.: Health information technology adoption in U.S. acute care hospitals. J. Med. Syst. **37**(2), 9907 (2013)
36. Tornatzky, L.G., Fleischer, M., Chakrabarti, A.K.: The processes of technological innovation (1990)
37. Purao, S., Storey, V.C.: Evaluating the adoption potential of design science efforts: the case of APSARA. Decis. Support Syst. **44**, 369–381 (2008)
38. Han, T., Purao, S., Storey, V.C.: Generating large-scale repositories of reusable artifacts for conceptual design of information systems. Decis. Support Syst. **45**, 665–680 (2008)
39. Skok, W., Kophamel, A., Richardson, I.: Diagnosing information systems success: importance-performance maps in the health club industry. Inf. Manag. **38**, 409–419 (2001)
40. Ahmadi, H., Nilashi, M., Ibrahim, O.: Organizational decision to adopt hospital information system: an empirical investigation in the case of Malaysian public hospitals. Int. J. Med. Inform. **84**, 166–188 (2015)
41. Amiri, M., Salehi, J., Payani, N., Shafieezadeh, M.: Developing a DEMATEL method to prioritize distribution centers in supply chain. Manag. Sci. Lett. **1**, 279–288 (2011)
42. Gregor, S., Hevner, A.R.: Positioning and presenting design science research for maximum impact. MIS Q. **37**, 337–355 (2013)
43. Gregor, S., Jones, D.: The anatomy of a design theory. J. Assoc. Inf. Syst. **8**, 312–335 (2007)

Easy Nutrition: A Customized Dietary App to Highlight the Food Nutritional Value

Mayda Alrige$^{(\boxtimes)}$ ⓘ and Samir Chatterjee ⓘ

Claremont Graduate University, Claremont, CA 91739, USA
{Mayda.alrige,Samir.chatterjee}@cgu.edu

Abstract. Healthy Eating is a two-part system that should strike a balance between food quality and food quantity. In this study, we have designed, developed, and evaluated a nutrition app called, Easy Nutrition to highlight the nutritional value/quality of the food we eat. We introduced the novel concept of Nuval rather than old concepts such as calorie counting. In this context, Easy Nutrition presents the food nutrition in a simple, easy to understand manner. Easy Nutrition also tackles the cultural differences by suggesting recipes tailored to users' food preferences. This paper delineates the build and evaluate phase of Easy Nutrition. Easy Nutrition has been evaluated from a sociotechnical perspective in for its of utility and quality. We conducted a cross-sectional study on Amazon Mechanical Turk platform to evaluate Easy Nutrition on a wide population. The results show that Easy Nutrition demonstrates a fairly high level of usability (SUS = 69.1), attractiveness (mean = 1.59), and hedonic and pragmatic quality.

Keywords: Health app · Nutrition · mHealth · Diet management
Calories

1 Introduction

Although genetics are an important consideration in health, during the past half-century our genes have not measurably altered, and yet we are significantly more overweight, obese, and prone to lifestyle-related diseases [1]. As of 2014, more than one-third (36.5%) of U.S. adults have obesity, according to the National Health and Nutrition Examination Survey data (2011–2014) [2]; 70.7% are overweight. [3]; and 29.1 million Americans (9.3% of the population) are diabetics (as of 2012) [4]. The root of the problem of all these conditions is a poor diet. Tackling this problem is by no mean easy and requires complex lifestyle changes. A healthy diet is a key component of a healthy lifestyle that can prevent the onset of chronic diseases or mitigate their severity [5]. A healthy lifestyle involves the ability to make healthy choices based on the awareness of the underlying nutrition of the food one consumes.

Most of the current computer-tailored dietary approaches deploy diet recalls and food records as the main dietary management approaches [9–11]. These approaches focus on the quantity of the food. That is, users are prompted to quantify the portion of the food consumed, for each nutrient. This way, users can keep track of their caloric intake by typing in every single item they eat. One of the critical issues in this context is time. It is very tedious and time-consuming to track food intake. Another problem in addition to the time it takes to track food is the issue of recall [5]. Users have to sit down at least once a day, remember what they had eaten during the day in correct portions, and type in their food intake. Despite their effectiveness, these tools require performing some tasks that are impractical to apply on a daily basis. Research suggests that too much detailed information on mobile phones may result in users being discouraged from using these tools [9]. The focus on food quantity in relation to the issues of time and recall has undermined the effectiveness of technology-tailored dietary tools.

The notion of nutrition profiling can alleviate these issues since it presents how healthy a food item is in a single measure that is easy to follow and intuitive to understand. Nutrient profiling is defined by the World Health Organization as the science of ranking foods according to their nutritional composition for reasons related to preventing disease and promoting health. By focusing on food quality instead of quantity, nutrient-profiling-based systems aim to educate users about the overall nutritional quality that constitutes a healthy or unhealthy food choice. In light of this notion, systems such as Nuval [10] (Nutritional Value) and ANDI [11] (Aggregate Nutrition Density Index) have been developed to rank foods according to their nutritional quality. These systems have been tested, and widely accepted in the market landscape to rank food products based on their nutritional content. However, no much work has been done to evaluate these systems in the literature.

This study aims to design, develop, and evaluate a nutrient-profiling app called Easy Nutrition. Easy Nutrition utilized the Intelligent Nutrition engine to classify food recipes based on their nutritional value[1]. This study explained how the app Easy Nutrition has been developed and evaluated through the DSR lenses (Sect. 3). The results are discussed in Sect. 4. Lastly, we conclude this paper by outlining new directions for future work inspired by some limitations we have faced during the study.

2   Background and Related Work

Nutrition profiling is one of the behavioral nutrition approaches that do not dictate to people what to eat or what not to eat. Rather, it aims at educating individuals about the overall nutritional quality of the food and leaving the choice of the meal to them. Nutrition profiling aims to rank food based on their nutritional quality. It is driven by the focus on food quality instead of quantity. Individuals who follow high-score food choices would most likely improve their dietary behavior.

Driven by the idea of nutrition profiling, the traffic-light diet was developed by Leonard H. Epstein and his colleagues in the 1970's. In this dietary approach, Epstein used a tri-color palette to create an easy-to-follow diet for overweight children. The notion of a traffic-light diet had inspired new research for two decades due to its

---

[1] The Intelligent Nutrition Engine is an algorithm developed by the authors and published before in the proceeding of AMIA 2017 [12].

groundbreaking nature. The traffic-light diet is a structured eating plan that divides food by the color of the traffic signals. Green is for low-calorie food (go) that can be eaten at any time, orange (caution) is for moderate-calorie food that can be eaten occasionally, and red (stop) is for high-calorie food that should be eaten rarely. Since it was launched, the Traffic Light Diet has been used widely by pediatricians to encourage healthy eating habits among their patients [13].

Many studies have been conducted utilizing the "Traffic-light" dietary approach and showed promising results. The traffic-light diet is used as a part of a comprehensive treatment, and the results show a significant decrease in obesity in preadolescent children [14–17]. Significant changes in eating patterns have been reported when comprehensive obesity treatment has been combined with the traffic-light diet. [18, 19]. Reductions in "red foods" have been observed after treatment with significant associations between changes in intake of "red food" and weight loss [18] or decrease in percent overweight [19].

In this study, we will adopt the approach of the traffic light diet to present nutritional information. However, it will not be a strict tri-color output. Rather, it will be a color-coded food rating scale of eight values as it takes into consideration five different nutrients and not only the caloric count. It scales food recipes based on its nutritional quality from red (for extremely unhealthy choices) to green (for optimal healthy choices) through intermediate colors.

3 Research Approach

3.1 Method and the Build Phase

The present study follows the design science research, DSR, approach suggested by Hevner and Chatterjee [20]. We adapted the design science research approach by Meth and colleagues [21] to illustrate the design process of Easy Nutrition. Each design cycle comprises six phases that iterate between conceptualization, development, and evaluation of the artifact, Easy Nutrition.

An intensive literature review demonstrates an initial awareness of the main problem. The domain of dietary management for diet-related chronic conditions presents a significant demand for behavioral nutrition approaches that shift out attention from the food quantity to the food nutritional quality [22]. After our first meeting with the domain experts Dr. Ernie Medina (former executive director of the Center for Nutrition, Healthy Life Style and Disease Prevention) and Dr. Jeje Noval (a registered dietician), it became clear that the notion of nutrition profiling would be a good research opportunity to address the problem. This phase resulted in a tentative design requirement, namely, a nutrient profiling system that highlights the nutritional quality of the food we eat. Current nutrient profiling systems, such as Nuval [10] and ANDI [11] guided our investigation of this topic.

Based on the main design requirements, we conducted a second literature review to identify general knowledge and theories that we could apply to address the identified problems. We also consulted the ADA to solicit their nutrition therapy recommendations. The domain experts also have helped us identify the criteria for the five nutrients considered in the Intelligent Nutrition Engine. Using this knowledge, we conceptualized preliminary design principles in the suggestion phase. These include customization and simplicity. We then mapped these design principles to design features that were implemented in Easy Nutrition during the development phase. For extended treatment for these design principles, requirements, and features please see Table 1.

Table 1. Design requirements, principles and features

Design principles	Design requirements	Design features
Customization	Recipes must be tailored to users' food preferences (ADA) [23]	Determination of favorite cuisines by users
	The use of menu plans as a dietary management approach (literature review) [22]	Menu planning feature
Simplicity	The recommended average of nutrients should be in line with ADA nutrition therapy recommendations (domain expert)	Traffic-light bar that represents the nutritional value of the recipe
	Ingredients have to be presented in an easy to understand manner (domain expert)	Picture of the ingredient will be shown next to each ingredient
		To visualize portion size, an image of a deck of cards will be presented to better estimate portion size
	The quantity of each nutrient has to be presented separately: fat, carbs, protein, dietary fibers, and sodium (domain expert)	Under the nutrition tab, users are allowed to see details of the five main nutrients comprising the nutritional value of the recipe

To collect feedback on the artifact's usability, we presented Easy Nutrition to the registered dietician. The feedback we obtained was mainly on the algorithm behind the Intelligent Nutrition Engine. Namely, we needed to change the weights of two nutrients: the protein and the dietary fibers. This is because, according to her, consuming too much protein increases the chance of renal disease. We traced the feedback she provided back to the related design feature. In the evaluation phase, we evaluated the prototype of Easy Nutrition in terms of its usability and understandability of its interfaces using "JustInMind" simulation, a prototyping tool for web and mobile apps. The results were presented in [12]. Section 3.3 in this paper presents the evaluation results of the final design cycle (Fig. 1).

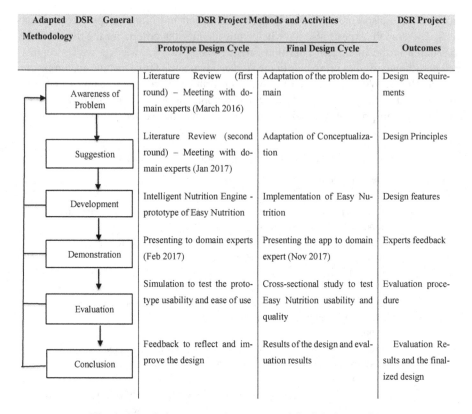

Fig. 1. The design process (prototype and final design cycle)

3.2   The Artifact: Easy Nutrition

Easy Nutrition is developed as a mobile-based application. Using Easy Nutrition, end-users will have the option to find online recipes that are tailored to their favorite cuisines and learn about their nutritional quality. In addition, users will have the option to plan their meals for a certain period of time in advance. This meal plan can be based on either their favorite recipes (chosen earlier) or their favorite cuisine. In both cases, the resulting recipe will be displayed along with their overall nutritional quality, in a traffic-light scale, as can be seen in Fig. 2. This scale gives the user an initial indication of how nutritious the chosen recipe is. If the user is interested to know more about the nutrients that lower the overall nutritional quality, he/she can click on the "nutrition" tab to find out which nutrient is beyond the recommended range, as can be seen in right picture in Fig. 3. Besides the nutritional quality, the pertinent information for each recipe is presented. These include the ingredients, instructions, and some healthy tips on how to maximize the nutritional value of the selected recipe.

The nutritional value of every recipe is presented in a single holistic measure. This measure is the output of an algorithm we had previously built called the Intelligent Nutrition Engine [12]. This algorithm considers the recipe's carbs (C_w), protein (P_w), fat (F_w), dietary fibers (Df_w), sodium (S_w), and total calories (Rc_w). The final formula encompassing all these contained nutrients as well as the calories produces a holistic number that represents the overall nutritional quality of a particular recipe (see Eq. 1). For the sake of simplicity, we presented this number in a traffic-light scale that ranges from red to green through some intermediate colors.

$$NV = \sum C_w + P_w + F_w + Df_w + S_w + Rc_w \qquad (1)$$

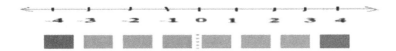

Fig. 2. The nutritional value presented behind a traffic-light scale.

The cursor would start right in the middle of the traffic-light scale as an initial score for any given food recipe, as can be seen in Fig. 2. The cursor would move to the right as a certain nutrient is within the recommended percentage/amount. On the other hand, the cursor would move to the left if a certain nutrient exceeds the maximum limit or fails to meet the minimum limit of the recommended range.

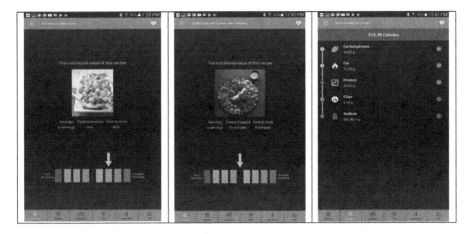

Fig. 3. The way of presenting the food nutrition in Easy Nutrition

Once into Easy Nutrition's home page, the user can either find online recipes (tailored to his/her favorite cuisines and body nutritional needs), browse the nutritional value of these recipes, or plan a weekly meal. This meal plan will be based on favorite cuisine and previously selected recipes.

3.3   Evaluate Phase

Evaluation is a significant part of any design science research. During this stage we have evaluated Easy Nutrition's utility and quality in a cross-sectional study conducted using two online research platforms: Amazon Mechanical Turk and TurkPrime.

Users

Users in this stage (n = 100) are adults with interest to better manage their diets and maintain a healthy life-style. We recruited subjects using purposeful sampling through an online research platform used for subject recruitment.

Procedures and Measures

The aim of this study is to evaluate the full version Easy Nutrition on a wider population. This study is conducted online using Amazon Mechanical Turk and TurkPrime. The first part of survey was launched to collect basic and demographic information from potentially interested subjects. Additionally, information about subjects' eating habits were collected to have a better sense of individuals' dietary behavior. We adopted the nutrition subscale from the Health Promotion Lifestyle Profile (HPLP) [24]. HPLP comprises the nutrition subscale which includes 10 items. This subscale measures the frequency of self-reported nutritional behaviors based on the Food Guide Pyramid recommendation (Cronbach's = 0.87). The items were scored from never (1) to always (4) with a higher score indicating a healthier dietary behavior (Fig. 4).

First Part. The first part of the survey was launched to everybody with only one qualification, which is having an Android as a primary phone. The attached consent form made it clear to the subjects that agreeing to participate in this study requires him/her to first download and use the app and second to complete a follow up survey, which asks the technical evaluation questions. Because this MTurk HIT (human intelligence task) asks users to download an app and use it for a few days, we assured them that we are a credible party and that the app, Easy Nutrition, can be safely

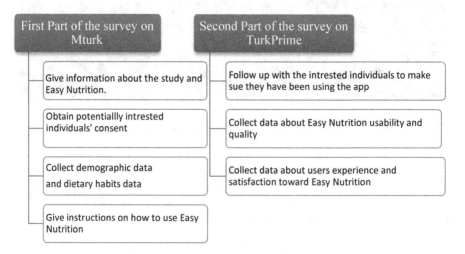

Fig. 4. The flow of this cross-sectional study

installed and reinstalled without leaving any remnants on the phone. We attached our contacts and affiliations in the main instructions page, so participants can follow up with any further questions regarding the nature and purpose of the study.

Second Part. The second part of the survey was launched using TurkPrime a week after launching the first part of the survey. TurkPrime is a platform that allows Mechanical Turk Requesters/Researchers to completely control and manage surveys by enabling selective recruitments. Using TurkPrime, we were able follow up with interested individuals by sending the second part of the survey to only Mturk worker who completed the first part of the survey and expressed an interest to download and use Easy Nutrition (n = 86). As opposed to Mturk, TurkPrime is a great platform for behavioral science research as it allows following up with the same cohort of people over a period of time. These tasks are common for social and behavioral research. Using TurkPrime, researchers can include participants on the basis of previous participation, run longitudinal studies, increase the speed of data collection by sending bulk e-mails and bonuses, enhance communication with participants, and monitor dropout and engagement rates.

This second part of the survey is basically composed of two segments. The first segment measures Easy Nutrition's classical usability and quality. We adopted the questionnaire of User Experience (QUE) to measure Easy Nutrition's overall quality. UEQ allows a quick assessment of the user experience of interactive products. The format of the questionnaire allows users to immediately express feelings, impressions, and attitudes that arise when they use the product under investigation. The UEQ contains 6 scales with 26 items. It seeks answers to the following questions:

- **Attractiveness:** Do users like or dislike Easy Nutrition?
- **Perspicuity:** Is it easy to get familiar with the Easy Nutrition? Is it easy to learn how to use Easy Nutrition?
- **Efficiency:** Can users solve their tasks without unnecessary effort?
- **Dependability:** Does the user feel in control of the interaction?
- **Stimulation:** Is it exciting and motivating to use Easy Nutrition?
- **Novelty:** Is Easy Nutrition innovative and creative? Does it catch users' interest?

The second segment concerns users' satisfaction toward Easy Nutrition with regards to two main concepts: customization and simplicity. By customization, users can find food recipes tailored to their food preferences and nutritional needs. By simplicity, users are able to learn about food nutrition in a simple, easy to understand manner. Also, we measured their behavioral intention to use Easy Nutrition for better dietary management.

Analysis

To gauge Easy Nutrition utility, we measured the system usability score. In addition, we investigated users experience, in terms of attractiveness, efficiency, stimulation, novelty, efficiency, perspicuity, and dependability. The mean score was calculated for each subscale.

4   Results and Analysis

The first survey was launched in Mturk (n = 100), in Dec/4/2017. 86 out of 100 participants completed the initial survey, indicated that they have an interest to participate in this study and use Easy Nutrition for a few days. Table 2 delineates the socioeconomic factors of the sample.

Table 2. Sample's descriptive statistics

		Value label	N
Income	1	<$50,000	62
	2	$50,000–$75,000	16
	3	>$75,000	8
Education	1	High school graduate	18
	2	Bachelor or associate degree	48
	3	Graduate degree	20
age	2	18–24	10
	3	25–34	54
	4	35–44	17
	5	45–54	3
	6	55 or older	2

The dietary behavior score is generated from the HPLP- Nutrition subscale. Based on users answers to this 10-items instrument, a score from 10–40 is assigned to indicate the dietary habits/behavior of the participants. The closer the score is to 40, the healthier the subject is. The score of the healthiest subject in our sample is 37 (Table 3). The dietary behavior of high school graduates tends to be stable with income have no discernible effect. For subjects with graduate degree, the data tells us that the income does have an effect on their dietary behavior as can be seen in Fig. 5. This opens the door for further discussion on the effect of income on dietary behavior.

Table 3. Dietary behavior descriptive statistics

N	Valid	86
	Missing	0
Mean		24.4884
Median		25.0000
Std. deviation		4.32705
Range		24.00
Minimum		13.00
Maximum		37.00

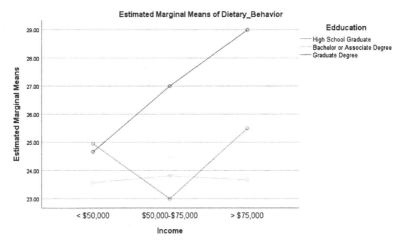

Fig. 5. Users dietary behavior

The second survey (Easy Nutrition Evaluation questions) was launched for this selective sample (n = 86) in Dec/14/2017. Out of 86, 42 subjects have used the app and completed the survey by Jan/8/2018. For this cohort of people, we investigated their user experience and satisfaction while interacting with Easy Nutrition.

4.1   Easy Nutrition: Utility and Quality

The SUS score of Easy Nutrition came to 69.1. This indicator shows that Easy Nutrition is technically usable and can fit the context of dietary management. In addition to the utility of Easy Nutrition, Users' Experience was investigated to measure Easy Nutrition's quality as a customized dietary tool. This quality was gauged to in terms of attractiveness, perspicuity, efficiency, dependability, stimulation, and novelty. Figure 6 shows the mean for every scale (−3. +3). Values between −0.8 and 0.8 represent a neural evaluation of the corresponding scale, values >0.8 represent a positive evaluation and values <−0.8 represent a negative evaluation. As you can tell from the table below, Easy Nutrition was found attractive to users (mean = 1.59). This gives us the indication that Easy Nutrition is user friendly and pleasing to interact with. In addition, Easy Nutrition was found perspicuous in content and easy to understand (mean = 1.66), efficient (mean = 1.41), dependable in the sense that users feel in control of the interaction (mean = 1.35), stimulating and motivating to utilize (mean = 1.24). Lastly, the way Easy Nutrition displays the overall nutritional value along with the nutrition breakdown was found novel for users (mean = 0.90). This implies that Easy Nutrition overall is innovative and creative and that the way the dietary information (recipes' nutrition breakdown) presented is leading edge.

Figure 6 shows a graphical benchmark and interpretation of the user experience 6 scales. The benchmark data set was developed to show how the investigated artifact, in this case Easy Nutrition, is compared with other studied artifacts. The comparison of

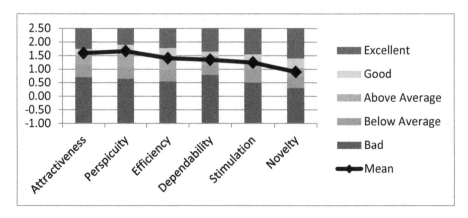

Fig. 6. Easy nutrition's quality against benchmark artifacts

the results for the evaluated product with the data in the benchmark allows conclusions about the relative quality of the evaluated product compared to other products.

Easy Nutrition's measured scales mean was compared in relation to existing values from a benchmark data set. This set contains data from 246 studies concerning different products, such as business software, web pages, social networks and many others. In comparison with these applications, Easy Nutrition's attractiveness and perspicuity was in the range of 25% of the best results. On the other hand, efficiency, dependability, stimulation, and novelty were in the range of the 50% best results (above average).

Scale	Mean	Std. dev.	Confidence	Confid. interval	
Attractiveness	1.590	1.063	0.322	1.268	1.911
Perspicuity	1.661	1.068	0.323	1.338	1.984
Efficiency	1.405	1.191	0.360	1.045	1.765
Dependability	1.345	0.859	0.260	1.085	1.605
Stimulation	1.244	1.319	0.399	0.845	1.643
Novelty	0.899	0.966	0.292	-	1.191

4.2   Users Satisfaction Toward Easy Nutrition

To gain a better understanding of their usage, users were asked to report the number of recipes they have learned about their nutrition from Easy Nutrition. About 95% of them have navigated the app and learned the nutritional value for up to 14 recipes (Table 4).

Table 4. Number of recipes users learned about their nutrition using Easy Nutrition

	Frequencies	Percent	Cumulative percent
<7 recipes	21	50.0	50.0
7–14 recipes	19	45.2	95.2
14–21 recipes	2	4.8	100.0
Total	42	100.0	

Table 5. Scaled users satisfaction

User satisfaction was investigated from two main perspectives: simplicity of the nutritional information, and the customization of the suggested recipes based on food preferences and body nutritional needs. The matrix in Table 5 summarized user satisfaction toward Easy Nutrition. The two upper bar charts demonstrate users' satisfaction toward Easy Nutrition customization based on body nutritional needs (to the left) and food preferences (to the right). About 81%of participants were satisfied with Easy Nutrition' customization based on their body nutritional needs. In the same vein, 76.2% of users found it tailored to their food preferences. The two lower charts demonstrate Easy Nutrition simplicity and hence ability to help users focus their attention toward nutrition (to the right) and make better healthier food choices (to the left). 81% of participants reported that Easy Nutrition was an enabling tool to focus their attention toward nutrition, while 90.5% found Easy Nutrition a powerful tool to help them choose better healthier food choices.

5 Discussion and Conclusion

Easy Nutrition is developed to introduce and apply the concept of Nutrient profiling in the domain of dietary management apps and investigate if this would influence users focusing their attention toward nutrition and hence making better, healthier food choices. In addition, it is developed with cultural differences in mind. That is, all food recipes suggested by Easy Nutrition are tailored to users' food preferences.

Using Easy Nutrition, the user can find online food recipes tailored to their food preferences, learn about their nutrition in a simple, efficient and easy to understand manner. The rigorous cross-sectional study presented in this paper shows that Easy Nutrition demonstrates a high level of usability, attractiveness, hedonic and pragmatic quality. Whiles the results of Easy Nutrition utility and efficacy are promising, there are some limitations that allows a room for further improvement.

First, Easy Nutrition presents the overall nutritional value in a traffic-light scale to promote simplicity. For people with color-blind, this present a huge issue. Another presentation mechanism, beside the traffic-light colors, should be added to the app like simple numerical values or emoji faces. Second, the nutritional value for every recipe does not allow ingredient substitution. That is, if the user ended up cooking one recipe but chose to substitute for example white rice with brown rice or decided to grill the chicken breast instead of frying it, the nutritional value is still the same. Dynamic nutritional value calculation would allow users to substitute ingredients and then adjust the overall nutritional value accordingly. Third and most importantly, Easy Nutrition at this stage is evaluated only for its utility and quality not for its impact on users. The aim at this stage is to investigate Easy Nutrition's quality and ensure its readiness for the next stage. The next stage of the study will evaluate its impact on behavior change. In particular, following stage will investigate the effect of Easy Nutrition on diabetics' eating habits and blood glucose level (glycemic A1C).

References

1. Eisenberg, D.M., Burgess, J.D.: Nutrition education in an era of global obesity and diabetes: thinking outside the box. Acad. Med. **90**(7), 854–860 (2015)
2. Ogden, C.L., Carroll, M.D., Fryar, C.D., Flegal, K.M.: Prevalence of obesity among adults and youth: United States, 2011–2014, November 2015. https://www.cdc.gov/nchs/data/databriefs/db219.pdf. Accessed 13 Dec 2016
3. Frieden, T.R., Rothwell, C.: Health, United States (2015)
4. American Diabetes Association: 2451 Crystal Drive, Statistics about diabetes. American Diabetes Association. http://www.diabetes.org/diabetes-basics/statistics/. Accessed 12 Dec 2016
5. Arens-Volland, A.G., Spassova, L., Bohn, T.: Promising approaches of computer-supported dietary assessment and management-current research status and available applications. Int. J. Med. Inf. **84**(12), 997–1008 (2015)
6. Ma, Y., et al.: PDA-assisted low glycemic index dietary intervention for type II diabetes: a pilot study. Eur. J. Clin. Nutr. **60**(10), 1235–1243 (2006)

7. Theng, Y.-L., Lee, J.W.Y., Patinadan, P.V., Foo, S.S.B.: The use of videogames, gamification, and virtual environments in the self-management of diabetes: a systematic review of evidence. Games Health J. **4**(5), 352–361 (2015)

8. El-Gayar, O., Timsina, P., Nawar, N., Eid, W.: Mobile applications for diabetes self-management: status and potential. J. Diab. Sci. Technol. **7**(1), 247–262 (2013)

9. Arsand, E., et al.: Mobile health applications to assist patients with diabetes: lessons learned and design implications. J. Diab. Sci. Technol. **6**(5), 1197–1206 (2012)

10. Nuval System

11. ANDI Food Scores: Rating the Nutrient Density of Foods. https://www.drfuhrman.com/learn/library/articles/95/andi-food-scores-rating-the-nutrient-density-of-foods. Accessed 31 Oct 2016

12. Alrige, M., Chatterjee, S., Medina, E., Nuval, J.: Applying the concept of nutrient-profiling to promote healthy eating and raise individuals awareness of the nutritional quality of their food. In: proceeding of AMIA2017, Washington, DC (2017)

13. Epstein, L.H., Myers, M.D., Raynor, H.A., Saelens, B.E.: Treatment of pediatric obesity. http://www.ohsu.edu/xd/outreach/oregon-rural-health/hospitals/chip/upload/Treatment-of-Pediatric-Obesity.pdf. Accessed 09 Dec 2016

14. Valocki, A.: Nutrient intake of obese children in a family-based behavioral weight control program. Int. J. Obes. **14**(8), 667–677 (1990)

15. Epstein, L.H., Wing, R.R., Koeske, R., Ossip, D., Beck, S.: A comparison of lifestyle change and programmed aerobic exercise on weight and fitness changes in obese children. Behav. Ther. **13**(5), 651–665 (1982)

16. Epstein, L.H., Wing, R.R., Steranchak, L., Dickson, B., Michelson, J.: Comparison of family-based behavior modification and nutrition education for childhood obesity. J. Pediatr. Psychol. **5**(1), 25–36 (1980)

17. Epstein, L.H., et al.: Effects of decreasing sedentary behavior and increasing activity on weight change in obese children. Health Psychol. **14**(2), 109 (1995)

18. Epstein, L.H.: Child and parent weight loss in family-based behavior modification programs

19. Duffy, G., Spence, S.H.: The effectiveness of cognitive self-management as an adjunct to a behavioural intervention for childhood obesity: a research note - Google Search. J. Child Psychol. Psychiatry **34**(6), 1043–1050 (1993)

20. Hevner, A., Chatterjee, S.: Design science research in information systems. In: Hevner, A., Chatterjee, S. (eds.) Design Research in Information Systems, vol. 22, pp. 9–22. Springer, Boston (2010)

21. Meth, H., Mueller, B., Maedche, A.: Designing a requirement mining system. J. Assoc. Inf. Syst. **16**(9), 799 (2015)

22. Bader, A., Gougeon, R., Joseph, L., Da Costa, D., Dasgupta, K.: Nutritional education through internet-delivered menu plans among adults with type 2 diabetes mellitus: pilot study. JMIR Res. Protoc. **2**(2), e41 (2013)

23. Evert, A.B., et al.: Nutrition therapy recommendations for the management of adults with diabetes. Diab. Care. **37**(Supplement_1), S120–S143 (2014)

24. Walker, S.N., Sechrist, K.R., Pender, N.J.: The health-promoting lifestyle profile: development and psychometric characteristics. Nurs. Res. **36**(2), 76 (1987)

Taxonomy Development for Virtual Reality (VR) Technologies in Healthcare Sector

Maram Almufareh, Duaa Abaoud$^{(\boxtimes)}$, and Md Moniruzzaman

Claremont Graduate University, Claremont, USA
{Maram.almufareh,Duaa.abaoud,Md.moniruzzaman}@cgu.edu

Abstract. The paper presents a Design Science Research (DSR) project, which was conducted to develop taxonomy for Virtual Realty VR technology in healthcare. In this paper, we discuss the process involved to design a comprehensive taxonomy framework of VR technologies that classify VR tools within the healthcare industry. The framework is intended to help practitioners, researchers, and developers to agree on a common language in order to analyze the usefulness and gaps in existing VR applications in healthcare. The taxonomy guide evaluates the process of VR tools to determine where each VR device fits in the healthcare industry; identifies the uniqueness and originality of new VR devices; and recognizes the needs and gaps for further VR application development within this industry.

Keywords: Design science research · Virtual reality · Technology
Healthcare · Taxonomy

1 Introduction

Currently, Virtual Reality (VR) technologies have emerged as an innovative mainstream tool with immense potential to transform the way human beings experience environments [1]. VR technology has the potential to revolutionize nearly every aspect of life, and healthcare (HC) is one of the main fields that has begun integrating VR technology into medical practice. Computer scientists and healthcare practitioners have been working to develop and implement applications using VR technologies to provide general and specialty health care services [6, 20].

There are many uses of VR in the HC industry. For example, VR is employed in surgical procedures to perform a remote surgery or telepresence, augmented or enhanced surgery, and for simulation as part of the planning process of operations. VR is utilized in other areas like medical therapy, preventive medicine, medical education and training, skill enhancement, rehabilitation, visualization of massive medical databases, and architectural design for health-care facilities [14, 20].

With this massive interest in VR, there is a need to build a classification framework of VR technologies to help practitioners, researchers, and developers agree to a common language in order to analyze the usefulness of existing VR applications, and to understand where a new application may fit with existing ones [17]. This urgent need for a useful taxonomy extends also to categorize and streamline current investigations

© Springer International Publishing AG, part of Springer Nature 2018
S. Chatterjee et al. (Eds.): DESRIST 2018, LNCS 10844, pp. 146–156, 2018.
https://doi.org/10.1007/978-3-319-91800-6_10

and practices in order to improve aspects of healthcare by extracting greater value from the existing information depository.

This paper presents the use of DSR to build and evaluate the taxonomy of VR technologies in healthcare. This proposed taxonomy would contribute new knowledge to design science research and Virtual Reality research in healthcare, as a taxonomy currently does not exist. The following sections elaborate on the development and evaluation processes, which will explain how our taxonomy was created and how it will solve the problems currently experienced [2].

2 Background

In 1987, Jaron Lanier introduced the term "Virtual Reality" through his Visual Programming Lab (VPL). Molin [14] defined Virtual Reality (VR) as "a fully three-dimensional computer-generated 'world' in which a person can move about and interact as if he were in an imaginary place." VR technologies have already expanded their reach into various domains for creative experiences, particularly in the healthcare field. However, to date research evaluating the full potentiality of VR in the healthcare field is still lacking. VR systems became popular because they are entirely different from interactive computer graphics or multimedia systems thanks, in part, to a sense of presence they create in a virtual world [14].

Over the past decade, VR applications have already penetrated fields from education and entertainment to critical applications like healthcare applications [8, 14]. Highlighting the importance of virtual environments and related technologies in medicine, we can point to the steady growth in use of VR by medical practitioners in order to help their patients [6].

Current VR literature provides a comprehensive review of existing and future trends applications in a wide-ranging industries, as previously mentioned [18]. The literature also identifies some essential characteristics and key elements of experiencing virtual reality that is not limited to immersion, sensory feedback, and interactivity. Sherman and Craig [18] categorized virtual reality systems according to the user interface involved with the VR experience, and focused mainly on the way participants interact with VR and how the user perceives the environment.

Gobbetti and Scateni [4] focused on virtual reality applications and discussed the characteristics of some past, present, and future VR products. Various existing virtual reality applications have been categorized in terms of user input (Position/Orientation Tracking, Eye Tracking, Full Body Motion) and sensory feedback (Visual, Haptic, Sound, etc.). Gobbetti and Scateni [4] argued that the complexity of VR tools make the selection of the ideal tool, with well-defined functionality, difficult. A significant step, then, would be to ease the investigation process by ensuring that the VR solution can be integrated smoothly with standard business practices. This study, then, will fill this need by comparing the features and abilities of VR tools with other competing technologies in an attempt to guarantee the selection of the right set of tools [19]. A systematic review of the existing literature on virtual reality in medicine reveals the lack of consensus on the meaning of VR and that there are no clear guidelines to characterize VR [21–25].

Duncan et al. [3] introduced training and education as critical dimensions of VR usage. Their research introduced six categories: population, educational activities, learning theories, learning environment, supporting technologies, and research areas [3]. Rehabilitation is another growing VR dimension. Kim [9] discusses many weaknesses, limitation and opportunities within the research concentrated on VR for rehabilitation and therapy, and argues that continued analysis of the files is critical for VR development. A classification framework, such as we posit, would aid decision-making about the use of VR as a tool for therapeutic intervention [11]. Computer-assisted surgery is another primary dimension in the literature. It has become one of the revolutionary technological developments in the medical field, but evaluation of the efficiency of training VR simulators for robotic surgery has not yet been confirmed [13].

Many researchers have standardized research approaches to address the need of their communities and to provide a clear and distinctive way for future developments like designing prototypes, models, products/applications, theoretical frameworks, and taxonomies [10, 17]. Taxonomies, as a tool, provide a structure and an organization to the knowledge of a field, thus enabling researchers to study the relationships between concepts and, therefore, hypothesize about these relationships [5]. Glass and Vessey [5] illustrated the use of taxonomies in understanding the science behind design principles of observed artifacts. Taxonomies are another consideration of grounded theory and help to explain any divergence from previous research findings.

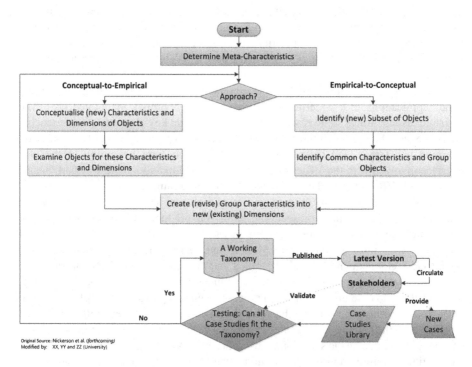

Fig. 1. Iterative process of selecting meta-characteristics [13]

Despite the fact that taxonomy plays a significant role in research to understand and analyze complex fields, to the best of our knowledge, to date there has not been any research focused on the taxonomy of recent VR technologies in healthcare [2]. To this end, our research will design a conceptual model to provide a classification framework, or taxonomy, for Virtual Reality technologies in the healthcare domain.

3   Research Questions

Emerging VR products make the development of a unified classification method, incorporating the specifics of each system, an extremely challenging task. That is why it is important to answer these questions: What are the different criteria or dimensions that can build a holistic taxonomy tool for VR technology in healthcare? What kind of virtual reality technologies are in use in the healthcare domain, and what are their value propositions? What are the needs and gaps for the future development of VR technology in healthcare?

4   Methodology

Design Science Research (DSR) is the adopted approach in this research. Design science is mainly a problem-solving paradigm that builds and evaluates artifacts. The artifact that is designed and evaluated in this study is a classification framework of Virtual Reality (VR) technologies in healthcare.

5   Design and Build Phase

Through our project, we aim to provide a clear and distinctive way for future developments in VR systems in the healthcare field. We have developed an efficient taxonomy by creating a construct and formulating a framework, thus designing a conceptual model for Virtual Reality technologies in the healthcare domain.

This artifact will provide in-depth insights into existing VR applications in healthcare and bring forward new development opportunities in this emerging field. This paper attempts to position itself as a pioneering research study in this proposition. In order to develop the proposed taxonomy, the following diagrams were used to elaborate the process of selecting meta-characteristics by analyzing features described in the literature and those included in existing VR technology.

To do that, we studied existing & prospective VR technology products by analyzing secondary data, and initially classified VR products by considering their utility/usability, user characteristics and the type of technology used. However, after a number of iterations using Bailey's model, we created the proposed solution [12]. This taxonomy adds to the knowledge of classification as well as Virtual Reality Systems to a great extent.

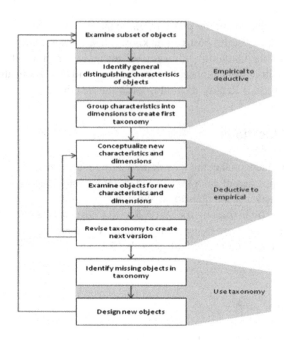

Fig. 2. Taxonomy development method [16]

In order to build the taxonomy, the following steps were conducted [15, 16]. To consider the characteristics, a tentative list of criteria was created at first. These criteria were chosen in light of both literature and industry. This list included the following items: utility, user characteristics (patients, surgeons, or physicians), and the purpose and type of technology used. We used Bailey's model in order to refine the criteria in the first step to determine the meta-characteristics. During this second phase, we came up with three major dimensions: user input, type of technology and application (Fig. 3).

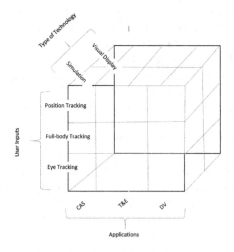

Fig. 3. 2nd iteration

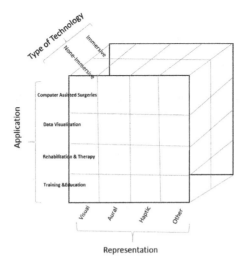

Fig. 4. 3rd iteration

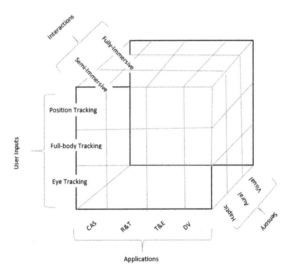

Fig. 5. 4th iteration (4-dimensional analysis of features of VR technologies)

1. In order to cross check the validity of our selection of meta-characteristics, we used two different iterative processes (Figs. 1 and 2) namely, empirical to deductive and deductive to empirical approaches which we found from previous literature [13, 16].
2. During the third iteration, after analyzing more characteristics, we further realigned the previously created dimensions into a set of three new dimensions with different sub-dimensions: type of technology, application, and representation. Figures 3 and 4 illustrate the development of taxonomy during the second and third iterations.
3. After the fourth and final iteration, a four-dimensional taxonomy was proposed (Fig. 5):
   (a) User Input: Position Tracking, Eye tracking & Full body motion
   (b) Interaction: Fully immersive, non-immersive and semi-immersive
   (c) Sensory: Visual, aural, and haptic
   (d) Application: Computer Assisted Surgeries (CAS), Data Visualization (DV), Rehabilitation & Therapy (R&T), Training & Education (T&E).

6   Evaluation Phase

Evaluation of the designed artifact is a key activity in Design Science Research (DSR) as it provides feedback for further development and assures the rigor of the research in the context of the knowledge it contributes to the knowledge base [2, 7]. The evaluation approach not only needs to address the quality of the artifact utility, but also the quality of its knowledge outcomes. This study has evaluated the artifact by mapping the commercial market products (industry-based VR technologies) to the taxonomy.

Table 1 Presents a market mapping that covered 17 different types of VR tools and technology using the developed taxonomy and shows how the current VR products fit within the designed artifact. Market mapping introduces a visual analysis of the current situation; the focus of VR development; and the market needs and gaps. Moving forward, this will enable us to seek and work with practitioners and researchers in the field to verify the efficiency of the taxonomy in practical use.

In this preliminary attempt, we have identified several key design dimensions and service provider objectives that play an important role in both the success of the service platform as well as the business. We have discussed these dimensions and objectives in order to provide some indication as to what role they might contribute to the overall design of digital services. In the near future, we hope to conduct detailed qualitative interviews and quantitative data collection from digital service companies to map the taxonomy, and uncover further interesting facets about their design, and continue breaking new ground in this critically important field.

Table 1. Commercial literature and market mapping

Virtual Reality Technologies	User input			Interaction		Sensory			Application			
	Position tracking	Eye tracking	Full body motion	Fully-Immersive	Semi-Immersive	Visual	Aural	Haptic	*CAS	*DV	*R&T	*T&E
Microsoft HoloLens (Headset)		⊞		⊞		⊞					⊞	⊞	
[VirtaMed ArthroS™ simulator				⊞		⊞		⊞	⊞	⊞		⊞
MAGNETOM Amira (MRI scans)									⊞	⊞	⊞	
Facebook Oculus Rift (Headset)	⊞	⊞		⊞		⊞				⊞	⊞	
Samsung Gear VR (Headset)		⊞		⊞		⊞				⊞	⊞	⊞
Google Glass (Headset)		⊞		⊞		⊞	⊞		⊞	⊞	⊞	⊞
Google Cardboard (Headset)		⊞		⊞		⊞				⊞	⊞	
Jaunt Neo (Camera systems)				⊞		⊞				⊞		⊞
Google Jump (Camera systems)				⊞		⊞				⊞		⊞
360cam(3D camera systems)				⊞		⊞				⊞		⊞
Microsoft Kinect(3D Depth Camera)				⊞		⊞				⊞		⊞
Da Vinci Robotic surgery				⊞				⊞	⊞	⊞		
MindMaze MindMotionPRO			⊞	⊞				⊞				

Product												
HTC Vive (Headset)		⊞		⊞		⊞				⊞	⊞	⊞
hapTEL virtual reality platform			⊞	⊞		⊞		⊞		⊞		⊞
Dexmo Dexta Robotics			⊞	⊞				⊞	⊞			⊞
iRobot RP-VITA								⊞			⊞	

*CAS – Computer Assisted Surgeries, DV – Data Visualization, R&T – Rehabilitation & Therapy, T&E – Training & Education

7 Conclusions

This taxonomy aims to raise awareness for its lack in this emerging technology's research. We categorized a list of the latest 17 VR technology products to test and evaluate our artifact. We understand that the proposed dimensions are not exhaustive. However, this taxonomy is expected to work as a guideline for future VR commercial and research development. In future, we hope to analyze more applications and research efforts so that our taxonomy can reach a wider audience. This study contributes to the existing knowledge base by creating a potential avenue for further research and sheds more light on a problem that is of increasing value.

We believe the taxonomy is a useful tool in evaluating the market presence and trajectory of various organizations involved in providing digital services. One of the values of the taxonomy is to give a more structured breadth to the evaluation of factors that might not be considered by the digital service designers. Likewise, we anticipate that designers with a more thorough understanding of the business and interaction objectives might be weak in understanding the technical objectives. Thus, one of the specific requirements proposed by this taxonomy is for developers to understand the business, technological, and interaction objectives of the organization.

Acknowledgements. The authors wish to thank Professor Samir Chatterjee for his technical support and periodic guidance in overcoming numerous obstacles we faced during our research.

References

1. Al-Kodmany, K.: Visualization tools and methods for participatory planning and design. J. Urban Technol. **8**(2), 1–37 (2001)
2. Alrige, M., Chatterjee, S.: Toward a taxonomy of wearable technologies in healthcare. In: Donnellan, B., Helfert, M., Kenneally, J., VanderMeer, D., Rothenberger, M., Winter, R. (eds.) DESRIST 2015. LNCS, vol. 9073, pp. 496–504. Springer, Cham (2015). https://doi.org/10.1007/978-3-319-18714-3_43
3. Duncan, I., Miller, A., Jiang, S.: A taxonomy of virtual world's usage in education. Br. J. Edu. Technol. **43**(6), 949–964 (2012)
4. Gobbetti, E., Scateni, R.: Virtual reality: past, present, and future. In: Virtual Environments in Clinical Psychology and Neuroscience: Methods and Techniques in Advanced Patient-Therapist Interaction (1998)
5. Glass, R.L., Vessey, I.: Contemporary application-domain taxonomies. IEEE Softw. **12**(4), 63–76 (1995)
6. Haluck, R.S., Marshall, R.L., Krummel, T.M., Melkonian, M.G.: Are surgery training programs ready for virtual reality? A survey of program directors in general surgery. J. Am. Coll. Surg. **193**(6), 660–665 (2001)
7. Hevner, A., March, S., Park, J., Ram, S.: Design science in information systems research. MIS Q. **28**(1), 75–105 (2004)
8. Janani, B., Arthy, R., Somasundaram, M.: Virtual World Technology for Healthcare: A Survey (2015). https://www.researchgate.net/profile/Muthuvel_Somasundaram/publication/260291595_Virtual_World_Technology_for_Healthcare_A_survey_B_Janani_R_Arthy_R_Sivakumar_and_M_Somasundaram/links/0c9605336963c3b7da000000/Virtual-World-Technology-for-Healthcare-A-survey-B-Janani-R-Arthy-R-Sivakumar-and-M-Somasundaram.pdf
9. Kim, G.J.: A SWOT analysis of the field of virtual reality rehabilitation and therapy. Presence **14**(2), 119–146 (2005)
10. Leston, J., Ring, K., Kyral, E.: Virtual Reality: Business Applications, Markets and Opportunities. Ovum Limited, London (1996)
11. Levac, D.E., Galvin, J.: Facilitating clinical decision-making about the use of virtual reality within pediatric motor rehabilitation: application of a classification framework. Dev. Neurorehabil. **14**(3), 177–184 (2011)
12. McKelvey, B.: Organizational Systematics–Taxonomy, Evolution, Classification. University of California Press, Berkeley (1982)
13. Moglia, A., Ferrari, V., Morelli, L., Ferrari, M., Mosca, F., Cuschieri, A.: A systematic review of virtual reality simulators for robot-assisted surgery. Eur. Urol. **69**(6), 1065–1080 (2016)
14. Moline, J.: Virtual reality for health care: a survey. In: Studies in Health Technology and Informatics, pp. 3–34 (1997)
15. Nickerson, R.C., Varshney, U., Muntermann, J.: A method for taxonomy development and its application in information systems. Eur. J. Inf. Syst. **22**(3), 336–359 (2013)
16. Nickerson, R., Muntermann, J., Varshney, U., Isaac, H.: Taxonomy development in information systems: developing a taxonomy of mobile applications. In: European Conference in Information Systems (2009)
17. Riva, G.: Virtual reality for health care: the status of research. Cyberpsychol. Behav. **5**(3), 219–225 (2002)
18. Sherman, W.R., Craig, A.B.: Understanding Virtual Reality: Interface, Application, and Design. Elsevier, New York (2002)

19. Pensieri, C., Pennacchini, M.: Overview: virtual reality in medicine. J. Virtual Worlds Res. **7**(1), (2014). https://doi.org/10.4101/jvwr.v7i1.6364. https://jvwr-ojs-utexas.tdl.org/jvwr/index.php/jvwr/article/view/6364

20. Vozenilek, J.J., Huff, S., Reznek, M., Gordon, J.A.: See one, do one, teach one: advanced technology in medical education. Acad. Emerg. Med. **11**, 1149–1154 (2004)

21. Muhanna, M.A.: Virtual reality and the CAVE: taxonomy, interaction challenges and research directions. J. King Saud Univ.-Comput. Inf. Sci. **27**(3), 344–361 (2015)

22. Pagliari, C., Sloan, D., Gregor, P., Sullivan, F., Detmer, D., Kahan, J.P., Oortwijn, W., MacGillivray, S.: What is eHealth (4): a scoping exercise to map the field. J. Med. Internet Res. **7**(1), e9 (2005). https://doi.org/10.2196/jmir.7.1.e9. https://www.ncbi.nlm.nih.gov/pmc/articles/PMC1550637/

23. McCloy, R., Stone, R.: Science, medicine, and the future: virtual reality in surgery. BMJ: Br. Med. J. **323**(7318), 912–915 (2001)

24. Reznek, M., Harter, P., Krummel, T.: Virtual reality and simulation: training the future emergency physician. Acad. Emerg. Med. **9**(1), 78–87 (2002)

25. Schultheis, M.T., Rizzo, A.A.: The application of virtual reality technology in rehabilitation. Rehabil. Psychol. **46**(3), 296–311 (2001)

Dengue Prediction Using Hierarchical Clustering Methods

S. Vandhana$^{(\boxtimes)}$ (iD) and J. Anuradha

Vellore Institute of Technology, Vellore 632014, Tamil Nadu, India
svandhana2012@gmail.com

Abstract. The occurrence of dengue is rapidly increasing in every year. Considering the welfare of the public, it is essential to have detailed study on the affected areas of dengue and its intensity for the control of disease. This paper uses hierarchical clustering technique to classify the data of dengue cases reported and deaths occurred in various states of India. An agglomerative clustering of ward method is used for clustering. The outcomes are represented in Indian map using shape file with RStudio. The data is predicted for 2018, by logarithmic transformation using linear models of regression. K-Nearest Neighbour algorithm is used for predicting the cluster data for 2018. The results have shown that the frequency of dengue happening or the intensity is considerably reduced in many states.

Keywords: Clustering · Prediction · Hierarchical clustering
Linear model · K-Nearest Neighbour (KNN)

1 Introduction

Clustering is defined as a descriptive task, used to find the homogeneous objects based upon the value of other attributes. In spatial data sets, clustering provides spatial component of explicit location and extension of spatial objects which define implicit relationship of spatial neighbours. Clustering is an unsupervised learning method which is different from classification. Unlike classification methods, clustering does not have specific class label. In clustering, large databases are isolated into the form of small different subgroups or clusters. Clustering divides the information in view of likeliness or similarity measure [16]. Tapia et al. analyzed the gene expression data with the help of new hierarchical clustering approach using genetic algorithm [17]. This paper predicts the occurrence of dengue for the year 2018. The data is collected for the dengue cases reported and deaths occurred between the year 2011–2017. Hierarchical clustering, Linear model and K-Nearest Neighbor (KNN) are used for cluster detection and prediction.

1.1 National Dengue Prevalence

Over a decade, the occurrence of dengue has drastically increased in India. This season dengue has shown its outbreaks in Kerala, Karnataka, Tamil Nadu and

S. Chatterjee et al. (Eds.): DESRIST 2018, LNCS 10844, pp. 157–168, 2018.
https://doi.org/10.1007/978-3-319-91800-6_11

West Bengal that are confronted with mosquito-borne infection. The distressing factor is that the three states Kerala, Karnataka and Tamil Nadu have recorded with the mosquito-borne infection. The three states account for more than half of India's 87,018 dengue cases and 151 deaths [13]. Recent study was made by Mutheneni [22] on different climatic zones and monthly mean temperature for states in India such as Punjab, Haryana, Gujarat, Rajasthan and Kerala. The association between precipitation and dengue cases was also observed. The results stated that temperature as an important factor in virus development which may be useful in understanding spatial-temporal deviations in dengue risk.

1.2 International Dengue Prevalence

Lindsay and Birley [11] built up a model on transmission of Plasmodium vivax with the effect of increase in temperature. Various environmental change, e.g. the maintained an Earth-wide temperature boost of $0.2\,^\circ C$ every decade, brings up many issues about how MBDs will be affected. For example, Hales et al. [6] demonstrated the recorded worldwide dissemination of dengue fever with the base of vapor weight, which is a measure of moistness. It also determined the topographical differences in dengue fever transmission and the quantity of individuals in danger of dengue by incorporating the future environmental change. The measure of population and environmental projections for 2085 demonstrated that 5–6 billion individuals would be in danger of dengue fever transmission by correlating with 3.5 billion individuals if environmental change did not occur [18].

2 Related Work

Clustering algorithms can be categorized into four main groups [15] as hierarchical clustering, partitional clustering, density-based clustering and grid-based clustering. Hierarchical clustering methods [5,21] can further be divided into agglomerative and divisive. In agglomerative clustering each point is considered as a separate cluster and successively performs a merging until the stopping criterion is met. Whereas divisive clustering considers all points as single cluster initially and splitting is performed until a termination criterion is met. The result of hierarchical clustering can be visualized by a tree like structure called dendrogram. This paper has used various methods in hierarchical clustering such as centroid, complete, median, average, and single and ward.D among which ward.D has shown better clustering. Partitional clustering method chooses a point into the cluster, such that the points in a cluster are more similar to each other than to points in different clusters. The arbitrary initial cluster is created and iteratively points are reallocated until a stopping criterion is met. Clusters with hyper spherical shapes are formed [10,14,20].

Density of points in a region is considered for clustering in Density-based clustering method. The dense regions that are similar to each other are merged to form clusters. Density-based clustering methods excel at finding arbitrary shapes of clusters [4, 8]. In Grid-based clustering method [1, 19], the clustering space is quantized into finite number of cells and then the clustering operation is done on the quantized space. Dense clusters are considered as the cells containing certain number of points. Figure 1 shows the combined chart of clustering techniques.

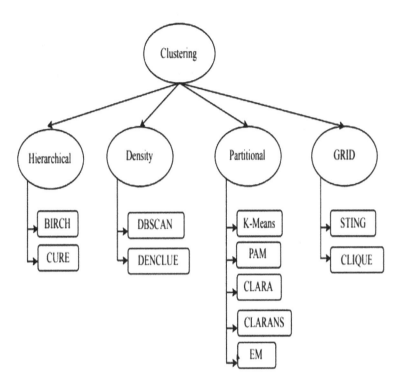

Fig. 1. Different clustering techniques.

Hybrid hierarchical clustering approach is proposed by Chipman and Tibshirani [3] developed a hybrid hierarchical clustering approach for analyzing microarray data. The new idea of mutual cluster is built. It combines the strength of bottom-up approach with that of top-down approach. Integrated hierarchical approach was proposed by Chen et al. for analyzing micro-array data. To improve the performance of analyzing large micro array data, the study combined both k-means and hierarchical clustering methods [2]. Liu et al. predicted the severity of disease by using Support Vector Machine and K-Nearest Neighbor in patients for gene expression profile having Rheumatoid Arthritis [12].

The hierarchical agglomerative algorithm that has several variations depending on the metric used to measure the distances among the clusters. The Euclidean distance is usually used for individual points. There are no known criteria of which clustering distance should be used, and it seems to depend strongly on the dataset. Among the most used variations of the hierarchical clustering based on different distance measures are average linkage, centroid linkage, complete linkage, single linkage and ward's method [9].

3   Implementation and Results

The different hierarchical methods used are average, centroid, complete, single and ward's method. Among which ward method has shown better results. The smallest of the sum of squared deviations from all the pairs is taken to merge the results and form clusters. It works on the clustering criterion [13] of ward method.

3.1   Average Linkage Clustering

The average value of the cluster is used for calculating the dissimilarity between the clusters. The distance between each point in a cluster and all other points in another cluster is the average distance between two clusters. The new cluster is formed by merging the two clusters having the lowest average.

3.2   Centroid Linkage Clustering

It is similar to that of average link. The centriod for each cluster is calculated. The centre of densely clubbed points is called as centroid. The distance between the two clusters is how far away the centroids are.

3.3   Complete Linkage Clustering (Maximum or Furthest-Neighbour Method)

The complete link cluster defines the distance between two clusters as the maximum over all the possible pairs x1 and x2 where x1 in cluster c1 and x2 in cluster c2 respectively. The dissimilarity between 2 groups is equal to the greatest dissimilarity between a member of cluster i and a member of cluster j.

3.4   Single Linkage Clustering (Minimum or Nearest-Neighbour Method)

The result of this method is of long chains which are loose and irregular in shapes. The dissimilarity between 2 clusters is the minimum dissimilarity between members of the two clusters.

3.5   Ward's Method

Cluster membership is assigned by calculating the total sum of squared deviations from the mean of a cluster. The criterion for fusion is that for different merging pairs we end up with different deviations and for clustering the smallest deviation is chosen.

Initially, each data point starts with its own cluster and the cluster starts to merge as the hierarchy goes up. The hierarchy is represented here as a tree called dendrogram. Implementation is for dengue cases prevailing in India from 2011–2017 and prediction is done for 2018. Data consist of reported cases and death occurred for all the consecutive years from 2011. The sample record is shown in Table 1. There are 28 states and 7 union territories. Data is collected for 8 consecutive years starting from 2011. The dengue cases occurred and the deaths reported are observed for each state and union territory. Figure 2 shows the plot of cases against death. On observing the pattern, reported cases are plotted against the death ratio, no pattern was identified as shown in Fig. 3. Logarithmic transformation has shown linear pattern (Fig. 4) for the cases reported and deaths occurred.

Table 1. Sample data on Dengue

States	Latitude	Longitude	Year	Cases	Deaths
Andhra Pradesh	15.9129	79.74	2011	1209	6
Arunachal Pradesh	27.84515	95.24735	2011	0	0
Assam	26.24416	92.53784	2011	0	0
Bihar	25.0961	85.3131	2011	21	0
Chattisgarh	21.29513	81.82823	2011	313	11
Andhra Pradesh	15.9129	79.74	2012	2299	2
Arunachal Pradesh	27.84515	95.24735	2012	346	0
Assam	26.24416	92.53784	2012	1058	5
Bihar	25.0961	85.3131	2012	872	3
Chattisgarh	21.29513	81.82823	2012	45	0
Andhra Pradesh	23.6102	85.2799	2013	910	1
Arunachal Pradesh	15.31728	75.71389	2013	0	0
Assam	26.24416	92.53784	2013	4526	2
Bihar	25.0961	85.3131	2013	1246	5
Chattisgarh	21.29513	81.82823	2013	83	2

Various hierarchical clustering methods such as Centroid, Complete, Median, Average, Single and Ward.D are implemented. The clustering is done for low, medium, high and no cases reported. Considering the 4 clusters for each year, the optimal number of clusters was obtained for Ward.D method (Fig. 5). The Table 2 shows the year wise clustering of low, medium, high and no cases between the years 2011–2017. For visualization of clusters, Indian shape file is fortified to fix it in a data frame. Now, the value of cluster is 0 for no cases reported and 3, 2, 1 for medium, low and high cases respectively. Figure 6 shows the plot of the cluster on Indian shape file. For 2018, the prediction is done using linear model. Linear model uses the previously recorded data and predicts the number of cases reported and deaths occurred for the year of 2018. Linear model is used when the response variable is logarithmically or exponentially related. The sample cases and the deaths predicted are given in the Fig. 7. By obtaining the cases and deaths of dengue for the year of 2018, clustering is done using K-Nearest Neighbour algorithm. Figure 8 shows the plot of cluster after prediction.

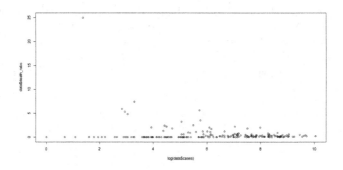

Fig. 2. Reported cases vs deaths occurred

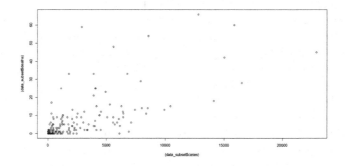

Fig. 3. Removing outliers

Figure 3 shows the plot of cases against deaths for all the years from 2011 to 2018. After removing the outliers the data is uniformly distributed. Now, to obtain the pattern a logarithmic transformation of the data is done. The logarithmic transformation shows the linear pattern or the linearity of the data and it is depicted in Fig. 4.

Observations from Fig. 6 have shown that the Southern parts of India and North-Western states were in great risk till the year 2016. In 2017, the states are recorded with low intensity of dengue. Moving to the North and North-East states such as Jammu Kashmir, Himachal Pradesh, Uttar Pradesh, Uttaranchal, Punjab, Haryana and Bihar have shown mixed results of high risk intensity and moderate intensity of dengue till the year 2016. The Eastern states of India have always recorded only with low and moderate dengue intensities. The notable

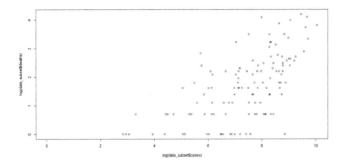

Fig. 4. Linear transformation

Table 2. Finding optimal method

Method	Tree cut	Clusters	Method	
			Dunn index	Silhouette coefficient
Centroid	4	>4	0.055	0.43
Complete	4	>4	0.049	0.46
Median	4	>4	0.048	0.45
Average	4	2 clusters	0.062	0.42
Single	4	2 clusters	0.085	0.49
Ward.D	4	4 (optimal)	0.045	0.41

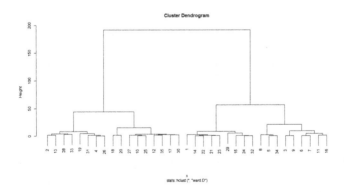

Fig. 5. Hierarchical clustering method ward.D

factor is that, Maharashtra, Gujarat, Orissa and West Bengal were always been in high risk till 2016. From the past to present the occurrence of dengue is drastically reduced from high risk to low risk in the states of Maharashtra, Gujarat, Orissa and West Bengal. The Southern part of India has also produced

Table 3. Year wise clustering

Hc_final, (cluster)	2011	2012	2013	2014*	2015	2016	2017
0	8	2	3	3	0	0	3
1	9	2	15	10	15	17	3
2	12	11	13	14	13	14	25
3	6	10	4	8	7	4	4

*Telangana was included after the year 2014. So till 2014 the records of Andhra Pradesh and Telangana are considered as same.

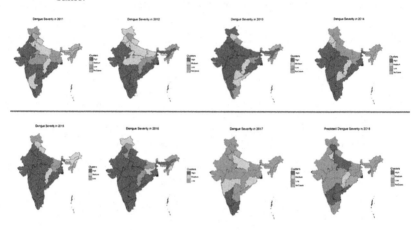

Fig. 6. Plot of year wise clusters

```
> test
   id year cases deaths class_prediction
1   0 2018     0      0                 0
31  1 2018   103      0                 1
2   2 2018  2491      0                 1
3   3 2018   514      0                 2
4   4 2018  2996      1                 2
5   5 2018  1248      0                 2
32  6 2018   771      0                 3
6   7 2018   251      0                 3
34  8 2018  2416      1                 2
35  9 2018    86      0                 2
33 10 2018  6328     20                 1
7  11 2018   245      0                 1
```

Fig. 7. Predicted data (2018)

mixed results of high and moderate intensities which are seen in the Fig. 9. The predicted data for the year 2015, 2016 and 2017 has shown slighter variations in the cases reported and deaths occurred.

Predicted Dengue Severity in 2018

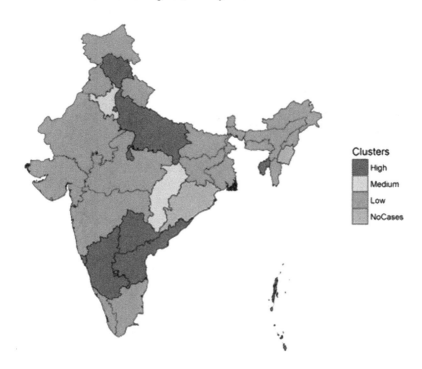

Fig. 8. Predicted dengue severity in 2018

	State	year	cases	deaths
1		2015	0	0
2	Andaman and Nicobar	2015	59	0
3	Andhra Pradesh	2015	1464	3
4	Arunachal Pradesh	2015	93	0
5	Assam	2015	1408	2
6	Bihar	2015	420	3
7	Chandigarh	2015	126	2
8	Chhattisgarh	2015	149	6
9	Dadra and Nagar Haveli	2015	283	1
10	Daman and Diu	2015	51	0
11	Delhi	2015	3752	6
12	Goa	2015	86	1
13	Gujarat	2015	3260	10

	State	year	cases	deaths
1		2016	0	0
2	Andaman and Nicobar	2016	78	0
3	Andhra Pradesh	2016	1865	3
4	Arunachal Pradesh	2016	400	0
5	Assam	2016	1380	2
6	Bihar	2016	796	2
7	Chandigarh	2016	261	1
8	Chhattisgarh	2016	225	4
9	Dadra and Nagar Haveli	2016	429	0
10	Daman and Diu	2016	74	0
11	Delhi	2016	4384	13
12	Goa	2016	141	1
13	Gujarat	2016	3658	9

	State	year	cases	deaths
1		2017	0	0
2	Andaman and Nicobar	2017	80	0
3	Andhra Pradesh	2017	2140	3
4	Arunachal Pradesh	2017	386	0
5	Assam	2017	1965	2
6	Bihar	2017	1014	1
7	Chandigarh	2017	453	0
8	Chhattisgarh	2017	262	3
9	Dadra and Nagar Haveli	2017	922	1
10	Daman and Diu	2017	76	0
11	Delhi	2017	4524	13
12	Goa	2017	146	0
13	Gujarat	2017	3917	9

Fig. 9. Predicted cases and deaths (2015, 2016, 2017)

On observing the predicted results for the year 2018 says that the dengue severity is greatly reduced. The states such as Karnataka, Andhra Pradesh, Telangana, Himachal Pradesh, Uttar Pradesh and Tripura are in risk for the year 2018. These states can take some precautionary measures so that the severity of dengue can be reduced or it can be prevented from spreading.

The model has also predicted for the years 2015, 2016, 2017. The test values predicted for the year is also given in Figs. 9 and 10 shows the predicted clustering. The visualization is done in Indian shape files.

Table 4 shows the observed and predicted values of cases and deaths for the year 2015, 2016, 2017. The predicted values are little higher than the original data.

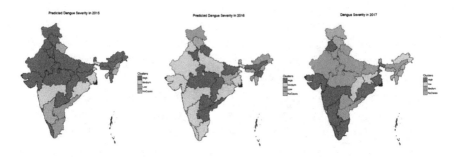

Fig. 10. Prediction using the model (year = 2015, 2016, 2017)

For measuring the accuracy of the model, prediction is done for the years 2015, 2016, 2017. The observed data is compared with the predicted values. Root Mean Squared Error is the accuracy measure used in calculating the error rate. Table 5 shows the measured error rate. While predicting the error rate for 2015, 2016 and 2017 varied. From the observed mean squared error the error rate is gradually decreased.

Table 4. Predicted deaths and cases reported

	Deaths occurred		
	2015	2016	2017
Observed	220	209	195
Predicted	232	220	201

Table 5. RMSE calculation

	Deaths		
	2015	2016	2017
RMSE	14.4595	11.01836	8.918

4   Conclusion

Clustering is a very good technique for visualization of various diseases. Hierarchical clustering works well with small set of data. In case of disease and disaster, the visualization can easily say about its intensity with the region or place of its occurrence and how the damage is recorded. This intern will provide a preventive measure and can make everyone precautious for saving many lives in future. For many years the occurrence of dengue was at its peak and thus it became the main aim to study the dengue intensities over the years, identify the patterns of its existence in overall India and predicting for the next coming years. The actual prediction for the year 2018 and the occurrence of dengue are consequently reduced in many states of India. The states Karnataka, Andhra Pradesh, Telangana, Uttar Pradesh, Tripura and Delhi are the states with high intensity of dengue. These areas have to be concentrated for the well-being of the public. In order to understand the reliability of the model, the prediction is also done for the years 2015, 2016 and 2017. The accuracy of the deaths occurred to the actual observed data is calculated using RMSE and the results with error rate are like 14.45 to 8.91%, which has shown a reduced error rate. The result reveals that the model is reliable and states that when the volume of data is increased the error rate is reduced as the model will be trained with continuous years of data. This paper shows that the government has to focus on the alarming effects of dengue for the betterment of human lives.

References

1. Agrawal, R., Gehrke, J., Gunopulos, D., Raghavan, P.: Automatic subspace clustering of high dimensional data for data mining applications. vol. 27. ACM (1998)
2. Chen, T.S., Tsai, T.H., Chen, Y.T., Lin, C.C., Chen, R.C., Li, S.Y., Chen, H.Y.: A combined k-means and hierarchical clustering method for improving the clustering efficiency of microarray. In: Proceedings of the 2005 International Symposium on Intelligent Signal Processing and Communication Systems, ISPACS 2005, pp. 405–408. IEEE (2005)
3. Chipman, H., Tibshirani, R.: Hybrid hierarchical clustering with applications to microarray data. Biostatistics **7**(2), 286–301 (2005)
4. Ester, M., Kriegel, H.P., Sander, J., Xu, X., et al.: A density-based algorithm for discovering clusters in large spatial databases with noise. In: KDD, vol. 96, pp. 226–231 (1996)
5. Guha, S., Rastogi, R., Shim, K.: CURE: an efficient clustering algorithm for large databases. In: ACM SIGMOD Record, vol. 27, pp. 73–84. ACM (1998)
6. Hales, S., De Wet, N., Maindonald, J., Woodward, A.: Potential effect of population and climate changes on global distribution of dengue fever: an empirical model. Lancet **360**(9336), 830–834 (2002)
7. Going viral: How dengue has widened its grip across India | health | Hindustan Times. https://www.hindustantimes.com/health/going-viral-dengue-widens-grip-across-india/story-qT4y5zXLzPtcSW6xOptKGO.html
8. Hinneburg, A., Keim, D.A., et al.: An efficient approach to clustering in large multimedia databases with noise. In: KDD, vol., 98, pp. 58–65 (1998)
9. Isa, D., Kallimani, V., Lee, L.H.: Using the self organizing map for clustering of text documents. Expert Syst. Appl. **36**(5), 9584–9591 (2009)
10. Kaufman, L., Rousseeuw, P.J.: Finding Groups in Data: An Introduction to Cluster Analysis, vol. 344. Wiley, Hoboken (2009)
11. Lindsay, S., Birley, M.: Climate change and malaria transmission. Ann. Trop. Med. Parasitol. **90**(5), 573–588 (1996)

12. Liu, Z., Sokka, T., Maas, K., Olsen, N.J., Aune, T.M.: Prediction of disease severity in patients with early rheumatoid arthritis by gene expression profiling. Hum. Genomics Proteomics: HGP, **2009** (2009)
13. Murtagh, F., Legendre, P.: Ward's hierarchical agglomerative clustering method: which algorithms implement ward's criterion? J. Classif. **31**(3), 274–295 (2014)
14. Ng, R., Han, J.: Efficient and effective clustering method for spatial data mining. In: Proceedings of the 20th International Conference on Very Large Data Bases, Santiago, Chile, pp. 144–155 (1994)
15. Shekhar, S., Chawla, S.: Spatial Databases: A Tour, vol. 2003. Prentice Hall, Upper Saddle River (2003)
16. Silver, M., Sakata, T., Su, H.C., Herman, C., Dolins, S.B., O'Shea, M.J., et al.: Case study: how to apply data mining techniques in a healthcare data warehouse. J. Healthc. Inf. Manag. **15**(2), 155–164 (2001)
17. Tapia, J.J., Morett, E., Vallejo, E.E.: A clustering genetic algorithm for genomic data mining. In: Abraham, A., Hassanien, A.E., de Carvalho, A.P.L.F. (eds.) Foundations of Computational Intelligence Volume 4, pp. 249–275. Springer, Heidelberg (2009). https://doi.org/10.1007/978-3-642-01088-0_11
18. Tonnang, H.E., Kangalawe, R.Y., Yanda, P.Z.: Predicting and mapping malaria under climate change scenarios: the potential redistribution of malaria vectors in Africa. Malaria J. **9**(1), 111 (2010)
19. Wang, W., Yang, J., Muntz, R., et al.: STING: a statistical information grid approach to spatial data mining. In: VLDB. vol. 97, pp. 186–195 (1997)
20. Witthen, I., Frank, E.: Data Mining-Practical Machine Learning Tools and Techniques with Java Implementations. Morgan Kaufmann Publishers, Burlington (2000)
21. Zhang, T., Ramakrishnan, R., Livny, M.: BIRCH: an efficient data clustering method for very large databases. In: ACM SIGMOD Record, vol. 25, pp. 103–114. ACM (1996)
22. Mutheneni, S.R., Morse, A.P., Caminade, C., Upadhyayula, S.M.: Dengue burden in India: recent trends and importance of climatic parameters. Emerg. Microbes Infect. **6**(8), e70 (2017)

Collaborative Literature Search System: An Intelligence Amplification Method for Systematic Literature Search

Andrej Dobrkovic[1]([✉]), Daniel A. Döppner[2], Maria-Eugenia Iacob[1], and Jos van Hillegersberg[1]

[1] Industrial Engineering and Business Information System, University of Twente, Enschede, The Netherlands
a.dobrkovic@utwente.nl
[2] Department of Information Systems and Information Management, University of Cologne, Cologne, Germany

Abstract. In this paper, we present a method for systematic literature search based on the symbiotic partnership between the human researcher and intelligent agents. Using intelligence amplification, we leverage the calculation power of computers to quickly and thoroughly extract data, calculate measures, and visualize relationships between scientific documents with the ability of domain experts to perform qualitative analysis and creative reasoning. Thus, we create a foundation for a collaborative literature search system (CLSS) intended to aid researches in performing literature reviews, especially for interdisciplinary and evolving fields of science for which keyword-based literature searches result in large collections of documents beyond humans' ability to process or the extensive use of filters to narrow the search output risks omitting relevant works. Within this article, we propose a method for CLSS and demonstrate its use on a concrete example of a literature search for a review of the literature on human-machine symbiosis.

Keywords: Intelligence amplification · Method
Collaborative literature search system · Human-machine symbiosis
Design science research

1 Introduction

Literature reviews are an essential part of the evolution of scientific knowledge as they summarize the state of the art, uncover knowledge gaps, and provide guidance for further research endeavors. By conducting a systematic literature review (SLR), researchers seek to systematically search, evaluate, and synthetize research evidence. This process remains predominantly "manual" because—for now—only human beings can review and evaluate the scientific material required by high-quality literature reviews. Consequently, this creates a limitation in the volume of scientific publications that can be processed.

Nevertheless, there are an ever-increasing number of research publications, which holds great potential for the synthesis of insightful knowledge. However, as the results

© Springer International Publishing AG, part of Springer Nature 2018
S. Chatterjee et al. (Eds.): DESRIST 2018, LNCS 10844, pp. 169–183, 2018.
https://doi.org/10.1007/978-3-319-91800-6_12

and quality of a literature review essentially depend on the literature selected, it becomes a complex and time-consuming challenge to identify the relevant publications in the jumble of documents that can amass in a literature search. This is reinforced by the fact that many research disciplines have become more interdisciplinary [1, 2], intertwining into an increasing variety of research communities. In this context, students and novice researchers may particularly struggle to get a clear overview of the existing research streams and underlying literature. A second challenge that comes with this problem is the use of different terms for similar or identical concepts.

With advancements in business intelligence, data mining, visualization, and technical computational power, it seems obvious that information technology can provide useful support for the literature-search task in the literature-review process. Indeed, there are a variety of tools that support or automate manual literature search conducted by humans (e.g., systematic literature search systems) [3]. However, since literature search is also a creative process to a certain extent (e.g., the identification of a starting point) [3], full automation is difficult to achieve [4]. Thus, the resulting design objective of this paper is to construct a method that combines the strengths of human and computers for conducting literature search for literature reviews.

Following the design science research (DSR) approach, which deals with the development of novel artifacts that solve or improve real-world problems [5–7], this paper makes two contributions to the DSR body of knowledge [5, 8]. First, we propose a method for conducting literature search while doing SLRs based on the collaboration between two entities: the human and the machine. Recognizing that each entity has different strengths and weaknesses, we propose a process that relies on the strengths of each entity to complement the weaknesses of the other such that the overall result is greater than what each entity could achieve on its own. Our approach is based on the idea of intelligence amplification—that is, the symbiotic interaction between human and machine [9] through which the processing power of computers to visualize and calculate measures in document networks and humans' creativity and visual perception for reasoning are merged to form a symbiotic entity, enabling superior literature search, exploration, and result selection. We refer to this class of literature search systems as *collaborative literature search systems (CLSS)*. Second, besides an abstract method description for CLSS, we present a prototypical instantiation of the method and demonstrate its applicability in practical case, which serves as validation for the proposed method.

The structure of the paper essentially follows the DSR process model from [7]. The problem definition is covered in the introduction (Sect. 1) and throughout the provided background knowledge on literature search in SLRs and human-machine symbiosis (Sect. 2). In Sect. 3, we describe the collaborative literature search method, which includes the objectives of the artifact and the essential components of its design and development. The demonstration and evaluation of the artifact is given in Sect. 4. Section 5 compares our solution with other approaches proposed in related work, and Sect. 6 provides some concluding remarks and pointers for future work.

2 Background

2.1 Literature Search in Literature Reviews

Literature reviews are an essential part of every research project [1]. They mainly comprise the following steps: (1) collecting data (search and select literature); (2) structuring, synthesizing, exploring, and analyzing data (summarize evidence); and (3) presenting results (disseminate results) [10].

The notable challenges in literature reviews include the increasing number of articles, information overload, increasing complexity, and pressure to obtain comprehensive coverage of article collections. Locating and identifying relevant documents are key factors in literature reviews. To support literature reviewers (from here on called reviewers), the academic literature provides a rich body of approaches and guidelines [11], emphasizing different literature-search strategies, such as keyword-based search, backward search, and forward search [1, 12]. There is also a broad range of software tools that support or automate the different phases of the literature-reviews process, including systematic literature search systems [3] and recommender systems aiding the identification of further potential citations [13]. Additionally, there are various approaches and techniques that help researchers structure and analyze documents and their contents, such as topic modeling [14], discipline structuring [15], authorship analysis [16], and knowledge diffusion [17], as well as tools to support the literature analysis [18]—for example, visualizing connections between research articles [19]. Nevertheless, although there are solutions for partial problems in the literature-review process, there is a lack of support for tasks that require human creativity (e.g., the so-called cold-start problem of determining a starting point for literature search), especially when the reviewer does not have in-depth knowledge of the field at hand.

2.2 Intelligence Amplification/Human-Machine Symbiosis

While the predominant system design approach is to automate as much as possible and reduce human intervention to increase efficiency [20], others recognize that humans play an important role in contexts that do not allow full automation [21]. For example, humans are better in creative tasks whereas machines are better in computational tasks [22].

The idea of intelligence amplification or human-machine symbiosis can be traced back to the work of Licklider [9] and is central to the vison put forward by the new smart industry paradigm. Unlike in artificial intelligence (AI), the goal of which is to create an artificial decision maker that mimics the human brain, intelligence amplification (IA) is based on the "human-in-the-loop" approach. In IA, both the human and the AI agent form a symbiotic partnership, in which the human entity defines strategy, oversees the AI agent, and corrects its decisions when needed, and the AI agent executes routine tasks according to the strategy. In [9], Licklider makes a fundamental observation: the time it takes a human to make a decision, regardless of the complexity, is negligible compared to the time required to complete the steps preceding the decision itself as well as the time for execution afterward.

To the best of our knowledge, no work exists that takes a symbiotic human-machine approach for designing a solution to support literature search and knowledge extraction. The need for such a method becomes especially evident in evolving and interdisciplinary fields for which the number of documents retrieved through rigorous keyword searches is beyond human processing abilities or for which the extensive use of filters to narrow the output risks omitting relevant concepts and publications coming from different scientific fields possibly using different yet semantically similar terminology. Machines can process huge data volumes quickly but lack the ability to reason and draw conclusions beyond the programmed parameters. Humans (experts in their fields) can evaluate any kind of material, but the volume they can handle is limited. Therefore, an ideal symbiotic partnership should be organized in such a way that the human sets the parameters the machine uses to mine the available scientific information and filter more relevant documents using basic reasoning, which will in turn allow the human to focus on the most important documents and complete the evaluation.

This paper addresses this shortcoming by proposing a CLSS that provides effective automation support through metadata extraction. The proposed method enables researchers to conduct faster and more thorough literature reviews as well as detect, extract, and connect interdisciplinary knowledge from different scientific fields.

3   Method

3.1   Seed-Based Search

A literature-search approach in SLR starts with the researcher selecting keywords and using them to search bibliographic databases for relevant scientific articles. This approach often returns a large number of articles that match the search criteria, so understanding their mutual dependencies becomes challenging. Therefore, we propose an alternative approach that emphasizes the relationships between documents based on their shared citations and references. In our seed-based approach, the idea is to start with an initial set of relevant documents (which we call seeds) and query bibliographic databases to conduct forward and backward literature search corresponding to a citation analysis. This initial set of articles can be, for example, the result of ad hoc keyword-based searches or recommended articles by colleagues. The result is transformed into a directed graph, in which each document is represented as a node and every citation and every reference becomes an edge. Through graph analysis, it is possible to identify the nodes that are most related (and possibly relevant) to the initial seed(s). The reviewer then performs a qualitative analysis of those documents. Each document that is identified as relevant for the literature review is added to the seed set and the process is repeated until a stop-criterion is achieved—that is, no additional seeds are discovered or a maximum search depth is achieved.

We illustrate this process with the following example (illustrated in Fig. 1). We assume that for a specific scientific field, the reviewer is familiar with three articles: A, B, and C. Two articles (A and C) are deemed to be influential and selected as seeds. Therefore, the initial graph contains two nodes. For this given example, article A is referenced by B and D, and article C is cited by B. After conducting the forward search for the next depth, articles B and D are added to the graph. Since B was already known to the reviewer, it is excluded from further consideration. However, this process also raises the reviewer's awareness about article D, which is related to the two already known and relevant articles.

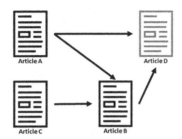

Fig. 1. Illustration of the discovery of the new articles through seed-based search

3.2 The Process

The search process contains four consecutive steps. In Step 1, the search parameters are determined. Expanding the document graph through forward and backward search of bibliographic databases is done in Step 2. In Step 3, found articles are analyzed, and the results are visualized in a way that allows quick understanding by the human. This step also includes highlighting potentially important articles based on the network analysis. Step 4 includes the examination of the extended list of articles and comparison with the current list of articles to determine if new search seeds can be identified. If there are new seeds, the process returns to Step 2 and is repeated until no new seed articles are found. Finally, articles are filtered (e.g., by publication year) to produce a final collection of articles that is manageable by the human. Afterward, the reviewer analyzes all articles in the list and moves on to the review. Figure 2 illustrates the steps of the intelligence amplification literature search and, most importantly, how they fit within the classical literature-review process. The proposed method replaces and automates search and acquisition and enhances some analysis and interpretation activities.

Since our method is based on the human-in-the-loop approach, in Step 1, human reviewers define the search criteria. As we base our search on citation analysis initiated by the given seeds, this step requires the reviewers to use their experience to identify the most relevant seed articles (sa) concerning the scientific field under review. To reduce unavoidable human bias, we recommend that more than one reviewer be involved in this step and that each creates a separate initial list of possible seeds, which will result in a consolidated collection of articles.

Step 2 and Step 3 are delegated to the machine. First, the intelligent agent queries bibliographic databases and performs forward and backward search based on the selected seeds and the depth set in Step 1. Forward search extracts all articles that cite the given seeds, and the backward search extracts all articles referenced in the seeds. Optionally, this search can be limited in depth and constrained with keywords to prevent it from exploding into literature retrieval from non-related scientific fields. The extraction is expected to generate potentially large lists of documents, which are not suitable for human evaluation. To address this issue, the intelligent agent is required to transform the list into a directed graph and cluster the nodes (i.e., documents) according to their relationships. This is done in Step 3. In Step 4, the reviewers examine the graph structure, but prior to that, additional visual cues need to be implemented to enable humans to quickly distinguish documents' publication year, number of connections, and relationship to the specific scientific field. One option is the use of visual markers to highlight potentially outstanding articles. These are typically so-called *bridging articles*—namely, documents that connect different scientific fields. Often, such papers lead to a *paradigm shift* and give rise to what Kuhn [23] calls a *scientific revolution* that significantly impacts a certain scientific field. Intelligent agents do not have humans' expertise to accurately determine such articles, yet machines can analyze the graph structure and provide visual cues for these "event nodes" (i.e., nodes representing paradigm-shifting articles) if certain conditions are met. Typically, these have a high number of citations and are the centers of a node cluster. We suggest that reviewers set a threshold (t) value, which is used to filter nodes by the number of different clusters each node is connected to.

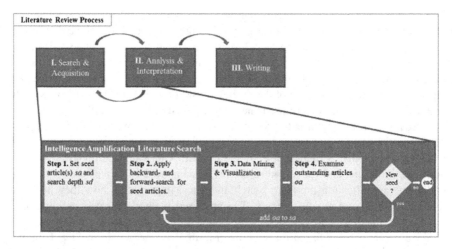

Fig. 2. Literature-review process and enhancement with intelligence amplification literature search

Aided by the visual cues and metadata extraction, in Step 4, the reviewers inspect the generated graph structure. Through the first level of publication filtering—by name and by abstract—the reviewers orient themselves to their potential areas of interest. As the documents are grouped within clusters, the reviewers can quickly decide to exclude unrelated document groups by inspecting cluster cores and the connected articles. By analyzing both highlighted articles and those they discovered by exploiting the graph structure, the reviewers can identify new seeds, and the process can be repeated from Step 2. If no new outstanding articles are found and/or the graph structure has converged toward a stable form, the process is finished, and all nodes in the structure become candidates for the literature review. At the end, the reviewers may opt to apply additional filters (e.g., publication year, connection strength between the article and the seeds) if the number of articles is still too high for human processing. Following that, the process provides the input for the next step of the literature-review process. The reviewers investigate each document thoroughly and formulate answers to their initial research question.

4 Demonstration and Evaluation

An essential component of every DSR project is an evaluation that rigorously demonstrates that the proposed solution addresses the stated problem [6]. The DSR literature proposes several approaches to plan evaluation strategies [24].

To demonstrate the effectiveness of our proposed method, we opted for a demonstration of the method by implementing a software tool that performs the machine's tasks. Like other studies in the field of scientometrics (e.g. [19, 25]), we demonstrate the method by providing details on an illustrative scenario, as described below [24].

The tool connects to the Scopus database via the official application programming interface (API), conducts the forward and backward search, and extracts the citation graph. The tool is used for Step 2 and Step 3 (see Sect. 3.2). The pseudo code for the document extraction is given in Fig. 3.

```
extract (seed_id, search_depth, keyword_list)
  set history_list, open_list to empty
    initialize Graph
    copy seed_id to open_list
    set depth to 0
    while depth < search_depth
        for each node in open_list
            neighbors = CALL_ADJECENT_API_SEARCH(node)
            append neighbors to adjacent_nodes
            for each n in neighbors
                if (KEYWORDS(n) in keyword_list) and (NOT(n in history_list))
                    Graph.add_edge (node, n)
                else delete n from adjacent_nodes
        append open_list to history_list
        copy adjacent_nodes to open_list
        set adjacent_nodes to empty
        depth = depth + 1
    return Graph
```

Fig. 3. Pseudo code for document extraction and graph generation via a database-specific API

Figure 4 shows the graph resulting from the search for two arbitrary seeds. Figure 4(a) shows the transformation of the extracted documents into nodes on the directed graph and their references and citations as graph edges. In Fig. 4(b), nodes have been clustered to make the structure more comprehensible for the human researcher. In Fig. 4(c), we use arrows to point to the visual cues given by the

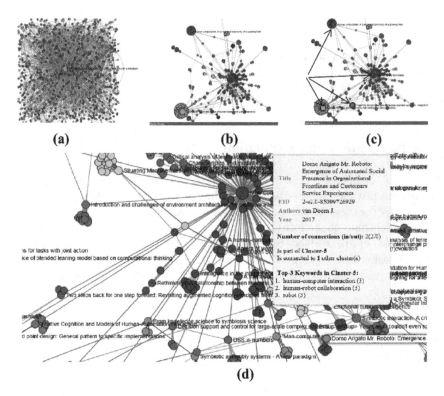

Fig. 4. Visualizing citation network as a directed graph with metadata

algorithm to indicate outstanding articles (*oa*), which are rendered as large squares instead of circles. Finally, in Fig. 4(d), we show how to zoom into the node structure and obtain specific document-related information.

We selected the literature from the field of human-machine symbiosis because we believe it is a good candidate to demonstrate our solution and evaluation as it (1) spans fields from theoretical computer science to practical robotics application and (2) is challenging for humans to fully process as a traditional keyword-based search returns well beyond thousands of articles. For simplicity, we decided to use a single seed for the initial search, and because Licklider is considered the most influential author for the origins of human-computer symbiosis, we used [9] (MCS) as the initial seed (cf. Step 1 in Sect. 3.2). In the following, we briefly describe the results of our execution of the defined method steps. Due to page constraints, each seed is coded using an acronym, while the full title, author(s), and publication year for each document is given in Table 1.

We used the Scopus database, set the algorithm to the maximum search depth of 2, and added a filter to exclude papers that do not have keywords related to human-machine symbiosis. The first iteration of Step 2 returned 753 documents. The analysis of these documents was done through the symbiotic partnership between us (i.e., the human reviewers) and the machine. The machine used a clustering algorithm

Table 1. Acronyms used for labeling event nodes

Acronym	Authors	Title	Year
MCS	Licklider	Man-computer symbiosis	1960
HC	Quinn and Bederson	Human computation: a survey and taxonomy of a growing field	2011
SI	Jacucci et al.	Symbiotic interaction: a critical definition and comparison to other human-computer paradigms	2014
EDP	Döppner et al.	Exploring Design Principles for Human-Machine Symbiosis: Insights from Constructing an Air Transportation Logistics Artifact	2016
FPS2MCS	Guo et al.	From participatory sensing to Mobile Crowd Sensing	2014
MCSC	Guo et al.	Mobile Crowd Sensing and Computing: The review of an emerging human-powered sensing paradigm	2015
DC	Hollan et al.	Distributed Cognition: Toward a New Foundation for Human-Computer Interaction Research	2000
Tl	Hornecker and Buur	Getting a grip on tangible interaction: A framework on physical space and social interaction	2006
AE	Kirsh	Adapting the environment instead of oneself	1996
IEPDL	Fast and Sedig	Interaction and the epistemic potential of digital libraries	2010
VABD	Ren et al.	Visual analytics towards big data	2014
MlwCEl	Smart	Situating Machine Intelligence Within the Cognitive Ecology of the Internet	2017
DCflV	Liu et al.	Distributed cognition as a theoretical framework for information visualization	2008

for the citation network analysis, which was combined with the human-defined threshold parameters to render the graph and to highlight the potentially most relevant articles in the structure. Detailed information about the input and output values per iteration, including suggested event nodes by the machine in response to the human-defined threshold t, is given in Table 2. Figure 5(a) shows the zoomed-out directed graph—that is, the result of Iteration 1—which contains information on 753 extracted articles and their correlation. We then explored the graph, focusing on the suggested event nodes.

As Iteration 1 had a few clusters, only low threshold parameters ($t = 3$ and $t = 4$) yielded outstanding articles (*oa*) beside the initial seed. We then inspected each node, checked the relevance of the title and abstract, and finally evaluated the content of the full article. We found SI [26] and HC [27] to be quite relevant to the search and good candidates for the next seed. HC has more citations, so more edges connect it with other nodes, and it also resides closer to the center of the graph. However, because we concluded that HC is a taxonomy paper from its content, we gave preference to SI as the next seed. In Fig. 5(b), we show how the tool provides analytical assistance to researchers by showing metadata about the highlighted node that can be inspected by humans. The view is zoomed in and rotated to show the connection between the new potential seed SI and the original seed MCS. From the tool, we obtained additional info about the node and its cluster: document title, author, number of connections, most common keywords, number of citations, and publication year.

Iteration 2 started with two seeds: MCS and SI. All other parameters remained unchanged. This resulted in 1,193 related articles. Exploring the structure with alternating event thresholds, two additional nodes were highlighted as potential paradigm shifts. These nodes are HC, which was already discovered in Iteration 1, and the new node: DC [28]. Based on the content of DC, we selected it as the most relevant node and added it to the seed list. Iteration 3 increased the node number to 2,427. Again, visual inspection of the results, together with experimenting with different thresholds, yielded three more seeds: HC, TI [29], and AE [30]. Based on the content, we found that these seeds are relevant, yet we noticed that their disciplinary focus is moving away from the core of human-machine symbiosis. We still proceeded to the Iteration 4 but reduced the search depth to 1, ultimately obtaining 2,427 nodes. As the graph structure and suggested event nodes remained similar to the previous iteration, we concluded that the structure converged toward a stable form and stopped the search. Figure 5(d) shows the zoomed-out view of the graph after concluding this phase.

Table 2. Input and output parameters for each iteration with suggested seeds per threshold level

		Iteration				
		1	2	3	4	filter
Input	Seed	MCS	MCS, SI	MCS, SI, DC	MCS, SI, DC, HC, TI, AE	MCS, SI, DC, HC, TI, AE
	Search depth	2	2	2	1	n/a
	Database	Scopus				
	Keywords filter	Intelligence amplification, Intelligence augmentation, Human-machine symbiosis, Human-computer symbiosis, Human-machine collaboration, Human-machine cooperation				
Output	No. nodes (documents)	753	1193	2427	2427	323
	No. edges (ref. + cit.)	842	1308	2847	2848	335
	No. clusters	38	30	48	52	6
Event nodes	t = 3	*MCS*, *SI*, HC, EDP, FPS2MCS, MCSC	*MCS*, *SI*, *DC*, HC	*MCS, SI, DC, HC, TI, AE*, IEPDL, VABD, MIwCEI, DCfIV, (+11)	*MCS, SI, DC, HC, TI, AE*, IEPDL, VABD, MIwCEI, DCfIV, (+14)	n/a
	t = 4	*MCS*, HC	*MCS, SI, DC*, HC	*MCS, SI, DC, HC, TI, AE*, IEPDL, VABD, MIwCEI, DCfIV	*MCS, SI, DC, HC, TI, AE*, IEPDL, VABD, MIwCEI, DCfIV	n/a
	t = 5	*MCS*	*MCS, SI*	*MCS, SI, DC, HC, TI, AE*, IEPDL	*MCS, SI, DC, HC, TI, AE*, IEPDL, VABD	n/a
	t = 6	*MCS*	*MCS, SI*	*MCS, SI, DC, HC, TI, AE*	*MCS, SI, DC, HC, TI, AE*, IEPDL	n/a

The final phase involved using the symbiotic human-machine partnership and narrowing down the set of extracted articles to one that is manageable by the human for full qualitative analysis. We used the tool to identify and select articles connected to the extracted seeds: MCS, SI, DC, HC, TI, and AE. We chose to keep only the documents

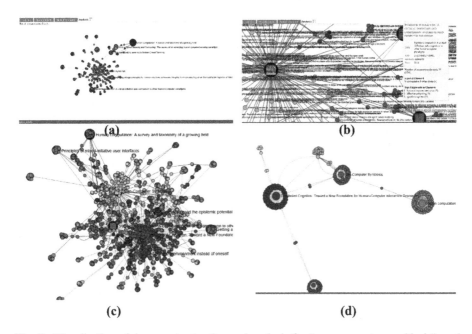

Fig. 5. Visualization of document extraction and analysis for "man-computer symbiosis" seed

published within the last five years and added the criterion that each must be connected to at least one seed. This gave us the structure shown in Fig. 5(d), which contains 323 documents. Following that, human expertise was required to assess the relevance of each article based on the title and abstract and to determine the final consolidated list.

5 Related Work

The research from the field of scientometrics is rich with publications focusing on measuring the impact of scientific publications [31]. Many research groups have investigated literature search and have produced software packages for mapping scientific field(s). For example, CiteSpace [25] provides keyword extraction, landscape, and timeline view from a variety of sources, such as Web of Science (WoS), Scopus, and PubMed. VosViewer [19] also uses data from WoS, Scopus, and PubMed and incorporates clustering and non-linear programming techniques to process and visualize the data. However, data extraction is not included in the process as these tools assume that the human reviewer obtains all the data and loads in one go, thus limiting the potential for sequential discovery.

Due to its powerful analysis features, easy and effective user interface, and ability to use data obtained from Scopus, we decided to use VosViewer [19] to demonstrate the execution of the process described in Sect. 4 based on the search spawning from Licklider's publication on man-computer symbiosis [9]. Thus, we explored the literature through search queries and extracted publication lists using Scopus' web interface.

The initial Scopus search using the query "TITLE-ABS-KEY (man-computer AND symbiosis)" returned 14 results, from which no significant correlation was found. Therefore, we obtained Scopus-specific unique paper identifiers (EID) for [9] (2-s2.0-84936949820) and used it to redefine the query, extracting MCS and all documents citing it. By running the following query, we obtained a list of 456 articles and exported it in .csv format: "REF (2-s2.0-84936949820) OR EID (2-s2.0-84936949820)." We then loaded this list in VosViewer, choosing the option to create the map based on the bibliographic data. We set the type parameter to citation analysis and set the unit parameter to documents. Finally, we set the minimal number of citations threshold to 0 and included all documents. The result is given in the Fig. 6(a) below.

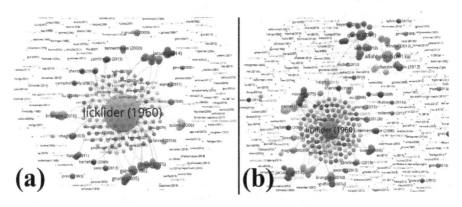

Fig. 6. Visualizing citation network for the man-computer symbiosis literature using VosViewer

Next, we examined the papers in the larger clusters of Fig. 6(a) and selected the publication by Jacucci et al. [26] (tagged as SI in Table 2). The paper HC [27] by Quinn and Bederson is in the list, but because only a few edges are connecting it with other nodes in the graph, it is not easily identifiable by the human. Nevertheless, we decided to include HC and SI in the next iteration to increase the complexity of the network and create a structure that is easier to compare with the graph we obtained after Iteration 3 and Iteration 4 in Sect. 4. We manually extracted all seed papers' unique EIDs and ran a new query in Scopus' browser interface: "REF (2-s2.0-84936949820) OR EID (2-s2.0-84936949820) OR EID (2-s2.0-84917733431) OR REF (2-s2.0-84917733431) OR EID (2-s2.0-79958083139) OR REF (2-s2.0-79958083139)." This search resulted in 825 papers, which VosViewer generated into the graph shown in Fig. 6(b).

After we examined new highlighted clusters and determined they were not relevant for further investigation, the search did not acquire new seeds and the process stopped. Thus, this process resulted in a list of 825 papers and no clear indication of how to proceed further with paper selection. These results contrasts with the more than 2,000 articles obtained through our CLSS after Iterations 3 and 4.

However, it should be noted that the capabilities of VosViewer exceed the visualization functionality included in our tool by far. The main advantage of our solution is thus not related to visualization per se but rather to the strategy we propose for searching and obtaining the data itself. The fact is that our method includes custom machine-assisted extraction, which can perform both forward and backward search and in larger depths, provides more data. Thus, it is possible for our tool to discover more clusters, and within those clusters, it can find outstanding articles that can be used as further seeds. As both VosViewer and CiteSpace are designed for data extracted manually by humans from pre-defined sources, they are constrained by that input. With an increasing number of seeds, this search process becomes more complex and creates more fatigue, ultimately causing the human component to be the bottleneck. Nevertheless, if VosViewer and CiteSpace enable custom data to be loaded, we expect that better (visualization) results could be obtained using our proposed extraction process and method together with the analytical functionality of those tools.

6 Discussion and Future Work

In this paper, we proposed a method for conducting collaborative literature search for SLRs using a symbiotic partnership between humans and machines. We showed that our method based on the principles of seed-based search and intelligence amplification (i.e., where machines augment the capabilities of human domain experts) has potential as a complementary approach to traditional search. Finally, we illustrated the method in a CLSS and demonstrated its application for obtaining an article list for a literature review in the field of human-machine symbiosis.

With our CLSS, we aim to provide efficient assistance for SLRs, particularly in interdisciplinary research domains as well as evolving scientific fields that typically use different terminology and keywords for similar concepts. When the literature review requires the processing of large amounts of publications beyond human capabilities, CLSS can be used by researchers to quickly identify potentially important publications. Through an interactive search of the generated directed graph, researchers can influence how the graph structure evolves as new seeds and paradigm shifts are identified. CLSS enables researchers to maintain a helicopter view of a large set of articles and aims at improving their ability to conduct SLR in an ever-increasing pool of scientific information while reducing the risk of potentially missing essential concepts and bridging articles.

In this paper, we demonstrated the first application of our proposed method and implemented an algorithm to retrieve important articles within a document collection. As we obtained data from a single bibliographic database, future work should focus on improving the scalability of the CLSS, examine further identification approaches, and expand literature sources. This would also strengthen the rigor required for SLR. In terms of performance, there is also room for improvement by adjusting the data mining (clustering) algorithms to enable real-time big data processing. This, together with improving the interface of the frontend component, would make interactive real-time content analysis possible, enabling researchers to dynamically add and remove seeds while exploring the literature landscape [32].

Gathering data about the usage of the CLSS, it might be interesting to analyze typical literature-exploration trajectories and train models that allow the machine part to recommend efficient trajectories (stronger assistance power). Shifting from a submissive role in the collaborative relationship, the system can become more powerful to guide the reviewer through the literature-search process. Because the focus of the proposed method is on the literature-search phase of SLR in this paper, it might be interesting for further research to use the lens of human-machine symbiosis and investigate its suitability for the design of IT support for the subsequent SLR phases.

References

1. Webster, J., Watson, R.T.: Analyzing the past to prepare for the future: writing a literature review. Manag. Inf. Syst. Q. **26**, 3 (2002)
2. Sheng, J., Amankwah-Amoah, J., Wang, X.: A multidisciplinary perspective of big data in management research. Int. J. Prod. Econ. **191**, 97–112 (2017)
3. Sturm, B., Sunyaev, A.: If you want your research done right, do you have to do it all yourself? Developing design principles for systematic literature search systems. In: Designing the Digital Transformation: DESRIST 2017 Research in Progress Proceedings of the 12th International Conference on Design Science Research in Information Systems and Technology. Karlsruhe, Germany, 30 May–1 June. Karlsruher Institut für Technologie (KIT) (2017)
4. Levy, Y., Ellis, T.J.: A systems approach to conduct an effective literature review in support of information systems research. Inf. Sci. **9**, 181–212 (2006)
5. Gregor, S., Hevner, A.R.: Positioning and presenting design science research for maximum impact. MIS Q. **37**, 337–355 (2013)
6. Hevner, A.R., March, S.T., Park, J., Ram, S.: Design science in information systems research. MIS Q. **28**(1), 75–105 (2004)
7. Peffers, K., Tuunanen, T., Rothenberger, M.A., Chatterjee, S.: A design science research methodology for information systems research. J. Manag. Inf. Syst. **24**, 45–77 (2007)
8. March, S.T., Smith, G.F.: Design and natural science research on information technology. Decis. Support Syst. **15**, 251–266 (1995)
9. Licklider, J.C.: Man-computer symbiosis. IRE Trans. Hum. Factors Electron. **1**, 4–11 (1960)
10. Boell, S.K., Cecez-Kecmanovic, D.: On being 'systematic' in literature reviews in IS. J. Inf. Technol. **30**, 161–173 (2015)
11. Boell, S.K., Cecez-Kecmanovic, D.: A hermeneutic approach for conducting literature reviews and literature searches. CAIS **34**, 12 (2014)
12. Jalali, S., Wohlin, C.: Systematic literature studies: database searches vs. backward snowballing. In: Proceedings of the ACM-IEEE International Symposium on Empirical Software Engineering and Measurement, pp. 29–38. ACM (2012)
13. Huang, W., Wu, Z., Mitra, P., Giles, C.L.: Refseer: a citation recommendation system. In: Proceedings of the 14th ACM/IEEE-CS Joint Conference on Digital Libraries, pp. 371–374. IEEE Press (2014)
14. Eickhoff, M., Neuss, N.: Topic modelling methodology: its use in information systems and other managerial disciplines. In: Proceedings of the 25th European Conference on Information Systems (ECIS), Guimarães, Portugal, June 5–10, pp. 1327–1347 (2017). ISBN 978-989-20-7655-3 Research Papers
15. Kulkarni, S.S., Apte, U.M., Evangelopoulos, N.E.: The use of latent semantic analysis in operations management research. Decis. Sci. **45**, 971–994 (2014)
16. Fischbach, K., Putzke, J., Schoder, D.: Co-authorship networks in electronic markets research. Electron. Mark. **21**, 19–40 (2011)

17. Xiao, Y., Lu, L.Y., Liu, J.S., Zhou, Z.: Knowledge diffusion path analysis of data quality literature: a main path analysis. J. Inform. **8**, 594–605 (2014)
18. Marjanovic, O., Dinter, B.: 25+ years of business intelligence and analytics minitrack at HICSS: a text mining analysis. In: Proceedings of the 50th Hawaii International Conference on System Sciences (2017)
19. Van Eck, N.J., Waltman, L.: Software survey: VOSviewer, a computer program for bibliometric mapping. Scientometrics **84**, 523–538 (2010)
20. Cummings, M.M.: Man versus machine or man + machine? IEEE Intell. Syst. **29**, 62–69 (2014)
21. Döppner, D.A., Gregory, R.W., Schoder, D., Siejka, H.: Exploring design principles for human-machine symbiosis: insights from constructing an air transportation logistics artifact. In: ICIS 2016 Proceedings, (2016)
22. Dobrkovic, A., Liu, L., Iacob, M.-E., van Hillegersberg, J.: Intelligence amplification framework for enhancing scheduling processes. In: Montes-y-Gómez, M., Escalante, H.J., Segura, A., Murillo, J. (eds.) IBERAMIA 2016. LNCS (LNAI), vol. 10022, pp. 89–100. Springer, Cham (2016). https://doi.org/10.1007/978-3-319-47955-2_8
23. Kuhn, T.S.: The route to normal science. Struct. Sci. Revolut. **2**, 10–22 (1970)
24. Prat, N., Comyn-Wattiau, I., Akoka, J.: A taxonomy of evaluation methods for information systems artifacts. J. Manag. Inf. Syst. **32**, 229–267 (2015)
25. Chen, C.: CiteSpace II: detecting and visualizing emerging trends and transient patterns in scientific literature. J. Assoc. Inf. Sci. Technol. **57**, 359–377 (2006)
26. Jacucci, G., Spagnolli, A., Freeman, J., Gamberini, L.: Symbiotic interaction: a critical definition and comparison to other human-computer paradigms. In: Jacucci, G., Gamberini, L., Freeman, J., Spagnolli, A. (eds.) Symbiotic 2014. LNCS, vol. 8820, pp. 3–20. Springer, Cham (2014). https://doi.org/10.1007/978-3-319-13500-7_1
27. Quinn, A.J., Bederson, B.B.: Human computation: a survey and taxonomy of a growing field. In: Proceedings of the SIGCHI Conference on Human Factors in Computing Systems, pp. 1403–1412. ACM (2011)
28. Hollan, J., Hutchins, E., Kirsh, D.: Distributed cognition: toward a new foundation for human-computer interaction research. ACM Trans. Comput.-Hum. Interact. (TOCHI) **7**, 174–196 (2000)
29. Hornecker, E., Buur, J.: Getting a grip on tangible interaction: a framework on physical space and social interaction. In: Proceedings of the SIGCHI Conference on Human Factors in Computing Systems, pp. 437–446. ACM (2006)
30. Kirsh, D.: Adapting the environment instead of oneself. Adapt. Behav. **4**, 415–452 (1996)
31. Harnad, S.: Open access scientometrics and the UK research assessment exercise. Scientometrics **79**, 147–156 (2009)
32. Ahmed, A.-I., Hasan, M.M.: A hybrid approach for decision making to detect breast cancer using data mining and autonomous agent based on human agent teamwork. In: 2014 17th International Conference on Computer and Information Technology (ICCIT), pp. 320–325. IEEE (2014)

Advances in Data Science and Analytics

ALDA: An Aggregated LDA for Polarity Enhanced Aspect Identification Technique in Mobile App Domain

Binil Kuriachan[1] and Nargis Pervin[2(✉)]

[1] Verizon Data Services, Chennai, India
[2] Indian Institute of Technology Madras, Chennai, India
nargisp@iitm.ac.in

Abstract. With the increased popularity of the smart mobile devices, mobile applications (a.k.a apps) have become essential. While the app developers face an extensive challenge to improve user satisfaction by exploiting the valuable feedbacks, the app users are overloaded with way too many apps. Extracting the valuable features from apps and mining the associated sentiments is of utmost importance for the app developers. Similarly, from the user perspective, the key preferences should be identified. This work deals with profiling users and apps using a novel LDA based aspect identification technique. Polarity aggregation technique is used to tag the weak features of the apps the developers should concentrate on. The proposed technique has been experimented on an Android review dataset to validate the efficacy compared to state-of-the-art algorithms. Experimental findings suggest superiority and applicability of our model in practical scenarios.

Keywords: Latent Dirichlet Allocation · App profiling · Mobile apps

1 Introduction

With the advent of Web 2.0, user generated content (reviews, blogs, etc.) has grown enormously. These publicly available user reviews about products have extensive impact on consumer decision making. Especially in the mobile app domain, app developers ought to be much more cautious in handling the dissatisfied app users. The reasons being multifaceted, firstly, mobile apps are inexpensive and easily substitutable in general. Secondly, the huge amount of reviews available makes it a daunting task for the developers to unravel the key aspects users are concerned of. On the other hand, the app users are facing immense information overload demanding a systematic construction of user profiles which would help to target users with personalized recommendations and real-time advertisements. An extremely rewarding scenario that would dramatically improve the performance is the consideration of timely and informative user feedbacks which would enable the fabrication of app profiles and help developers fix bugs, improve graphics, performances, etc. Although most of the app

© Springer International Publishing AG, part of Springer Nature 2018
S. Chatterjee et al. (Eds.): DESRIST 2018, LNCS 10844, pp. 187–204, 2018.
https://doi.org/10.1007/978-3-319-91800-6_13

stores have categorized the apps, problem is still not resolved as in top categories like Games, Tools, Entertainment, etc., the number of apps is gigantic. Several studies have been conducted to alleviate this problem by recommending the apps to the users using the download history, ratings, etc. [1]. However, the existing solutions do not take into consideration the opinions of the users about the apps and ignore the root cause of exasperation. This shows the problem relevance [2] and scope for further research [3] in this area.

In this study, we propose a text-mining based approach using Latent Dirichlet Allocation (LDA) [4] to profile mobile apps and its users that consist of respective key features. We conceptualize the problem as follows: first, from the massive set of user reviews, non-informative reviews are filtered out. Non-informative reviews are the ones which does not help developers to improve the apps. For example, *'The app is crap'* does not say much about the reason of disliking, whereas, the review *'The app consumes too much of battery'* conveys that the user is concerned about the battery life of mobile device. We build a classification model to segregate the informative reviews about apps. Next, LDA has been employed on text reviews aggregated at user and app levels separately. It should be noted that LDA models have been employed in each mobile app category distinctly as the features and associated concerns differ across categories. For example, users using game app might be concerned about speed, difficulty in levels, etc. while users using a travel app will be concerned about privacy settings, up to date information, interface usability, etc. Once the user and app profiles are generated, sentiment analysis has been performed on app aspects to identify the key features developers should focus on. The proposed model has been evaluated against the state-of-art algorithms (in both review classification and aspect identification stage) to demonstrate the efficacy of the proposed approach, *Aggregated LDA (ALDA)* using real mobile app review data collected from Android app store. The experimental findings reveal that *User Level LDA (ULDA)* and *Sentiment App Level LDA (SALDA)* can effectively identify key issues like connectivity, sound effects, memory card, etc. Compared to other methods, *ULDA* and *SALDA* show better predictive power and semantic coherence measured by perplexity and word-intrusion score, respectively.

The rest of the paper is structured as follows: literature pertaining to this work has been discussed in Sect. 2. Section 3 covers the solution overview followed by solution details in Sect. 4. Dataset used in this study is described in Sect. 5 and the experimental findings in Sect. 6. Finally, Sect. 7 concludes with future work recommendations.

2 Literature Review

We group the related works into two major categories as described below.

2.1 Review Classification

Reviews posted in the app marketplace contain latent information such as positive comments, suggestions, grievances about apps and its various features.

Hence, mining the unstructured data help us to identify the key aspects of the apps and concerns of the users. While app store has many reviews for most of the apps, majority of them are not much informative. For example, *'App not working'* doesn't tell us much about the feature user is concerned about and hence, it is not informative. However, the review *'Application consumes battery a lot'* is informative as it specifies the particular aspect, battery life. Several prior works have applied sentiment analysis on reviews to determine the semantic orientation [5–7] and polarity (positive or negative) for a given review. In another work done by Oh et al. [8], they focused on developer's point of view alone and treated reviews reporting issues alone as informative and others as non-informative. This method discards all the positive aspects which are useful in profiling both apps and users. In our work we classify user reviews into either informative or non-informative based on usefulness of content rather than polarity of reviews. A closely related work is reported by Chen et al. [9], in which they created a semi-supervised model to filter out non-informative reviews and then identified and ranked the key topics for individual apps. This strategy requires a distinct labeled dataset for each app. However, the usability of such method is limited in practical scenarios as manual annotation for each app is not feasible. To mitigate this issue, we build a L2 regularized logistic regression based classification model built for all apps together.

2.2 Aspect Identification

Considering the amount of reviews available, identifying the key aspects from the filtered out reviews is still a cumbersome process. Several approaches have been adopted by researchers for extracting key topics from the reviews. Based on app usage pattern of users, Yan and Chen [10] developed a collaborative filtering based recommender system. Even though basic details of apps and users are used for profiling, the latent features in app reviews are not considered. In another study by Ikeda et al. [11], tweets of users in Japanese language along with other community related information are used for identifying the demography of users using supervised text classification algorithm. To build the app profiles, prior studies [12] have employed certain linguistic rules and LDA [4] to identify feature requests and requirement demanded by the users. In particular, Galvis Carreño et al. [13] have proposed an Aspect Sentiment Unification Model to disclose requirement evolution from user reviews. But these works focus only on single app. Vu et al. [14] proposed a keyword based method for mining user opinions. Knowing the keyword is a prerequisite for this work and they do not focus on identifying the unknown aspects which are latent in the user reviews. In another study done by Liu et al. [15], they proposed a model to identify the sought after changes of apps and their respective sentiments from the reviews based on a hot entity discovery, but their work is focused only on entities which are occurring highly frequent among the reviews and moreover, this work doesn't consider the user level aspects. Our work can be differentiated from the prior works discussed in the preceding section in following aspects:

1. We aim to find the requirement related functionalities along with other latent aspects.
2. Aspect identification is a unified model where all the apps are considered together.
3. Profiling for both apps and users are executed and sentiment is integrated with app profiles to examine the efficacy of app features.

3   Solution Overview

3.1   Problem Formulation

We are given a set of r user comments $R = \{r_1, r_2, \ldots, r_n\}$ written by n users $\in U = \{u_1, u_2, \ldots, u_n\}$ for m apps $\in A = \{a_1, a_2, \ldots, a_m\}$. These are comments or user reviews that represent the user's key preferences about the apps. The aim of this study is to identify k_u key preferences/aspects for users U and k_i key aspects for applications I. Moreover, it is interesting to know which aspects of the apps are perceived positively or negatively. So overall, the goal is to:

1. generate personalized profile for users and apps over the k_u and k_i dimensions respectively.
2. find the sentiment associated with the app aspects.

However, all the reviews are not informative for others to assess about the apps. To profile the users and apps, we first filter out the non-informative app reviews. Next we aggregate the review text to user and app level and apply LDA [4] to identify the key aspects.

3.2   Latent Dirichlet Allocation

Topic modeling is a probabilistic model for identifying the hidden aspects or topics that occur in a collection of documents and to derive hidden patterns exhibited by the text corpus. It is an unsupervised approach used for identifying the group of words (called "topics") in large corpus of texts. The LDA model proposed by Blei et al. [4] is the most widely used algorithm for topic modeling. The model identifies distribution of probability over words for each topic, and further infers the distribution of each documents over topics. The interaction between hidden topic structure and observed documents is manifested in the probabilistic generative process associated with LDA. Let M, N, K, and V be the number of documents in a corpus, number of words in a document, number of topics, and the vocabulary size respectively. The notations $Dirichlet(\cdot)$ and $Multinomial(\cdot)$ represent Dirichlet and multinomial distribution with parameter $(\cdot)$ respectively. The notation β_k is the V -dimensional word distribution for topic k, and θ_d is the K-dimensional topic proportion for document d. The notation η and α represent the hyperparameters of the corresponding Dirichlet distribution. Figure 1 shows the graphical representation of LDA model [16] and the corresponding generative process [16] is shown as follows:

1. For each topic $k \in \{1, \ldots K\}$,
   (a) draw a distribution over vocabulary words
   $$\beta_k \sim Dirichlet(\eta)$$
2. For each document d,
   (a) draw a vector of topic proportions $\theta_d \sim Dirichlet(\alpha)$
   (b) For each word $w_{d,n}$ in document d,
      i. draw a topic assignment $z_{d,n} \sim Multinomial(\theta_d)$
      ii. draw a word $w_{d,n} \sim Multinomial(\beta_{z_{d,n}})$

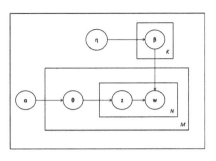

Fig. 1. Graphical model of LDA

4   Solution Details

The LDA based user and app profiling approach groups the reviews of apps posted by users to identify user an app specific aspects separately. The overview of the proposed approach has been presented in Fig. 2. The proposed approach consist of two main modules - (a) Classification Module, (b) Aspect Level Sentiment Generation Module. The first step is to clean and process the text reviews and second step is to filter out the non-informative reviews for which the review classification model is created. The reviews filtered using the classification model are then stored into *Filtered Review (FR)* database. It is worthy to note that the aspects for apps are very different for each category they belong to. For example, if an app belongs to *Games* category, aspect like speed, difficulty in levels of Game will be important, whereas if the app belongs to category like *Utilities*, the aspects will be very different from Games. Therefore, we envisage that, for each category of the apps, a separate LDA model should be executed. In the third step, informative reviews are grouped into user and app levels. LDA is applied to the preprocessed grouped data to identify the key aspects. Further, the associated sentiments are generated for each aspect. The steps are described in details below.

4.1   Review Cleaning

Preprocessing of text is vital for the performance when it comes to identifying key information from the text, exploratory text analysis, etc. [17]. In the real user text data, one needs to deal with misspelled words, for e.g., 'aaawwwwsssss-soooooommmmeeee', 'bbbeeeessstttt', 'batery', etc. Since many of those words either capture the aspects or sentiments, transforming them to the correct form is of utmost importance. As a first step in cleaning the review, spell correction has been carried out using a simple heuristic as shown below.

1. For each review $r \in R$
2. $tokens \leftarrow WordTokenize(r)$

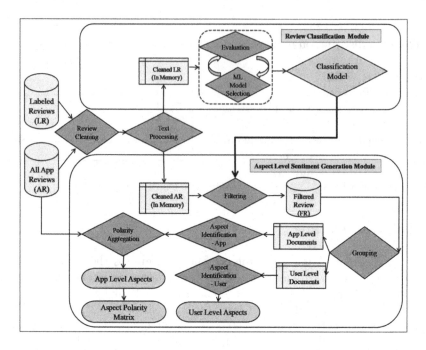

Fig. 2. Overview of proposed method

(a) For each token $t \in tokens$
 i. Remove more than two consecutive occurrence of character
 ii. identify best suggested word using *Hunspell* [18]

Next, stop words [19] are removed from the review corpus. User reviews as well contains many domain specific terms, for e.g., the brand of phone, model number, etc. Such words are replaced with its most common general form using a bag-of-word approach. So, occurrences like 'samsung', 'htc', etc. are replaced as 'device'. Name of the apps are also removed from the corpus as part of cleaning. Cleaned reviews are stored into in-memory storage.

4.2 Text Processing

The cleaned text reviews are fed to the text processing module. Each review is tokenized to sentences and Part-Of-Speech (POS) tagger [19] has been used to tag the correct POS for each word. POS except noun, verb, adjective and adverb are removed from the text data as they contribute little to understand the meaning and context of the reviews [20]. Further lemmatization [21] and stemming [22] has been performed to get the root words. The whole corpus has been weighted using Term Frequency-Inverse Document Frequency (TF-IDF) [23]. In the TF-IDF representation, Inverse Document Frequency (IDF) is used to normalize the Term Frequency(TF) of each word. IDF normalization helps to penalize the weights of common words in the corpus. This process reduces the importance of words which are common and give importance to the rare words across the document collection.

4.3   Review Classification

In this step, our goal is to create a classifier that can automatically identify and filter out non-informative reviews. Informative reviews corresponds to the ones that have constructive information about the app and non-informative is the vice-versa. In order to filter out the non-informative reviews, a classification model is created. In the work done by Chen et al. [9], Expectation Maximization Naive Baye's was used to classify app reviews which used a semi-supervised technique. The method had been experimentally validated with four apps where for each app, a separate model was created. Applications of such method in practice is limited as the number of apps is huge and annotating the train set for each app is not practically feasible. In our study, we have used the dataset provided by Chen et al. [9] which has reviews of different apps along with the label indicating whether the review is informative or no-informative. We have focused on building a more generalized model which is trained on historical labeled data using machine learning techniques and can filter out the non-informative reviews of all apps at once. In this study, all the labeled reviews provided in the dataset are combined together to create a single and large corpus (Table 1).

For creating the classification model, unigrams and bigrams are created from the cleaned review and then weighted using TF-IDF as the first step. Next, count of noun, verb, adjective, and adverb is computed for each review text and added along with the length of the raw review to create the feature matrix. For building the classifier, different machine learning classification models namely Support Vector Machines (SVM), Logistic Regression with L2

Table 1. Informative and non-informative reviews

Class	Real example
Non-informative	This is the best game ever
Non-informative	I love this game!!!
Non-informative	Can i have my money back
Non-informative	Frustrating, fun, addictive!
Informative	It's freezing
Informative	App closes all the time and progress is lost
Informative	Great game but force close since last update
Informative	Level advertising make game crash

regularization, and Naive Baye's which are popular in text classification problems are evaluated. Based on experimental findings, logistic regression model with L2 regularization penalty value 5 is chosen as the final model which is discussed in the Sect. 6.

4.4   Aspect Level Sentiment Generation

In this module, we discuss about the aspect identification and polarity aggregation. As a first step, non-informative reviews are filtered out using the classification model created in the Sect. 4.3. Filtered reviews are then grouped into user and app level for aspect identification. User level aspects provide the key concerns or preferences of each user. However, aspects identified at app level are further processed to measure the sentiment polarity which gives the sentiment distribution of reviews for each features or functionalities of the app.

Filtering. After creating the classifier model as explained in Sect. 4.3, it has been used to filter out non-informative review records of all apps. As a result, from a total of 1048576 review records, we retain 181630 informative reviews (17.32%). The reviews are then stored into database for further processing.

Group Reviews. App developers can place their apps in specific categories like Games, Entertainment, etc. which is available on the mobile app marketplace. User reviews provide the latent preferences of users as well as apps. To profile the users and apps using LDA, we define the document for each of these two models in an aggregated level. Let $R_{u_i} \in R$ be the reviews authored by user $u_i \in U$. We merge R_{u_i} into a single document. In this process, $|R|$ number of reviews are grouped in $|U|$ documents. Similarly, let $R_{a_i} \in R$ be the reviews for app $a_i \in A$. We merge R_{a_i} into a single document reducing the document space to $|A|$ documents. It should be noted that for both users and apps, we want to profile separately. Hence the merging processes are independent for these two operations.

Aspect Identification. In this step, we identify the key aspects present in the reviews at both app and user level separately. Aspect identification at the user level generates the latent aspects or preferences of users. Likewise, app level aspects give the preferences or functionalities of apps. The common aspects occurring at both levels help us to analyze further how app's features or functionalities match with user's preferences. In order to identify the key topics, we use LDA [4], a probabilistic model which is one of the most widely used unsupervised learning method for text mining. In contrast to supervised learning methods which assume a predefined set of categories, unsupervised learning methods learn underlying features of text without defining the categories explicitly. Unlike clustering which assumes each category as exclusive, in topic modeling, a topic is defined by a group of words with each word in the group having a probability of occurrence for the given topic, and different topics have their respective group of words along with corresponding probabilities. In LDA, each document is considered as a mixture of topics and each word in a document is considered randomly drawn from document's topics. The topics are or latent which is uncovered via analyzing joint distribution to compute the conditional distribution of hidden variables (topics) given the observed variables, i.e., words in documents. From a collection of document, LDA infers per word topic assignment, per document topic proportion, and per corpus topic distribution. The process for identifying user and apps is described below.

1. For each user $u_i \in U$
   (a) merge all reviews given by u_i as single document //user level

2. For each app $a_i \in A$
   (a) merge all reviews received a_i as single document //app level
3. Compute LDA with user level documents
4. Compute LDA with app level documents

Labeling Topics. The topics learned by the model need to be labeled before using so that we could understand what each topic measures. Automatic labeling methods are not suitable for our study as it requires domain knowledge (mobile apps related). In topic modeling, it has become customary to manually label topics ensuring better labeling quality.

Algorithm 1. Polarity Aggregation

Input: Topics T, Words W, Topic-Word distribution Matrix $TWM_{W \times T}$, Aggregated Reviews at app level R
Output: Aspect Polarity Matrix $APM_{R \times T}$

```
 1: Initialize [APM_{R×T}] ← NULL
 2: for r ∈ R do
 3:     for s ∈ SentenceTokenize(r) do
 4:         Initialize topic, prob ← 0
 5:         polarity ← PolarityIdentification(s) [24]
 6:         tokens ← WordTokenize(s)
 7:         CommonTokenVector ← W
 8:         for ct ∈ CommonTokenVector do //Create (W × 1) vector of 0 and 1
 9:             if ct ∈ tokens then
10:                 ct ← 1
11:             else
12:                 ct ← 0
13:             end if
14:         end for
15:         Prob_{1×T} ← trans(CommonTokenVector_{W×1}) × TWM_{W×T}
16:         topic ← argmax(Prob)
17:         APM_{r,topic}.sentiment ← APM_{r,t}.sentiment + polarity
18:     end for
19: end for
```

Polarity Aggregation. In this step, we identify the polarity of app level reviews for each aspects being identified and aggregate them. We have used dictionary based sentiment classifier [24] to identify the polarity of reviews at sentence level. TextBlob, a python implementation of sentiment detection task returns polarity score within the range $[-1.0, 1.0]$ where value less than 0.0 is negative and greater than 0.0 is positive. In this step, for each sentence of the reviews, sentiment is identified and then the topic closely associated with the sentence is determined. Next, sentiment polarity is aggregated to the identified topic. The sentiment values for aspects corresponding to each apps are stored as *Aspect Polarity Matrix, APM*.

Algorithm 1 explains the process of identifying and aggregating polarity of aspects. Sentiment of review is identified at sentence level after tokenizing each review text into sentences [line numbers 2–5]. Next, a matrix of dimension $W \times 1$ is created by assigning values 1 and 0 whereas 1 implies topic-word is present in current sentence and 0, otherwise [line numbers 6–14] where W represents the set of all words in the corpus. For each sentence, we need to identify the closely associated topic which can be conceptualized as the set of words in a sentence which attain highest probability in a topic. In order to do so, we sum the topic-word probability of matching words in the sentence for each topic and the one having highest value is selected [line numbers 15–16]. Once topic is determined, polarity value is aggregated to the $r, topic$ entry of aspect polarity matrix where r represent the review record and *topic* corresponds to the topic.

5 Dataset Description

Table 2 shows the statistics of labeled review dataset. Our proposed algorithm executes in two levels: first we segregate the informative reviews from the non-informative ones. Secondly, we identify the aspects and associated sentiment from the reviews. In the first stage, to train the model, a

Table 2. Statistics of labeled review dataset

Dataset	SwiftKey	Facebook	Temple Run2	TapFish
Train	1000	1000	1000	1000
Test	2000	2000	2000	2000

labeled dataset containing 9000 reviews obtained from [9] has been used. Labels of the dataset indicate whether the review is informative or non-informative. In the second stage, we use a mobile app review dataset [25] of 21624 mobile apps with AppID, UserID, app rating, textual review etc. Without loss of generality, we have considered only the 'Games' category for identifying the aspects and polarity. From the selected category, we have taken applications which have received at least 1000 reviews and for those with more than 2000, a random sample of 1500 reviews is taken for our analysis.

6 Experimental Details

Comprehensive experiments are conducted to evaluate our proposed approach. First, we describe the filtering process where a classification model is created to filter out non-informative reviews. Second, we compare our proposed method for aspect identification with two benchmark models, original LDA and Local LDA. Finally, we evaluate the polarity associated with the identified aspects.

6.1 Experimental Settings

For this study, Windows 10 operating system with 8 GB RAM has been used. Python 3.5 is used for text preprocessing and creating review classification model while R 3.4.2 is used for topic modeling.

6.2 Review Classification

The first task is to filter the non-informative reviews for which we build a classification model using machine learning techniques namely L2 regularized Logistic Regression (LRL2), SVM and Naive Bayes. To identify the best classifier, we train each of these three models separately on dataset mentioned earlier [9] and evaluate using standard metrics as mentioned below

$$Precision = \frac{(TP)}{(TP + FP)}, \; Recall = \frac{(TP)}{(TP + FN)}$$

$$Accuracy = \frac{(TP + TN)}{(TP + FP + TN + FN)}, \; F\text{-}Measure = \frac{(2 * Precision * Recall)}{(Precision + Recall)})$$
(1)

where TP, FP, TN and FN represent the number of true positives, false positives, true negatives and false negatives respectively. Figure 3 depicts the variation of F-measure for different values of L2 penalty. From the plot it is evident that F-Measure attains its highest value for L2 penalty = 5.

Experiments have been conducted on the models as shown in Table 3 and respective F-Measures are compared. Results show that for all the four apps, F-Measure is the highest for logistic regression with l2 regularization. Other evaluation metrics have been shown in the Table 4 for logistic model. Therefore, we choose LRL2 as the classifier model for informative review filtering. It should be noted that this experiment as well depicts the superiority of this approach compared to EMNB presented by Chen et al. [9]. Also [9] presented one model for each app

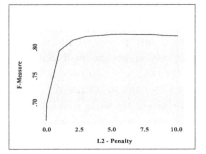

Fig. 3. Logistic regression with L2 regularization

which limits the applicability in the practical scenario. On the other hand, LRL2 performs consistently good even on the combined model with F-Measure = 0.83

Table 3. Model comparison with F-measure

	All reviews	Facebook	Temple Run2	SwiftKey	Tap Fish
LRL2	0.83	0.885	0.831	0.77	0.789
SVM	0.81	0.884	0.813	0.721	0.788
Naive Bayes	0.8	0.844	0.815	0.727	0.748
EMNB	NA	0.877	0.797	0.764	0.761

Table 4 shows a detailed performance metrics of LRL2 which include precision, recall, accuracy, and f-measure on each apps individually and combined.

Table 4. L2 regularized logistic regression

	All reviews	Facebook	Temple Run2	SwiftKey	Tap Fish
F-measure	0.83	0.885	0.831	0.77	0.789
Precision	0.806	0.875	0.843	0.745	0.744
Recall	0.86	0.892	0.818	0.795	0.84
Accuracy	0.873	0.877	0.89	0.855	0.897

6.3 Aspect Level Sentiment Generation

Filtering. LRL2 has been employed as the classifier to filter out the non-informative reviews yielding a F-Measure of 0.79. From a total of 1048576 review records 181630 are identified as informative which is 17.32% of the total reviews.

Aspect Identification. After filtering out non-informative reviews, common aspects in the reviews are identified using Latent Dirichlet Allocation across apps and user level. Aspects at app and user level give the key topics being discussed with respect to the apps as well as the user perspective. In this study, we have compared our proposed method with review level LDA and local LDA [26], respectively. In review level LDA, each review is considered as a single document. In local LDA, each sentence is considered as one document. In app level, reviews received by each application is considered as one document while in user level, reviews given by each user is one document. Figure 4 shows the word cloud of app, user, review and local LDA corpus. Size of words in the word cloud correspond to relative frequency of their occurrence. From the picture, it is clear that many instances of words like time, level, update, load, freeze, player, etc. are very frequent in all the corpus.

Herein, we aim to identify important aspects from large set of reviews using LDA, an unsupervised text clustering technique. The metrics to evaluate the quality of the topics generated have been discussed below.

– Perplexity

The standard assessment of topic models involves measuring how well the model performs when unseen documents are predicted. More specifically, a model trained on a set of documents should give high probability while testing on held-out documents. One of the most common metric used in language models to measure the predictive power is perplexity [27], which is the probability of test set normalized by the number of words. It can be understood as the predicted number of equally likely words for a word position on average, and is a monotonically decreasing function of the log-likelihood. Thus, a lower perplexity over a held-out document is equivalent to a higher log-likelihood, which indicates better predictive performance. For a test data or unseen set of M documents, the per-word perplexity is defined as

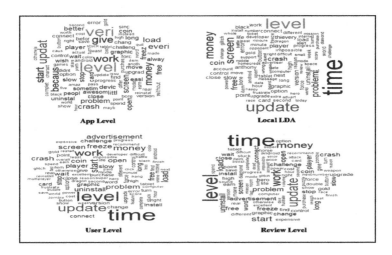

Fig. 4. Word cloud of app, local, user and review level LDA

$$Perplexity(test) = exp\left(- \sum_{d=1}^{M} \frac{log\ p(w_d)}{\sum_{d=1}^{M} N_d} \right) \qquad (2)$$

where N_d is the number of words in document d.

– Word Intrusion

For measuring the quality of topics, the most important indicator is the semantic coherence of words present in each topic. For a topic, semantic coherence can be understood as how well a topic is represented by a set of words and understood by human subject. In order to measure the semantic coherence quantitatively, word intrusion task designed by Chang and Chien [28] is used. In the word intrusion task, the subject is provided with six randomly ordered words with an intruder word not present in the topic. The task of subject is to identify the intruder word. An intruder word is selected at random from a pool of words with low probability in the current topic but high probability in some other topic so as to ensure that the intruder is not rejected solely due to rarity. All six words are then shuffled and presented to the subjects. The model precision MP_m^k of the kth topic inferred by model m in word intrusion task is defined as the fraction of subjects agreeing with model

$$MP_m^k = \frac{1}{S} \sum_s I(i_{k,s}^m = w_k^m) \qquad (3)$$

where $i_{k,s}^m$ is the intruder word selected by subject s among S subjects, w_k^m is the actual intruder word, and $I(\cdot)$ is an indicator function. $I(\cdot) = 1$ if condition holds true and 0 otherwise.

Selecting Topic Number: In order to identify the key aspects from the reviews, we are using LDA which is parametric and topic number should be given. The most challenging part in unsupervised learning is determining the number of clusters (here, topics). Though there are methods which automatically identify the number of clusters using statistical fit like perplexity, multiple studies [28, 29] show that, statistical fit alone is not an ideal choice and rather suggested to take in account both statistical as well as sub-

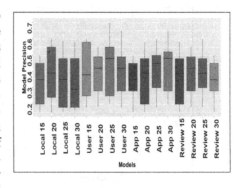

Fig. 5. Model precision for word intrusion

stantiate fit (semantic coherence). Choosing topic number by perplexity relies solely on the predictive power alone of the model, but our goal is to identify the latent aspects which are semantically relevant. For this task, we use substantiate fit which involves human judgment. Since measuring the substantiate fit is time consuming, we have used perplexity value to limit the number of models to be evaluated. Herein, we have measured the perplexity values of held-out documents and used those values to reduce the set of models that needs to be evaluated for semantic coherence. Figure 6 shows the perplexity value of held-out documents with different topic number for each LDA models. For all of the models, change in the perplexity values are very minimal after topics 15. Hence, we perform substantiate fit for numbers in the range of 15 to 30 as perplexity value is almost steady after topic 30.

Figure 5 shows box-plots of four model's (*Local, User level, App Level* and *Review Level LDA*) precision with different topics. It is clear from the plot that *User Level LDA* which has each user's review combined and the *Aapp level LDA* where reviews received by each app aggregated separately perform better than *Local LDA* and *Review Level LDA* with 25 and 30 topics respectively.

Aspects are identified using *User* and *App level LDA*. Aspects identified from *App Level LDA* is further used to measure the sentiment polarity with respect to each of them.

Figures 7 and 8 shows random 4 aspects identified using *User* and *App Level LDA*, respectively. Each aspect is represented by list of words in the barchart. One can easily note that many of them are common. While User Level LDA renders the key preferences by user, *App Level LDA* delineates general opinion of all the users using that app. For example, the aspect 'Graphics & Control' in *User Level LDA* shows that some users are concerned about the particular feature which can be inferred from the topic probability distribution. On the other hand, 'Graphics & Control' in *App level LDA* indicates a large number of users is discussing about that feature. To know the sentiment associated with this aspect, polarity aggregation step has been performed as discussed below.

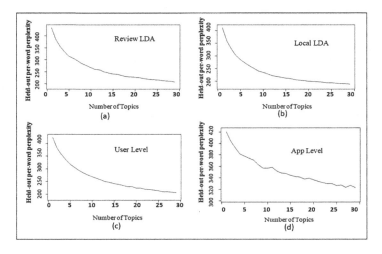

Fig. 6. Held-out per-word perplexity vs number of topics of (a) app level, (b) user level, (c) review level and (d) local LDA

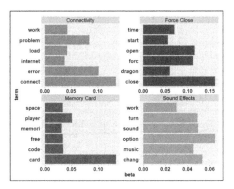

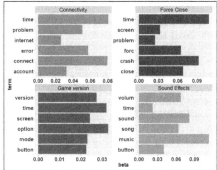

Fig. 7. User level - topics   **Fig. 8.** App level - topics

Polarity Aggregation. Aspects of *App level LDA* is further processed to identify the sentiment polarity. For measuring the sentiment of the review sentence, we have used a dictionary based sentiment classifier implementation of TextBlob [24]. Polarity is identified for each sentence of the review. After identifying the polarity, we have associated it with the closest aspect. Table 5 shows a sample result of app level polarity aggregated matrix normalized to the number of sentences in the reviews. It shows the sentiment distribution for 5 random topics which are selected from the available 30 aspects. Each row in the table shows sentiment polarity distribution of aspects for individual app. The value in the parenthesis represent the positive and negative sentiment for each aspect, respectively. For example, the third review in Table 5 discusses about the annoying advertisements in a game app. It is evident from the review text that the users of the app are dissatisfied with this particular aspect which is captured in the polarity aggregation technique with negative sentiment score $= 0.18$. It can be explained similarly for the other two reviews.

Table 5. Sample of app polarity matrix normalized by number of sentences

No:	Review snippet	Topics			
		Force close	Game version	Sound effects	Advertisement
1	App frequently exits without any error message on my device, frustrating. Tablet running the latest version of the original rom. Please fix this in next update...	(0.01, 0.15)	(0.15, 0.18)	(0.00, 0.00)	(0.00, 0.00)
2	Screwed up my sound card, now bad touchscreen sounds. Poor volume...	(0.01, 0.07)	(0.02, 0.05)	(0.04, 0.15)	(0.01, 0.06)
3	Too many seizure triggering flashing advert. The adds are very annoying i don't want to keep winning each game...	(0.00, 0.00)	(0.00, 0.07)	(0.00, 0.00)	(0.01, 0.18)

7   Conclusion and Future Work

Considering the vast amount of reviews available in the app marketplace, both users and app require personalized profiles. Prior works on app profiling have mainly constructed models on single app which lacks generalizability and applicability in practical scenarios. In this work we proposed an Aggregated LDA (*ALDA*) for apps (*SALDA*) and users (*ULDA*), separately. Unlike local LDA model which considers topic modeling at sentence level, this approach aggregates reviews for an app as a single document in *ALDA* and groups reviews for users as a single document in *SALDA*. Moreover, sentiment has been associated at aspect level for mobile apps. This in turn improves the interpretability of the identified topics. Experimental findings on a mobile app review dataset collected from Android app store demonstrate that *SALDA* and *ULDA* can effectively identify the latent topics. In future work, we plan to apply the user and app profiles to improve the personalized app recommendations. The model will further be applied on different app categories to understand how user requirements vary across popular categories in app store.

References

1. Ruiz, I.M., Nagappan, M., Adams, B., Berger, T., Dienst, S., Hassan, A.: An examination of the current rating system used in mobile app stores. IEEE Softw. **33**(6), 86–92 (2017)
2. Von Alan, R.H., March, S.T., Park, J., Ram, S.: Design science in information systems research. MIS Q. **28**(1), 75–105 (2004)
3. Gregor, S., Jones, D.: The anatomy of a design theory. J. Assoc. Inf. Syst. **8**(5), 312 (2007)
4. Blei, D.M., Ng, A.Y., Jordan, M.I.: Latent Dirichlet allocation. J. Mach. Learn. Res. **3**(Jan), 993–1022 (2003)
5. Guzman, E., Maalej, W.: How do users like this feature? A fine grained sentiment analysis of app reviews. In: 2014 IEEE 22nd International Requirements Engineering Conference (RE), pp. 153–162. IEEE (2014)
6. Fu, B., Lin, J., Li, L., Faloutsos, C., Hong, J., Sadeh, N.: Why people hate your app: making sense of user feedback in a mobile app store. In: Proceedings of the 19th ACM SIGKDD International Conference on Knowledge Discovery and Data Mining, pp. 1276–1284. ACM (2013)
7. Panichella, S., Di Sorbo, A., Guzman, E., Visaggio, C.A., Canfora, G., Gall, H.C.: How can I improve my app? Classifying user reviews for software maintenance and evolution. In: 2015 IEEE International Conference on Software Maintenance and Evolution (ICSME), pp. 281–290. IEEE (2015)
8. Oh, J., Kim, D., Lee, U., Lee, J.G., Song, J.: Facilitating developer-user interactions with mobile app review digests. In: CHI 2013 Extended Abstracts on Human Factors in Computing Systems, pp. 1809–1814. ACM (2013)
9. Chen, N., Lin, J., Hoi, S.C., Xian, X., Zhang, B.: AR-miner: mining informative reviews for developers from mobile app marketplace. In: Proceesings of the 36th International Conference on Software Engineering, pp. 767–778. ACM (2014)
10. Yan, B., Chen, G.: AppJoy: personalized mobile application discovery. In: Proceedings of the 9th International Conference on Mobile Systems, Applications, and Services, pp. 113–126. ACM (2011)
11. Ikeda, K., Hattori, G., Ono, C., Asoh, H., Higashino, T.: Twitter user profiling based on text and community mining for market analysis. Knowl.-Based Syst. **51**, 35–47 (2013)
12. Iacob, C., Harrison, R.: Retrieving and analyzing mobile apps feature requests from online reviews. In: Proceedings of the 10th Working Conference on Mining Software Repositories, pp. 41–44. IEEE Press (2013)
13. Galvis Carreño, L.V., Winbladh, K.: Analysis of user comments: an approach for software requirements evolution. In: Proceedings of the 2013 International Conference on Software Engineering, pp. 582–591. IEEE Press (2013)
14. Vu, P.M., Nguyen, T.T., Pham, H.V., Nguyen, T.T.: Mining user opinions in mobile app reviews: a keyword-based approach (t). In: 2015 30th IEEE/ACM International Conference on Automated Software Engineering (ASE), pp. 749–759. IEEE (2015)

15. Liu, Y., Li, Y., Guo, Y., Zhang, M.: Stratify mobile app reviews: E-LDA model based on hot "entity" discovery. In: 2016 12th International Conference on Signal-Image Technology & Internet-Based Systems (SITIS), pp. 581–588. IEEE (2016)
16. Bao, Y., Datta, A.: Simultaneously discovering and quantifying risk types from textual risk disclosures. Manag. Sci. **60**(6), 1371–1391 (2014)
17. Srividhya, V., Anitha, R.: Evaluating preprocessing techniques in text categorization. Int. J. Comput. Sci. Appl. **47**(11), 49–51 (2010)
18. Németh, L.: Hunspell. Dostupno na: http://hunspell.sourceforge.net/. Accessed 01 Oct 2013 (2010)
19. Bird, S., Loper, E.: NLTK: the natural language toolkit. In: Proceedings of the ACL 2004 on Interactive Poster and Demonstration Sessions, p. 31. Association for Computational Linguistics (2004)
20. Feldman, R., Sanger, J.: The Text Mining Handbook: Advanced Approaches in Analyzing Unstructured Data. Cambridge University Press, Cambridge (2007)
21. Miller, G.A.: WordNet: a lexical database for English. Commun. ACM **38**(11), 39–41 (1995)
22. Porter, M.F.: Snowball: a language for stemming algorithms (2001)
23. Ramos, J., et al.: Using TF-IDF to determine word relevance in document queries. In: Proceedings of the First Instructional Conference on Machine Learning, vol. 242, pp. 133–142 (2003)
24. Loria, S., Keen, P., Honnibal, M., Yankovsky, R., Karesh, D., Dempsey, E., et al.: TextBlob: simplified text processing. Secondary TextBlob Simplified Text Processing (2014)
25. Chen, N., Hoi, S.C., Li, S., Xiao, X.: SimApp: a framework for detecting similar mobile applications by online kernel learning. In: Proceedings of the Eighth ACM International Conference on Web Search and Data Mining, pp. 305–314. ACM (2015)
26. Brody, S., Elhadad, N.: An unsupervised aspect-sentiment model for online reviews. In: Human Language Technologies: The 2010 Annual Conference of the North American Chapter of the Association for Computational Linguistics, pp. 804–812. Association for Computational Linguistics (2010)
27. Azzopardi, L., Girolami, M., van Risjbergen, K.: Investigating the relationship between language model perplexity and IR precision-recall measures. In: Proceedings of the 26th Annual International ACM SIGIR Conference on Research and Development in Information Retrieval, pp. 369–370. ACM (2003)
28. Chang, Y.L., Chien, J.T.: Latent Dirichlet learning for document summarization. In: IEEE International Conference on Acoustics, Speech and Signal Processing, ICASSP 2009, pp. 1689–1692. IEEE (2009)
29. Grimmer, J., Stewart, B.M.: Text as data: the promise and pitfalls of automatic content analysis methods for political texts. Polit. Anal. **21**(3), 267–297 (2013)

Development of a Data-Driven Business Model Transformation Tool

Dominik Augenstein[(⊠)], Christian Fleig, and Alexander Maedche

Karlsruhe Institute of Technology (KIT),
Institute of Information Systems and Marketing (IISM), Karlsruhe, Germany
dominik.augenstein@kit.edu

Abstract. Rapidly changing environments and customer demands force companies to transform their business models in ever shorter periods of time. However, existing approaches like the business model canvas and corresponding tools mainly focus on documentation on a strategic level and do not actively support the business model transformation process from a current state towards a target state. To address this problem, we derive requirements for a business model transformation tool. We translate these requirements into design principles and present a toolset for data-driven business model transformation. This toolset enables companies to extract status quo business models from existing operational information systems. Furthermore, it allows the representation of explicit relationships between the different value dimensions of a business model and enables quantifying the impact of changes. The result of this paper is a set of requirements, design principles as well as a tool instantiation, which can actively support the business model transformation process.

Keywords: Business model · Transformation · Design science

1 Introduction

Increasing global competition and new challenges driven by a growing number of services and digitalization force companies to adjust their business models (BM) steadily to the new environment. The combination of traditional products with (digital) services becomes more and more important for companies. As consumers are more than ever able to compare products and services on the markets, companies have to rethink their traditional way of doing business [1]. Thus, companies increasingly redesign their BMs and focus on digital services [2]. To support business modelling in general, several methods, techniques and tools exist [3]. The most well-known is the Business Model Canvas (BMC) by Osterwalder [4].

Although BMs have been intensively investigated in the information systems discipline as well as strategic management, entrepreneurship and marketing, there is still a gap with regards to the question how actual transformation of BMs can be better supported [5]. Having a closer look at the often cited BMC by Osterwalder, it becomes obvious that the focus of the concept is rather strategic and less focused on the operationalization of the defined BMs [4]. Thus, different advancements and frameworks have been suggested to make the concept more operational [3, 6]. Zott et al. [7]

© Springer International Publishing AG, part of Springer Nature 2018
S. Chatterjee et al. (Eds.): DESRIST 2018, LNCS 10844, pp. 205–217, 2018.
https://doi.org/10.1007/978-3-319-91800-6_14

further mention the need of an increased flexibility in BMs to improve the support for transformation processes. As a result, the knowledge of BM transformation (BMT) can be used by practitioners. This knowledge can be used to extend the current BM concepts from the strategic level to the operational level. This is because current BM concepts like the BM canvas [8] or the BM cube [6] are inflexible in the way that these concepts focus mainly on the strategic view of a company [8]. In sum, most of these models provide guidance rather on a higher abstraction level, like the BMC as a first outline of the planned value creation in a start-up phase. IS research started to link the operational level to the rather strategic BM level and emphasizes the importance of making BMs more operational for example through considering the dependencies of lower levels [9, 10]. Implementing a higher degree of operationalization in existing BM concepts would support a better comprehension of the transformation process [5]. Having a look at strategy execution research, Richardson [11] stresses the need of supporting the execution of strategic frameworks. He further claims, that a BM is neither a strategy nor a table of actions to execute the strategy (see also [9, 12]). The key question is, how to make BMs more executable, considering operational levels in organizations to emphasize the path from strategy to execution [7, 13]. In particular, there is a need to develop a framework, which supports a transformation through clear rules. So, in this work we want to answer the question:

What are relevant meta-requirements and design principles for business model transformation tools and how can they be instantiated?

To answer this question, we follow a design science research (DSR) approach. In this paper, we first describe conceptual foundations (Sect. 2). In Sect. 3, we elaborate on the underlying DSR methodology and specifically describe the activities performed in cycle 1 of the entire DSR project. Sect. 4 presents the meta-requirements and design principles. Subsequently, we give an overview about the instantiation of the design principles in a concrete business transformation toolset (Sect. 5) and provide an outlook and a final conclusion (Sect. 6).

2   Conceptual Foundations

2.1   Business Model Tools

Business models (BM) focus on providing a transparent representation of how a company actually creates value [16]. For Timmers [17], a BM is "an architecture for the product, service and information flows, including a description of the various business actors and their roles; and a description of the potential benefits for the various actors; and description of the sources of revenue". Facing disruptive changes, companies can influence such changes through extensive adjustments of their BMs [17]. Existing approaches try to support this through a representation of the value creation process of a company [16] and facilitating a mediation between strategic and operational levels [9]. However, actual support for this mediation process is lacking [3]. Contemporary business model research focuses on the challenge by adapting business models according to disruptive situations [18]. Both in practice and theory, the aim is to demonstrate the interaction of business model components and the development of the entire business model so that changes in the environment and the associated development can be viewed better [15].

Osterwalder's ontology for BMs [4] and the related book [8] is most likely the most visible framework in research and practice. Today, more than twenty BM frameworks with various purposes of use and field of study exist [15]. Specifically, scholars added further dimensions to transform the one-dimensional BMC to a multidimensional cube. In this cube concept, the categories of the BMC are reorganized in a way, that they show relations and support BM implementations [6]. A practical tool, which is using this BM cube, is for example the "NEFFICS platform" [19]. This reflects the logic, how value is created in more detail, but also requiring higher modelling effort [6]. The basic idea of this tool is to make the entire model more operational and allow connections between the different elements of the model [20]. However, these extensions and improvements come at the expense of simplicity, which is provided through the established BM canvas [8]. An adequate tool should therefore consider the principles of operationalization as well as simplicity.

2.2   Business Model Transformation

In general, we define business model transformation (BMT) as a transformation process of the value creation caused by external or internal changes [18]. Especially, disruptive changes can affect companies in a way that they have to adapt and change their BMs significantly [15]. For this definition of BMT, we adapt the definition of Lindgardt et al. [21] for BM innovation (BMI): "A business model consists of two essential elements – the value proposition and the operating model – each of which has three sub-elements. [...] Innovation becomes BMI when two or more elements of a business model are reinvented". However, if at least one element changes, one has to adapt the BM, which we define as BMT. Consequently, BMI is part of BMT when the value creation changes tremendously [22].

Three kinds of resource flows in BMs are considered: Flow of goods, representing the way of products, ownership and risk; flow of information as well as flow of funds [23, 24]. In the BMC, the categories "Key Activities" and "Key Resources" build partial models, which have interlinks between each other, because the resources are used in the activities or at least address the same questions of customer relationship and revenue streams [8]. The intention in practice as well as in theory is to show the interaction of BM parts and the development of the whole BM, so changes in the environment and the related development can be understood better [15]. This means for BMT, that the user should not only have an idea of the value creation process, but also should understands the individual partial models. This understanding is not only necessary at one single point of time, but during the entire transformation process. Scholars in BMI are aware of this requirement: They propose information about the flow of goods, information and funds as design elements and consider effects of the corresponding activities in the business model innovation process [18, 26]. As a result, the implementation of BMI using a transformation tool should follow a systematic management process [18, 22]. Thus, business model comprehension should be enabled for the corresponding users of the BMT tool during the whole transformation process.

Existing approaches try to provide a clear and transparent representation of how a company creates value [16, 27, 28]. However, they come with limitations with regards to the end-to-end perspective. An advanced BM tool should take into account the current and target state of a company and orientate itself on the processes at the operational level [3].

3 Methodology

We follow the Design Science Research framework suggested by Vaishnavi and Kuechler [29]. The overall DSR project consists of two design cycles as depicted in Fig. 1. In our research we specifically target real-world-challenges of companies in the manufacturing industries. In particular, we put a specific focus on the implementation of strategic changes of their organization triggered by changes in the BM. We tightly cooperate with industry partners in this DSR project. Each design cycle consists of a problem awareness phase to determine the needs for a comprehensive BMT tool to overcome the weaknesses of current approaches. In this paper, we specifically focus on the **first design cycle** and discover requirements and design principles for a BMT tool through the analysis of real-world cases research complemented with a literature study. The second design cycle will build on the first design cycle and deliver a complete software artefact for BMT.

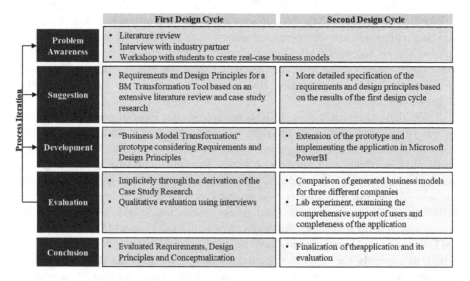

Fig. 1. DSR cycles based on Vaishnavi and Kuechler [29]

We suggest meta-requirements and design principles based on existing literature and interviews with industry partners. Furthermore, we perform a qualitative validation of the identified design principles by investigating real-world- transformation cases.

Case studies are investigations of "contemporary real-life phenomenon through detailed contextual analysis of a limited number of events or conditions, and their relationships" [30]. Studying companies, for instance by means of a customer database, and generalizing the results is a common approach. Specifically, we leverage real-world cases to validate our identified design principles. Focus of these cases is the transformation of an existing BM. We select a wide range of cases from the manufacturing sector. We focus on this sector, because for us the comparability between companies of the same sector is higher than across different sectors. The main information of the transformation in the cases is derived from public available reports [31–37]. Additionally, information is derived from public Web pages, publications of the companies and business performance reports. The companies are located all over the world, e.g. United States, India or Europe. A majority of the cases is from the automotive sector, but the rest is spread in other fields of manufacturing. Therefore, we want to guarantee a higher generalizability of the results.

4   Suggestion Phase

In this section we describe the meta-requirements and design principles for a BMT tool. As mentioned above, a BMT tool in general should demand the two mentioned main needs: Getting an objective overview of the current situation and supporting users throughout the entire transformation process.

4.1   Requirements for BM Transformation Tools

We proposed five requirements (RQ) for business model transformation tools. Three requirements focus on extracting the status quo business models from existing organizational information systems and two for supporting the actual BMT process. As mentioned earlier the use of the BMC is quite common in companies. However, BMC's are created top-down and therefore contain subjective data. This is because the BM is depending on the involved people and their actual knowledge about the value creation process. Existing literature addresses such challenges as the formation and adaption of BMs [5]. As a result, there is no evaluation step included and people involved in the transformation do not know, if they start with a complete and correct capturing of the initial situation.

A possible solution can be the use of company data from organizational information systems. In particular, information systems such as enterprise resource planning (ERP) systems can be leveraged. They provide a huge amount of data follow a more objective data-driven BM approach. Thereby, one has to take care, that relevant data is used, which provides detailed information about the current value creation process. The key challenge hereby is to identify appropriate data sources containing the relevant information of the company's BM. This, we articulate the first meta-requirement:

RQ 1.1: To enable bottom-up creation of a business model leverage existing data.
The results of this bottom-up approach have to be compared and rated towards the top-down approach. Therefore, the extracted data should be structured in some way. With that, not only a comparison between the top-down approach, but also with other BMs is important. In BMT, one typically compares the initial situation with the target state. Current BM approaches like the BMC [8] or the BM cube [6] are able to provide such a structure. Furthermore, a defined structure of the extracted data is also contributing to the comprehension for its users. Thus, we articulate

RQ 1.2: To guarantee comparability of top-down and bottom-up business model creation approaches, the extracted data should be structured in a unified way.
Not only a easy-to-understand structure of the business model is important. Too much information can negatively influence business model comprehension of a user. For example, the BMC is kept easy to fill in and to understand, so that users are more likely to use it [8]. This is in contrast to the BM cube, which is a more dimensional BM representation. Nevertheless, in this representation also the information is aggregated [6]. In general, to reduce an overload of information, the given data should be provided in a way such that the user has the necessary information in an aggregated form:

RQ 1.3: To report relevant information, the collected data should be aggregated.
Existing BM research deals with challenges such as the formation and adaptation of BMs in different business areas [5]. It is relatively easy to model the current state and a target state that represents the future to-be situation of the company [8]. However, there are specific challenges in the transformation process. For example, when mapping the actual and target situation, some elements in their context cannot be reused or are outdated. This results in a number of gaps that force decisions, e.g. by means of leveraging internal or external capacities [21]. Thus, we articulate the following requirement:

RQ 2.1: In order to increase the executability, the status quo of a companies' business model(s) should be explicitly interconnected to the target business model(s).
Mapping is difficult because the focus is mainly on the logic of value creation [4, 17]. However, the mapping of the current BM with the target BM is important because one can quickly see which elements are not mapped. We understand the "as-is state" BM to be representative of the current operational level of a company, since it represents the existing value creation logic. For us, the target state model is a representation of the company's goals. Consequently, mapping the elements means linking the different levels of an enterprise as required by a BM. Thus it is possible to mediate between these levels and to show how the different levels interact [4, 17]. For example, a company can choose between an internal or external resource with different effects on revenues and costs. After the mapping of the elements, it should be possible to carry out a gap analysis, which shows the need for action to transform towards the target state:

RQ 2.2: In order to increase mediation of different business levels, business model configuration should explicitly show the consequences of alternatives (Table 1).
An overview on the described requirements is listed in Table 1.

Table 1. Requirements for business model transformation tools

RQ	Description
1.1	To enable bottom-up creation of a business model leverage existing data
1.2	To guarantee comparability of top-down and bottom-up business model creation approaches, the extracted data should be structured in a unified way
1.3	To report relevant information, the collected data should be aggregated
2.1	In order to increase the executability, the status quo of a companies' business model(s) should be explicitly interconnected to the target business model(s)
2.2	In order to increase mediation of different business levels, business model configuration should explicitly show the consequences of alternatives

4.2   Design Principles for BM Transformation Tools

After the derivation of the requirements we propose design principles. The requirements (RQs) 1.1–3 will be factored in the design principles (DP) 1.1–4 and analogously RQ 2.1 and 2.2 will be translated in DP 1.1–3.

For the RQs focusing on data-driven status quo capturing of business models, it is of particular importance to use suitable data that reflects the logic of a company's value creation process. It is also important that the data is correct and complete. In order to meet the requirement RQ 1.1, we suggest for DP 1.1 that data from existing organizational information system (IS) is used. This data is typically based on transactions and represents an unbiased view from the real world. In addition to the use of the corresponding data, the way in which they it is structured is important, as articulated in RQ1.2. Since the BMC is frequently used in practice and is often quoted [34], we consider the BMC categories as an adequate structure. This structure enables users to find relevant information according to the established BMC concept (DP 1.2).

Next to this, the consolidation of data is important to avoid a information overload for users. In addition, not all data can be captured by the model. Since the goal of the BMT tool is to give the user a quick and comprehensive overview of the BM [10], the extracted data should be consolidated. As a criterion for this consolidation, the various categories of BMC should be automatically populated in with aggregated information. This information can be obtained by using calculation and aggregation methods within business model extraction process. For example, important customer segments can be defined as a segment with which a company generates the majority of its sales. That is why we articulate DP 1.3. In addition, business-model-related data is distributed across different storage locations within organizational information systems. The artifact must therefore know which different tables need to be merged in order to obtain relevant information about the business model. DP 1.4 therefore requires the artifact to provide proxies on how to retrieve the dimensions of a business model, and to know from which data sources and tables in the enterprise system the information can be retrieved. These four DPs contribute to the automatic creation of a BM. Reducing effort and increasing accuracy are the two main advantages of this approach. These principles build the first part of the BMT tool. It guarantees, that the user does not have to rely on his or her feelings and knowledge, but is supported by mining algorithms.

In order to support responsible people involved in the BMT process, the target BM and the current state of the value creation should be comparable. Additionally, users should be able to work with both BMs in parallel. One possibility is the use of a semantic relationship model, as it contains the relationships between the elements and a base for comparison of different BMs. Based on a semantic relationship model for the current and the target BM, one can also support different configurations (DP 2.1). In general, the semantic models enable a more precise representation of how a company performs its business today and in the future. Subsequently, the various elements (e.g. common elements) and their categorization as well as other relevant aspects have to be considered [6]. In addition, it represents also a basis for a gap analysis if the elements of different BMs are represented. The two semantic graphs of the current and target state can then be compared with each other. This means that the same notes are recognized in both graphs. So, one can quickly see where adjustments need to be made in the target state. This should also lead to a better understanding of the transformation dependencies (DP 2.2). The mapping of the different situations allow a better comparison of existing, obsolete and missing elements in different situations. Based on a comparison between an actual and a target state, it shows the need for action. In particular, a gap analysis could show that there is a need for action in designing the implementation of the target state. If there are different alternatives to the implementation of the model, it would be helpful to see the effects of the individual alternatives on the selected KPIs [5]. This demand for DP 2.3 enables changes in the BM to be detected quickly. For a transformation and long-term observation of BMs it is very helpful, but requires that each element is linked to at least one KPI, so that the meaning of an element is visible in the model [15]. All in all, these three DPs build the second part and should consider the support of the user during the BMT process. All DPs and their related requirements are shown in Table 2.

Table 2. Design Principles and the related Requirements

RQ	DP	Description
1.1	1.1	In order to satisfy the demand for suitable data, existing raw data should be extracted from organizational information systems
1.2	1.2	In order to meet the requirement for a uniform structure, the business model canvas structure should be used
1.3	1.3	In order to meet the need for relevant information, calculation and consolidation functions must be provided
1.4	1.4	To meet the demand for relevant business model data, the artifact requires a knowledge base of the sources of business model information and a merge logic to recombine existing the information
2.1	2.1	Status quo and target business models should be captured using semantic models to allow different configurations
2.1	2.2	A mapping between status quo and target business models should be enabled to understand transformation dependencies
2.2	2.3	Business implications of changes performed within the transformation should be reflected in KPIs referring to the corresponding business model elements

We performed a qualitative validation of the proposed design principles on the basis of real-world transformation cases. Selected results of the case analysis are depicted in Fig. 2. The basic idea is that we analyzed the cases with regards to the relevance of the proposed design principles. We rated each case from 1 (low), 2 (medium) to 3 (high) if some reference was mentioned and "X" if it is not mentioned. These proposed numbers should not be considered as formal measures, but rather reflect the tendency of the relevancy of the proposed design principles in the specific cases.

Nr.	Evaluated element	TRUMPF GmbH + Co. KG	SEW-Eurodrive GmbH & Co KG	Daimler AG	Grand Rapids Chair Company	Menlo World-wide Logistics, LLC	Delphi Corp.	Procter & Gamble Service GmbH
1.1	Available data	2	3	3	2	2	2	3
1.2	Structured data	1	2	2	1	1	2	2
1.3	Consolidated information	2	3	3	1	1	2	3
1.4	Knowledge Base	1	2	2	X	1	1	2
2.1	Configuration	3	3	3	2	2	2	3
2.2	Mapping	2	3	3	1	1	2	3
2.3	Changes	1	2	2	X	X	2	2

Fig. 2. Aggregated results of case analysis

Getting relevant data to actually model the current state seems to be possible and relevant in all cases. However, the degree of structuration of the data is varying. For the underlying knowledge base, there are some potentials for improvement. The data quality varies across the cases. However, nearly all information is spread over different sources and is typically provided in spreadsheets or PDF-based documents.

Many limitations exist with regards to the ability to actually perform business model transformation (2.1–2.3). In many cases it remains questionable whether a structured business model transformation process has taken place at all. Looking at the changes (2.3), a partly high potential for impact monitoring with KPIs is existing. This relates also to our assumption, that some measures for transformation were not evaluated and not observed with KPIs.

Overall, the analyzed cases provide evidence for the suggested design principles. Enough data (besides KPIs for supervising the transformation) is available and provided. However, this data is often unstructured, unconsolidated and spread across different data media as Excel, PDFs etc. The BMT tool should help here, to get a complete and structured overview about the current situation. Furthermore, the BMC seems to provide an accepted structure, which can be used as a base for a transformation. Furthermore, configuration, mapping and continuous evaluation of changes is not done and supported enough.

5   Instantiation

As mentioned earlier, a BMT tool in general should (i) support users in getting an objective and complete overview of the current business model and (ii) empower users to execute the business model transformation process. Our overall BMT tool instantiation is implemented in a toolset that currently consists of two loosely coupled tools. First, a business model mining tool implementing DP 1.1–1.3. We do not further elaborate here on this instantiation, as it has been introduced and described in Augenstein and Fleig [38]. Second, a Business Model Analyzer tool that builds up the business model mining results and supports users in actually running the transformation process. With regards to DP 2.1 and DP 2.2. the tool explicitly captures and depicts semantic relations between the different elements following a hyperlink approach in order to allow for mapping and configuration. Through the linkage between the elements, one established a semantic relationship network, which can also be mapped to other BMs. Clicking on one element shows the predecessors and successors of this element in the semantic relationship network. Furthermore, this builds also the foundation for configuration features.

Furthermore, a dedicated KPI category based on DP 2.3 is introduced. In this category, the user can include further KPIs in order to explicitly capture changes in the transformation activities. Leveraging this KPI category, changes can be captured more accurately than with the existing value capturing dimensions of the BMC. Figure 2 depicts a screenshot of the Business Model Analyzer (Fig. 3).

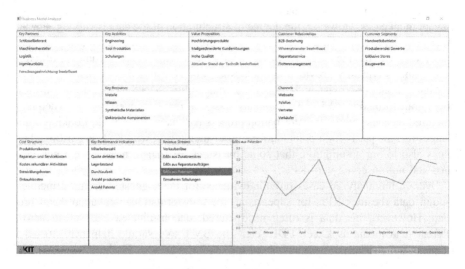

Fig. 3. Business model analyzer tool

6   Conclusion

Companies have to adapt their business models in ever shorter time intervals. Existing tools do not fully unleash the potential for a comprehensive support of such transformation processes. In this paper, the requirements and design principles for a BMT toolset have been identified and described. We present our implemented BMT toolset and specifically describe advanced mapping and evaluation features. Future work will include the evaluation of this toolset as well as advancing configuration functions as well as analytical features with regards to prognostic functions for the KPIs category and extended business model mining algorithm.

Our work in its present form comes with several limitations. First, the data required for the tool must be consistent. While downloading and consolidating data from organizational information system is a minor challenge in tool development, the real challenge is to identify business model relevant data within the various source systems. In order to "compute" business models from data, our approach must "proxy" the elements and dimensions of a business model from data. Furthermore, several business models can coexist within an organization. In addition, the current status of the prototype is not able to distinguish between the different business models in an information system and to merge business models from different source systems. A challenge will therefore be to find a way to choose and differentiate between different business models and to merge several sub-business models from several information systems.

To conclude, we believe the presented DPs for BMT tools contribute to the organizational capability to generate knowledge about the organization itself, and offer a solid base for improving transformation decisions by providing an alternative to "de jure", top-down models in "de facto" and bottom-up models. Practitioners as well as scholars can build on the presented design knowledge in order to build corresponding BMT tools addressing their challenges.

References

1. Piccinini, E., Gregory, R.W., Kolbe, L.M.: Changes in the producer-consumer relationship-towards digital transformation (2015)
2. Ostrom, A.L., Parasuraman, A., Bowen, D.E., et al.: Service research priorities in a rapidly changing context. J. Serv. Res. **18**(2), 127–159 (2015)
3. Ebel, P., Bretschneider, U., Leimeister, J.M.: Leveraging virtual business model innovation: a framework for designing business model development tools. Inf. Syst. J. **26**(5), 519–550 (2016)
4. Osterwalder, A.: The business model ontology – a proposition in a design science approach (2004)
5. Veit, D., Clemons, E., Benlian, A., et al.: Business models - an information systems research agenda. Bus. Inf. Syst. Eng. (2014)
6. Lindgren, P., Rasmussen, O.H.: The business model cube. J. Multi Bus. Model Innov. Technol. **1**(2), 135–182 (2013)
7. Zott, C., Amit, R., Massa, L.: The Business model: recent developments and future research. J. Manag. **37**(4), 1019–1042 (2011)

8. Osterwalder, A., Pigneur, Y.: Business Model Generation: A Handbook for Visionaries, Game Changers, and Challengers. Toronto (2010)
9. Di Valentin, C., Burkhart, T., Vanderhaeghen, D., et al.: Towards a framework for transforming business models into business processes. In: AMCIS 2012 Proceedings (2012)
10. Bonakdar, A., Weiblen, T., Di Valentin, C., et al.: Transformative influence of business processes on the business model: classifying the state of the practice in the software industry. In: 46th Hawaii International Conference on System Sciences (HICSS 2013), pp. 3920–3929. IEEE, Piscataway (2013)
11. Richardson, J.: The business model: an integrative framework for strategy execution. Strateg. Change 17(5–6), 133–144 (2008)
12. Morris, M., Schindehutte, M., Allen, J.: The entrepreneur's business model: toward a unified perspective. J. Bus. Res. 58(6), 726–735 (2005)
13. Alt, R., Zimmermann, H.-D.: Introduction to special section–business models. Electron. Mark. 11(1), 3–9 (2001)
14. Doz, Y.L., Kosonen, M.: Embedding strategic agility: a leadership agenda for accelerating business model renewal. Long Range Plan. 43(2), 370–382 (2010)
15. Wirtz, B.W.: Business Model Management: Design - Instruments - Success Factors, 1st edn. Gabler, Wiesbaden (2011)
16. Kley, F., Lerch, C., Dallinger, D.: New business models for electric cars - a holistic approach. Energy Policy 39(6), 3392–3403 (2011)
17. Timmers, P.: Business models for electronic markets. Electron. Mark. 8(2), 3–8 (1998)
18. Zott, C., Amit, R.: Business model design: an activity system perspective. Bus. Models 43 (2–3), 216–226 (2010)
19. NEFFICS Platform—NEFFICS. http://neffics.eu/platform/. Accessed 15 Nov 2016
20. Value Management Platform - VDMbee. https://vdmbee.com/work/value-management-platform/. Accessed 15 Nov 2016
21. Lindgardt, Z., Reeves, M., Stalk, G., et al.: Business model innovation. When the game gets tough, change the game. The Boston Consulting Group (2009)
22. Johnson, M.W., Christensen, C.M., Kagermann, H.: Reinventing your business model. Harv. Bus. Rev. 86(12), 57–68 (2008)
23. Berman, B.: Marketing Channels. Wiley, London (1996)
24. Rosenbloom, B.: Marketing Channels. Cengage Learning, Boston (2012)
25. Magretta, J: Why Business Models Matter. Harvard Business School Publishing, Brighton (2002)
26. Zott, C., Amit, R.: Business model design and the performance of entrepreneurial firms. Organ. Sci. 18(2), 181–199 (2007)
27. Kinder, T.: Emerging e-commerce business models: an analysis of case studies from West Lothian, Scotland. Eur. J. Innov. Manag. 5(3), 130–151 (2002)
28. Akkermans, J.M., Gordijn, J.: Value-based requirements engineering: exploring innovative e-commerce ideas. Requir. Eng. 8(2), 114–134 (2003)
29. Vaishnavi, V., Kuechler, W.: Design science research in information systems (2004)
30. Zainal, Z.: Case study as a research method. J. Kemanus. 9, 1–6 (2007)
31. Kaliudis, A.: TRUMPF realisiert Pilotfabrik für Industrie 4.0 (2016)
32. Soder, J.: Use case production: Von CIM über Lean Production zu Industrie 4.0. In: Bauernhansl, T., ten Hompel, M., Vogel-Heuser, B. (eds.) Industrie 4.0 in Produktion, Automatisierung und Logistik, pp. 85–102. Springer, Wiesbaden (2014). https://doi.org/10. 1007/978-3-658-04682-8_4
33. Steegmüller, D., Zürn, M.: Wandlungsfähige Produktionssysteme für den Automobilbau der Zukunft. In: Bauernhansl, T., ten Hompel, M., Vogel-Heuser, B. (eds.) Industrie 4.0 in

Produktion, Automatisierung und Logistik, pp. 103–119. Springer, Wiesbaden (2014). https://doi.org/10.1007/978-3-658-04682-8_5

34. Miller, G., Pawloski, J., Standridge, C.R.: A case study of lean, sustainable manufacturing. J. Ind. Eng. Manag. **3**(1), 11–32 (2010)
35. Bartholomew, D.: Putting Lean Principles in the Warehouse (2008)
36. Marchwinski, C.: Following Four Steps to a Lean Material-Handling System Leads to a Leap in Performance (2003)
37. Marchwinski, C.: Toothbrush Plant Reverses Decay in Competitiveness (2004)
38. Augenstein, D., Fleig, C.: Exploring design principles for a business model mining tool. In: International Conference on Information Systems 2017, Seoul, South Korea (2017)

Towards Collaborative Data Analysis with Diverse Crowds – A Design Science Approach

Michael Feldman$^{(\boxtimes)}$, Cristian Anastasiu, and Abraham Bernstein

Department of Informatics, University of Zurich, Zurich, Switzerland
{feldman,bernstein}@ifi.uzh.ch,
cristiananastasiu@googlemail.com

Abstract. The last years have witnessed an increasing shortage of data experts capable of analyzing the omnipresent data and producing meaningful insights. Furthermore, some data scientists mention data preprocessing to take up to 80% of the whole project time. This paper proposes a method for collaborative data analysis that involves a crowd without data analysis expertise. Orchestrated by an expert, the team of novices conducts data analysis through iterative refinement of results up to its successful completion. To evaluate the proposed method, we implemented a tool that supports collaborative data analysis for teams with mixed level of expertise. Our evaluation demonstrates that with proper guidance data analysis tasks, especially preprocessing, can be distributed and successfully accomplished by non-experts. Using the design science approach, iterative development also revealed some important features for the collaboration tool, such as support for dynamic development, code deliberation, and project journal. As such we pave the way for building tools that can leverage the crowd to address the shortage of data analysts.

Keywords: Collaborative data analysis · Crowdsourcing · Design science

1 Introduction

Data analysis is a complex task that touches on many skills. Experts conducting data analysis are, therefore, expected to be proficient not only in the domain of their interest, but also in other disciplines such as statistics, computing, software engineering, and algorithms [1]. These high expectations make data scientist scarce, leaving their valuable services out-of-reach for a big share of public. This also means that the way to become data analysis expert is extremely complex and the specialization cannot be easily gained.

In this paper, we introduce an approach for collaborative data analysis *to allow non-experts to cooperate on data analysis projects*. In contrast to the lack of data scientists, there are many freelancers or enthusiasts that have some basic coding skills obtained either in introductory classes during their studies or self-acquired throughout the course of their life. While those non-experts do not have all necessary skills to perform end-to-end data analysis projects, they can be involved in some parts where their skills are sufficient. Specifically, we argue that non-experts with some coding skills can be especially helpful in the *data preprocessing* stage of data analysis. In this step data

© Springer International Publishing AG, part of Springer Nature 2018
S. Chatterjee et al. (Eds.): DESRIST 2018, LNCS 10844, pp. 218–235, 2018.
https://doi.org/10.1007/978-3-319-91800-6_15

scientist transforms raw data into a data suitable for statistical modelling, as it is often inconsistent, incomplete and contains many errors. It is, therefore, likely that prior to statistical modelling, which requires significant knowledge in statistics and computer science, there is a need in "data wrangling" – transforming and editing raw data until it is suitable for data analysis [2].

At the same time, data preprocessing and the following statistical analysis cannot be decoupled. Often, in order to apply certain statistical approaches, the data has to be previously transformed and organized accordingly. For instance, to apply a statistical model that assumes linearity the dependent variable often has to be transformed first. Moreover, data analysis is an iterative process where data preprocessing and modelling are intertwined: the results of data analysis lead to new ideas on how better to analyze data, which in turn leads to additional data preprocessing. Therefore, it is important that experts and non-experts cooperate and efficiently coordinate tasks. Following these considerations, we propose a process where data analysis projects are divided into sub-tasks and each is assigned to a freelancer with limited knowledge in data analysis and (some basic) coding skills. While the participants are assigned to different tasks, they interact through various communication channels in order to draw on their collective knowledge [3], and thus, reach the desired results. Dividing the project into several simple tasks allows project manager – a data analysis expert responsible for the whole data analysis project – to distribute and coordinate the tasks. This way the manager can take advantage of various workers' abilities in order to conduct data analysis. In our experiments, we explore whether the results of non-expert teams orchestrated by manager are comparable to the results produced by experts handling the whole project. Therefore, our goal is to propose a practical solution to the problem of shortage of data scientists and allow non-experts to take part in the process of data analysis.

Our contributions are as follows: First, we present a method for collaborative data analysis in online freelance setting. Second, through a set of experiments, we show that the proposed approach is both cost-effective and can produce results with equivalent quality to those produced by data scientists. Finally, following a design-science approach, we develop a platform that supports collaborative data analysis with mixed-level expertise.

2 Literature Review

In the following section, we introduce prior work on which we based our study. Its subsections review the success factors of online collaboration, describe the existing solutions for collaborative data analysis, and discuss the theoretical underpinnings that informed our method.

Online Collaboration: The advances of communication technology as well as a spread of sociotechnical systems made it possible for workers effectively collaborate within a distributed environment. Rather than meeting face-to-face, workers can rely on various communication channels such as emails, teleconference software or chat tools to cooperate in various tasks [4]. Many domains adopted computer mediated collaboration as a useful tool for reaching goals. Scientists use different online tools to engage in research discussions and activities [5]. Educators take advantage of online collaborative learning techniques to support students in achieving competence and foster skills like team working and group decision making [6]. Moreover, online collaborative tools facilitate marketing and decision making activities by, for instance, allowing better understanding of shopping behavior and predicting demand for products [7]. Previous research has identified multiple factors that impact successful online collaboration. First, a team has to be supported by senior member or manager who is facilitating the progress of the task and provides feedback [8]. Second, the members have to make themselves familiar with each other, which in turn should lower the psychological barrier of estrangement and promote cooperation over time [9]. Third, well-established communication is essential to avoid disagreements about the priorities and strategy to achieve pre-set tasks [10]. Fourth, trust along the group members supports the feeling that all members work towards the same goal and make every effort to achieve the best possible outcome in order to earn trust among team members. Finally, the last element is well established organization of the team. A competent leader will support the team in the process of developing manageable and effective workflow to accomplish the task in short time end with reasonable efforts [8, 9]. We considered all these factors during the design of the artifacts that will support collaborative data analysis with non-experts.

In crowdsourcing literature, a few notable methods to support crowd-collaboration have been proposed. For instance, Turkomatic is a tool that utilizes crowdworkers to plan and execute complex tasks. Requesters can watch workers decomposing and solving tasks in real time, either collaboratively or independently. Requesters can intervene to modify tasks or request new solutions to subtasks as needed [11]. Another framework, CrowdForge, introduces a map-reduce paradigm to split complex work into small parts and solve it in crowdsourcing setting. The task is broken into multiple subtasks that are concurrently solved and verified by other workers, and eventually merged into a cumulative output. However, although the framework relies on a powerful paradigm of parallel work execution, it assumes that complex work can be decomposed into lots of merely dependent micro tasks – an assumption that is often violated [12]. Other notable examples of online collaboration in crowdsourcing are CrowdWeaver – supporting with visual interface for real-time managing both human and machine crowdtasks within an integrated workflow [13], and Soylent – a word processing interface, implementing the Find-Fix-Verify crowd programming pattern, which splits tasks into a series of generation and review stages and utilize the collaboration among crowdworkers through independent voting and agreement to produce reliable results [14].

Existing Solutions for Collaborative Data Analysis: One of the most well-known examples of collaborative data analysis is Kaggle [15]. Kaggle is a web platform for data analysis that allows organizations to post their data projects and invite enthusiasts all around the world to participate in contests. Participants experiment with different techniques and compete against each other to produce the best models. For most competitions, submissions are scored immediately, based on their predictive accuracy relative to a withhold test-set of data, and summarized on a live leader-board. Once the deadline is over, the competition host pays prize money in exchange for the winning model [16]. Participants are allowed to team up together to collaborate on projects, and thus improve their chances to win the contest. Other solutions, such as Sense.us [17] or Many Eyes [18], have been proposed for collective data analysis by enabling crowds visually inspect data. For example, [19] presented CommentSpace, a collaborative tool for visual analysis that allows to annotate graphic content with tags and links that reflect the relationship between comments and visualizations. Wisteria and Wrangler are example of two human-in-the-loop systems that involve crowds in data cleaning by inferring the operations performed manually by crowds and extrapolating them to the whole dataset [2, 20]. Collaborative data analysis can be seen as an offshoot of distributed software projects. However, despite the evolution of advanced collaboration and software engineering tools (e.g., GitHub, Jira), software development is still mostly a prerogative of experts and does not involve laymen.

All mentioned solutions fall short on supporting collaborative data analysis by relying on crowds with mixed expertise. While platforms such as Many Eyes or Wrangler appeal to crowds without any prior expertise, platforms like GitHub require substantial skills in order to be able efficiently collaborate using their functionalities. Moreover, web-portals for crowdsourced data science such as Kaggle or TopCoder are rather a meeting point for data scientists and customers and, by and large, do not support the teams with any functionalities throughout data analysis.

Theoretical Underpinnings: Tasks can be complex and may involve the coordination of a large number of participants with different capabilities. Therefore, different scientific communities have made efforts to associate tasks by decomposing them into the sub-tasks required to complete the full task [21, 22]. For instance, within the AI community, Chandrasekaran et al. [23] proposed a hierarchical task-method decomposition, which recursively links a task to alternative methods and their subtasks. This method emphasizes modeling of domain knowledge by utilizing tasks and methods as mediating concepts and, therefore fits our scope of the data analysis domain. Stefik [24] proposed an approach of constraint hierarchical planning where the constraints are dynamically formulated and propagated as the process proceeds. Subsequently, these constraints are used to coordinate the solutions of defined sub-tasks. The organizational approach, as presented in the Handbook of Organizational Processes of Malone et al. [25], in contrast, introduces methodologies to represent and codify organizational processes and provides different perspectives on how business processes might be decomposed into sub-activities. A difference between these two approaches lies in their different purposes: while AI is focused on building computer systems that automatically execute processes, the organizational approach advocates building systems to support people to plan and execute processes. Howison and Crowston [26] propose a theory of collaboration through open superposition. Developed in the context of open source software development, this theory emphasizes that tasks that appear too large for individual are likely to be postponed until they redefined such that they can be performed by single member, and that most of the tasks are indeed accomplished with only a single programmer.

These theories inform our solution in a few ways. (A) decomposition of ill-defined task has to be tied into domain knowledge. (B) the envisioned system should enable experts to decompose the task in efficient manner (e.g. through taxonomy or by utilizing expert's knowledge). (C) There is a need for efficient coordination and communication in order to enable unimpeded process of data analysis (D) data analysts working on a well-defined task will prefer to work on their own rather than collaboratively in an online team. However, they will be interested to coordinate the outputs of their task, to discuss possible solutions, and to receive feedback to their job. (E) every task assigned to a worker should be well adapted to the skills and needs of the worker, with a clear specifications and task manager that can supervise and help with advice and guidance.

3 Research Design

The research design presented here follows a design-science research approach in information systems as presented by Hevner et al. [27]. The authors describe design-science process as a sequence of expert activities that produces a set of artefacts with the following evaluation and feedback in order to improve both the quality of the artefacts and the design process. According to the theory taxonomy proposed by Gregor [28], the proposed research resides within the *theory for design and action* by contributing to knowledge via addressing the considerations of (a) the utility to a community of users, (b) the novelty of the artefact, and (c) the persuasiveness of claims that it is effective. As the goal to define and develop artefact that supports a novel approach of *collaborative data analysis with mixed-expertise crowds*, design can be seen as a search process involving an iterative evaluation and refinement of artefacts [27, 29]. The research methodology we adopted follows Peffers et al. [30] and includes six steps: problem identification and motivation, definition of the objectives for a solution, design and development, demonstration, evaluation, and communication (see also Fig. 1).

Following the figure, we start by laying out the research motivation: (a) to enable collaborative data analysis by crowds with different expertise, (b) the lack of platforms that support an efficient environment for data analysis for non-experts in a dynamic manner, and (c) to leverage the crowdsourcing and citizen science phenomena of

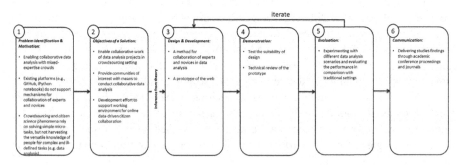

Fig. 1. Research methodology (Following Peffers et al. [35])

harvesting knowledge that is hard to reach. We then define objectives of the solution: (a) to enable collaboration on data analysis tasks on web, (b) to provide communities of interest with means to conduct collaborative data exploration, and (c) to propose a web environment for online collaboration. At the design stage, to the best of our knowledge, no dominant method has been identified so far to incorporate people with diverse skills into data analysis. Hence, the major challenge of this paper is defining and evaluating the needs for collaborative data analysis, accounting for the diverse nature of crowd workers. To do so, we start with the top-down approach of expert managing the novices and gradually explore the predominant factors for successful collaboration and tasks' coordination. The results will be demonstrated through the web application prototype built based on the discussed artefacts and set of experiments in which we evaluate the crowd's performance on a series of data analysis projects to check whether the designed prototype satisfies the prerequisites.

4   Conceptualization of the Artefact (Data Analysis Tool)

In this study we present a framework that allows non-experts to work on data analysis projects. Our framework (i) supports a project manager in decomposing complex tasks into small and facile sub-tasks, (ii) supports coordination and supervision by project manager, and (iii) enables an iterative development of the data analysis project. The methodology we propose implies that the project manager defines a project and distributes assignments to workers in a top-down approach. A top-down approach is considered as more appropriate for well-specified, rather than ill-defined problems [31]. However, we decided in favour of this method, as the scenario we envision is of non-experts that are competent to perform preprocessing tasks only with the appropriate supervision. It is, therefore, necessary to impose task decomposition hierarchy to be able to manage the complexity of task on the expense of its flexibility. In addition, as our approach implies iterative exploring of the success factors for the scenario we investigate, the top-down approach is better suited for understanding how strictly hierarchical approach can transition into more collaborative one. For instance, it allows to see throughout the iterative development and evaluation, where the expert oversight can be replaced with peer-review of other novices, how decisions made throughout data analysis can be informed by the broad knowledge of the crowd to enrich expert's decisions, or how to establish effective communication to unleash the untapped knowledge of project members. Following the design science approach, we conducted two iterations of prototype development with consequent evaluations. In the following we first describe the general workflow and then the evolvement of the prototype and of the methodology after each iteration.

Figure 2 describes the workflow of the envisioned collaborative data analysis project. The figure presents both schematic workflow of the process on the top and the corresponding print-screens of the prototype on the bottom. The first part of the workflow is focused on the project definition, task decomposition and sub-tasks assignment processes done by the project manager. The second part focuses on the iterative collaboration on the project, enabling the manager and team to refine the implementation and output through multiple iterations.

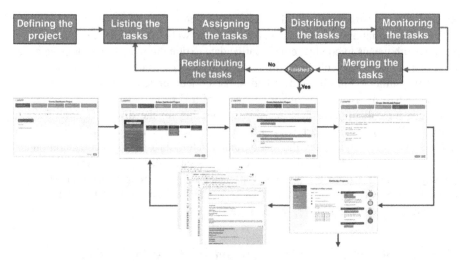

Fig. 2. Process workflow

Next, we go through each of the workflow steps and explain them. First, the project manager defines the project by entering all relevant details, such as the software language to be used, the project name, and the project description. This step also provides some validations, ensuring that all necessary information is present. Next, the manager lists and defines the actions that need to be done. An action is the smallest unit of sub-task and an assignment is a composition of actions assigned to a worker. An example of an action would be *loadFromCSV*, which receives as input the path of the CSV file and returns a data-frame. Splitting assignments into small actions, especially in the preprocessing part, allows the project manager to distribute them to non-expert workers and supervise their execution throughout the assignment. Further, **tasks are assigned** to suitable workers. The assignment of tasks to workers follows a top-down approach and can be done on the basis of different criteria such as worker or task attributes, or by taking into consideration external factors such project deadlines or budget. The **tasks are then distributed** among the workers by virtue of email invitation to the IPython (or Jupyter) Notebooks that are created and contain all the required information. At this point the workers can work on their personal notebooks stored on their personal cloud storage (Google Drive) and interact with each other through the shared notes-board. They can also review others notebooks and comment on the relevant code using side-comments. All throughout the project, manager can **monitor the progress** of the workers and guide them towards the desired output. Finally, the tasks are merged into one notebook which allows a manager to run the end-to-end implementation. Project managers can then verify that the output meets their expectations and that the interaction between different assignments works properly. Otherwise, if the goal has not been reached, the implementation of the tasks will be changed or new **tasks will be redistributed** and the project will enter a new iteration.

5   Iterative Development-Demonstration-Evaluation

The proposed solution has been developed in two iterations by improving the method and the web-prototype for collaborative data analysis in a consecutive manner. Based on the evaluation of each iteration, we focused on advancing the artifact with respect to the following two criteria:

First, the proposed methodology and web-prototype should enable coordination and successful completion of data analysis projects with diverse crowds. Specifically, typical data analysis projects should be decomposed into subtasks such that they will be simple enough to be performed by non-experts. We evaluate these criteria qualitatively, through a user study by answering the following hypothesis:

> *H1: It is possible to decompose typical data analysis projects into small enough tasks such that the complexity of these tasks is substantially reduced.*

Second, the proposed solution has to be comparable in quality to traditional expert-based data science projects. To answer whether the proposed methodology is feasible and can reach the desired output of collaborative data analysis with mixed-level expertise teams, we propose the following hypothesis:

> *H2: The quality of the results produced by a team of non-non experts is comparable to the one achieved by experts.*

In the following we will present three versions of the prototype and discuss their performance according to these measures. Note that we tested all iterations on real-world examples chosen from Kaggle based on the following criteria: (a) the projects should be implemented either in R or Python, as these are the most popular languages in data analysis, (b) the projects should contain a relatively large preprocessing part, as that has been found to be a major part of data [32], (c) the projects should encompass various types of data analysis such as descriptive statistics, visualization, and prediction, (d) the projects should be conducted by individuals that can be considered as experts, either based on their verified biography or because of their high ranking on Kaggle, and (e) the projects should not be trivial (i.e., we limited the minimal size of the project to be about 150 lines of code, chose projects with significant number of up-votes, and history of comments such that it can be assumed that the code went through a substantial public review).

5.1   The Pilot Study

Following to literature review we designed the first prototype of our tool. The web-platform is based on the Jupyter Notebook (colloquially known as IPython notebook) and available online. Jupyter is a command shell for interactive computing in multiple programming languages that offers enhanced introspection, media, additional shell syntax, tab completion, and rich history. Using Jupyter, researchers can capture data-driven workflows that combine code, equations, text and visualizations and share them with others. We decided in favor of this platform due to the following reasons. First, it is a browser-based notebook with support for code, text, mathematical expressions, inline plots, and other rich media. These functionalities are essential for collaborative data analysis as they allow participants to exchange results and easily communicate their findings and difficulties. Second, although initially designed for Python, the platform is language agnostic and provides the ability to be extended with additional interpreters such as R and Ruby. Third, this platform supports an interactive data visualization toolkit, often required in data analysis.

To better understand the requirements of the proposed solution, *we conducted a user-study with three graduate students supervised by a Ph.D. student.* As part of their course work, the students conducted data analysis project that involved substantial data preprocessing followed by network analysis. The supervisor was managing the task decomposition and divided the project among the group members with further coordination of the process up to its successful accomplishment (following the process presented in Fig. 2).

The goal of pilot study was twofold. First we wanted to reach a proof-of-concept, showing that our approach is feasible and data analysis projects can be successfully accomplished with non-experts. Therefore, we alleviated some constrains such as performing the experiment in real-world setting using freelancers/crowdworkers or assuring that the analysis has been performed exclusively on our platform. Second, we aggregated the feedback to better understand the requirements of the proposed tool and to evaluate the workflow. In addition, the feedback received from this iteration helped us to simplify the coordination process and to resolve some technical issues.

Conclusions/Requirements Drawn from Pilot Study and Their Addressing: First, all participants pointed to the need for collaboration and communication tools. While some can be externally used (e.g., forums, video chats), some tools have to be embedded into the platform to support effective coordination between team members. Especially, since the assignments distributed to workers are often interdependent, it is important to allow team members to comment on the relevant code-blocks of their peers. To address this need, *we developed features that allow workers better to collaborate.* For instance, we presented "sticky notes" – a note that every team member can leave next to the code-box of a Notebook. Second, another point, raised by the manager, is to improve the control over the project by enabling easy access to the notebooks, evaluating the current results, and (re)distributing the tasks. We, therefore, *added a functionality to automatically merge the notebooks into a master notebook that includes all notebooks in predefined order.* This allows to run all distributed assignments at one run and quickly identify bugs and inconsistencies. To redistribute the tasks with new instructions, we implemented a feedback loop (see Fig. 2) that allows easily to redistribute the tasks to team members with new instructions and based on the previously submitted code. Third, to improve the collaboration, team members pointed to the need to have access to the instructions every team member received from the manager as well as have the opportunity to intervene in order to clarify what in their opinion has to be done. To address this, *we added a project journal, where all project participants can add their comments.*

Note, while such functionalities exist in professional software development platforms such as GitHub, our goal is to enable *non-experts* to collaborate instantly on data analysis projects in easy and interactive way with no knowledge on the principles of distributed software development. In the following iterations, we qualitatively evaluated the proposed features and extend our platform according to the additional feedback provided by crowdworkers in the real-world setting. Most of the attention in the following two iterations though, is devoted to testing the postulated hypotheses.

5.2 First Iteration - Three Data Analysis Projects

For a real-world evaluation, we selected three data analysis projects that represent various types of data analysis. Projects were taken from a large crowdsourcing data science platform, Kaggle. In these experiments, a data analysis expert (also a co-author) assumed the role of the project manager and the workers are recruited through the Upwork[1] platform. As of today, Upwork is the biggest online labor market and contains online freelancers in different domains. Data analysis is one of its most common domains and has a large pool of freelancers with different level of expertise willing to work on data analysis projects [33]. These tasks can be classified as of moderate complexity as they involved mainly data preprocessing and visualization, and did not require any advanced knowledge in data analysis.

Task #1: Earnings Chart by Occupation and Sex[2]: The aim of the first project is to create a chart showing the earnings of the population by occupation and gender, using the data of the latest US census from 2014. The original Kaggle project analyzes 24 occupation categories, while in our project we randomly selected 11 categories. The workers had to classify the list of the professions into these 11 job categories (e.g., management, science, military) and plot a chart of the earnings for each occupation with respect to the gender. This project is the easiest and was accomplished in two days.

We split the project into three assignments. The first assignment involved data loading and cleaning with the primary goal of identifying the correct industry code ranges and sub-setting the data. It consisted of five actions. The first was to *Identify Occupation Industry Codes*, and *Subset data* and the output of this task was a file containing the information about the population working in the 11 industries relevant for our chart. The second task focused on the data transformation and had only two actions –*Mean* and *Save results*. The output of this task was an aggregated data set containing the mean earnings of men and women per industry. In the last task, the crowdworker had to plot the data as a bar chart diagram in descending order, showing the distribution of men and women per industry and their average earnings. It consists only of one action – *Bar Chart*, and produced as output a bar-chart similar to the one in the Kaggle project.

The main focus of this project was to find the right occupation categories and to subset the data accordingly. The project used a random 1% sample of the US census data from 2014. In order to compare the results, we evaluated both implementations (Kaggle's and non-experts' team) on the same data (Fig. 3). The team of non-experts managed successfully to finish the project and their results were similar to those published on Kaggle, resulting in the Pearson correlation coefficient $\rho = 0.8$.

---

[1] www.upwork.com/.

[2] www.kaggle.com/wikunia/d/census/2013-americancommunity-survey/earnings-by-occupation-sex/.

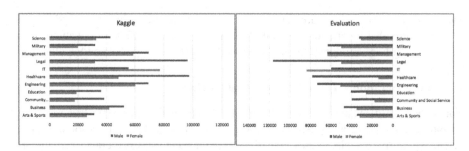

Fig. 3. Pearson correlation coefficient ρ = 0.8

The differences in the results can be traced back to the nuance that two implementations perform the data subsetting in different way. Each occupation in the data set is identified by a code. The 11 categories used in the project are quite generic, so it is user's responsibility to find the occupations which belong to the respective category. While Kaggle solution identifies only one occupation for each category, the Upwork team's implementation aggregates multiple occupation codes under the same category.

Task #2: Hillary Clinton's Emails[3]: This project explores the content of Hillary Clintons emails which were released by her in response to a Freedom of Information Act (FOIA) request, and produces a heat-map of the countries that often appear in the emails. The dataset for this project is available on Kaggle. This project was also split into three assignments. The first assignment focused on data loading and cleaning, and consisted of three actions. The output of this task was a cleansed subset containing only the emails sent by Hillary Clinton and a list of all the countries in the world and their alternative spellings and abbreviations. The second task focused on identifying countries in the email data set and contained two actions – *Subset* and *Calculate occurrences*. The output of this task was a country occurrence list, containing the number of times each country is mentioned. The last task focused on the visualization part and consisted of two actions. The output was a sorted histogram and a heat-map in form of a world map, similar to the output of the Kaggle project.

The team of non-experts managed successfully to finish the project and the output of their work was similar to the results published on Kaggle (see Fig. 4). In both implementations, the heat-map is based on a country occurrence list. We compared the results by calculating the Pearson correlation coefficient between the two lists with country occurrences which resulted in ρ = 0.72.

Similar to the previous project, the difference in the results is caused by the way two implementations identify the countries mentioned in the emails. The project on Kaggle and the team of non-experts use different approaches to identify countries abbreviations which lead to difference in the results.

---

[3] https://www.kaggle.com/ampaho/d/kaggle/hillary-clinton-emails/foreign-policy-map-through-hrc-s-emails/code.

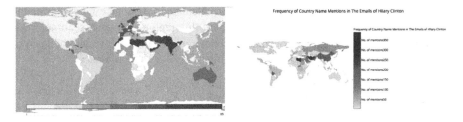

Fig. 4. Pearson correlation coefficient ρ = 0.72

Task #3: Reddit Sentiment Analysis[4]: The purpose of this project was to create a chart showing which Reddit comments receive the highest scores, based on the sentiment of the comment. Reddit is a large social network where users can submit content. The dynamics of this website is solely dependent on the number of up/down votes that the content receives. The content or comment with the highest number of votes is shown at the top. The categorization into three sentiment categories – objective, negative, and positive – was performed using the designated software package. The initial dataset includes Reddit comments from May 2015 and available on Kaggle.

The goal of *Reddit Sentiment Analysis* is to create a chart showing which Reddit comments receive the highest scores, based on the sentiment of the comment. Three sentiment categories were defined – objective, positive and negative. As in the previous project, we used a random sample of the May 2015 dataset. Both implementations were tested and evaluated using the same dataset. As it can be seen in Fig. 5, the results are very similar – the average ranking scores for the positive, negative and objective comment categories are 6.18, 6,78, and 5.96 in the Kaggle project, and 5.75, 6.22, and 6.34 in the Upwork project performed by non-expert team.

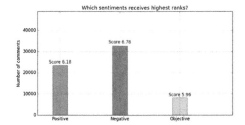 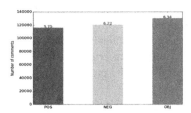

Fig. 5. Equivalence tests: comparison of Kaggle with non-experts results

We also compared the ranking values in each sentiment category by performing equivalence tests on the results of the two projects [34]. The goal of equivalence tests is to statistically test the equivalence of the variables. This was achieved by setting the

---

[4] https://www.kaggle.com/lplewa/d/reddit/reddit-comments-may-2015/communication-styles-vs-ranks/code.

equivalency region δ and testing whether the calculated confidence intervals for the differences between the two variables are within this region. For each sentiment category, we set the δ to be the average standard deviation of the Kaggle and the team of non-experts results. All the intervals are calculated with 95% confidence:

- Positive: CI_{poss} (−0.21, 1.07) ⊆ (−S.D.$_{poss}$, S.D.$_{poss}$)
- Objective: CI_{obj} (−1.16, 0.4) ⊆ (−S.D.$_{obj}$, S.D.$_{obj}$)
- Negative: CI_{neg} (−0.17, 1.29) ⊆ (−S.D.$_{neg}$, S.D.$_{neg}$).

In all cases the confidence intervals are contained within the equivalency region, meaning that there is no difference between the ranking means in each sentiment category.

Note that the implementation, the classification of the comments into one of the three sentiment categories was done differently. In Kaggle project, the comments are classified by selecting only the comments with values above average (top quartile or top 3/8) for each sentiment, while the in project done by the non-expert team, sentiment scores are first normalized (through division by mean), and only then the comments are classified. Nevertheless, the results are almost identical.

Conclusions: At the end of this iteration, we qualitatively evaluated the features previously developed via a questionnaire, where we asked the participants open-end questions related to the use of the system. Specifically, we asked them to describe the features they found useful, difficulties they experienced in using the platform, and what are the functionalities that are missing or insufficient. We used the feedback received in this iteration to improve our prototype and to add missing functionalities. For example, *we added a notification that the worker has finished his part such that the manager can review the output* and *the worker responsible for the next step can start working with the provisional results*. We also *added a notification to inform the owner of the notebook via email every time a "sticky-note" is attached*.

Regarding H2, all three experiments present substantial similarity between the experts' and non-experts' results. The similarity in the results of task #1 and task #2 is shown through significantly high correlation between the results – 0.8 and 0.72 correspondingly. Similarly, the results of task #3, compared using equivalence tests, indicate equivalence of the results. Altogether, the results of experiments support our hypothesis that crowds with mixed expertise are able to produce outputs comparable with the results produced by experts.

5.3 Third Iteration – Fully Autonomous Data Analysis Project

The last experiment we conducted was *Prediction in the Republican Primaries*[5]. The goal of this evaluation was to predict the results of the Republican Primaries 2015 in different counties. This experiment can be seen as full end-to-end data analysis project that includes all elements of data analysis, starting with data preprocessing, visualization, and up to building prediction models. The manager in this project, an expert worker from the crowd, was also responsible for building the prediction model. This

---

[5] https://www.kaggle.com/apapiu/d/benhamner/2016-us-election/predictions-in-the-republican-primary.

setting allows the expert to better define the requirements of the activities, as he will use the processed data to build prediction models. In this project the manager was responsible both for hiring the crowdworkers and defining assignments without intervention. Eventually, the project was split into three assignments performed by manager and two crowdworkers.

The first assignment focused on activities of *data loading, subsetting, and aggregating data* from different sources, such that the resulting data can be used for further analysis. The output of this task was a data-frame that included information about the primaries winner in every county and state as well as the demographic data of regions extracted from different data sources. This task required significant efforts and took about 5–7 h of work. The second assignment was mainly about visualization of the data and descriptive statistics and resulted in various visualizations describing the relationship between population features of counties (e.g., residents' ethnicity or education, population density) and candidates' voting patterns. The duration of this task was about two hours. The last assignment was to build models predicting vote rates of each candidate. This task included training prediction models and testing them, similarly to Kaggle solution, on the test-set with reporting prediction qualities, such as Mean Absolute Error (MAE) and Root Mean Square Error (RMSE).

The overall results of the prediction errors of the crowd and the experts are very similar. The mean absolute error of the Kaggle solution is $MAE_{Kaggle} = 6.5\%$ while the solution of the non-experts team yields $MAE_{Upwork} = 6\%$. The root mean square errors of both solutions are almost identical with $RMSE_{Kaggle} = 8\%$ in the Kaggle solution and $RMSE_{Upwork} = 7.7\%$ in the model produced by crowdworkers.

Regarding H2 we can, hence, again conclude that the results produced by non-experts are comparable in their quality to those produced by data scientists.

5.4   Summary and Discussion of Results

Evaluation of H1: We tested the first hypothesis by reviewing the task decomposition output. Specifically, we aimed to ascertain whether it is possible to decompose the selected data analysis projects into sub-tasks such that the complexity of the sub-tasks is reduced compared to the overall complexity of the project. We asked the crowd-workers to report about the perceived complexity of the project and the sub-tasks. Following, we aggregated the results and analyzed them.

It was possible to split all projects into actions. Also, all of the workers were able to successfully complete their assignments. They rated the complexity of their assignment with an average of 2.25 (S.D. = 0.96) out of 5. The project, on the other hand, was rated higher than the assignment complexity, with 2.42 out of 5 (S.D. = 0.67). Despite the lack of significance (possibly due to the small sample size), we believe the results indicate a trend, that the method might work. Based on our evaluation and echoed by the literature review, we conclude that data analysis can be split into less complicated sub-tasks and accomplished by non-experts.

Evaluation of H2: To test the second hypothesis, we statistically compared the results of the projects conducted by experts with the results of non-experts that used our platform. As the data analysis projects we used for evaluation are publicly available on Kaggle, we explicitly asked the participants to not search and browse for the solutions on Kaggle. We also compared the code and the solutions' logic to assure that the code has not been inspired by the original solution. As already described in the iterations above, we attempted to cover a range of typical data analysis projects with complexity that meets real-world scenarios. Moreover, in order to ensure that the similarity is not a result of naturally limited space of solutions (which could lead to highly correlated results), we compared the results of other authors to see whether there is a natural variance in results.

Discussion: Both hypotheses have been empirically supported, meaning that data analysis projects can be effectively decomposed and accomplished with good quality. However, we found that the success of a project also greatly depends on other factors. The decomposed-tasks have to be effectively coordinated and timely adapted for the changing needs of data analysis. This is due to the dynamic/iterative nature of data analysis, where new insights, resulting from intermediate results, inspire new ideas on how to proceed with analysis. This, in turn, often requires additional data wrangling and sparks new iterations of work. While this work is performed in distributed way by non-experts, there is a need to support such process with appropriate coordination tool that will facilitate the process.

Moreover, the total cost of the experiments excluding manger was about 120 USD per project (the projects were split between three crowdworkers), where every worker has been paid 40 USD to accomplish her part, and each project required on average about 12 h of work. In the project that involved the freelance manager, additional cost of 100 USD was paid for about 8 h of manager's work. This makes the projects economically competitive, especially in the light of the soaring data scientists' wage.

We also collected information about the background and skills of the crowdworkers that participated in our experiments. Most of them are bachelor or master students in their twenties, studying IT, computer or exact sciences and working part-time as freelancers (13 h per week on average). The workers perceive themselves mildly proficient in coding (self-rated with 3.2 out 5) and have basic background in data analysis, usually limited to introductory class in statistics or online course. Even though we have not conducted in-depth study on the demographics of online freelancers working in data analysis, our strong impression was that most of them can be characterized as part-time workers with average coding skills and very limited statistical/data analysis education with expected remuneration similar to the one in our experiments. This can be seen as evidence for the existence of sufficient talent to support the scenario we propose.

6 Limitations and Future Work

The proposed methodology has the following limitations. First the proposed top-down approach is not necessarily the optimal structure and other alternatives might be explored. For example, to allow workers to pick a task they want to work on in a self-managed manner and accompany the execution with managerial oversight. Second, we showed that the tasks can be decomposed into multiple simple sub-tasks. However, were not able to confirm this statistically. It is unclear whether this is due to a small sample of respondents (12). Future work might explore this by increasing the sample size and with recording additional data indicating the complexity of tasks. Third, to better evaluate the proposed platform, additional evaluation of the proposed scenario with other systems can be performed. For instance, the experiment where the coordination is done through a version control system that is used for software development such as GitHub[6]. Lastly, further research is needed to better understand the trade-off between the managerial overhead and saved costs due to outsourcing to non-experts.

7 Conclusion

This paper presents an approach of collaborative data analysis that involves data analysis novices with initial coding skills to participate in the process. We propose and evaluate the scenario where teams of non-experts are guided by expert throughout the process of data exploration and preprocessing. The proposed framework was evaluated with an especially data designed tool and by virtue of multiple experiments, where the constraints are gradually released: first a pilot study where we control for both the workers and the manager, then three experiments, where only the project manager is controlled, and ultimately, a data analysis project, where both the project manager and the workers are hired and perform the task without any external interference. The results demonstrate the feasibility of the proposed approach and support the hypothesis that the output of teams with mixed-level expertise is equivalent to the results achieved by experts. Moreover, through various data analysis projects we show that it is possible to decompose them into simpler sub-tasks that can be then successfully accomplished by non-experts. Additionally, we found that the following features were valuable for collaborative data analysis with crowd workers: support for dynamic development, code deliberation, communication, and a journal with decisions made throughout the project.

In summary, we believe that our study paves the way for including non-expert crowd workers in data analysis tasks. As such, we hope to contribute to the research studying the requirements for building tools that can leverage the crowd to address the shortage of data analysts.

Acknowledgments. This work was supported by the Swiss National Science Foundation under contract number 14341.

References

1. Davenport, T.H., Patil, D.J.: Data_Scientist-the_Sexiest_Job_of_the_21St_Century.Pdf (2012)
2. Kandel, S., Paepcke, A., Hellerstein, J., Heer, J.: Wrangler: interactive visual specification of data transformation scripts. In: Human Factors in Computing Systems, pp. 3363–3372. ACM (2011). https://doi.org/10.1145/1978942.1979444

---

[6] https://github.com/.

3. Bernstein, A., Klein, M., Malone, T.W.: Programming the global brain. Commun. ACM **55**, 41 (2012). https://doi.org/10.1145/2160718.2160731

4. Sere, F.C., Swigger, K., Alpaslan, F.N., Brazile, R., Dafoulas, G., Lopez, V.: Online collaboration: collaborative behavior patterns and factors affecting globally distributed team performance. Comput. Hum. Behav. **27**, 490–503 (2011). https://doi.org/10.1016/j.chb.2010.09.017

5. Van Noorden, R.: Online collaboration: scientists and the social network. Nature **512**, 126–129 (2014). https://doi.org/10.1038/512126a

6. MacDonald, J.: Assessing online collaborative learning: Process and product. Comput. Educ. **40**, 377–391 (2003). https://doi.org/10.1016/S0360-1315(02)00168-9

7. Yadav, M.S., Pavlou, P.A.: Marketing in computer-mediated environments: research synthesis and new directions. J. Mark. **78**, 20–40 (2014). https://doi.org/10.1509/jm.12.0020

8. Tseng, H., Wang, C.-H., Ku, H.-Y., Sun, L.: Key factors in online collaboration and their relationship to teamwork satisfaction. Q. Rev. Distance Educ. **10**, 195–206 (2009)

9. Salehi, N., McCabe, A., Valentine, M., Bernstein, M.S.: Huddler: convening stable and familiar crowd teams despite unpredictable availability. In: Proceedings of the 20th ACM Conference on Computer Supported Cooperative Work & Social Computing (2016)

10. Yukl, G.: Leadership in organizations. In: Personnel Psychology, 7th edn, p. 542 (2001). https://doi.org/10.1016/1048-9843(95)90027-6

11. Kulkarni, A., Can, M., Hartmann, B.: Collaboratively crowdsourcing workflows with turkomatic. In: Proceedings of the ACM 2012 Conference on Computer Supported Cooperative Work - CSCW 2012, p. 1003 (2012). https://doi.org/10.1145/2145204.2145354

12. Kittur, A., Smus, B., Kraut, R.: CrowdForge Crowdsourcing complex work. In: Proceedings of the 2011 Annual Conference Extended Abstracts on Human Factors in Computing Systems - CHI EA 2011. p. 1801 (2011). https://doi.org/10.1145/1979742.1979902

13. Kittur, A., Khamkar, S., André, P., Kraut, R.E.: CrowdWeaver: visually managing complex crowd work. In: Scenario, pp. 1033–1036 (2012). https://doi.org/10.1145/2145204.2145357

14. Bernstein, M.S., Little, G., Miller, R.C., Hartmann, B., Ackerman, M.S., Karger, D.R., Crowell, D., Panovich, K.: Soylent: a word processor with a crowd inside. In: Proceedings of the 23nd Annual ACM Symposium on User Interface Software and Technology, pp. 313–322 (2010). https://doi.org/10.1145/1866029.1866078

15. Carpenter, J.: May the best analyst win. Science (New York) **331**, 698–699 (2011). https://doi.org/10.1126/science.331.6018.698

16. Dissanayake, I., Zhang, J., Gu, B.: Virtual team performance in crowdsourcing contests: a social network perspective. In: ICIS 2015 Proceedings, pp. 1–16 (2014)

17. Heer, J., Viégas, F.B., Wattenberg, M.: Voyagers and voyeurs: supporting asynchronous collaborative visualization. Commun. ACM **52**, 87–97 (2009). https://doi.org/10.1145/1240624.1240781

18. Viegas, F.B., Wattenberg, M., Van Ham, F., Kriss, J., McKeon, M.: Many Eyes: a site for visualization at internet scale. IEEE Trans. Vis. Comput. Graph. **13**, 1121–1128 (2007). https://doi.org/10.1109/TVCG.2007.70577

19. Willett, W., Heer, J., Hellerstein, J.M., Agrawala, M.: CommentSpace: structured support for collaborative visual analysis. In: Proceedings of the SIGCHI Conference on Human Factors in Computing Systems, pp. 3131–3140 (2011). https://doi.org/10.1145/1978942.1979407

20. Haas, D., Krishnan, S., Wang, J., Franklin, M.J., Wu, E.: Wisteria: nurturing scalable data cleaning infrastructure. In: Proceedings of the 41st International Conference on Very Large Data Bases, vol. 8, pp. 2004–2007 (2015). https://doi.org/10.14778/2824032.2824122

21. dos Santos, F., Bazzan, A.L.C.: An ant based algorithm for task allocation in large-scale and dynamic multiagent scenarios. In: Proceedings of the 11th Annual conference on Genetic and evolutionary computation - GECCO 2009, p. 73 (2009). https://doi.org/10.1145/1569901.1569912

22. Campbell, A., Wu, A.S.: Multi-agent role allocation: issues, approaches, and multiple perspectives. Auton. Agents Multi-Agent Syst. **22**, 317–355 (2011). https://doi.org/10.1007/s10458-010-9127-4

23. Chandrasekaran, B., Josephson, J.R., Benjamins, V.R.: Ontology of tasks and methods. Knowl. Acquis. 1–25 (1998). Spring symposium series technical report (AAAI Technical Report SS-97-06)

24. Stefik, M.: Planning with constraints (MOLGEN: part 1). Artif. Intell. **16**, 111–139 (1981). https://doi.org/10.1016/0004-3702(81)90007-2

25. Malone, T.W., Crowston, K., Lee, J., Pentland, B., Dellarocas, C., Wyner, G., Quimby, J., Osborn, C., Bernstein, A., Herman, G., Klein, M., O'Donnell, E.: Tools for inventing organizations: toward a handbook of organizational processes. Manag. Sci. **45**, 425–443 (1999)

26. Howison, J., Crowston, K.: Collaboration through open superposition. Mis Q. **38**(1), 29–50 (2014)

27. Hevner, A.R., March, S.T., Park, J., Ram, S.: Design science in information systems research. MIS Q. **28**, 75–105 (2004). https://doi.org/10.2307/25148625

28. Gregor, S.: The nature of theory in information systems. MIS Q. **30**, 611–642 (2006). https://doi.org/10.2307/25148742

29. Reinecke, K., Bernstein, A.: Knowing what a user likes: a design science approach to interfaces that automatically adapt to culture. MIS Q. **37**, 427–453 (2013)

30. Peffers, K.E.N., Tuunanen, T., Rothenberger, M.A., Chatterjee, S.: A design science research methodology for information systems research. Decis. Sci. **24**, 45–77 (2008). https://doi.org/10.2753/MIS0742-1222240302

31. Redmiles, D.: Software requirements for supporting collaboration through categories (2000)

32. Krishnan, S., Wang, J., Franklin, M.J., Goldberg, K., Kraska, T., Milo, T., Wu, E.: SampleClean: fast and reliable analytics on dirty data. Bull. IEEE Comput. Soc. Tech. Comm. Data Eng. **38**(3), 59–75 (2015)

33. Agrawal, A., Horton, J., Lacetera, N., Lyons, E.: Digitization and the contract labor market: a research agenda. NBER Working Paper, vol. 37 (2013). https://doi.org/10.3386/w19525

34. Mascha, E.J.: Equivalence and noninferiority testing in anesthesiology research. Anesthesiology **113**, 779–781 (2010). https://doi.org/10.1097/ALN.0b013e3181ec621

35. Peffers, K., Tuunanen, T., Rothenberger, M.A., Chatterjee, S.: A design science research methodology for information systems research. J. Manag. Inf. Syst. **24**(3), 45–77 (2007)

ICT for Development

An Argument for Post-Hoc Collective Intelligence

Dean J. Jones$^{(\boxtimes)}$ and Gunjan Mansingh

Department of Computing, The University of the West Indies,
Mona Campus, Jamaica
{dean.jones03,gunjan.mansingh}@uwimona.edu.jm

Abstract. Despite the advancement of artificial intelligence there are still some problems which are beyond current computing capabilities including some high dimensional pattern recognition tasks and those that require creativity or intuition. These problems are often delegated to interested participants through carefully engineered human computation systems, crowdsourcing systems or collective intelligence systems. However, all these systems require a fore-planned platform to coordinate the production of the intellectual product such as a vote or a statement from the human participants. Outside of these platforms, however, there is a vast amount of independently created intellectual products, for example in tweets, YouTube comments, online articles, internal company reports and minutes. These are largely untapped due to a lack of awareness of the potential that exists within them and the inaptness of the tools and techniques that would be required exploit the data. In this paper we propose Post-Hoc Collective Intelligence (PHCI) as a novel research and argue that it has important distinctions from the closely related research areas. In so doing we present an informed argument for the PHCI framework having 5 components which give structure to implementation and research pursuits.

Keywords: Post-Hoc Collective Intelligence · PHCI · Collective Intelligence
Natural language processing · Cognitive biases

1 Introduction

Humans are incredible creatures who are uniquely adept at problem-solving and, unsurprisingly, considered amongst the most successful species on our planet. However, humans have limitations in their cognitive resources such as memory, speed, etc., and in a demonstration of their problem-solving prowess devised mechanisms to delegate specific tasks. In the 1700s human computers were used to undertake computing tasks [1] until the advent of the 'automatic computer' in the 1900s [2], with the latter being so designated to distinguish it from the human computers. The 'automatic computers', now known as just computers, have since become astronomically more advanced and are able to tackle a wide variety of problems with great speed, efficiency and reliability and retain vast amounts of knowledge. Nonetheless, there are many problems which are easy for humans but are difficult for even the most advanced computers and computer algorithms [3]. These problems include tasks such as

© Springer International Publishing AG, part of Springer Nature 2018
S. Chatterjee et al. (Eds.): DESRIST 2018, LNCS 10844, pp. 239–252, 2018.
https://doi.org/10.1007/978-3-319-91800-6_16

perceptual tasks, natural language analysis and cognitive tasks such as planning and reasoning [3]. Humans have exploited this ability by including other humans in Human Computation systems such that the parts that are suited to the digital computer is done by it and the human-suited parts are done by the human. Humans have further exploited their problem-solving ability through the development of Crowdsourcing and Collective Intelligence systems that allow them to exchange ideas and collaborate towards solving problems. Spreading the load across many humans in this way enables many of their limitations to be mitigated. However, these systems require careful engineering to pull the humans in and channel their efforts towards a task so expressions of human intellect that fall outside of these systems remain largely untapped, presenting an opportunity for a new era of advancement in problem-solving capabilities.

In this research we describe how the intellect of humans that are embedded in various expressions and scattered across different sources can be exploited in a process we call Post-Hoc Collective Intelligence (PHCI) and present an argument for considering it as a distinct research area. We demonstrate this by describing closely related research areas and illustrating the differences between what exists and what is being proposed. In particular, we show that the characteristics of crowd control and the nature of the aggregation are critical differences which have significant implications for the applicability of existing theories. This framework is a useful start towards the understanding of this nuanced type of Collective Intelligence (CI) and by putting the spotlight on it we hope to further direct interest into the problem for the benefit of researchers, practitioners, businesses and the wider public.

The paper is organized as follows. First, we explore relevant literature on Collective Intelligence and its related areas. Next we provide an overview of Design Science Research Methodology used to develop an artifact. We then present the PHCI framework and evaluate the artifact by using informed arguments and, finally draw conclusions.

2 Background

The subject of this research cross-cuts several research areas. The body of research on Big Data is relevant as it describes the opportunities that are waiting to be exploited and the challenges surrounding them. The production of Big Data is trending upwards [4]. Big Data in the unstructured form is difficult to analyze and techniques are "relatively experimental" [4] and the skills to utilize them are "in short supply" [5].

Collective Intelligence (CI), and closely related research areas, are of great importance because they describe how the intellect of humans are applied to problems. Understanding them is a prerequisite to understanding their limitations which warrant this work. CI, has been described and defined by several over the years [1, 5–8]. Malone et al. [9] defined CI simply as "groups of individuals doing things collectively that seem intelligent". It is an emergent phenomenon where the overall judgement of a group of people is more accurate than that of individuals alone [9]. The chief motivation behind exploiting CI comes from the premise that "no one knows everything, everyone knows something, all knowledge resides in humanity" [8].

The other closely related but distinct ideas related to the broader concept of CI are Social Computing, Crowdsourcing, Crowd Intelligence and Human Computation. Figure 1 [10] shows the relationships between the concepts. The descriptions and examples described show that there are overlaps between each of the concepts.

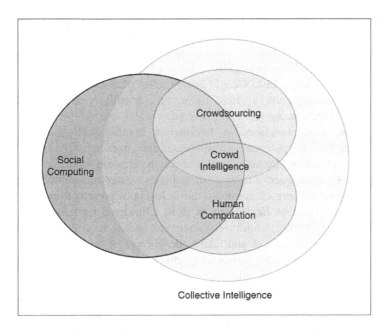

Fig. 1. Collective Intelligence and related areas [10]

Social computing is "a sort of collective intelligence, which provides users a way to gain knowledge through collective efforts in a social interactive environment" [10]. Online forums and Community Question and Answer sites Stack Exchange (http://www. stackexchange.com) are instances of such social environments that allow users to contribute their ideas towards answering users' questions or rank other proposed answers.

Crowdsourcing is "the act of taking a task traditionally performed by a designated agent (such as an employee or a contractor) and outsourcing it by making an open call to an undefined but large group of people" [11]. Wikipedia (http://wikipedia.org) is the most popular example within this category. It allows individuals to contribute his/her ideas and editing skills towards encyclopedia articles by submitting new content or content supplied by someone else. Github (http://www.github.com) allows individuals to contribute their programming skills towards software projects.

Crowd intelligence "emerges from the collective intelligent efforts of massive numbers of autonomous individuals, who are motivated to carry out the challenging computational tasks under a certain Internet-based organizational structure" [10]. Amazon Mechanical Turk (AMT) and reCAPTCHA are two well-known platforms that implement crowd intelligence.

Human computation is "harnessing human intelligence to solve computational problems that are beyond the scope of existing Artificial Intelligence (AI) algorithms"

[3]. It involves breaking the task into well-defined, much smaller 'microtasks' that do not require much time on the part of each 'worker.' Amazon Mechanical Turk (AMT) and reCAPTCHA are two notable examples. In AMT humans offer their time in exchange for monetary reward to complete tasks such as tagging images, transcribing audio and completing surveys [3]. reCAPTCHA is used to get humans to label characters that are difficult for optical character recognition (OCR) algorithms [3, 9]. Humans are typically presented with a known Completely Automated Public Turing test to tell Computers and Humans Apart (CAPTCHA) challenge alongside an image requiring labelling. The humans label the unknown image, and may not know that they are contributing to a larger task. Google Search relies on decisions made by users to construct future search results [9]. Here, again, the user is likely unaware of the effect that they have on influencing the larger outcome.

When faced with abundance of information humans will employ cognitive heuristics which have the potential to cause biases and errors in judgement [6, 12, 13]. This is humans' significant limitation and it affects the creation and evaluation of ideas [14]. There are CI techniques to mitigate these biases – outreach, additive aggregation and self-organization. Outreach speaks to the inclusion of persons from diverse areas that typically would not be likely sources to be considered for generating ideas or evaluating/deciding on them. Additive aggregation speaks to collecting information from a large number of sources and taking the average of the responses. This only succeeds with the right balance between expertise and diversity, and its effect is rendered null if all members are ignorant and the results may be affected if distribution of perspectives are skewed in some way [14]. Diversity has the potential of to mitigate the effects of self-serving and belief perseverance biases [14]. Self Organization is the third mechanism that allows for interaction in the form of adding to or subtracting from the ideas of others in the group. This is potentially problematic when the effect of groupthink comes into play [14].

The literature to date have explored factors needed for traditional CI ecosystems to work and what problems they can be applied to [10, 14]. In Crowd Intelligence the following are the chief research concerns [10]:

1. How can the crowd be effectively organized? This problem is concerned with the interaction patterns such collaboration, coordination and competition.
2. How can the crowd be effectively incentivized to drive predictable emergence of CI.
3. How can the quality of the output be assured? This problem is mainly concerned with assessment and treatment of the submissions by individuals.

Previous research [14] have put forward applications of CI and the factors needed for collective intelligence ecosystems to work. The overarching gap is that none of these theories answer address these concerns for data that resides outside the CI platforms. This is the gap that this research seeks to fill.

3   Research Methodology

This work is based on the Design Science Research Methodology (DSRM). It is primarily about solving a problem within the Information Technology and Information Systems disciplines. It seeks to address the problem through research activity that culminates in the creation of some artifact as the solution. An artifact is "any designed object with an embedded solution to an understood research problem" [15]. It may be constructs, models, methods or instantiations [16] or "new properties of technical, social, and/or informational resources" [17]. The DSRM guides the research process through conceptualization and representation of the problem, selection and application of appropriate methods to search for a solution and, finally, evaluation of the solutions using appropriate means [18]. This process involves six activities [15]: (1) Problem identification and motivation, (2) Definition of the objectives for a solution, (3) Design and Development, (4) Demonstration, (5) Evaluation, (6) Communication. For a full description of the methodology see [15, 16].

The use of appropriate methods to evaluate research artifacts is an integral part of rigorous scientific research [19], the absence of which is a common weakness of Information Systems research [19]. In this work we therefore endeavoured to introduce this rigor through careful selection of our evaluation methods. The presentation of the framework in Sect. 4 employs the informed argument [16] evaluation method to show the goodness of the PHCI framework, whose primary utility centers around developing the understanding of this nuanced type of CI and prompting further research. This is a descriptive method that is appropriate in cases where the innovative nature and form of the artifact makes it infeasible to use other methods [16], such as this. We compare the framework to similar frameworks and show how they are incompatible with the features of the problem that PHCI solves and the solutions that are based on them. Indeed, the other artifacts created are prompted by questions that emerged from this PHCI framework.

4 The Post-Hoc Collective Intelligence Framework

4.1 Distinctions Between PHCI and Related Concepts

In background section we described the related concepts such as Social Computing, Crowd Sourcing, Crowd Intelligence and Human Computation. While PHCI shares characteristics of each of these there are key differences that make it distinct from each of them. Figure 1 illustrates the defining characteristics (with a highlighted cell) and shows where the characteristics overlap or are incompatible.

Crowd Intelligence [10], for instance, requires massive numbers of independent persons working towards some goal. It requires AI to integrate with human intelligence in some way such as (1) the human helping to improve the AI or (2) AI helping the crowd by coordinating and mediating it. Resultantly, research topics for this area will therefore include: determining how to dynamically assign members to the crowd; dynamic adjustments of the monetary incentives; quality control [10]. PHCI does not require this coordination between the humans and AI and therefore these concerns do not apply.

PHCI bears a similarity to Crowd Sourcing's defining feature of being a technique for using a crowd to perform an activity that would traditionally be done by a specific individual or group of individuals [11]. In many cases, what would have been done by individuals within an organization is being issued to the wider public. In PHCI the crowd can be any group of persons having sufficiently diverse perspectives. It could be members of the board or committee, or a group of experts who have communicated their thoughts about a subject matter. It could also be a broader group of internet users who have independently offered their thoughts on the same matter (Table 1).

Table 1. Defining features of PHCI and CI-related concepts

Feature/Concern	PHCI	Collective Intelligence	Crowd Intelligence	Crowd Sourcing	Human Computation	Social Computing
Intelligent outcome resulting from the group of individuals	Yes	Yes [9]	Yes	Yes	Yes	Not necessarily
Technology/Human Relationship:						
Integration of human intelligence with computing intelligence			Yes [10]			
Who performs the task:						
Activity shifted from specific person having that role to a large undefined group of persons				Yes [11]		
Crowd Characteristics:						
The crowd consists of large numbers of people			Yes [10]		Not necessarily [3]	
Members of the crowd may not know each other	Yes		Yes	Yes [10]	Yes [3]	Yes
Crowd Control:						
There is control over what ideas are created	No	Yes	Yes	Yes	Yes – strong control [3]	Yes
There is control over the how the ideas are created	No	Yes	Yes	Yes	Yes, strong control [3]	Yes
There is control over how the human intelligence is captured	No	Yes	Yes	Yes	Yes, strong control [3]	Yes
There is control over who creates the ideas	No*	Yes	Yes	Yes	Yes, strong control [3]	Yes
Human-Human Interaction Characteristics:						
Members of the crowd interact/communicate with each other to produce the output	No	Not necessarily	Yes	Not necessarily	Not necessarily	Yes
Platform:						
Some Platform is used to facilitate the communication between the participants	No		Yes	Yes		Yes
Platform must be internet based			Yes [10]			
A computer based interactive environment is used			Yes			Yes [10]
Task Type:						
Centered around goal of having humans perform tasks that are difficult for computers					Yes [3]	
Aggregation:						
Humans will coordinate, aggregate the ideas	No					Yes

Social Computing is a "broad concept that covers everything to do with social behavior and computing" [3]. Therefore, any interaction by humans that involve a virtual platform can be classified as a Social Computing System. Unlike CI, there is no requirement on the characteristics of the process or the outcome. Therefore, some Social Computing systems can be CI systems but this is not necessarily so. Social Computing differs from PHCI firstly in that CI needs to be achieved in the outcome. Secondly, in Social Computing there is interaction between the human participants while in PHCI there is none. While many Social Computing platforms are not designed for and do not produce an intelligent collective output in that platform PHCI can combine the KNs from many of these platforms to artificially produce CI. Research applicable to Social Computing such as group dynamics and platform design therefore do not apply to PHCI.

Human Computation is the process in which humans perform computation, defined as the "mapping of some input representation to some output representation using an explicit, finite set of instructions" [3]. Human computation systems are "intelligent systems that organize humans to carry out the process of computation" [3]. It is concerned with integrating a computational task with humans who perform some step that is presently difficult for computers. Computers are good at processing large volumes of data. They can also accurately and consistently sense the world through various sensors. For example, they can measure temperature, wind speed, and humidity, count the cars on a highway and record their registration numbers, detect changes in ambient lighting and sound levels. In many cases, however, human intellect is often required for the higher level task of perceiving what is taking place and making decisions based on them. Humans will use their knowledge, past experiences and expectations – for better or worse – to ascribe meaning to stimuli. It is this unique capability of humans that PHCI, like human computation aims to exploit. However, in human computation there is strong and explicit control over the process that allows the humans to generate their knowledge [3] while in PHCI there is only control in the selection and use of the existing information. Open problems in HC include how to determine which tasks will benefit from human intellect, how to develop and assign tasks to the human participants and how to keep them sufficiently motivated to continue to perform [3]. A common problem between Human Computation and PHCI includes the question of determining how to aggregate knowledge in the absence of ground truth and how to model the expertise of the humans.

4.2   What is PHCI?

CI is characterized by there being groups of individuals doing things collectively that seem intelligent [9]. Extending this generalized definition, we define Post-Hoc CI as:

the output of a computational process in which multiple, diverse, stored representations of human intellect are used outside the context which it was originally captured for and combined in some way to produce output which seems intelligent with respect of the task being performed.

The diversity may be achieved from multiple humans, from the perspectives of a human taken over time, or a combination of both. Using a PHCI process, the KN is made to perform some secondary function beyond what it was originally supplied and stored for. For example, in an automatic witness report processing system the report (which embodies human intellect used in perceiving an event) would have been submitted simply as a capture of the experiences of the witness for later use by an investigator or to be heard by jurors – its primary purpose. However, with PHCI, multiple witness perspectives can be combined and used to highlight false statements – a secondary purpose.

4.3   The Components of the PHCI Framework

Text produced by humans embody their knowledge and views about a particular subject matter. Given the abundance of data in this form it is a worthwhile place to start the exploration of PHCI. Our framework is focused on this type of data source and on arriving at reliable output from multiple natural language sources that may each have questionable veracity. In future research we will extend and adapt it to other unconventional forms of knowledge.

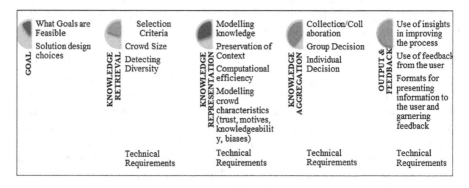

Fig. 2. A framework for PHCI

Our framework, summarized in Fig. 2, structures PHCI design considerations into: Goal, Knowledge Retrieval, Knowledge Representation, Data Aggregation, Output and Feedback. We elaborate on each below and use informed arguments to evaluate the need for the different components in the framework.

Goal. There are two key concerns within the Goal component of the framework that has implications for research and praxis. Firstly, the goals that the PHCI can be successfully applied to must be determined and, secondly, the goal will determine implementation choices for the solution. There are many potential goals that PHCI may be applied to but in its infancy as a research area these goals have not yet been well defined and verified. Computers and computer systems promise extending human capabilities so that they may be more effective at solving various problems that they face. The decision making process [20], which is embedded within the larger problem-solving process, consists of three phases – research[1], design and choice.

---

[1] The first stage of the decision making process is generally referred to as "intelligence" but it is generally accepted that in that context it refers to process of gathering information about the environment and the problem. Thus, to avoid confusion with the use of "intelligence" in this work we refer to this step as "research".

The research phase involves collecting information about the environment so serve as a basis of identifying a problem or possible solutions. The design phase involves identifying/creating alternative solutions. Lastly, the choice phase involves selecting the best of the proposed solutions. Implementation and monitoring generally follow the decision making process. Other forms of CI, having been around for some time, have been tested against various problems establishing theories that can be applied in the real world. Crowdsourcing, for instance, has been successfully applied to the different phases of the process [20].

It is then worth exploring how effective PHCI can be at the stages within the decision making process. PHCI aims to collect and concentrate the intellect that is scattered across different sources and direct it towards the task at hand. This prompts questions such as:

- What types of activities is this type of CI applicable to?
- Can PHCI be successfully applied to idea creation task (as opposed to decision)?
- How effective is PHCI in improving decision-making?
- Can PHCI provide useful output in the absence of 'ground truth'?

Some of the literature surveyed in section have demonstrated that CI can be applied to choice. The works by [21–23], in particular, use the individual solutions provided by members of the crowd to choose the best answer. These we retrospectively classify as PHCI, given that individual solutions provided by the crowd have no explicit choice being made by the humans who supplied the information originally (but is instead done by the aggregation functions) and the final output of their process is intelligent. The research and design decision-making phases also require exploration. To date, it has been a challenge for computers to generate solutions beyond what is explicitly selected from the pool human solutions [21].

The goals or tasks that PHCI is used for will dictate how the solution is implemented. Two possible tasks are Question Answering and Knowledge Exploration. For Question Answering the process may start with a user's query which may be in a structured format or in Natural Language. The query may then be expanded to broaden the search scope. If the goal of PHCI is Knowledge Exploration then the user may not have a specific question to be answered. Instead, they may be interested in mining insights from some Knowledge Source which they will supply.

Knowledge Retrieval. Data must be retrieved from some Knowledge Source using some means. The Knowledge Source may be supplied by the user in the form of collections of natural language texts or some structured database. The information may also be sourced from the open internet using appropriate information retrieval techniques [24].

In traditional question answering of factoid information the information retrieval process often needs to only identify a single, 'good' source that provides the information being sought. Once the knowledge source is considered to be reputable the search can terminate here. However, in seeking the answers from a crowd with unknown reliability the system must sample a myriad of independent sources. For CI to manifest it is important that a diverse and well informed information source is used [14]. Therefore, at this stage it is important that the knowledge source contains metadata such as those indicating the source data's creation time and characteristics about the author. Temporal metadata is used to determine temporal diversity. Characteristics about the author can help to determine characteristics of the individuals within the source. It is also important, especially where data is sourced from the internet, that the system is able to identify copies of information originating from the same source so as not to introduce a skew towards the same, regularly sampled information. 'Source Insights' are used at this stage to determine what sources are to be included or excluded in further processing. The insights may be in the form of preprogrammed or learned heuristics for distinguishing between low and high quality sources. It may also be supplied by the user of the system who manually labels a source as good or bad by interacting with the system's initial or previous output using some interface of the PHCI system.

It is important to note that we do not expect that the average, or the middle ground between stupid and intelligent contributions to be the intelligent collective solution. Collective stupidity is likely to result from a crowd that is completely ignorant [14]. However, outright exclusion of poor-quality sources may not always be the right method. Even poor quality submissions can add value to the solution and in cases where only low-quality data is available mechanisms must be put in place to extract useful information from that [10]. For example, Prelec et al. [7] used low quality contributions in their "Surprisingly Popular" algorithm to improve their selection of the correct solution. In other words, the low-quality contributions helped to identify the high-quality ones. It is the responsibility of the aggregation step further in the process to determine how these will be used to arrive at the intelligent output. This component overlaps the 'who' and 'why' genes in [9] as well as the crowd category in [20] such as motive and trust of the participants.

In all other forms of CI those in charge can structure the task to control the crowd and their tasks, albeit more strictly in some than in others. In human computation this is precisely engineered while in social computing control is often more relaxed. For PHCI there is no possibility to control what ideas are created, who creates them, how they are created or how they are stored. Instead, this control must be concentrated in the selection and retrieval of the ideas. This results in research problems centered around adapting to these limitations. The following questions result:

- What criteria can be used to determine which participants and perspectives are to be included?
- Given that the system has no control over the selection of the crowd participants or how they provide their information before-hand how can characteristics of the participants be identified from the source?

Knowledge Representation. The Knowledge Nugget (KN) to be used in further processing must be in a form that may be processed by the computer. We consider the Knowledge Nugget to be the result of the intellect of a human. Examples include: a number (e.g. 1337) or sentence (e.g. "Over ten thousand as of 2016.") submitted to answer a question (e.g. "How many satellites are in the sky?"); a single vote cast to up-vote or down-vote an answer in a CQA system; a line of code to implement a feature. Numeric information can be easily processed by a computer but knowledge embedded in text requires advanced NLP to convert the idea into various forms such as formal logic or as assertions. It is important for metadata to be captured with the KN itself to preserve the context of the knowledge and to capture the characteristics of the participants as these will be needed in the aggregation step.

Knowledge Aggregation. In other forms of CI, aggregation can be pre-engineered or be designed to occur 'naturally' through human interaction. Much research has gone into designing and controlling the interactions to allow a constructive feedback to occur between motivated humans while mitigating the side-effects of group interactions such as groupthink, human biases and cheating in the crowdsourcing processes [20] until some final aggregate output is reached. For example, in human computation a reCAPTCHA task could simply count the number of persons that identify an unknown character until some predefined threshold of certainty is reached, and no person to person interaction is needed. In social computing and crowd sourcing the crowd, possibly supported by some hierarchy of persons, will interact back and forth until they agree on the final result as a group.

In the PHCI aggregation process the side-effects that can result from human-interaction are non-existent since all interactions are managed by the system itself. It is the system that is organizing the ideas of the crowd, as opposed to organizing the crowd so that they can provide and refine ideas organically. For example, in the voting system of Yelp the KN is the rating submitted by a user; in a public Github repository the KN is the line of code that adds to the feature set of a software being developed; in Wikipedia the KN is a paragraph or citation added to an article which improves its quality. In some cases it may require the KN be enhanced over several iterations or enhancements over time before it reaches what could be considered intelligent. A Wikipedia article may start as a 'stub' containing a single paragraph. After a series of revisions are made the article will eventually cross a threshold beyond which one would consider it a good article, at some time tint. Figure 3 depicts a CI system in which KNs (represented by a square, circle, triangle, and diamond) are supplied over time t_0 to t_n. The KNs interact in some way, reinforcing or cancelling out each other. After sufficient KNs have been supplied the KNs remaining at t_n will, collectively, represent the intelligent output of the system. That is, $t_{int} = t_n$. This is akin to how the first of a series of fair coin-flips may be biased in one direction but once sufficiently large numbers of flips are done the average will converge on the unbiased expected result. In other cases all the KNs are available at the same instant and their aggregate represents the intelligent output. In this case $t_{int} = t_0$. It is here that novel techniques are needed to combine the ideas.

In cases such as independent accounts of some event temporality may be of no significance and all KNs can be assumed to have time of t_0. It can be important in other cases where a newer source could invalidate an older source either because new information was received, giving a clearer or more accurate view, because the state of the world has changed or because the original information was incorrect. For example: in a Github project, code implementing a newly established best-practice can warrant new code to replace it; a reviewer in a forum changes his opinion after learning the correct operation of the item bought; in a Wikipedia article a false fact may be replaced by someone more knowledgeable. A successful PHCI system must account for both independent and related knowledge.

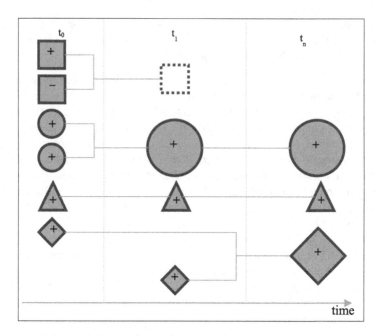

Fig. 3. Depiction of changes in collective knowledge over time

With Natural Language data sources the ideas expressed in the text are the KNs to be aggregated. Yi, Steyvers [21] identified two aggregation methods that can be used on non-discrete information – Local Decomposition Aggregation (LDA) and Global Similarity Aggregation (GSA). This framework component overlaps with the considerations of the 'how' gene in [9] and the process category in [20].

In PHCI this aggregation must be engineered using the preexisting information. Important problems that arise are as follows:

- How can the ideas of the humans be represented so that they can be evaluated against each other?
- In what ways can the information be combined to yield output relevant to the task and should some carry greater weight than others?
- How can the technical challenges associated with this type of processing be overcome in this type of processing?
- How do characteristics of the crowd relate to the appropriateness of aggregation method?
- How do characteristics of the task relate to the appropriateness of the aggregation method?

Output and Feedback. After going through the processes above the system will yield its output. A researcher or practitioner must therefore give consideration to the appropriateness of the output format. This is as important as in crowdsourcing [20] and human computation systems [3]. In some cases, a command line application may produce an effective output while in others a sophisticated, interactive user interface may be needed to adequately communicate the output of the system. This output can be used to identify good/bad individual Knowledge Nuggets or Knowledge Sources. This can itself be the output of the system or this insight can be used as feedback to the data aggregation or source data retrieval procedures above for subsequent iterations of the process. This may cue the system to expand its search of the Knowledge Source for further information. The user of the system may also have knowledge about the information nuggets or data sources that they can introduce to the process as insights. For example, in evaluating witness reports the investigator may mark a fact reported as false if he/she has first-hand/ground-truth knowledge of its falsehood. Excluding this false information nugget could allow other nuggets to emerge in the output. It could also be used to identify and exclude sources that are bad overall and their exclusion in the subsequent iterations could remove any skew they may have caused.

5 Conclusion

In this work, we proposed a framework for extracting CI from stored information in the form of natural language. This framework, called PHCI, was created from a synthesis of existing CI frameworks and other areas of study. We showed by analysis of these areas which concepts are adaptable and which areas are incompatible with the characteristics of PHCI, thereby justifying its creation. The framework proposed may be used by practitioners and researchers for implementing an end to end PHCI process. The framework highlights the categories of technical capabilities that are likely needed to implement PHCI successfully.

One emerging research question seeks to determine the goals that PHCI can be used to achieve. To further evaluate our framework we plan on applying this framework to witness statements for an event in Jamaica. The experiment will demonstrate how PHCI could be used to perform the functions of humans or to aid them. Initial results have shown that PHCI can be successfully applied to the task. We hope the work here will catalyze future research into the area and spawn new types of solutions that can leverage our collective human intelligence.

References

1. Grier, D.A.: When Computers were Human. Princeton University Press, Princeton (2013)
2. Denning, P.J., Martell, C.H.: Great Principles of Computing. MIT Press, Cambridge (2015)
3. Law, E., Ahn, L.V.: Human computation. Synth. Lect. Artif. Intell. Mach. Learn. 5(3), 1–121 (2011)
4. Bulger, M., Taylor, G., Schroeder, R.: Data-driven business models: challenges and opportunities of big data. Oxford Internet Institute (2014)
5. Schroeck, M., et al.: Analytics: the real-world use of big data. IBM Global Bus. Serv. 12, 1–20 (2012)
6. Tversky, A., Kahneman, D.: Judgment under uncertainty: heuristics and biases. Science 185 (4157), 1124–1131 (1974)
7. Prelec, D., Seung, H.S., McCoy, J.: A solution to the single-question crowd wisdom problem. Nature 541(7638), 532–535 (2017)

8. Pierre, L.: Collective Intelligence: Mankind's Emerging World in Cyberspace. Perseus Books, Cambrigde (1997)
9. Malone, T., Laubacher, R., Dellarocas, C.: Harnessing crowds: mapping the genome of collective intelligence (2009)
10. Li, W., et al.: Crowd intelligence in AI 2.0 era. Front. Inf. Technol. Electron. Eng. **18**(1), 15–43 (2017)
11. Howe, J.: Crowdsourcing: How the Power of the Crowd is Driving the Future of Business. Random House, New York (2008)
12. Peer, E., Gamliel, E.: Heuristics and biases in judicial decisions. Court Rev. **49**, 114 (2013)
13. Ramprasath, M., Hariharan, S.: A survey on question answering system. Int. J. Res. Rev. Inf. Sci. (IJRRIS) **2**(1), 171–179 (2012)
14. Bonabeau, E.: Decisions 2.0: the power of collective intelligence. MIT Sloan. Manag. Rev. **50**, 45–52 (2009). Winter
15. Peffers, K., et al.: A design science research methodology for information systems research. J. Manag. Inf. Syst. **24**(3), 45–77 (2007)
16. Hevner, A.R., et al.: Design science in information systems research. MIS Q. **28**(1), 75–105 (2004)
17. Järvinen, P.: Action research is similar to design science. Qual. Quant. **41**(1), 37–54 (2007)
18. March, S.T., Smith, G.F.: Design and natural science research on information technology. Decis. Support Syst. **15**(4), 251–266 (1995)
19. Hart, D., Gregor, S.: Information Systems Foundations: The Role of Design Science. ANU E Press, Canberra (2010)
20. Chiu, C.-M., Liang, T.-P., Turban, E.: What can crowdsourcing do for decision support? Decis. Support Syst. **65**, 40–49 (2014)
21. Yi, S.K.M., et al.: The wisdom of the crowd in combinatorial problems. Cogn. Sci. **36**(3), 452–470 (2012)
22. Steyvers, M., et al.: The wisdom of crowds in the recollection of order information. In: Advances in Neural Information Processing Systems (2009)
23. Faisal, C.M., et al.: A novel framework for social web forums' thread ranking based on semantics and post quality features. J. Supercomput. **72**(11), 4276–4295 (2016)
24. Kolomiyets, O., Moens, M.-F.: A survey on question answering technology from an information retrieval perspective. Inf. Sci. **181**(24), 5412–5434 (2011)

An Ontological Approach to Classifying Cybercrimes in an ICT4D Context

Charlette Donalds[1](✉) ⓘ and Kweku-Muata Osei-Bryson[2]

[1] University of the West Indies, Mona Kingston, Jamaica
charlette.donalds02@uwimona.edu.jm
[2] Virginia Commonwealth University, Richmond, USA
KMOsei@VCU.edu

Abstract. While the phenomenon of cybercrime remains a challenge for governments worldwide, it is even more of a challenge for countries in an ICT4D context since they possess limited technical skills and resources to respond to, investigate and prosecute nefarious cyber activities. Despite the challenges, governments have responded by establishing legal frameworks and Computer Security Incident Response Teams. However, scholars argue that the cybercrime phenomenon is still not well understood; which is compounded by the lack of an accepted, uniform cybercrime classification scheme or ontology with which to classify cybercrimes. While few classification schemes have been published, same are limited in that they are not comprehensive; i.e., they are unable to account for the range of and ever changing types of cybercrimes and, the schemes are largely incompatible, focusing on different perspectives. This makes holistic and consistent classification improbable. To address these gaps we propose a formal cybercrime classification ontology, expressed in OWL Ontology Language. In designing our ontology we were guided by the steps of the design science research methodology. This paper contributes a formal ontology of a 'shared conceptualization' of cybercrimes by police practitioners and researchers. The ontology presented here is improved over prior works since it incorporates multiple perspectives and its design is better able to handle existing and future cybercrimes, a most salient feature given the dynamic nature of cybercrimes. We demonstrate the ontology by applying it to an actual cybercrime case. The designed ontology effectively classifies the cybercrime and has the potential to improve cybercrime classification in ICT4D and developed contexts.

Keywords: Cybercrime classification · Ontology · Developing country

1 Introduction

Cybercrime remains a fundamental concern for citizens, organizations and governments worldwide. With the increasing proliferation of integrated digital technology into objects and the World Wide Web being the universal medium for conducting business and for socialization, security issues such as unauthorized access to, interception of, interference with data, computer related fraud and forgery, et al., are now major challenges. Also, the financial consequences of cyber-related incidents are dire and is

© Springer International Publishing AG, part of Springer Nature 2018
S. Chatterjee et al. (Eds.): DESRIST 2018, LNCS 10844, pp. 253–267, 2018.
https://doi.org/10.1007/978-3-319-91800-6_17

worsening. According to the Ponemon Institute and Accenture [1], cybercrimes cost organizations, on average, US$11.7 million in 2017, representing a 23% increase over 2016.

An upsurge in cybercrime in some Commonwealth Caribbean countries has also been reported. According to the Commonwealth Cybercrime Initiative, some reported incidents in the region include the theft of US$150 million from the Bank of Nova Scotia in Jamaica in 2014; individuals claiming to be local ISIS supporters hacked government websites in 2015; and, in the same year, tax authorities in the region were infected by ransomware, which blocked users from accessing their systems and demanded money for users to regain access [2]. This trend in the Caribbean is even more troubling than for developed nations as more and more governments increase the use of Information and Communication Technologies (ICTs) to deliver services to its people without the commensurate technical and administrative capabilities to combat these emergent threats. Notwithstanding, the Caribbean counties have formally recognized that combatting cybercrimes and strengthening their cyber resilience are imperatives to economic and social development; democratic governance, and national and citizen security [3].

In response to cybercrimes, governments worldwide and in the Caribbean specifically, have in recent years developed legal frameworks and established Computer Security Incident Response Teams (CSIRTs also commonly referred to as CERTs or CIRTs) to better respond to, investigate, and prosecute nefarious cyber activities or crimes involving the use of ICTs [3]. However, scholars argue that the phenomenon of cybercrime is still not well understood. In fact, they posit that a better understanding of cybercrimes is necessary: (1) to develop appropriate legal and policy responses; (2) to develop better estimates of the economic costs of cybercrimes on society; and (3) for educating the public about the types of cybercrimes [4]. Researchers argue further that the problem is compounded by the lack of an accepted, uniform cybercrime classification scheme or ontology with which to classify cybercrimes. According to Ngo and Jaishankar [5], a universally agreed-upon classification scheme is necessary to advance our knowledge and the scholarship of cybercrime. Other scholars [6] posit that a consistent classification scheme is needed for cross jurisdictional cooperation, information sharing and for the successful prosecution of cybercriminals.

Despite the magnitude of the cybercrime phenomenon, there is a dearth of research focusing on a cybercrime classification scheme [see 4, 7–9] and even fewer yet on a cybercrime ontology [see 4]. Albeit, the published classification schemes are limited in that they are not comprehensive; i.e., they are unable to account for the range of and ever changing types of cybercrimes. Further, these classification schemes are incompatible, focusing on different perspectives and/or using varying terminologies interchangeably, even though they refer to the same thing. This makes consistent and repeatable cybercrime classification difficult. However, consistent and repeatable classification is salient to the area. Arguably, it can enable researchers and practitioners to predict the direction of future cybercrimes as well as formulate novel and timely solutions [5]. To achieve repeatable and consistent classifications, their needs to be a shared conceptualization of cybercrimes. This shared conceptualization provides a common, consistent language that can be used by all cybercrime stakeholders.

To address these research gaps, we develop a comprehensive cybercrime classification ontology, expressed in OWL ontology language. Furthermore, this work is part of a larger project that aims to develop a cybercrime reporting tool for a police organization in a Caribbean country. The objective is that the cybercrime tool will be able to collect, classify and provide trending information about cybercrimes. This ontology then, is an initial step towards such an effort; and aims to provide a 'shared conceptualization' of cybercrimes by police practitioners and researchers. A conceptualization has been described by Gruber [10] as an abstract, simplified view or model of a domain of interest.

An ontology is described as an "an explicit specification of a conceptualization" [10] which captures objects, concepts, entities and the relationships that hold among them. Some advantages presented in the literature [11] for adopting an ontology are: (1) Common vocabulary - it defines a common vocabulary for stakeholders who need to share information in a domain. (2) Sharing – facilitates the sharing of a common understanding of the structure of information among stakeholders in a domain or software agents; (3) Reuse – enables the reuse of domain knowledge; and (4) facilitates the analysis of domain knowledge.

The remainder of this paper is organized as follows: in Sect. 2 we present our research approach and works related to our study. Section 3 describes the research methodology and in Sect. 4 we present the conceptual model of our ontology, represented as an entity relationship diagram (ERD). In Sect. 5 we then present our ontology, expressed on Protégé OWL and demonstrate the efficacy of our ontology by using it to classify an actual cybercrime. We present concluding remarks and future research plans in Sect. 6.

2 Research Approach and Related Work

2.1 Research Approach

Our cybercrime classification ontology is based primarily on the taxonomy presented by Donalds and Osei-Bryson [7], hereafter referred to as the base taxonomy. That is we adopt/adapt the taxonomic characteristics proposed by [7]. Notably, in this study other related works augment our proposed ontology. We believe that the base taxonomy is a good starting point for several reasons: (1) during its development the authors incorporated properties of a sufficient and acceptable taxonomy in its design (such as 'useful', 'accepted', 'unambiguous', 'established terminologies', 'complete', et al.); (2) it incorporates several perspectives to more holistically classify cybercrimes (such as 'attacker', 'victim', 'offense', 'objective', 'tactic and tool', 'impact', et al.); (3) its uses the concept of characteristic structure, i.e., it classifies properties about that which is being classified and not the object itself, making it easily extendable.

The approach in grounding our work on a taxonomic structure is acceptable and is also described as an important step in the ontology development process. For instance, researchers [12] indicate that a "baseline taxonomy" forms the basis of the "seed ontology" (i.e., the initial ontology) in the ontology development process. Other researchers [13, p. 2] note that "an ontology subsumes a taxonomy" and Noy and

McGuinness [11, p. 3] indicate that building an ontology includes "arranging the classes in a taxonomic (subclass – superclass) hierarchy". Further, this approach has also been used in other works [see for example 4, 14].

2.2 Related Work

While there is a growing body of literature about cybercrimes, not much focus has been given to the use of ontologies for the classification of such crimes. However, some prior works have been done in the area of network and computer related attacks, which we think are pertinent and are therefore included in this review. Network and computer attacks are relevant to this area since they too are described as types of cybercrimes. For instance, in the Convention on Cybercrime [15] these types of cybercrimes are described as attacks against computer systems, networks and infrastructure.

Donalds and Osei-Bryson [7] proposed a taxonomy with nine characteristics, which arguably provides a more holistic classification scheme for cybercrimes. This taxonomy provides assistance in improving the classification of cybercrimes as well as consistency in language with regards to cybercrime events. Specifically, *Victim, Attacker, Objective, Tool & Tactic, Impact, Result, Relationship, Target* and *Offence* are the proposed taxonomic characteristics. While improved, the taxonomy is still limited. For instance, it does not address vulnerabilities via which the cybercrimes may occur nor identify the types of impacts that may affect a victim.

van Herdeen et al. [14] presented a computer network attack taxonomy and ontology with *Attack Scenario* as the core class to characterize and classify network attacks. Other taxonomy and ontology classes include, *Actor, Actor Location, Motivation, Target, Aggressor, Vulnerability, Phase, Attack Goal, Automation Level, Attack Mechanism, Effects, Sabotage, Scope and Scope Size*. Some classes also had sub-classes; for instance, the Actor class was divided into subclasses: *Group Actor, Hacker, Insider* and *Unknown Actor* and the Aggressor class: *State, Commercial Aggressor, Individual Aggressor, Self Instigator* and *Unknown Aggressor*. This network attack taxonomy and ontology is useful in that additional classes not previously identified for cybercrimes can now be incorporated in future works. For instance, in our ontology we incorporate *Vulnerability* and our *Attack_Event* is analogous *to Attack Scenario*. Notwithstanding, this ontology also has limitations. For instance, it is not able to classify cybercrimes against individuals and therefore lacks pertinent information that would be beneficial for knowledge bodies such as CSIRTs that classify cybercrimes on a day-to-day basis, and for the type of organization that our ontology is being developed for.

Using facet theory and multidimensional scaling (MDS) Kjaerland [16] analyzed cyber-intrusions reported to a CERT and identified a four faucet cyber incident taxonomy. The four facets are: *Source, Impact, Target* and *Method of Operation*. Using the four facets, Kjaerland analyzed government incidents vis-à-vis commercial. This taxonomy is useful in several ways: (1) it identifies new concepts that improve or knowledge and that which can also be incorporated in future works on cybercrime classification; and (2) it attempts to classify cybercrimes based on characteristics. However, the taxonomy is limited. Like most other cybercrime classification taxonomies, it too focuses on only few areas via which to classify cybercrimes, thus it is lacking the details needed for thorough insight into and complete classification of cybercrimes.

Barn and Barn [4] presented a taxonomy for cybercrimes, which formed the basis of their proposed cybercrime classification ontology. The ontology presented the following classes: *Agent, Action, Contact, External Observer, Impact, Location, Motivation, Target, Technology Role* and *Viewpoint*. To evaluate their proposed ontology, the authors used two well-known cybercrime examples: the Nigerian 419 scam and the CryptoLocker malware. The authors present an informative ontology which uses several perspectives with which to classify cybercrimes. Additionally, it identifies additional concepts that improves our understanding about cybercrimes. Notwithstanding, this ontology is limited; it lacks the details needed for thorough insights into cybercrimes. For instance, it does not capture the various types of attackers (e.g., blackhat, script kiddies, et al.) nor does it distinguish between a target and the victim; both are not necessarily one and the same. Additionally, the authors present a high level view of *Viewpoint* without providing enough detail about *Action_View* and *CrimeView*, subclasses of *Viewpoint*.

Our ontology is improved over existing works in several areas: (1) it incorporates varying and multiple cybercrime perspectives and therefore should provide a more holistic and complete scheme with which to classify cybercrimes; (2) its' structure is flexible, i.e., our ontology classifies cybercrimes based on properties of the cybercrime and not the actual cybercrime itself. Therefore, it is arguably better able to handle existing and future cybercrimes, a most salient feature given the dynamic nature of cybercrimes; and (3) it is adaptable, i.e., it can be easily extended in terms of new concepts and new types of cybercrimes.

3 Methodology

In this research we adopt a design science (DS) approach in designing our cybercrime classification ontology (CCO). DS, as conceptualized by Simon [17], is a research paradigm that produces innovative artifacts to solve real-world problems. Additionally, DS involves a rigorous process to design artifacts to solve observed problems, to make research contributions, to evaluate the designs, and to communicate the results to appropriate audiences [18]. Artifacts can take several forms and may include constructs, models, methods and instantiations [18, 19]. In this research, the artifact is the cybercrime classification ontology expressed in the OWL Ontology Language (OWL).

We applied the design science research methodology (DSRM) proposed by Peffers et al. [19] in developing our artifact. We chose the DSRM since: (1) it builds upon the strengths of prior efforts that proposed guidelines for conducting DS research; and (2) we concur with others [20] that it provides a useful synthesized general model. In Table 1 we indicate the steps of the DSRM and discuss how it is applied to this research.

Table 1. DSRM steps and application.

DSRM Step	Research application
Problem identification and motivation	In Sects. 1 and 2 we have established the importance and relevance of our research problem
Define solution objectives	The objectives of the solution have been inferred from the problem definition, which seeks to explain how the artifact would address the stated problem(s). The objectives of the study addresses current research gaps by proposing a more comprehensive artifact with which to classify cybercrimes; and, is more adaptive in that new terms and concepts can be easily added
Design and development	In Sects. 4 and 5 we have presented the conceptual design as well as the cybercrime artifact, respectively
Demonstration	In Sect. 5 we have demonstrated the use of the artifact by classifying an actual cybercrime.
Evaluation	Evaluation of the effectiveness of the artifact and possible redesign will be conducted in our next step after the artifact is implemented in a developing country police organization and used by cybercrime investigators to classify cybercrimes
Communication	This paper represents an attempt to communicate the problem and its importance, the artifacts' design and its effectiveness to the research community

4   Conceptual Model

In this section we present the conceptual model of our cybercrime classification ontology. Figure 1 provides a general overview of the ontology with the main concepts and the relationships between them. Below, each concept in the conceptual model is discussed.

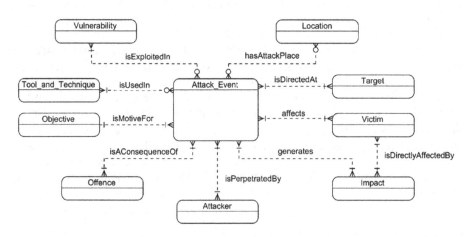

Fig. 1. Cybercrime classification conceptual model.

4.1   Attack_Event

The *Attack_Event* is central to our conceptual model and is used to capture the type of cybercrime/action that has been perpetrated by an *Attacker*. Examples of *Attack_Events* are: virtual sit-ins, hacking of email servers, denial of service (DoS), website deface-ment, site redirects, et al. Properties about the *Attack_Event* such as the start and end dates of the attack event will be captured, if known. This type of meta-data could aid in the identification of trends and patterns by police investigators overtime.

4.2   Attacker

An *Attacker* is an entity that attempts to or commits a cyber *Attack_Event* to achieve an *Objective*. Donalds and Osei-Bryson [7] classified *Attackers* into the following groups: *Corporate Raider; Hacktivist, Political Activist; Script Kiddie, Newbie, Novice; Cyber-punk, Coder, Writer; Insider, User Malcontent; White Hat Hacker, Old Guard, Sneaker; Black Hat Hacker, Professional, Elite; Cyber Terrorist, Cyber Warrior, Information Warrior; Digital Pirate, Copyright Infringer; Online Sex Offender, Cyber Predator, Pedophile*. We have mostly adopted this classification and have also extended same to include *Unknown Attacker* and *Group Attacker*. The *Attacker* in a cyber *Attack_Event* may be unknown to the *Victim* and the *Attack_Event* may also be committed by a group, therefore their inclusion. Attack_Events committed by indi-viduals are accounted for in the other adopted categories [7].

4.3   Objective

An *Objective* can be considered as the primary driving force why an *Attacker* commits the cyber *Attack_Event*. We have adopted/adapted and extended prior works on the classification of *Objective* [7] to include the following: *Curiosity, Challenge, Thrill; Political, Ideological, Moral; Status, Fame-seeking, Self-aggrandizement; Financial Gain; Anger, Revenge; Sexual Impulses*.

4.4   Victim

A *Victim* is an entity that is affected in some way by a cyber *Attack_Event*. Victims could be individuals, groups, organizations and government entities. A *Victim* may be the same as or differ from a *Target*. A *Victim* could be specifically targeted, and, would be the same as the *Target* in such an instance. However, when a *Victim* is affected by a virus that is mass distributed, for example, the *Victim* is not necessarily the specific *Target* but is affected due to a weakness or weaknesses exploited in the system.

4.5   Target

A *Target* can be described as an entity towards which the cyber *Attack_Event* is directed. Infrastructure, organization, state, target individual [4], personal computer, network infrastructure device, server and industrial equipment [14] are proposed as types of *Target*. In this study a *Target* can be of type *Infrastructure, Personal Device, Network Device, Site, Organization, Government, Group* and *TargetIndividual*.

4.6 Impact

An *Impact* can be described as the direct effect of a cyber *Attack_Event* on a *Victim*. Researchers propose differing categories for *Impact*. For instance Kjaerland [16] classifies *Impact* as *Disrupt*, *Distort*, *Destrust*, *Disclosure* and *Unknown* while Simmons et al. [9] propose two broad categories: *Operational Impact* and *Informational Impact*.

They further sub-divide *Informational Impact* into categories *Distort*, *Disrupt*, *Destruct*, *Disclosure* and *Discovery*, while *Operational Impact* is subdivided into categories such as *Installed Malware*, *Denial of Service* and *Web Compromise*. In this study we adopt the *Informational Impact* category proposed by Simmons et al. [9] with the values proposed by Kjaerland [16], which we also extend to include *Discovery* and *UnknownImpact*. Since Simmons et al.'s [9] *Operational Impact* values, in general, identify actions perpetrated in a cybercrime and is covered by our *Attack_Event* concept, we exclude this category. We also include the class *Psychological Impact* [4]. Examples of *Psychological Impact* are *fear, reputational damage, anxiety, depression* and *loss of trust*.

4.7 Location

Location refers to where (i.e., country generally or specific address) the cyber *Attack_Event* occurs. Location has been classified as either *Physical Location* or *Cyberspace* [4]. Additionally, *Location* refers to the country or specific address of the *Victim* that experiences the cyber *Attack_Event*. We note however, that while it may be possible to identify the *Location* from where a cyber *Attack_Event* occurs, this may not correspond to the actual *Location* of the *Attacker* and that a cyber *Attack_Event* via the Internet could be launched from multiple sources.

4.8 Tool and Technique

Tool and Technique can be thought of as the method(s) employed by the *Attacker* in a cyber *Attack_Event*. The categories proposed by Donalds and Osei-Bryson [7] are adopted in this study and are: *Attack Vector* (such as viruses, worms and malware); *Tool* (such as packet sniffers/injectors, password generators and key loggers); *Illicit Collusion* (a term used to describe parties willing to exploit network technology for illicit activities such as communication or data distribution and could include peer-to-peer data sharing, email and Internet Relay Chat (IRC)); and *Social Engineering* (such as impersonation, email and phising). We note that an *Attacker* may use multiple methods in a cyber *Attack_Event*.

4.9 Vulnerability

A *Vulnerability* can be described as a weakness or weaknesses in the system exploited by an *Attacker* in a cyber *Attack_Event*. Therefore, *Vulnerability* is only applicable to Attack_Events committed against ICTs. We adopt the categories of *Vulnerability* proposed by Howard [21]: *Implementation Vulnerability*, *Design Vulnerability* and *Configuration Vulnerability*.

4.10   Offence

An *Offence* can be described as a cyber *Attack _Event* that has been perpetrated by an *Attacker* against a *Victim* that is punishable by law. *Offence* often vary by jurisdiction; examples of *Offence* in the developing country for which this ontology is being developed include: Access with intent to commit or facilitate commission of offence; Computer related fraud or forgery; and, Unlawfully making available devices or data for commission of offence.

5   Ontological Representation and Cybercrime Classification

In this section we present our cybercrime classification ontology (CCO), implemented in Protégé OWL, as well as demonstrate the CCO by using it to classify an actual cybercrime event.

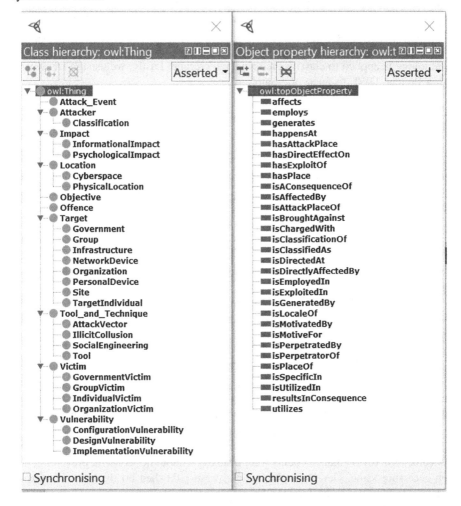

Fig. 2. Classes and properties in the cybercrime classification ontology.

Figure 2 shows the ontological representation of our CCO. This step translates the conceptual model developed from the previous stage (see Fig. 1) to an ontology– based representation using Protégé OWL. Protégé OWL (http://protege.stanford.edu/) is a tool that supports the development of a formal ontology and can be used to model domain concepts as well as the construction of a knowledge-based application, one of our future goals. The OWL ontology typically includes classes along with their descriptions, properties, instances as well as role restrictions. Examples of classes in our CCO includes Attack_Event, Attacker, Victim, Tool_and_Technique. Object properties are used to link two instances together. For instance the property is Charged With links Ronald Oates the instance unauthorised access. Our CCO then is the explicit formal specification of the terms for cybercrime classification (respresented as classes) and the relationships among them.

To demonstrate the artifact, we classify an actual cybercrime using our CCO. The actual cybercrime information is obtained from the print media in a developing country, Jamaica. The case scenario, outlined below, is a synopsis of the cybercrime details printed in two newspapers. Using said details, we instantiate our ontology by adding individuals or instances of classes as appropriate. Subsequently, we demonstrate how the ontology is applied to classify the actual cybercrime. Lastly, we use the DL Query tool in Protégé OWL to query the ontology.

5.1 Actual Cybercrime Synopsis: – Emails Hacked: Nude Photographs Uploaded [22, 23]

The police, on Monday August 27, 2012 arrested and charged a 27-year-old man, Ronald Oates, of a Kingston address, with unauthorised access, unauthorised obstruction and unlawfully making available data for the commission of an offence, all under the Jamaican Cyber Crime Act.

It is alleged that Mr. Oates hacked into the email accounts of his victims, gaining access to their nude photographs. He would then contact the women threatening to upload the photographs to a local website, if he is not paid a certain sum of money, or he would upload the photos and then demand money for them to be removed from the website.

According to the police, Mr. Oates often demanded between $10,000 and $20,000 from his victims, which has amounted to some $150,000 in total. Police say those targeted were mainly from Kingston and St. Andrew and St. Catherine, but the crime also stretched as far as Manchester.

The arrest of alleged computer hacker Ronald Oates has provided some measure of relief for popular entertainer Denyque. Denyque, who was one of the first women to come forward with claims that she was being extorted by the operators of a website that had obtained nude pictures of her, is also appealing to other victims to come forward.

Bianca Bartley owner and designer of a popular jewelry line Peace-is-of-Bianca, is one of the complainants in the matter involving Ronald Oates. Bianca reported that the passwords to her two email accounts were changed without her consent, preventing her from accessing same. Her nude photographs were published on the sites: "Jamiaca-girlsexposed.blogspot.com" (created by the accused), "myfreeblack.com" and "jcan-girls.blogspot.com".

5.2   Applying CCO to Classify an Actual Cybercrime

How can the CCO shown in Fig. 2 be used to classify the cybercrime presented in the scenario above? To do this we ask a series of questions and create individuals/instances of the appropriate class/classes. Table 2 illustrates the questions and the individuals created along with their classes. Further, we use the class hierarchical structure in our ontology model in Protégé and the conceptual model together to classify and store the cybercrime.

Table 2. Cybercrime classification questions and individuals.

Question	Instance	Class/subclass
What action/cybercrime has been committed?	Emails hacked: nude photos uploaded	Attack_Event
What entity perpetrated the action/cybercrime?	Ronald Oates	Attacker
What is the main motive of the perpetrator?	Financial gain	Objective
How is the perpetrator classified?	Black hat, professional, elite	Classification
What entity was affected by the action/cybercrime?	Bianca Bartley and Denyque	Victim
What is the type of entity affected by the action/cybercrime?	Bianca Bartley and Denyque	IndividualVictim
What entity was the action/cybercrime directed at?	Bianca Bartley and Denyque	Target
What is the type of entity that the action/cybercrime was directed at?	Bianca Bartley and Denyque	TargetIndividual
What effect did the action/cybercrime have on the entity?	Reputational damage Disclosure	PsychologicalImpact InformationalImpact
Where did the action/cybercrime take place as reported by the affected entity?	Social networking site	Cyberspace
What method did the perpetrator use in the action/cybercrime?	Social networking	SocialEngineering

5.3   Querying and Searching the CCO

An important feature of the ontology is the retrieval of results. The DL Query tab in Protégé provides an interface for searching and querying the ontology. Of note, the ontology must be classified by a reasoner before it can be queried in the DL Query tab. Below are examples of queries that can be performed on the CCO.

Q1: "Which attackers used social engineering as a tool/technique in committing a cybercrime?" The result is shown in Fig. 3.

Q2: "Which cybercrimes were committed and resulted in offence(s) being brought against an attacker?" The result is shown in Fig. 4.

Q3: "Which victim was affected by a specific cybercrime [for instance "Emails Hacked: Nude Photos Uploaded"] and has been impacted by same?" The result is shown in Fig. 5.

Q4: "Which cybercrime and attacker are motivated by financial gain?" The result is shown in Fig. 6.

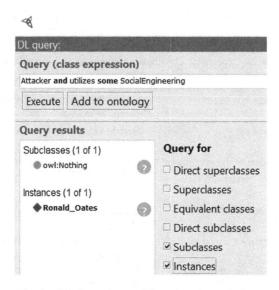

Fig. 3. Attacker using social engineering technique.

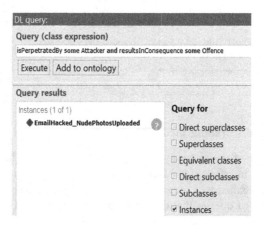

Fig. 4. Cybercrime resulting in offences brought against an attacker.

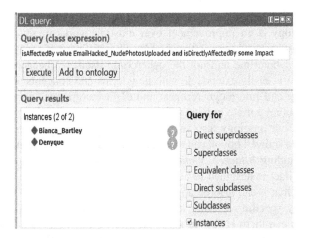

Fig. 5. Victim impacted by specific cybercrime.

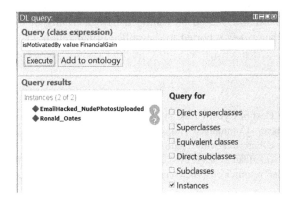

Fig. 6. Cybercrime and attacker motivated by financial gain.

6 Conclusion and Future Work

While few cybercrime classification schemes exist, they are largely incompatible. Further, their focus is generally narrow, concentrating on a single perspective, such as *attacker*, *defender* or *role of the computer*, or they use different terminologies, even though they refer to the same thing. This makes consistent and holistic classification unlikely.

To achieve repeatable and consistent classifications, their needs to be a shared conceptualization of cybercrimes, i.e., an ontology for cybercrime classification. This ontology will provide a common, consistent language that can be used by all cybercrime stakeholders. Without which, the same cybercrime may be classified differently by investigators and can result in inaccurate identification of cybercrime trends and patterns; prerequisites for better allocation of resources to combat cybercrimes. A most salient consideration, especially given the resource constraints that generally confront developing countries.

In this paper we propose an ontology to improve the classification of cybercrimes, CCO. This ontology is an improvement over existing works in several areas: (1) it utilizes a characteristic structure with which to classify cybercrimes; i.e., it classifies properties about cybercrime and not the cybercrime itself; (2) because of its classification structure, it is easily extendable with new terms and concepts and is better able to handle existing and future cybercrimes; and (3) it incorporates varying cybercrime perspectives, enabling a more holistic scheme with which to classify cybercrimes. The demonstration of our ontology also supports the claim that it is an improved classification scheme; we showed how it can be applied to classify a cybercrime from multiple perspectives (including *Attacker*, *Victim*, *Impact*, *Objective*, et al.).

While the artifact is designed to address cybercrime classification in a developing context, we note that it can also be applied to the developed context. Generally, there are many country specific reporting mechanisms of cyber incidents and not enough coordination between them [16]. Our study has, however, provided a formal ontology that may enable improved cybercrime threat assessments if cybercrime information is standardized and shared across jurisdictions. In future we intend to formally evaluate the artifact by implementing same in a developing country police organization. The evaluation would be mainly based on testing the functionality of the artifact to adequately classify cybercrimes reported to the police organization's CSIRT.

References

1. Accenture: 2017 Cost of Cyber Crime Study. Ponemon Institute LLC and Accenture (2017)
2. Caricom Caribbean Community. https://caricom.org/communications/view/caribbean-to-tackle-escalating-cybercrime-with-regional-approach. Accessed 17 Mar 2017
3. Organization of American States (OAS) & Symantec. http://www.symantec.com/content/en/us/enterprise/other_resources/b-cyber-security-trends-report-lamc.pdf. Accessed 17 Feb 2015
4. Barn, R., Barn, B.: An ontological representation of a taxonomy for cybercrime. In: 24th European Conference on Information Systems (ECIS), İstanbul, Turkey (2016)
5. Ngo, F., Jaishankar, K.: Commemorating a decade in existence of the international journal of cyber criminology: a research agenda to advance the scholarship on cyber crime. Int. J. Cyber Criminol. **11**(1), 1–9 (2017)
6. Stabek, A., Brown, S., Watters, P.A.: The case for a consistent cyberscam classification framework (CCCF). In: Symposia and Workshops on Ubiquitous, Autonomic and Trusted Computing, UIC-ATC 2009, Brisbane, Australia (2009)
7. Donalds, C., Osei-Bryson, K.-M.: A cybercrime taxonomy: case of the Jamaican jurisdiction. In: CONF-IRM 2014 Proceedings, p. 5 (2014)
8. Land, L., Smith, S., Winchester, D., Pang, V.: The construction of identity offences taxonomy: an Australian context. In: 25th Australasian Conference on Information Systems, Auckland, New Zealand (2014)
9. Simmons, C., Ellis, C., Shiva, S., Dasgupta, D., Wu, Q.: AVOIDIT: a cyber attack taxonomy. Technical report: CS-09-003, University of Memphis (2009)
10. Gruber, T.R.: Toward principles for the design of ontologies used for knowledge sharing. Int. J. Hum.-Comput. Stud. **43**(5–6), 907–928 (1995)

11. Noy, N.F., McGuinness, D.L.: Ontology development 101: a guide to creating your first ontology. Stanford knowledge systems laboratory technical report KSL-01-05 and Stanford medical informatics technical report SMI-2001-0880, vol. 15, p. 25, Stanford, CA (2001)
12. Staab, S., Studer, R., Schnurr, H.-P., Sure, Y.: Knowledge processes and ontologies. IEEE Intell. Syst. **16**(1), 26–34 (2001)
13. Undercoffer, J., Pinkston, J., Joshi, A., Finin, T.: A target-centric ontology for intrusion detection. In: IJCAI-2003 Workshop on Ontologies and Distributed Systems, pp. 47–58 (2004)
14. van Herdeen, R., Irwin, B., Burke, I.D., Leenen, L.: A computer network attack taxonomy and ontology. Int. J. Cyber Warfare Terrorism **2**, 12–25 (2012)
15. Council of Europe.: Convention on Cybercrime. http://conventions.coe.int/Treaty/en/Treaties/Html/185.htm. Accessed 20 July 2012
16. Kjaerland, M.: A taxonomy and comparison of computer security incidents from the commercial and government sectors. Comput. Secur. **25**(7), 522–538 (2005)
17. Simon, H.: The Sciences of Artificial. MIT Press, Cambridge (1996)
18. Hevner, A.R., March, S.T., Park, J.: Design science in information systems research. MIS Q. **28**(1), 75–105 (2004)
19. Peffers, K., Tuunanen, T., Rothenberger, M.A., Chatterjee, S.: A design science research methodology for information systems research. J. Manag. Inf. Syst. **24**(3), 45–78 (2007)
20. Gregor, S., Hevner, A.R.: Positioning and presenting design science research for maximum impact. MIS Q. **37**(2), 337–355 (2013)
21. Howard, J.D.: An analysis of security incidents on the Internet 1989–1995. Engineering and Public Policy, Doctor of Philosophy, pp. 1–319. Carnegie Melon University, Pittsburg (1997)
22. Jamaica Information Service: COPS Make Major Breakthrough in Cybercrime. JIS Service. http://jis.gov.jm/cops-make-major-breakthrough-in-cybercrime/. Accessed 6 Dec 2016
23. The Gleaner: Denyque Praises Cops On Porn Hacker Case. http://jamaica-gleaner.com/gleaner/20120905/lead/lead6.html. Accessed 6 Dec 2016

Extending DSR with Sub Cycles to Develop a Digital Knowledge Ecosystem for Coordinating Agriculture Domain in Developing Countries

Tamara Ginige[1]([⊠]), Lasanthi De Silva[2], Anusha Walisadeera[3], and Athula Ginige[4]

[1] Australian Catholic University, North Sydney, Australia
tamara.ginige@acu.edu.au
[2] University of Colombo, Colombo, Sri Lanka
lnc@ucsc.cmb.ac.lk
[3] University of Ruhuna, Matara, Sri Lanka
waindika@cc.ruh.ac.lk
[4] Western Sydney University, Sydney, Australia
a.ginige@westernsydney.edu.au

Abstract. Still a large percentage of the world population, especially in developing countries are depending on agriculture for their livelihood. The agriculture domain in many developing countries is not well coordinated leading to over and under production of crops resulting in widely fluctuating market prices, waste and economic hardship for farmers. Rapidly growing Smartphone usage among farming community has opened new possibilities to develop a mobile based artefact to coordinate the agriculture production. We have developed an overall artefact; a Digital Knowledge Ecosystem using Design Science Research (DSR) methodology to solve this complex problem. The main project had many research challenges to solve and they were assigned to several sub-projects to address. The outputs of sub-projects created several artefacts. They were integrated to develop the overall artefact to achieve the main goal of the overall project. Managing the complexity of the overall project was a challenge. For this, we had to split three main cycles of DSR: Relevance, Design and Rigor into 6 DSR sub-cycles; Relevance – Problem Understanding and Relevance – Suitability Validation, Rigor – Learning and Rigor –Contribution, Design - Heuristic Search and Design - Functional Validation. This split enabled us to better coordinate the activities to address different aspects of the problem performed by different researchers, often in parallel at multiple geographical locations. The resulted mobile based Digital Knowledge Ecosystem initially developed for farmers in Sri Lanka is now being trialled in India and adapted to develop a Mobile based Information System for Nutrition Driven Agriculture for African Countries.

Keywords: Digital Knowledge Ecosystem · DSR sub-cycles
Coordinating agriculture domain

© Springer International Publishing AG, part of Springer Nature 2018
S. Chatterjee et al. (Eds.): DESRIST 2018, LNCS 10844, pp. 268–282, 2018.
https://doi.org/10.1007/978-3-319-91800-6_18

1 Introduction

World population grew to 7.06 billion in mid-2012. Developing countries accounted for 97% of this growth. At present, about 60% of these people are classed as rural; of whom around 85% are agricultural. It is estimated that across the developing world, a total of 1.2 billion people live in poverty. The evidence is clear that broad-based agricultural development provides an effective means of both reducing poverty and accelerating economic growth [1].

In Sri Lanka, agriculture is one of the important sectors and approximately 33% of the total labour force is engaged in agriculture [2]. Coordinating the agriculture production characterized by a large number of small land holdings is a major problem. One major symptom of an uncoordinated agriculture domain is over production of some crops while some others are in short supply, leading to widely fluctuating market prices. A deeper analysis of the problem revealed that the root cause of the problem was farmers and many other stakeholders in the domain not receiving correct, up-to-date, complete information in a suitable modality on time. Inspired by the rapid growth of mobile phone usage in Sri Lanka [3] including among the farming communities, a mobile-based solution was sought to overcome this information gap. Farmers need published information (quasi static) about crops, pests, diseases, land preparation, growing and harvesting methods, and real-time situational information (dynamic) such as current crop production and market prices. This situational information is also needed by agriculture department, agro-chemical companies, buyers and various government agencies to ensure food security through effective supply chain planning whilst minimising waste.

In 2011, an international collaborative research team with members from Sri Lanka, Australia, Italy and United States, embarked on a project to address this problem by developing a mobile-based artefact to enhance the flow of information among stakeholders in the agriculture domain. This was a complex problem with many research challenges. We had to divide the main project into many sub projects to address each of these challenges. We used Design Science Research (DSR) to discover a suitable artefact. Due to complexity of factors that affect supply and demand in the agriculture domain it was very difficult to identify the deeper requirements an artefact should address to achieve a good coordination between the two. Thus we used an iterative process building many functional prototypes and validating the relevance of these artefacts to address certain symptoms of the problem to finally discover the requirements the overall artefact should fulfil and build the artefact [4].

This research was carried out by five higher degree research students (4 PhDs and 1 Master) from Sri Lanka, Australia and Italy. Each investigated a different research challenge that produced several new artefacts. These new artefacts were integrated to create a new mobile-based solution that was later conceptualised as a Digital Knowledge Ecosystem [5]. This system can now predict current production situation in near real time enabling government agencies to dynamically adjust the incentives offered to farmers for growing different types of crops to achieve sustainable agriculture production through crop diversification [6]. In 2016, the Sri Lankan Government announced this as a National Project in that year's Budget Speech. The system that was originally developed for farmers in Sri Lanka is now being trialled by 5000 farmers in India and also adapted by South Africa, Kenya and Nigeria to combat "Hidden Hunger Problem" by developing a Mobile based Information System for Nutrition driven Agriculture.

This paper describes how we had to extend the DSR with sub-cycles to manage the complexity of the research process. The emphasis is on the process rather than the two major tightly coupled artefacts that resulted from the process; the mobile based artefact to empower farmers and Digital Knowledge Ecosystem that connect all stakeholders in the domain including farmers via the mobile based artefact. This Digital Knowledge Ecosystem provides a mechanism for effective exchange of actionable information in real time [7]. As the project activities were carried out in different countries by multiple researchers, reflecting on the overall process provided very valuable insights on how to develop artefacts using DSR methodology for very complex problems by a geographically dispersed team working on different sub projects.

2 Literature Review

Design Science research is a constructive research method in that it produces an innovative artefact as its constitutive and distinctive research output [8, 9]. Design Science research has been defined as a research paradigm in which a designer answers questions relevant to human problems via the creation of innovative artefacts, thereby contributing new knowledge to the body of scientific evidence. The designed artefacts are both useful and fundamental in understanding that problem [8].

Design Science Research is said to stem from a desire to complement mainstream behavioural orientation of information systems research with a more design-oriented approach. It is fundamentally a problem-solving paradigm. Design Science Research encompasses the idea that doing innovative design that results in clear contributions to the knowledge base constitutes research. Design science research projects are often performed in a specific application context and the resulting designs and design research contributions may be clearly influenced by the opportunities and constraints of the application domain.

The fundamental principle of design science research is therefore that knowledge and understanding of a design problem and its solution are acquired in the building and application of an artefact. The term artefact is central to design science research and is used to describe something that is artificial, or constructed by humans, as opposed to something that occurs naturally. In design science, as a research activity, the interest is on artefacts that improve upon existing solutions to a problem or perhaps provide a first solution to an important problem. At least five types of artefacts are typically identified [8]; Constructs (vocabulary and symbols), Models (abstractions and representations), Methods (algorithms and practices), Instantiations (implemented and prototype systems) and Design theories (improved models of design, or design processes).

DSR framework is bounded by the practical environment and the available knowledge base at that point in time. The *environment* defines the problem space in which the phenomena of interest reside. In information systems research, the environment is comprised at least of people, organisational structures, and technologies. It thereby establishes the relevance of design science research. The *knowledge base* provides the materials from and through which design science research is accomplished. That is, prior research and results from relevant disciplines provide foundational theories, frameworks, instruments, constructs, models, methods, and instantiations that can be used in the design phase. The *knowledge base* therefore assists the design science in achieving rigor. Design science research is comprised of activities related to building and evaluating artefacts designed to meet the identified business needs. Thus DSR framework can be depicted by 3 cycles.

The *relevance cycle* bridges the contextual environment of the research project with the design science activities. The *rigor cycle* connects the design science activities with the knowledge base of scientific foundations, experience, and expertise that informs the research project. The central *design cycle* iterates between the core activities of building and evaluating the design artefacts and processes of the research. In a design science research project, these three cycles must be present and clearly identifiable [9].

3 Conceptual Solution and Formulation of Sub Research Projects

As explained in the introduction, in our initial investigation, we identified the root cause for uncoordinated agriculture sector in developing countries is lack of timely access to context specific information that can assist in making informed decisions. We started our research project to discover a suitable mobile artefact to address this root cause with the 1st *Relevance Cycle*. We conducted surveys and interviews with farmers and agriculture extension officers to find out how farmers decide what crops to grow. From the information that we gathered, we identified the factors that influence farmers when deciding crops to grow, with an aim of achieving their final goal of a larger revenue. To better depict the problem domain we also created a set of typical scenarios and personas of actors based on data gathered from the surveys [19].

In the 1st *Design Cycle* we used the scenario transformation approach of Rosson and Carrol to design the first set of interfaces [10]. We investigated how information deficiencies in the earlier identified scenarios can be mitigated by providing missing information and created a set of transformed scenarios. Based on original scenarios and personas, we also identified the usability requirements. Next, we used transformed scenarios and usability requirements to develop the first set of user interfaces. Transformed scenarios indicated that farmers need to know what crops will grow in their farm in that season and current production level of each crop. That way they can decide on suitable crops to grow while avoiding an overproduction situation and selecting crops that are in undersupply. Figure 1 shows the mobile screen of the crop catalogue listing crops that will grow in their farm. Icons were used to describe crops and a coloured background to indicate the approximate quantity of each crop already in production. The colour scale ranges from white indicating no data, green indicating low, yellow indicating medium and red indicating intensive production.

After selecting a crop, users can navigate to the next interface (Fig. 2) to obtain a more detailed description of the selected crop. It also had a mechanism to indicate the quantity of crop that they wanted to cultivate. This information could then be aggregated

Fig. 1. Crop catalogue (Color figure online)   **Fig. 2.** Details of the crop selected

to derive the current production levels of a crop in real time and display it in the crop catalogue using the colour codes. This design gave the research team a clearer and better idea about how user input can be captured and aggregated information can be displayed.

In the 2nd *Relevance Cycle* we first evaluated the suitability of the solution by showing it to sample of potential users. We realised that it is very effective to use colour to communicate the current production levels to the farmers. If farmers use the current production levels in their decision-making process, it may lead to diversification of crops being grown, thus achieving some degree of coordination of the agriculture domain and stability in market prices. Having established the suitability of the developed conceptual solution to better coordinate the agriculture domain and avoid symptoms such as overproduction, we next wanted to find out how this conceptual solution can be realised in practice. This led to formulation of 3 sub research questions.

1. What are the information needs of a farmer throughout the crop life cycle, when do they need them (in what context) and what are the effective formats to present the information?
2. How can we obtain or generate the information that farmers need?
3. How can we motivate farmers to act on this information?

To address these research questions three different yet integrated research projects were formulated that directly resulted in 3 successful PhD completions in 2016.

- Project A - Holistic Information Flow Model to Enhance Livelihood Activities of Sri Lankan Farmers
- Project B - User Centered Agriculture Ontology for Sri Lankan farmers
- Project C - An Empowerment Framework for Developing Mobile-based Applications: Empowering Sri Lankan farmers in their Livelihood Activities

4   Creation of DSR Sub-cycles

From the aspect of research process, we had two major challenges to tackle.

1. This was an ill-structured problem with unclear and undefined user requirements. Therefore, each investigation had to iterate through several cycles of learning established theory, understanding the problem, designing and building prototypes, validating its functionality and field testing them to validate its suitability in the environment.
2. There were 3 sub research projects that were carried out in 3 different geo-locations which shared much of the problem understanding activities and needed to contribute to an integrated artefact at the end. To establish the suitability of the artefact, during intermediate stages and at the end, the artefact had to undergo through *Relevance Cycles* that involved farmers in Sri Lanka (i.e. in a Single geo-location which gave rise to some logistical challenges).

It became clearer to us that we require a more granular structure to the DSR cycles to better manage and coordinate activities that are happening across multiple sub projects. For this we divided each of the main DSR cycles in to two sub-cycles.

As shown in Fig. 3, the Relevance cycle was divided into two sub cycles: *Relevance – Problem Understanding (RePU)* and *Relevance – Suitability Validation (ReSV)*. In *Relevance – Problem Understanding (RePU)* sub-cycle, the problem, opportunities and obstacles that existed in the agriculture domain were clearly identified. When a solution was designed and tested for an immediate goal, its suitability was validated in the environment in *Relevance – Suitability Validation (ReSV)* sub-cycle.

The Rigor cycle was split in to *Rigor – Learning (RiLE)* and *Rigor –Contribution (RiCO)* sub-cycles. When in *(RePU)* sub-cycle trying to understand the problem, it is important to refer to the past knowledge base of theories, existing artefacts, foundations and methodologies. This happens in the *Rigor – Learning (RiLE)*sub-cycle. After suitability validation *(ReSV)* sub cycle, all new knowledge gained is contributed back to the knowledge-base in the *Rigor –Contribution (RiCO)* sub-cycle.

The Design cycle too was split into two sub-cycles: *Design - Heuristic Search (DeHS)* and *Design - Functional Validation (DeFV)*. In *Design-Heuristic Search (DeHS)* sub-cycle, when a suitable design for an immediate goal was identified, it was designed and implemented. In this sub-cycle, various heuristic search methods were applied to design this artefact. In *Design - Functional Validation (DeFV)* sub-cycle, the research team evaluated its functional validity. The constructed artefact was iterated many times between these two sub-cycles to confirm its functional validity and to produce an error free artefact. Then only the research process moved to *Relevance – Suitability Validation (ReSV)* sub-cycle to establish the relevance of the designed artefact as a means to solve the problem at hand. When the designed artefact has no functional aspects such as conceptual models or paper prototypes of User Interfaces there is no need for a *Design - Functional Validation sub-cycle*. After *Design - Heuristic Search (DeHS)* sub cycle the research process can move onto a *Relevance – Suitability Validation (ReSV)* sub-cycle.

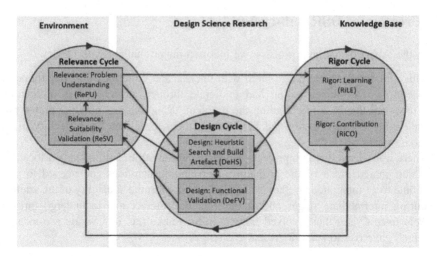

Fig. 3. Design science research (DSR) sub-cycles and interactions among them

4.1 Application of DSR Sub-cycles to Sub Research Projects

This section describes how we carried out the 3 integrated research projects identified above to discover an artefact that can be used to effectively coordinate the agriculture domain in developing countries. First a brief description of the research that was carried out in each project is given and how each of the sub research questions were investigated using set of DSR sub-cycles is explained in a tabular form.

4.2 Project A – Holistic Information Flow Model to Enhance Livelihood Activities of Sri Lankan Farmers

In project A, a detailed investigation was carried out to understand what information farmers need, when they need them, how do they currently receive information and in which format, and the currency and relevance of the information. This resulted in discovering open-ended and inefficient information flow model with limited collaboration among stakeholders [11, 12]. Further it revealed that farmers were not receiving current, accurate, complete and relevant information to make informed decisions in all stages of a crop cycle [13]. This led to another investigation that resulted in discovering all the stakeholders involved in agriculture domain, what type of information they need to carry out their tasks and what type of information they produce while carrying out their tasks. This resulted in creating a farmer-centric information flow model for the farmers [14]. Table 1 below shows how DSR sub-cycles were used to achieve the goals in project A.

Table 1. Research questions of Project A and relevant DSR sub-cycles

Research question	Relevant DSR sub-cycle
RQ1: How do farmers currently receive information and how this information flow can be enhanced?	• RePU1(A) – Application domain was analysed in detail to investigate how farmers currently receive information and current information flow among farmers in Sri Lanka • DeHS1(A) – A farmer-centric information flow model was derived to enhance the flow of information to farmers from officials and other sources within the agriculture domain
RQ2: How to structure and provide relevant information using mobile technology?	• RePU2(A) – Agriculture domain was further studied to understand which information is needed in different stages of a farming cycle. This information was categorized and structured to meet the exact needs of farmers • DeHS2(A) – Initial set of interfaces of the mobile artefact were designed • DeFV1(A) – The correct functionality of the first prototype of the mobile artefact was validated by the research team • ReSV1(A) – First prototype of the mobile artefact was field tested with 32 farmers in Sri Lanka in Dec 2012 • RePU3(A) – Learning from 2012 field trails • DeHS3(A) – From the feedback from 2012 field trials, the design and the functionality of the mobile artefact was enhanced • DeFV2(A) – The new functionality of the mobile artefact was validated by the research team • ReSV2(A) – The enhanced mobile artefact and additional paper-based mobile interfaces (paper prototype) were field tested with 50 farmers in Sri Lanka in Dec 2013 • RePU4(A) – Learning from 2013 field trails • DeHS4(A) – From the feedback from 2013 field trials, the overall design and the functionality of the mobile artefact was enhanced • DeFV3(A) – The correct functionality of the mobile artefact was validated by the research team
RQ3: How to achieve a sustainable flow of information within the agriculture domain?	• RePU5(A) – Agriculture domain was further studied via interviews and surveys to investigate ways to increase the sustainability of the current information flow model • DeHS5(A) – A stakeholder centric information flow model was designed to increase the efficient information sharing among all stakeholders. It was discovered by using mathematical and logical operators, "aggregation" and "disaggregation" from the information produced by some stakeholders the information needs of some others can be fulfilled • ReSV3(A) – The stakeholder centric information model was validated with 20 stakeholders • ReSV4(A) – The fully developed mobile artefact was deployed in March 2015 with 30 farmers. Data was collected in March and October for evaluation purposes of Project A

4.3   Project B – User-Centered Ontology for the Sri Lankan Farmers

The advantage of a farmer-centric information flow model can only be fully realised if it can be used to deliver the context specific information that a farmer needs. Therefore, the researchers in project B first gained an understanding of domain-specific information needs of farmers in context. For example, a typical question often asked is: "what crops will grow in my farm". "My farm" can be characterised by climatic conditions for the planned season, type of soil and water availability at the location. This forms the context for the query. The Agriculture Department: a major stakeholder in the domain has published how to grow various crops, required climatic conditions, suitable soil type, watering methods, fertilizer and pesticides to be used as documents on their website and booklets [2]. Since this knowledge is scattered and in document form, it is not possible to query it in context. Therefore, it has to be extracted and organized into a suitable granular representation so that one can query this information in context. For this, user-centered ontological knowledge base was developed [15, 16]. Now when the question "what crops will grow in my farm" is asked via a mobile phone, first it is necessary to capture the geo-coordinates of the farm, and using these geo-coordinates to find the corresponding agro-ecological zone that farm belongs to. Next "my farm" has to expand with corresponding climatic and soil parameters stored in the context model for that agro-ecological zone. With this expanded information ontological knowledgebase can be queried to obtain a list of crops that will grow in that farm. Table 2 shows how DSR sub-cycles were used to achieve the goals of Project B.

Table 2. Research questions of Project B and relevant DSR sub-cycles

Research question	Relevant DSR sub-cycle
RQ1: How to model a user's context with respect to the domain of agriculture?	• RePU1(B) – An understanding of needs of farmers in context and domain specific knowledge were gathered from a variety of reliable sources • DeHS1(B) – Required information for each stage of a crop cycle was broadly categorized into two types: published literature (quasi-static) and situational knowledge required to generate in real time (dynamic). From this analysis, information important to the farmers was identified as a set of questions
RQ2: How to represent agricultural information and relevant knowledge in context	• RePU2(B) – A deeper understanding of Ontology and its development process were gained • DeHS2(B) – A user-centred Ontology to organise domain knowledge and events of a crop life cycle was developed
RQ3: How to evaluate the artefact developed in RQ2?	• RePU3(B) – An understanding of ontology validation and evaluation methods were gained • DeFV1(B) – The Ontology created was internally evaluated for its validity, correctness and user satisfaction using Delphi method • ReSV1(B) – The Ontology was externally field tested with 32 farmers in 2012 for one major event called Crop Selection

(continued)

Table 2. (*continued*)

Research question	Relevant DSR sub-cycle
	• RePU(4) – Learning from 2012 field trails
	• DeHS3(B) – From the feedback from the field trial, the Ontology was enhanced to accommodate more events
	• DeFV2(B) – The enhanced Ontology was internally evaluated for functional correctness
	• ReSV2(B) – The Ontology was externally field tested with 50 farmers in 2013 to assess user satisfaction for information provided
	• RePU5(B) – Learning from 2013 field trails
	• DeHS4(B) – From the feedback from the field trial, the Ontology was further enhanced
	• DeFV2(B) – The Ontology was internally evaluated for its validity and correctness
RQ4: How to maintain the artefact developed in sub-question Q2?	• RePU6(B) – An understanding of how to manage a large, user-centered ontology was gained
	• DeHS5(B) – An architecture of an ontology management system was designed
	• ReSV3(B) – The fully developed mobile artefact in which the Ontology is a part of was deployed in March 2015 with 30 farmers. Data was collected in March and October for evaluation purposes of Project B

4.4   Project C – an Empowerment Framework for Developing Mobile-Based Applications: Empowering Sri Lankan Farmers in Their Livelihood Activities

In this project, we investigated how to motivate the stakeholders to act on the information to generate transaction data. The rapid growth of Social Networks is a result of user empowerment due to symmetric information flow and the associated communication and collaboration patterns. This led us to carry out a detailed study of psychological empowerment to understand the various components of psychological empowerment, key drivers and influences of empowerment and their relationships to each other [17–19]. The objective of Project C was to create an artefact that would empower farmers to achieve their meaningful goals. This led us to first understand and learn about the meaningful goals of farmers, the issues and challenges they face in their livelihood activities, and how they have been using technology in their daily activities in detail [20]. With these insights and the knowledge gained from empowerment theory, we have implemented empowerment-oriented processes in the mobile artefact that are closely aligned with the meaningful goals of the farmers [21]. Further, these processes were embedded with choices, supported with relevant, accurate and timely knowledge, to make informed decisions. The goals achieved in Projects A and B were necessary to achieve the goals in Project C. Table 3 below shows how goals of Project C were achieved via DSR sub-cycles.

Table 3. Research questions of Project C and relevant DSR sub-cycles

Research question	Relevant DSR sub-cycle
RQ1: How can farmers be empowered in their livelihood activities?	• RePU1(C) – An understanding of the agriculture domain knowledge, issues of farmers, their technology usage and empowerment theory were gained • DeHS1(C) – From the information gathered, a conceptual empowerment model for the Sri Lankan farmers was developed. A web based profit calculator was designed to ascertain technology usage of farmers and how it might help in their decision-making process • DeFV1(C) – The functionality of the profit calculator was validated by the research team • ReSV1(C) – Profit calculator implemented as a mobile artefact was field tested with 32 farmers in Sri Lanka in Dec 2012. In addition, data was collected to understand how farmers make decisions, their new user requirements and feedback on the interfaces of the mobile artefact • RePU2(C) – Learning from 2012 field trial • DeHS2(C) – An enhanced empowerment model and a cultivation planning application were designed. The cultivation planning application incorporates new user requirements and has processes to support all stages of a crop cycle • ReSV2(C) – An enhanced mobile artefact with cultivation planning application was validated with 50 farmers in Sri Lanka in Dec 2013
RQ2: How to design a suitable mobile-based information system (artefact) to empower farmers?	• RePU3(C) – An understanding of how to design empowerment-oriented processes of the mobile artefact, supported with different types of knowledge required to enhance decision making were gained • DeHS3(C) – The empowerment processes embedded with choices, and personalised, factual and procedural knowledge for the mobile artefact were designed (Empowerment framework). The mobile artefact was implemented fully with enhanced interfaces to support HCI principles • DeFV2(C) – The functionality of the artefact with empowerment processes was validated by the research team
RQ3: How to evaluate the effectiveness of the empowerment framework?	• RePU4(C) – An understanding of how to measure empowerment and suitable instruments were gained • DeHS4(C) – The instruments to measure empowerment were designed • ReSV3(C) – The fully developed mobile artefact implemented based on empowerment framework was deployed in March 2015 with 30 farmers. Data was collected in March and October for evaluation purposes of Project C

Figure 4 shows the DSR sub-cycles of the three projects and their integration to create the final artefact – Digital Knowledge Ecosystem. As explained in Sect. 3, at the beginning of our investigation, we created a conceptual solution for the main project. This initial investigation consists of *1st Relevance Cycle, 1st Design Cycle and 2nd Relevance Cycle*. In Fig. 4 they are shown as *Relevance Understanding 1 (Main), Design Heuristic Search 1 (Main) and Relevance Suitability 1(Main)*. The three individual projects denoted using A, B and C, progressed through the DSR sub-cycles to achieve their individual yet connected goals of the *Main* project. The outcomes of one project became important inputs to another.

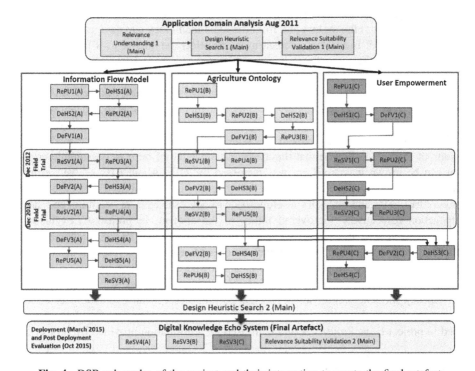

Fig. 4. DSR sub-cycles of the project and their integration to create the final artefact

In 2012 and 2013 field trials, each sub project validated their designs and implementations independently for suitability and gathered information to learn and improve the design of the artefacts. (at *ReSV* DSR sub-cycle). At the *2nd Design Heuristic* cycle of the *Main* project, all the outputs of three sub projects were integrated to create the final artefact: Digital Knowledge Ecosystem. This was deployed in March 2015 among 30 farmers and survey instruments were used to collect data required to establish their current level of empowerment and knowledge about crops and agriculture practices. In Oct 2015, 6 months after initial deployment, similar survey was carried out to ascertain the effectiveness of the developed artefact.

Throughout this investigation, the research team referred to the existing knowledge base to learn and gather relevant knowledge (*RiLE DSR sub-cycle*). Similarly, new knowledge was created by the research team as they progressed through the investigation and that was contributed to the knowledgebase via 4 PhD theses, 1 Master's thesis, and 26 book chapters, journal and conference publications (*RiCO DSR sub-cycle*). However, *RiLE* and *RiCO* DSR sub-cycles are not shown in Fig. 4 as it was necessary to maintain clarity in the diagram.

5   Integrated Artefact and Impact

Some user interfaces of the Mobile based Information System are shown in Fig. 5. Farmers can log into the system and from the main menu they can navigate to different functions provided. In the login screen user can select the language. If farmer selects "Crop Selection", the crops that will grow in that farm (previously registered – these UI are not shown) will be listed with colour coding. There are UIs (not shown below) for them to obtain the varieties and the cost of production by providing the planed cultivation extent. The UI showing the summery cost based on planned extent is shown below. This planned extent of farming is used to predict the current production level of a crop.

The results of post deployment assessments were very positive. The evaluation results of Project A showed that the average knowledge of farmers on suitable crops that can be grown in one's farm was increased by 21%. About 61% of the farmers reported that they would like to receive information via the mobile. Farmers reported 98%, 70%, 68% and 98% for usefulness, ease of use, ease of learning and user satisfaction respectively for overall utility of the artefact. In project C, evaluation results showed a relative positive change of 11%, 6% and 25% for empowerment outcomes such as sense of control, motivation and self-efficacy respectively for the farmer group. Further, September 2015 data, showed a significant correlation among empowerment outcomes. These results are consistent with the growing evidence that self-efficacy influences motivation [17, 22–25]. The successful evaluation results of projects A and C also validated the suitability of the User-Centered Ontology developed in project B, as Projects A and C utilised the information provided by Project B.

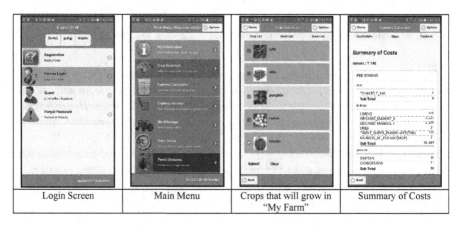

| Login Screen | Main Menu | Crops that will grow in "My Farm" | Summary of Costs |

Fig. 5. Selected screens of the mobile artefact

6 Conclusions

In this paper, we have shown how an artefact can be developed using DSR to solve a complex problem. The main problem had many research challenges and they were assigned to several sub projects to address. The outputs of individual projects were integrated to achieve the main goal of the larger project. For this purpose, we had to split three main cycles of DSR: Relevance, Design and Rigor into 6 DSR sub-cycles. This split enabled us to perform the necessary activities to address different aspects of the problem by different researchers, often in parallel, at multiple geographical locations.

Having a well-coordinated effective agriculture production system is a key requirement for achieving at least 3 of the United Nations Sustainable Development Goals; No Hunger, Zero Poverty and No Malnutrition. Finding solutions to these problems require multi nation, multi-disciplinary approaches. The work presented in this paper highlights the suitability of extended DSR methodology for discovering artefacts to address such complex and challenging problems and finding possible solutions can make an immense contribution to humanity.

References

1. Dixon, J.A., Gibbon, D.P., Gulliver, A.: Farming Systems and Poverty: Improving Farmers' Livelihoods in a Changing World. Food & Agriculture Org, Rome (2001)
2. Agriculture: Department of Agriculture, Sri Lanka, 20 February 2015. http://www.agridept.gov.lk/
3. ITU: Country ICT Data, 23 January 2018. https://www.itu.int/en/ITU-D/Statistics/Pages/stat/default.aspx
4. De Silva, L., Ginige, T., Giovanni, P.D., Mathai, M., Goonetillake, J., Wikramanayake, G., et al.: Interplay of requirements engineering and human computer interaction approaches in the evolution of a mobile agriculture information system. In: Ebert, A., Humayoun, S.R., Seyff, N., Perini, A., Barbosa, S.D.J. (eds.) UsARE 2012/2014. LNCS, vol. 9312, pp. 135–159. Springer, Cham (2016). https://doi.org/10.1007/978-3-319-45916-5_9
5. Ginige, A., Silva, L.D., Ginige, T., Giovanni, P.D., Walisadeera, A.I., Mathai, M., et al.: Towards an agriculture knowledge ecosystem: a social life network for farmers in Sri Lanka. In: 9th Conference of the Asian Federation for Information Technology in Agriculture - 2014, Perth, Australia, pp. 170–179 (2014)
6. Ginige, A., Walisadeera, A., Ginige, T., Silva, L.D., Giovanni, P.D., Mathai, M., et al.: Digital knowledge ecosystem for achieving sustainable agriculture production: a case study from Sri Lanka. In: Presented at the the 3rd IEEE International Conference on Data Science and Advanced Analytics Montreal, Canada (2016)
7. Ginige, A.: Digital knowledge ecosystems: empowering users through context specific actionable information. In: Presented at the 9th International Conference on ICT, Society and Human Beings (ICT 2016), Madeira, Portugal (2016)
8. Hevner, A., March, S., Park, J., Ram, S.: Design science in information systems research. MIS Q. **28**, 75–105 (2004)
9. Hevner, A.: A three cycle view of design science research. Scand. J. IS **19**, 87–92 (2007)
10. Rosson, M.B., Carrol, J.M.: Scenario-Based Design: The Human Computer Interaction Handbook. Lawrence Erlbaum Associates, New Jersey (2002)

11. Lokanathan, S., Kapugama, N.: Smallholders and Micro-enterprises in Agriculture. LIRNEasia, Colombo (2012)
12. Jensen, R.T.: The digital provide: information (technology), market performance and welfare in the South Indian fisheries sector. Q. J. Econ. **122**, 879–924 (2007)
13. De Silva, H., Ratnadiwakara, D.: Using ICT to reduce transaction costs in agriculture through better communication: a case-study from Sri Lanka (2008)
14. De Silva, L., Goonetillake, J., Wikramanayake, G., Ginige, A.: Towards an agriculture information ecosystem. In: 25th Australasian Conference on Information Systems (2014)
15. Walisadeera, A.I., Ginige, A., Wickramanayake, G.: Conceptualizing crop life cycle events to create a user centered ontology for farmers. In: Presented at the Computational Science and Its Applications (ICCSA 2014), Poroto, Portugal (2014)
16. Walisadeera, A.I., Wikramanayake, G.N., Ginige, A.: An ontological approach to meet information needs of farmers in Sri Lanka. In: Presented at the International Conference on Computational Science and its Applications, Ho Chi Minh City, Vietnam (2013)
17. Bandura, A.: Self efficacy mechanism in human agency. Am. Psychol. **37**, 122–147 (1982)
18. Zimmerman, M.A.: Psycological empowerment: issues and illustrations. Am. J. Commun. Psychol. **23**, 581–600 (1995)
19. Deci, E.L., Schwartz, A., Sheinman, L., Ryan, R.M.: An instrument to assess adults' orientations toward control versus autonomy with children: reflections on intrinsic motivation and perceived competence. J. Educ. Psychol. **73**, 642–650 (1981)
20. Cattaneo, L.B., Chapman, A.R.: The process of empowerment: a model for use in research and practice. Am. Psychol. **65**, 646–659 (2010)
21. Ginige, T., Richards, D., Hitchens, M.: Cultivation planning application to enhance decision making among Sri Lankan farmers. In: Presented at the Pacific Rim Knowledge Acquisition Gold Coast, Australia (2014)
22. Schunk, D.H.: Self-efficacy and achievement behaviors. Educ. Psychol. Rev. **1**, 173–208 (1989)
23. Corno, L., Mandinach, E.B.: The role of cognitive engagement in classroom learning and motivation. Educ. Psychol. **18**, 88–108 (1983)
24. Pintrich, P.R., Schunk, D.H.: Motivation in Education: Theory, Research, and Applications. Merrill, Minnesota (2002)
25. Cohen-Mansfield, J., Marx, M.S., Guralnik, J.M.: Motivators and barriers to exercise in an older community-dwelling population. In: JAPA 2003, vol. 11, pp. 242–253 (2003)

Designing Cybersecurity

Strategic Planning for IS Security: Designing Objectives

Gurpreet Dhillon[1(✉)], Gholamreza Torkzadeh[2], and Jerry Chang[2]

[1] University of North Carolina at Greensboro, Greensboro, USA
gdhillon@uncg.edu
[2] University of Nevada Las Vegas, Las Vegas, USA

Abstract. Management of information systems (IS) security in organizations has been hampered by the apparent lack of inclusion of organizational security objectives in the traditional strategic planning process. In order to improve IS security strategic planning, we argue that there should be a renewed emphasis on security planning objectives. In this paper we present two sets of objectives – fundamental and means. We then define an evaluation mechanism for assessing the security posture of a firm. Based on case work in healthcare, we illustrate the usefulness of the security evaluation method for designing enterprise security.

Keywords: IS security strategic planning · Value-focused thinking
IS security objectives

1 Introduction

Strategic planning has long been considered as an important activity in management of organizations [4]. The Information Systems (IS) literature has recognized that strategic planning helps in reducing uncertainty [2], ensuring co-ordination [39], maintaining business process integrity [30] and facilitating good communication among stakeholders [21]. While the need to undertake strategic planning in the context of IS has been well appreciated, the same strategic planning focus has not been extended to IS security. This absence of inclusion of security planning has occurred in spite of the fact that security has been considered as a key enabler in the management of organizations [16, 63].

It is possible that the increased organizational reliance on information technology combined with realistic security concerns has resulted in a more immediate techno-centric security orientation by management. Instead, organizations would be better served with the adoption of a long-term strategic vision for this important aspect of IS management. The attention that has traditionally been rendered to IS security has largely focused on specifying requirements (i.e., confidentiality, integrity, availability of information) rather than larger security objectives that serve the organization as a whole. Dominant IS security research has also largely been technical in nature, with limited consideration of people and organizational objectives.

One of the main reasons for the lack of a strategic planning focus in managing IS security is that security has often been considered as an 'afterthought'. Baskerville [6] terms this as 'developmental duality' when design of systems and security are not integrated and follow independent paths. Furthermore, security breaches trigger

© Springer International Publishing AG, part of Springer Nature 2018
S. Chatterjee et al. (Eds.): DESRIST 2018, LNCS 10844, pp. 285–299, 2018.
https://doi.org/10.1007/978-3-319-91800-6_19

implementation of remedial measures in a reactive manner, not necessarily aligned with the overall strategic plan. There is no doubt that security breaches can cause huge monetary losses and disrupt critical business processes. Nevertheless, it is also prudent to proactively consider IS security that facilitates smooth operation of the organization. This necessitates not only the need for strategic planning and definition of a set of strategic objectives [3], but also the need to establish a strategic security planning process to identify corresponding IS security objectives and mechanisms to ensure realization of security measures within organizations.

In this paper, we call for strategic planning for IS security in organizations. Based on research from Dhillon and Torkzadeh [20], we design a conceptual artifact to undertake a security posture assessment of a firm. The output of the assessment framework allows us to comment on the discrepancies and hence suggest security strategic planning opportunities.

2 Literature Review

The major focus within the strategic management literature has been to conceptualize dimensions of the planning process and then define the associated effectiveness measures [34]. However, Lederer and Sethi [36] and Grover and Segars [25] noted that in the IS literature, focus has been more on the development of tools and methodologies for undertaking strategic planning. Although it has been argued that IS strategic planning and organizational strategic planning is largely similar (e.g. [26]) and should be conceptualized in the same way, some researchers would however contend that this has not been the case [50]. Despite repeated calls for strategic planning for IS security (e.g. see [1, 11, 26]), there has been little progress in conceptualizing and developing tools and methodologies for the strategic IS security planning processes.

In fact, the majority of IS security research has focused on security policies as a proxy for IS security strategy. For example, Baskerville and Siponen [9] call for information security meta-policies, essential for thinking strategically about IS Security. Siponen and Iivari [52] also propose theories for developing security policies and guidelines. Although policy formulation is an important aspect of IS security, it needs to be undertaken within the context of strategic planning. As Baskerville and Dhillon [8] note, "we can have a strategy for creating organizational security policies, and we can have a strategy for implementing security policies. This means that organizational strategy will help determine the security policies, and these policies may in turn embody a determination for the strategy for carrying out the security policies." Similarly, Anderson and Choobineh [1] make a call for security "actions and tactics" to be bounded by the enterprise security strategy.

In reviewing IS security research related to strategic aspects, we draw upon strategic management and IS strategy literature to identify broad categories or schools of thought. Opinions are divided as to the number and scope of schools of thought. The strategic management field, for instance, considers anywhere between five and eleven schools of thought (see [33]). In the IS strategy literature, Segars and Grover [50] identify five planning philosophies, including design, planning, positioning (based on [41]), learning, and political. Adapting from Mintzberg's work, we classify IS security research into three essential schools of thought that includes the design school, planning school, and emergent positioning school, with the emergent position school of thought incorporating the learning and political aspects. We discuss each of these approaches to security planning below.

2.1   Design School of Thought

This category of research relates to the design of IS security and is largely technical in nature. The emphasis here is on designing artifacts that help in ensuring security. The very nature of this strand of research results in focusing more on identifying and fulfilling requirements for ensuring IS Security. The design school that inspired IS Security research can be traced back to the early 1970s when the US Department of Defense (DoD) undertook proactive steps to define confidentiality requirements for data residing in its systems. The DoD intention was to protect the unwanted exposure of secure information within systems, which in turn would ensure overall information security. The outcome of this early DoD work was the Bell-LaPadula model that defined multilevel security in the form of a state transition model. Here, a set of access control rules used security labels on objects and access clearances for subjects [10]. In subsequent years, additional information security models were developed. For example, the Biba Integrity Model [11] defined access control rules to ensure data integrity. The Biba model groups data and subjects in ordered levels of integrity, i.e. subjects may not corrupt or alter data that is at a level higher than the subject. At the heart of a Biba Integrity Model are three goals: prevent data modification by unauthorized parties; prevent unauthorized data modification by authorized subjects; and ensure that the data reflects the real world. In addition to the confidentiality (Bell-LaPadula) and integrity (Biba) security models, availability of data has also been considered closely. Availability refers to ready accessibility to data existing in tables and files where it is supposed to be and has not been inadvertently or purposefully deleted. Prominence of availability as a requirement for security emerged following concerns for increased processing power of computer systems and the corresponding reduction in access time to disks (see [58]). Moreover, the DoD requirements called for timely availability of data at all times while attempting to curtail denial of service attacks. The disaster recovery planning process (DRP) and information assurance management, including COBIT (ISACA model for Control Objectives for Information and related Technology) also addresses various aspects of the design school of thought.

Undoubtedly requirements such as confidentiality, integrity, and availability (CIA) have been considered as cornerstones for good IS security (see [12]). Numerous products and services have attempted to incorporate these requirements into their specifications (for instance IBMs System-managed storage model, Hewlett-Packard's DataMesh project, the RAID project at UC Berkley, among numerous others). However, some have argued that an exclusive focus on CIA requirements has been considered as limiting the ability to ensure good security. For example, Parker [42, 43] considers the CIA model to be a rather limited list of requirements and suggests three additional requirements - possession or control, authenticity, and utility. Additionally, for the past several years, many researchers have highlighted the importance of possession as a requirement because it connotes a senses of data stewardship (e.g. [29, 49]). Authenticity refers to the correct attribution or provenance of information while utility means usefulness, which suggests that while data may meet all other requirements, it still may not be useful in that form.

While the IS security requirements that have emerged from the design school have helped in developing good security artifacts, products and services, their relevance in multiple contexts remains questionable. It is argued that the context of information use can change the validity or worth of the formal security models [60]. Dhillon [17] notes, "A challenge, however, exists when business organizations are using models based on a different reality." Further, Wing [59] argues that when large and complex software systems are being specified, special care is needed to explicitly state the assumptions about the context. Wing notes, "Unfortunately, when specifying a large system, specifiers too often forget to explicitly state the circumstances under which the system is expected to behave properly." (p. 20). Hence, the literature supports the idea that the design of IS security requirements has to be grounded in specific organizational contexts.

2.2   Planning School of Thought

This category of research relates to the planning of IS security that treats formulation of strategy as a formal process. The planning school of thought for IS security has largely focused on identifying vulnerabilities, conducting risk analysis, and ensuring compliance with internal and external standards. Such activities are typically undertaken both at the system and organizational level. Interestingly, research in the planning school of IS security has unquestionably drawn on the security requirements established by their design school counterparts. This means that identification of security vulnerabilities, security risk analysis, and compliance have all been centered around CIA and their purported extensions. In many ways confidentiality, integrity, availability, possession, authenticity, and utility requirements for ensuring IS security have taken the form of IS security objectives for defining security programs in organizations. While one may argue that such an approach is valid, researchers consider this to be atheoretical and based on ill-formed constructs. In reference to the CIA constructs, Backhouse and Dhillon [5] consider security programs based on such requirements to lack an understanding of substantive questions. Choobinen et al. [14] maintain, "Over the past several decades, the field of information security management has suffered because of a lack of theoretical conceptualizations. While many researchers have offered interesting insights, there are as yet no well-established principles that define 'good' information security management" (p. 963).

The preponderance of the requirement-centered orientations in IS security research in both the design and planning school have been highlighted in major IS security literature reviews (see [10, 19, 53]). Baskerville [7] terms it a general disconnect between systems development methods and security design and calls for integrating security considerations into systems development. Even after two decades, this call has not been entirely heeded to. Dhillon and Backhouse [19] classify most of the current approaches as 'functionalist' in nature and hence suggest that the context of use needs to be adequately considered. Siponen [53] reiterates the need for a socio-organizational perspective and in developing deep insights into organizational situations for understanding security. Both the Dhillon and Backhouse [19] and Siponen [53] calls have been partially heard, particularly in terms of understanding behavioral aspects of security compliance [27] and awareness [44].

Both the design school and planning school categories of research ultimately aspire to inform IS Security policy formulation, implementation, and strategic planning. In the case of the design school, the center of attention is on eliciting the security requirements at a system level. The implicit assumption is that security of systems within an organization will help in protecting the overall organization. Researchers in this category therefore tend to take a technical requirements based mode of inquiry. On the other hand, the planning school of thought reviews the requirements identified within the design school and plans for security both at system and organizational level. Researchers in this category tend to develop organizational security policies that help in ensuring system security. Neither the design school nor the planning school rise above the technical and operational level to address security needs at the strategic level.

2.3   Emergent Positioning School of Thought

Research in the emergent positioning category considers IS security plans to emerge based on the context and the relative positioning of a range of issues and stakeholder values. With the emergent positioning view, planning of IS security strategy is considered to be largely an analytical process. There have only been isolated attempts in the literature that call for identifying and defining objectives or for strategizing about security from the perspective of emergent positioning school of thought (cf. [41]). Rees et al. [47], for instance express their frustration by stating that, "the prevalent model within many organizations appears to be an ad hoc approach to security, where the latest breach becomes the model for future occurrences" (p. 101). While Rees et al. [47] present a policy framework and suggest that proper strategizing needs to be undertaken, they fall short of actually presenting security objectives that organizations could adopt. This they feel should be the focus of future research initiatives.

Baskerville and Siponen [9] also call for meta-strategizing about security policies. Incorporating prior work undertaken at the US Department of Defense, they identify various security policy requirements, which include identification and classification of security subjects and objects, the need for a design process for development and implementation of policies, and the need for implementation and testing processes. Baskerville and Siponen [9] highlight the need for a process and the form a given security strategy needs to take. However, they do not comment on the content of the security strategy and/or the planning process.

Similarly, Straub and Welke [54] present a security planning approach. They argue that the "scholarly and consulting literatures on security do not provide a commonly agreed upon conceptual model for the security planning process" (p. 450). Even after a decade of research efforts, the state of security planning has not significantly changed. While many researchers have proposed one form of planning approach or the other, they have usually fallen short of defining objectives that need to inform any kind of a planning process.

Given the need to establish objectives for IS security, we systematically identify values, synthesize these and then present a consolidated set of fundamental and means objectives. We found instilling a certain set of ethical values, assuring identity management, promoting positive attitude, and improving technology competency to be fundamental objectives for any IS security strategy. We also identified elevating awareness, honoring individuality, establishing censure, appreciating reciprocity, promoting openness, encouraging compliance, reducing apathy, clarifying accountability, and developing mutual understanding as means objectives for IS security. The combination of the fundamental and means objectives forms the basis for an IS security strategic plan.

3 Value-Focused Thinking Approach and IS Security Objectives

In 2006, Dhillon and Torkzadeh [20] undertook an extensive study where 103 interviews were conducted to identify individual values for ensuring IS security. Their systematic application of Keeney's [31] methodology resulted in 430 values, which were consolidated into 86 micro level objectives. These micro level objectives were then clustered into 25 categories, which they termed "high-level objectives." They then classified these, based on the concept of Why Is This Important (WITI) test proposed by Keeney, into 9 fundamental and 16 means objectives.

Dhillon and Torkzadeh [20] illustrate the usefulness of IS security objectives with numerous examples. For instance, they identify "Enhancing integrity of business processes" as a fundamental objective that helps in ensuring IS security. Integrity of business processes can be enhanced if stakeholders: (1) understand the expected use of available information; (2) are aware of the procedures and codes of conduct; and (3) ensure that appropriate organizational controls are in place. They also call for "enhanced management development practices". By enhancing the competence of staff and providing legitimate opportunities for financial gain, it is possible to ensure security and curb internal threats. In a final synthesis, Dhillon and Torkzadeh [20] suggest that their objectives and the associated sub-objectives form a good basis for organizations to plan for security. Additionally, D'Aubeterre et al. [15] highlight the importance of information and proper design of activities in enhancing business process security. Launching from this research work, Kolkowska et al. [32] use the objectives identified by Dhillon and Torkzadeh [20] to define a range of IS security goals for Swedish hospitals. Herath and Rao [45] and Drevin and Steyn [22] use some of the same concepts to study aspects of IS security policy.

The objectives described by Dhillon and Torkzadeh [20] provide a useful basis for undertaking strategic planning for IS security. Value based objectives have been extensively used to develop strategic plans for a number of areas. Merrick et al. [37] for instance, define objectives for identifying and improving watershed needs leading to a strategic plan for the Upham Brook Watershed in the Richmond, Virginia area. Ramanujam et al. [46] present a multi-objective assessment of planning systems and reassert the need for a multidimensional view of planning. While the mainstream IS literature has made significant progress in defining multi-objective perspectives for IS planning, more research is clearly needed on strategic planning for IS security. Using different terminology, many authors have made such calls (e.g. [9, 23, 51, 54, 57], among others).

4 Strategic Planning Using IS Security Objectives

In this section, we illustrate an applied use of value-focused IS security objectives. The main purpose of this section is to demonstrate the usefulness of the objectives in terms of engaging in a strategic planning exercise. The illustrative example is drawn from the healthcare sector. This sector has an overabundance of IS security issues that need consideration. In the USA, for example, a "leak" of a HIV Positive diagnosis, alarmed public and a series of public hearings culminated in the 1996 HIPAA (Health Insurance Portability and Accountability Act) legislation. HIPAA incorporates within itself a privacy rule, which addresses how and when patient records may be used or disclosed.

Healthcare organizations need to institute strong information security mechanisms. IS security objectives are central to a security based IS strategic planning initiative. Based on the parsimonious set of objectives from the Dhillon and Torkzadeh study, we undertook an IS security assessment. We identified two organizations for the research based, applied assessment - a US based Medical College (MC) and a US based Cancer Institute (CI).

MC is constituted of 19 departments (ranging from Anesthesiology and Dermatology to Radiology and Surgery). We sampled 38 individuals across the departments (1 physician and 1 nurse from each department). A total of 26 usable responses were received. At CI a cross section of health care providers was identified and 14 usable responses were received. The assessment instrument was the same for both sites and was administered about a year after the first study. The 13 objectives were organized into 2 categories - fundamental objectives (with 26 sub-objectives) and means objectives (with 36 sub-objectives). Each objective was assessed on a 5 point Likert-type scale where 1 indicates strongly disagree and 5 denotes strongly agree.

Figure 1 is a graphical representation of our findings from the MC and CI illustrative cases. Three profiles for fundamental and means objectives are presented (original study sample responses, MC and CI data). The findings provide a useful basis for strategic planning for IS security. To the extent that the large sample represents a variety of industry from banking and insurance to healthcare to manufacturing, these findings are generalizable. Follow up studies can focus specifically on a single industry by collecting data from that industry. The intent for our healthcare specific data collection is to provide an example of a single industry results and be able to interpret those results relative to our results from the large sample.In collecting data, we asked representatives of MC and CI to assess their organizations in terms of fundamental and the means objectives based on the original survey. There were multiple respondents from each organization and the collective view of the respondents is reflective of the organization in general. In the literature typically a single informant is used to provide an organizational view [35]. In our study however we had several informants who provide an organizational view [56]. The following interpretations can be drawn.

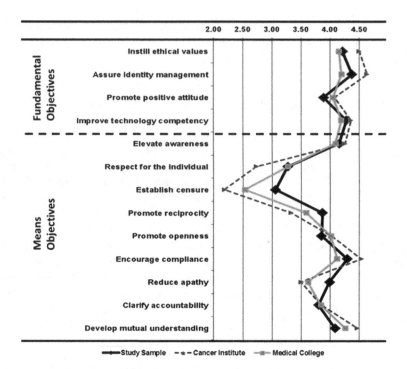

Fig. 1. An illustrative IS security profile

(1) If the employees conform to the general patterns (the study sample in our case), then this might suggest that the organization is more or less performing satisfactorily in relation to the given objective. With respect to *improving technology competency*, the study sample and data from MC and CI seem to converge, indicating that all constituents consider this objective to be of similar importance. If the respective organizations do not have adequate mechanisms or programs in place to improve technology competence, then they should proactively engage in this effort. As previously discussed, we know that technology competency helps in improving IS security.

(2) It is interesting to note how the responses differed for the *establish censure* objective. Censure ensures IS security by instilling fear, possible excommunication, and prospects of losing one's job. While our large sample showed somewhat average importance of this objective, respondents from CI did not consider this objective to be that important. The MC respondents felt this was more important compared with CI. We feel (as have Herath and Rao [45] along similar lines) that ensuring censure can possibly result in good IS security, particular in achieving objectives such as *promoting positive attitude* and *assuring identity management*. Therefore a higher score on censure is ideally needed. However it may just be that in healthcare, establishing censure may not have high relevance. One could possibly explain this based on what Mintzberg [38] terms as power residing in the *system of expertise*. Mintzberg argues that in high expertise domains (*viz.* healthcare), by virtue of the inherent expertise, some individuals and groups wield a lot of power. Both the MC

and CI groups had a high concentration of experts, who were perhaps less worried about censure relative to say compliance. Nevertheless, failure to address such issues and understand potential impact of other means and fundamental objectives could prove detrimental to the organization.

(3) In our original sample, we found *reducing apathy* to be an important objective. While the average benchmark from the study sample was fairly high, both MC and CI scored lower. Reducing apathy helps promote a *positive attitude* and *instill ethical values*, which in turn helps in assuring good IS security. A low score on apathy suggests that respondents are indifferent towards security violations, which could have corresponding impact on compliance and censure. In a 2004 Global Information Security Survey, Ernst & Young found that while management is hesitant to assign priority to human capital, it was more than willing to invest on various security technologies. The study also noted that management's apathetic attitude was resulting in pathetic consideration of IS security [62]. Certainly we corroborated this view, and believe that it is therefore prudent to understand apathy issues and their potential impact on other objectives and how strategic planning could be undertaken.

In this illustrative example we see three most noticeable differences relative to the large sample results in IS security means objectives - *establish censure*, *promote reciprocity*, and *reduce apathy*. This research work indicates that perhaps healthcare professionals consider these three objectives less important than security professionals in our larger sample. We do not wish to impose any judgment with respect to the efficacy of the value perception in the healthcare industry, but merely want to use the example to demonstrate the usefulness of the two sets of objectives. The specific profile can provide focus for firms in conducting their IS security strategic planning. In setting strategy for IS security for healthcare industry, the sample results seem to suggest greater emphasis on means objectives such as *awareness* and *compliance* and less emphasis on *censure* and *individuality*. Comparison with subsequent profiles would offer evidence of the effectiveness of implemented security measures for continuous improvements.

5 Discussion

On the Socio-Technical Nature of IS Security. It is interesting to observe that most of the value-focused IS security objectives presented in this study span across technical and social aspects of IS security. This research outcome is consistent with what mainstream IS security literature has to say about the nature of IS security. While the literature has long recognized the increasing importance of non-technical, people related issues in ensuring IS security (e.g. see [28]), the objectives have not been conceptualized). For instance, Rindfleisch [48] in the context of healthcare comments:

> *Technology can help to ensure that only health care personnel access information they have a right and need to know, and that information gets from one place to another accurately and securely. But technology can do very little to ensure the person receiving the information will handle it according to confidentiality standards. That depends on ethics and an effective supervisory and legal structure that provides sanctions against detected misuse (p. 99).*

While our study presents technically and organizationally/socially grounded IS security objectives, these are not necessarily in contradiction with the traditional exclusively technical world-view of IS security. Instead, it augments it with a fresh dimension that stems from the social system and technical system interaction, rather than just from the technical system. As Keeney [51] suggests, the best way to know the real concerns of the users in order to arrive at good decisions is to ask them. Similarly the best way to anchor user perception and to obtain their judgment is to focus on their value-base. A value-based approach is expected to be stable with long lasting effects. Clearly, some of the elements derived from a techno-centric orientation are essential in the overall management of IS security, but it is important to begin thinking about the values prior to discussing alternatives - for an exclusive techno-centric orientation only allows identification of requirements for IS security.

We have argued earlier that a requirements based design orientation may result in excellent and elegantly designed secure systems, but may not fulfill the need to think strategically about IS security. We wish to emphasize that a broader socio-technical perspective that includes the individual values, as well as the technical elements, is necessary for forming long term strategic plans in an enterprise (see [13]). Ultimately, it is the individuals that cause, and are affected by, the security threats [18]. The more we understand an individuals' value system, the better we might be at developing responsive information systems security plans.

IS Security Objectives and the Content of Strategic Planning. Following Mintzberg [41] we identified design, planning, and emergent position as three schools of thought informing IS security research. While each school of thought offers interesting insights for IS security, being aware of the pitfalls and adopting a user/stakeholder value-based (c.f. Gregory and Keeney [24]) perspective allows for identifying IS security objectives in a proactive manner.

As the health care example illustrates, results of an assessment using our objectives can help in developing IS security profiles. Such profiles suggest the employee's perceived importance of these objectives. Strategic decisions can then be taken to address the areas that need attention. Periodic collection of data with the same instrument would provide information for evaluating the results of implemented IS security measures. Our survey results can also serve as a baseline for comparison purposes. Various scholars of strategic management, irrespective of their philosophical orientation, have considered objectives as a useful basis to define strategic plans (e.g. see works of [2, 3, 40, 45, 61] to name a few).

While the IS security objectives appear to be generic enough to guide strategic planning, the balancing of the IS security objectives with other strategic opportunities/ threats, resources and organizational capabilities, may impact the values of individuals and hence redefine the objectives over time [3]. Periodic reassessment of objectives would be a useful exercise since values and objectives may change over a period of time (similar observations are made by Tan and Hunter [55] and Keeney [51]). Ansoff [3] summarizes the intricate relationship of objectives, resources, opportunities, and capabilities succinctly when he notes:

> *The interaction between objectives and opportunities ... shows the key variable which determines the strategy. The need to balance four variables against one another (the environmental threats/opportunities, the firm's objectives, its present capabilities, and its future resources) during formulation of strategy explains much of the complexity (p. 179).*

Therefore, it is prudent to remain cognizant of not only the IS security objectives, but their possible evolution over time. In the interim however, the IS security objectives provide a useful basis to engage in discussions, undertake assessments and provide guidelines for IS security strategic planning.

Is Security Objectives and the Structure of Strategic Planning. The security objectives defined in the current research allow organizations to structure their security related strategic planning. In this section we suggest possible ways in which the objectives could be used to facilitate security strategic planning.

(1) Reconsideration of near term and long term IS security goals. The thirteen fundamental and means objectives, along with all the sub-objectives are a useful basis for an organization to assess their current security policies and provide input for future security policy conceptualization. Rather than begin with a clean slate, the objectives are a reasonably good starting point to assess what is in place for a given enterprise and what more needs to be done, especially in terms of formal programs that should be initiated. While objectives are a useful starting point to engage in strategic planning, this orientation has come under criticism from emergent positioning school of thought researchers. Hence, the objectives need to be considered in the context of a portfolio analysis of activities discussed next.

(2) Engage in a comparative portfolio analysis. The profiles developed for individual organizations and their comparison with a baseline (see Fig. 1), are useful for defining a portfolio of activities that any firm should have. For example, instilling the importance of ethical values to IS security is one of the fundamental objectives. One way to ensure that all employees in the organization have the same understanding is to promote awareness. If this means objective is considered lacking in an organization, one strategy could be to raise employee ethical value with a variety of promotional campaigns. Resources would then be allocated to design effective campaigns. One such campaign could aim at raising employee awareness on the inappropriateness for sharing password among coworkers. Additional policies and procedures may also be implemented to help reinforce or maintain high level of ethical value in the organization. While we do suggest that comparative portfolio analysis should be undertaken, presenting a detailed strategic plan is beyond the scope of this paper.

(3) Engage in a IS security technology review. A clearer view of what an organization may aspire to achieve helps in identification and subsequent realization of mechanisms needed to achieve the objectives. This helps with a clear definition of the kind of technical solutions that may be required for achieving the purpose. For instance, implementing a biometric access control system should not determine how identity management should be accomplished. On the other hand, focusing on clarity of accountability structures helps in appropriately using access control systems, for they do impact reporting and responsibility structures, which in turn will help in assuring censure, thus leading to good identity management.

Limitations. Like any research, our study has some limitations. We are clearly bounded by the conceptualization of fundamental and means objectives from Dhillon and Torkzadeh [20]. It is possible that the value-focused thinking approach runs the risk of personal biases influencing the qualitative interpretations. However, Dhillon and Torkzadeh [20] did note that they were cognizant of the limitations and that their method helped in addressing some of the concerns.

The Dhillon and Torkzadeh [20] study offered 25 fundamental and means objectives, which emerged into 13 (4 fundamental and 9 means) in this study. While systematic quantitative data analysis helped us in defining a more parsimonious list, we may have lost some of the richness that was integral to the original set of objectives. Nevertheless, a smaller statistically valid set of objectives would form a good basis for further research.

While the development of the strategic planning for IS security assessment was grounded in the responses of the IS security professionals, our illustrative application to engage in strategic planning was based on data from non-IS security professional perspective. Such an orientation is useful particularly since it provides insight into the value gap between the IS security and non-IS security professionals.

6 Conclusions

We presented a set of 4 fundamental and 9 means objectives based on survey responses by 253 security professionals. While fundamental objectives provide an overall picture of what is important for IS security, means objectives offer suggestions on how to accomplish those objectives. respondents' profile suggests that these objectives are applicable to most industries. Organizations can review existing IS security policies and procedures against these objectives and identify areas where objectives were not met. Strategies could then be formulated and actions taken to address the lacking objectives.

Empirically grounded, comprehensive IS security objectives for planning have not been proposed in the literature. At best, a number of requirements for IS security have been established. A requirements based strategic planning seeks to only find alternative based objectives. In this research and in line with Keeney [51], we presented the view that a value-focused perspective in strategic planning helps in creating a richer and a more robust set of objectives. We believe that the objectives presented in this research will significantly help in IS security strategic planning, and have demonstrated the use of these objectives in an applied case.

References

1. Anderson, E.E., Choobineh, J.: Enterprise information security strategy. Comput. Secur. **27** (1–2), 22–29 (2008)
2. Andrews, K.R.: The Concept of Corporate Strategy. Irwin, Homewood (1987)
3. Ansoff, H.I.: Corporate Strategy. Penguin Books, Harmondsworth (1987)
4. Ansoff, H.I.: Strategic Management in a Historical Perspective. Wiley, Chichester (1991)
5. Backhouse, J., Dhillon, G.: Structures of responsibility and security of information systems. Eur. J. Inf. Syst. **5**(1), 2–9 (1996)
6. Baskerville, R.: Designing Information Systems Security. Wiley, New York (1988)

7. Baskerville, R.: Information systems security design methods: implications for information systems development. ACM Comput. Surv. **25**(4), 375–414 (1993)

8. Baskerville, R., Dhillon, G.: Information systems security strategy: a process view. In: Straub, D.W., Goodman, S., Baskerville, R. (eds.) Information Security: Policy, Processes, and Practices. M E Sharpe, Armonk (2008)

9. Baskerville, R., Siponen, M.: An information security meta-policy for emergent organizations. Logistics Inf. Manag. **15**(5/6), 337–346 (2002)

10. Bell, D., Padula, L.: Secure Computer Systems: Unified Exposition and Multics Interpretation. MITRE Corp, Bedford (1976)

11. Biba, K.J.: Integrity considerations for secure computer systems. The Mitre Corporation (1977)

12. Bishop, M.: Computer Security. Art and Science. Addison-Wesley, Boston (2003)

13. Bostrom, R.P., Heinen, J.S.: MIS problems and failures: a socio-technical perspective. Part I: The causes. MIS Q. **1**(1), 17–32 (1977)

14. Choobinen, J., Dhillon, G., Grimaila, M., Rees, J.: Management of information security: challenges and research directions. Commun. AIS **20**, 958–971 (2007)

15. D'Aubeterre, F., Singh, R., Iyer, L.: Secure activity resource coordination: empirical evidence of enhanced security awareness in designing secure business processes. Eur. J. Inf. Syst. **17**(5), 528–542 (2008)

16. Dhillon, G.: Managing Information System Security. Macmillan, London (1997)

17. Dhillon, G.: Information Security Management: Global Challenges in the New Millennium. Idea Group Publishing, Hershey (2001)

18. Dhillon, G.: Violation of safeguards by trusted personnel and understanding related information security concerns. Comput. Secur. **20**(2), 165–172 (2001)

19. Dhillon, G., Backhouse, J.: Current directions in IS security research: towards socio-organizational perspectives. Inf. Syst. J. **11**(2), 127–153 (2001)

20. Dhillon, G., Torkzadeh, C.: Value focused assessment of information system security in organizations. Inf. Syst. J. **16**(3), 293–314 (2006)

21. Donnellon, A., Gray, B., Bougon, M.G.: Communication, meaning, and organised action. Adm. Sci. Q. **31**, 43–55 (1986)

22. Drevin, L., Kruger, H., Steyn, T.: Value-focused assessment of information communication and technology security awareness in an academic environment. In: Fischer-Hübner, S., Rannenberg, K., Yngström, L., Lindskog, S. (eds.) SEC 2006. IIFIP, vol. 201, pp. 448–453. Springer, Boston, MA (2006). https://doi.org/10.1007/0-387-33406-8_40

23. Gerber, M., Solms, R.: From risk analysis to security requirements. Comput. Secur. **20**(7), 207–214 (2001)

24. Gregory, R., Keeney, R.L.: Creating policy alternatives using stakeholder values. Manag. Sci. **40**, 1035–1048 (1994)

25. Grover, V., Segars, A.H.: An empirical evaluation of stages of strategic information systems planning: patterns of process design and effectiveness. Inf. Manag. **42**(5), 761–779 (2005)

26. Henderson, J.C., Sifonis, J.G.: The value of strategic IS planning: understanding consistency, validity, and IS markets. MIS Q. **12**, 187–200 (1988)

27. Herath, T., Rao, H.R.: Encouraging information security behaviors in organizations: role of penalties, pressures and perceived effectiveness. Decis. Support Syst. **47**(2), 154–165 (2009)

28. Hitchings, J.: The need for a new approach to information security. In: 10th International Conference on Information Security (IFIP Sec 1994), Curacao, NA, 23–27 May (1994)

29. Hoven, J.: Information resources management: stewards of data. Inf. Syst. Manag. **16**(1), 88–90 (1999)

30. Kaplan, R.B., Murdock, L.: Rethinking the corporation: core process redesign. McKinsey Q. **2**, 27–43 (1991)

31. Keeney, R.L.: Value-Focused Thinking. Harvard University Press, Cambridge (1992)
32. Kolkowska, E., Hedström, K., Karlsson, F.: Information security goals in a Swedish hospital. In: Asproth, V. (ed.) Proceedings of IRIS 31 - The 31st Information Systems Research Seminar in Scandinavia, Åre, Sweden (2008)
33. Koontz, H.: The management theory jungle revisited. Acad. Manag. Rev. 5(2), 175–187 (1980)
34. Kukalis, S.: Determinants of strategic planning systems in large organizations a contingency approach. J. Manag. Stud. 28, 143–160 (1991)
35. Kumar, N., Stern, L.W., Anderson, J.C.: Conducting interorganizational research using key informants. Acad. Manag. J. 36(6), 1633–1651 (1993)
36. Lederer, A.L., Sethi, V.: Key prescriptions for strategic information systems planning. J. Manag. Inf. Syst. 13, 35–62 (1996)
37. Merrick, J.R.W., Parnell, G.S., Barnett, J., Garcia, M.: A multiple-objective analysis of stakeholder values to identify watershed improvement needs. Decis. Anal. 2(1), 44–57 (2005)
38. Mintzberg, H.: Power in and Around Organizations. Prentice-Hall, Englewood Cliffs (1983)
39. Mintzberg, H.: Structures in Fives: Designing Effective Organizations. Prentice-Hall, Englewood Cliffs (1983)
40. Mintzberg, H.: Crafting Strategy. Harvard Business Review, Boston (1987)
41. Mintzberg, H.: Strategy formulation: schools of thought. In: Fredrickson, J.W. (ed.) Perspectives on Strategic Management. Harper Business, New York (1990)
42. Parker, D.B.: Restating the foundation of information security. In: Gable, G.G., Caelli, W. J. (eds.) Eighth IFIP International Symposium on Computer Security, IFIP Sec 1992, Singapore, 27–29 May 1992, pp. 139–151. Elsevier Science Publishers B.V. (North Holland) (1992)
43. Parker, D.B.: Toward a new framework for information security. In: Bosworth, S., Kabay, M.E. (eds.) The Computer Security Handbook. Wiley, New York (2002)
44. Puhakainen, P., Siponen, M.: Improving employee's compliance through IS security training: an action research study. MIS Q. 34(4), 757–778 (2010)
45. Quinn, B., Mintzberg, H., James, R.M.: The Strategy Process - Concepts, Contexts and Cases. Prentice-Hall, Englewood Cliffs (1988)
46. Ramanujam, V., Venkatraman, N., Camillus, J.C.: Multi-objective assessment of effectiveness of strategic planning: a discriminant analysis approach. Acad. Manag. J. 29(2), 347–372 (1986)
47. Rees, J., Bandyopadhyay, S., Spafford, E.H.: PFIRES: a policy framework for information Security. Commun. ACM 46(7), 101–106 (2003)
48. Rindfleisch, T.C.: Privacy, information technology, and health care. Commun. ACM 40(8), 93–100 (1997)
49. Sammon, D., Finnegan, P.: The ten commandments of data warehousing. ACM SIGMIS Database 31(4), 82–91 (2000)
50. Segars, A.H., Grover, V.: Profiles of stratgic information systems planning. Inf. Syst. Res. 10(3), 199–232 (1999)
51. Siponen, M.: Five dimensions of information security awareness. Comput. Soc. 31(2), 24–29 (2001)
52. Siponen, M., Iivari, J.: Six design theories for IS security policies and guidelines. J. Assoc. Inf. Syst. 7(7), 445–472 (2006)
53. Siponen, M.T.: An analysis of the traditional IS security approaches: implications for research and practice. Eur. J. Inf. Syst. 14(3), 303–315 (2005)
54. Straub, D.W., Welke, R.J.: Coping with systems risks: security planning models for management decision making. MIS Q. 22(4), 441–469 (1998)

55. Tan, F.B., Hunter, M.G.: The repertory grid technique: a method for the study of cognition in information systems. MIS Q. **26**(1), 39–57 (2002)
56. Van Bruggen, G.H., Lilien, G.L., Kacker, M.: Informants in organizational marketing research: Why use multiple informants and how to aggregate responses. J. Mark. Res. **39**(4), 469–478 (2002)
57. Von Solms, R., Van de Haar, H., Von Solms, S.H., Caelli, W.J.: A framework for information security evaluation. Inf. Manag. **26**(3), 143–153 (1994)
58. Wilkes, J., Stata, R.: Specifying data availability in multi-device file systems. ACM SIGOPS Operating Syst. Rev. **25**(1), 56–59 (1991)
59. Wing, J.M.: A specifier's introduction to formal methods. Computer **23**(9), 8–24 (1990)
60. Wing, J.M.: A symbiotic relationship between formal methods and security. In: Proceedings from Workshops on Computer Security, Fault Tolerance, and Software Assurance: From Needs to Solution, CMU-CS-98-188, December 1998
61. Wrapp, H.E.: Good managers don't make policy decisions. In: Mintzberg, H., Quinn, J.B. (eds.) The strategy process, pp. 32–38. Prentice-Hall, Englewood Cliffs (1991)
62. ZDNet Australia. Security's pathetic while management's apathetic: Ernst & Young. ZD Net Australia, Australia (2004)
63. Zuccato, A.: Holistic security management framework applied in electronic commerce. Comput. Secur. **26**(3), 256–265 (2007)

A Prediction Model of Privacy Control for Online Social Networking Users

Rohit Valecha[1(✉)], Rajarshi Chakraborty[2], H. Raghav Rao[1], and Shambhu Upadhyaya[2]

[1] University of Texas at San Antonio, San Antonio, TX 78249, USA
{rohit.valecha,hr.rao}@utsa.edu
[2] State University of New York at Buffalo, Buffalo, NY 14260, USA
rajarshic@gmail.com, shambhu@cse.buffalo.edu

Abstract. With the growing popularity of social network sites (SNS), organizations have started to leverage them for encouraging both personal and professional data sharing. However, inherent privacy problems in social networks have become a concern for organizations deploying them. So companies have started investing in systems for evaluating employees' behaviors on SNSs. In evaluating employees' behaviors on SNSs, this study aims at developing a mechanism for learning users' behaviors on SNS and predicting their control of privacy on SNS. Privacy prediction is based on the revelation of actual privacy characteristics of users through the analysis of their SNS usage patterns. Using the Design Science research methodology, this study presents the design and instantiation of a prediction model that is trained using survey data and SNS data of graduate students from a prominent Northeastern University in the United States, which is used to generate class labels associated with their privacy control. The prediction model provides a data analytics component for reliable predictions of users' privacy control using Machine Learning algorithm SVM and a randomized ensemble of decision trees. The results suggest that the prediction model represents a reliable method for predicting privacy control based on user actions on SNS.

Keywords: Privacy control · Social networks · Prediction model
Machine learning · Design science

1 Introduction

Recent surveys indicate that a large majority of companies are actively using, or evaluating the use of social networking sites (SNSs). According to a report from September 2017, 52% of businesses say social media positively influences revenue and sales. In addition, about 58% of business-to-consumer companies consider investing time and money in social media[1]. These companies are viewing SNSs as "[…] a new method of communication between colleagues, encouraging both personal and professional sharing [of information]" (DiMicco et al. 2009, p. 711). SNSs offer many benefits to both companies and their employees – create working relationships, provide

---

[1] https://clutch.co/agencies/social-media-marketing/resources/social-media-survey-2017.

© Springer International Publishing AG, part of Springer Nature 2018
S. Chatterjee et al. (Eds.): DESRIST 2018, LNCS 10844, pp. 300–315, 2018.
https://doi.org/10.1007/978-3-319-91800-6_20

social support, generate capital and foster corporate citizenship behaviors (DiMicco et al. 2009; Skeels and Grudin 2009), and generate job satisfaction, allow work freedom and create an environment of fun (Koch et al. 2015; Tan et al. 2009). SNSs are keeping employees engaged as well as companies efficient and effective (Wehner et al. 2017). Thus, by blurring of work and social boundaries, SNSs are paving the way for companies to extend their efforts regarding "crowdsourcing, open innovation, or the inclusion of external experts in internal processes" (Koch et al. 2015, p. 151).

Many researchers have focused on privacy issues in SNS use (Acquisti and Grossklags 2004; Brandimarte et al. 2013; Gross and Acquisti 2005). SNS users share all kinds of personal details about themselves (including their likes, dislikes, friends, education, etc.). Some SNS users also share sensitive information such as their birthdays, addresses and other location details (Dong et al. 2015). Wang et al. (2011) have demonstrated empirically that SNS users often share something publicly, which they later regret. This points to the fact that users fail to manage their privacy by failing to control or restrict information from certain other users (Compano and Lusoli 2010). Some of the users often avoid the hassle of controlling information altogether when faced with numerous and complex privacy decisions. Such users that are negatively predisposed towards controlling their information are considered to be more prone to manifest privacy mishaps on the SNSs.

It is essential to assess users' control on SNS in order to prevent privacy mishaps that may threaten corporate reputation. Privacy researchers have often linked the concepts of privacy and control (Laufer and Wolfe 1977). They state that control is a key factor that shapes privacy. Margulis (2003a, b) has also pointed out that privacy is a control-related phenomenon. Xu et al. (2011) state that "the element of control is embedded in most privacy conceptual arguments and definitions, and has been used to operationalize privacy in numerous studies (Culnan 1993; Malhotra et al. 2004; Sheehan and Hoy 2000)" (p. 804). In this paper, we define "control" based in terms of how well the users can control their information on the SNS (henceforth referred to as "privacy control").

Estimating users' privacy control on SNS is a complex task, particularly because privacy control is subjective. Subjective evaluation of privacy control requires experiments or surveys with users (see Hoadley et al. 2010 and Xu 2007), which can be affected by many factors such as experimental setting, subjects' mood, and other contextual elements. As a result, subjective evaluation of privacy control can be an inconvenient, costly and time-consuming operation to perform, thereby making it impractical for large-scale study or real-world applications. It will be more practical (as well as considerable improvement) to design objective models that are able to predict privacy control in a consistent manner and that can automate assessment of users' privacy control on SNS.

Towards that end, we evaluate how accurately a machine learning model can predict human judgment about privacy control (i.e. perceived privacy control) on SNS. The main objective of this paper is to test whether the machine learning (objective) model matches the privacy control perceived by the user (subjective) on SNS. The contribution of this paper is a machine learning model (classifier) to classify users into privacy control groups based on an analysis of their SNS usage. Such a classifier spells out the actual privacy-related characteristics of users. It would allow organizations several benefits such as: studying users under the prism of predisposition towards privacy mishaps, getting an evaluation of users' privacy attitude, training users to control information based on their professional activities, tailoring system designs to respond to individual behavioral dynamics, and promoting privacy-conscious practices in data-collecting environments.

Using the Design Science Research (DSR) methodology (Hevner et al. 2004; Peffers et al. 2007), the machine learning classifier was devised in two phases: (1) a survey to subjectively assess users' perception of privacy control on SNS, and (2) a theory-guided approach for feature selection to create a predictive function. In the survey phase, SNS users identify their level of privacy control on SNS. In the feature selection phase, we adapt Communication Privacy Management (CPM) theory for selecting SNS interactions as feature vectors to a Support Vector Machine (SVM) classifier. The SVM classifier is trained using the survey instrument and the selected SNS interactions. The SVM classifier uses a predictive function that automatically assigns privacy control labels for SNS users with an F-score of 71%. The SNS usage-related features (visits and durations) are found to be more effective for the objective (machine learning-based) model of privacy control.

In order to facilitate the direct observation of users' actions, we developed an SNS. We formed a community of SNS users involving graduate students in a prominent Northeastern University in the United States, and collected traces of interactions among them. Our results suggest that the machine learning classifier (objective) represents a reliable method for predicting SNS users' perception of privacy control (subjective) based on their actions on the SNS usage. In accordance with McLaren (2011), the rest of this paper loosely follows a structure prescribed as optimal for demonstrating design science research work (Gregor and Hevner 2013). We look at the extant literature on privacy control in the Literature Review section. Subsequently, we present the description of the machine learning classifier in detail. Evaluation of this prediction model is presented through a case study with a student population. The paper concludes with remarks about limitations of the current state of the artifact and its evaluation so far. We also highlight the potential for possible future research directions taking advantage of the software setup designed for this paper.

2 Literature Review

In this section, we discuss the extant literature on privacy control. Then we provide the theoretical underpinnings of the privacy profiling model.

2.1 Privacy Control

A control-centered privacy definition has its roots in Westin's (1967) and Altman's (1975) theories of general privacy (as elaborated by Margulis (1977)). This definition equates privacy with control. The later studies have focused on privacy as the ability to control (Malhotra et al. 2004; Smith et al. 1996; Xu et al. 2011). Some scholars have also linked privacy with control by positioning control as a key factor shaping privacy

(Laufer and Wolfe 1977; Margulis 2003a, b). Margulis (2003a, b) has also pointed out that very little research has focused on the nature of control in the privacy context.

The few research papers that are exceptions (to name a few, see Dinev and Hart 2004; Johnson 1974; Xu et al. 2011) have looked into the nature of control in the privacy context through a psychological lens. Following this perspective, privacy control has been interpreted as "a perceptual construct with emphasis on personal information as the control target" (Xu et al. 2011, p. 804). Along these lines, it is obvious that privacy control has been assessed through a subjective evaluation using survey or experimental design focusing on perceptions of privacy control using questions such as "I can control over my personal information" or "I have control over what personal information is released" (Xu 2007).

As stated earlier, subjective evaluation of privacy control achieved in this way can be inconvenient because it gets affected by the experimental setting, subjects' mood, and other contextual elements. It can also turn out to be a costly and time-consuming operation to perform owing to the human-in-the-loop element, thereby making it impractical for real-world applications. To best of our knowledge, there has been very little research in predicting privacy control. Along this backdrop, we investigate the nature of privacy control on SNS from a computational viewpoint that allows us to interpret privacy control as an objective construct and emphasizes on users' interactions on SNS. In particular, we propose a machine learning model for predicting users' privacy control based on their interactions on SNS.

In order to derive the features affecting users' privacy control on SNS, it is important to understand how SNS users manage private information. Communication Privacy Management (CPM) Theory helps in understanding how users make decisions about revealing and concealing their private information through the use of boundary metaphor (Petronio 2002), as explained in next sub-section. In line with this discussion, we resort to the literature on CPM Theory to create the machine learning model to automate the subjective assessment of privacy control.

2.2 Communication Privacy Management (CPM) Theory

CPM theory aims to understand how users make decisions about controlling information within interpersonal relationships. This theory uses the metaphor of boundaries to define privacy as the process of opening and closing boundaries to others (Petronio 2002). When the boundary is open, information flows freely and when it is closed, the information flow is restricted (Xu et al. 2011). CPM theory is based on two main principles: ownership and control. Ownership suggests that people believe they own their private information, and control suggests that they believe they have the right to control it (Petronio 2002). Taken together, CPM theory proposes that individuals develop information spaces with clearly defined boundaries around the information spaces (Xu et al. 2011).

In constructing privacy boundaries, people develop privacy rules to impose control by concealing or revealing their private information. Petronio (2002) argues that individuals create and apply rules that effectively control information based on goals, context, and attitudes. In particular, she has identified five factors – culture, gender, motivation, context, and risk/benefit ratios – which have been shown to be responsible for the differences in the way people create privacy rules. Mullen and Hamilton (2016) also state that "[privacy] rules are influenced by culture, context, and gender and are driven by motivation that often applies a risk-benefit ratio" (p. 166). In addition to this, Westin (2003) explicates the effect of social values in controlling information. Westin states that at the social level, factors related to crowd capacity shape the opportunities people have to claim control of information from observation of others (Westin 1967; Westin 2003). Borrowing from Westin's definition of control, we examine how social factors play a role in setting privacy rules.

On SNSs, information can be controlled through several options. First, a user can choose what information to control. Intuitively, people would be more likely to control sensitive information. However, Brandimarte et al. (2013) show otherwise. Second, for every piece of information, the user can select a specific audience. Kostakos et al. (2011) suggest network structure may be used as a basis for predicting disclosures amongst individuals. Wellman and Wortley (1990) also indicate that there is less control of information for stronger ties. Finally, the user can also decide the frequency of the SNS use. Staddon et al. (2012) suggest that avid users of SNSs are less likely to control their personal information with others on the network. Kisekka et al. (2013) also investigate this relationship and report an opposite finding that using more than one SNS increases the likelihood of information control. Recently, SNSs have added numerous mechanism to control information at social levels by restricting friends' and groups' access to information. One such example is that of "circles" in Google+, which have been added for social privacy control (Kairam et al. 2012). The various factors, such as personal, social, environment, culture, context, setting, content, technology, network and SNS use, can be instantiated through the use of privacy preferences and settings through which users can create boundaries to control their information. Margulis (2003a, b) describes privacy control as regulating access to self through interactions. In the context of this study, we conceptualize privacy control as the regulation of the personal information within social circles through the capabilities afforded by the technology. In essence, we consider three factors that influence privacy control on SNSs: technology, information and network-related. Technology use is represented by the SNS usage, information factors include profile fields, and network-related factors account for features such as friends and groups.

3 Methodology

To create a machine learning model for predicting users' privacy control based on their interactions on SNS, the prediction model requires micro- and macro-level understanding of the users. We custom-built an SNS that captured two main sources of data – SNS interactions and perceptions of privacy control. In this section, we discuss the data collection methodology for assessing perception of privacy control on SNS. This section also discusses the objective data in the form of SNS interactions.

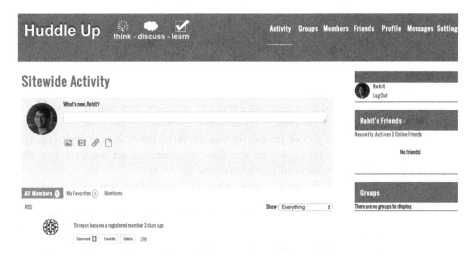

Fig. 1. Activity page of a signed in HuddleUp user

3.1   Custom-Built SNS – HuddleUp

There are several existing SNSs available, such as Facebook, MySpace, etc., that can be used to conduct a study on users' privacy behaviors. However, they do not provide flexibility in controlling the configuration settings. Furthermore, such systems also have hefty restrictions on the level of access to the data. Consequently, in order to achieve full control over the users' social data, we custom built an SNS called HuddleUp (details on the architecture of HuddleUp is available upon request).

HuddleUp was built upon an open-source website platform called WordPress. The desired features in HuddleUp were obtained through WordPress' add-ons (more precisely "plug-ins"). The fundamental social networking feature was enabled through a popular plug-in called "BuddyPress". However, the "BuddyPress" plug-in alone was not sufficient to implement all the features, such as friending, liking, commenting, etc. required for modern social networking experience. For this purpose, we relied upon several BuddyPress-specific plugins.

Some of these plugins were from BuddyPress enthusiasts, while the rest were commercial. A key plug-in was called "BuddyPress Activity Plus" that allowed the website to have an "activity feed" the same way Facebook has a News Feed. This feed kept users updated about the latest developments depending on the filter chosen (e.g. activities of friends, public activities of non-friends, etc.). The "Like" button revolutionized the concept of bookmarking user actions in social networking. "BuddyPress Like" plug-in allowed for taking advantage of the same bookmarking feature.

The various plug-ins made it possible to record each and every social update from the users and their visibility perimeter (public/private) of those updates within the database. As with a multitude of SNSs, HuddleUp supported the various social features like "friending" of other people, individual profile page for each user, media sharing in the form of photo and list sharing, and an updating news feeds page (Geyer et al. 2008). Some of the features of HuddleUp are shown in Fig. 1.

3.2 SNS Interaction Data

We formed a community of SNS users involving graduate students in a prominent Northeastern University in the United States. There were a total of 84 students who participated in this study. The participating students created online accounts and developed friendships amongst themselves. From the launch of the website, they interacted with the SNS and each other for about one semester. Any activity beyond the end of the semester was not considered for analysis, even though many of the students had got used to the SNS as part of their daily routine. After the SNS was deployed, the next step was to collect and aggregate the data on their interactions to create the objective method for assessment of privacy control on SNS.

We collected various facets of user data: (1) user data that contained the user-specific and profile-related information (such as profile picture), (2) site data that generated all the information regarding interactions of SNS users with HuddleUp (for e.g. visit duration), (3) friends' data that consisted of information about the users' friends, (4) activity data that consisted of the information that users shared or created on the website (for example friend requests), (5) group data that includes information about all the groups the user forms and takes part in (such as group participation). One of the authors of this paper, who was handling HuddleUp, at the time of data collection was a Ph.D. student. No faculty members had access to HuddleUp. Given that HuddleUp was devoid of any faculty participation, the class students freely communicated on HuddleUp. A perusal of the content shows that information sharing was freely practiced.

3.3 Privacy Control Data

In machine learning applications, one or more experts assign labels to training data points. However, this method is not scalable if each data point pertains to an individual user. So, we asked the users to rate themselves regarding their privacy control, i.e. the extent of control the participants had on their information in the context of HuddleUp. For this purpose, we utilized survey instruments published in Information Systems literature (Xu et al. 2011) to measure it. The privacy control survey consisted of four questions on a 5-point Likert scale: I have control over – (1) who can get access to my personal information collected by this SNS, (2) what personal information is released by this SNS, (3) how my personal information is used by this SNS, and (4) my personal information provided to this SNS.

In order to create labels for privacy control based on the responses to the four questions, we resorted to z-transformation. It makes mean and variance equal for all respondents making it possible to compare their perception of privacy control on the SNS (Mohammadi et al. 2014). The z-transformation standardizes the privacy control scores in a way that the value 0 denotes the mean and the difference from the mean signifies the standard deviation from the mean. We dichotomize the users' responses into two labels: "high" privacy control where the z-scores are positive and "low" privacy control where the z-scores are negative. In other words, by z-transforming the privacy control responses, we acquired self-reported class labels in terms of what the users perceived their control of private information on HuddleUp was.

3.4   Data Descriptive

A total of 40 students were identified as having low privacy control on the SNS, while 44 students had high privacy control when using the SNS. Table 1 provides a description of users' behavior on the SNS.

Table 1. Data descriptive (N = 84)

Best features	Min	Max	Mean	Std. Dev.
Visits	1	109	25.33	20.09
Visit duration (in seconds)	282	63063	17465.63	14827.10
Groups	1	23	11.88	5.753
Profile fields	1	20	9.49	4.56
Friends	9	89	54.65	18.42
Comments	0	43	8.44	9.49
Likes	0	23	4.54	4.63

4   Prediction Model

In this section, a prediction model (objective method) is used to evaluate users' privacy control on HuddleUp. The goal of the prediction model is to predict users' privacy control accurately and automatically as compared to the subjective assessment (involving survey). In other words, it should be able to mimic users' perception of privacy control. Figure 2 provides a methodological overview of the design of the prediction model. First, we extract the best features from the Extra-Trees feature selection. Then, we utilize the Support Vector Machine (SVM) model for classification.

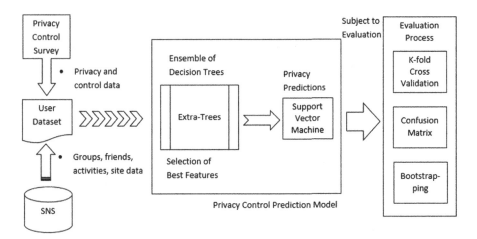

Fig. 2. Conceptual model of privacy prediction

4.1   Selection of Best Features – Decision Trees (Extra-Trees)

Most data sources in the world produce raw data that always has some level of redundancy. In the process of prediction, it is important to extract non-redundant features so as to improve predictability and generalizability of models (Tuv et al. 2009). This has made the sub-field of dimension reduction important in machine learning. Reduction of dimensions (or features) in a dataset allows for selecting the features that will be used in the final prediction model. In an effort to extract non-redundant features from the feature-set so as to improve predictability and generalizability of models, we apply Extra-Trees ensemble method (Geurts et al. 2006) that allows for selecting best performing features from the dataset.

The Extra-Trees (ET) method, a randomized ensemble of decision trees, has been shown to be computationally efficient in reducing the redundancy of the final model. ET provides prediction through a two-step process – selecting the features, and splitting the dataset based on a certain threshold value(s) of the features. The goal of both these steps is to get closer to the true class of each data point. Thus, the ET method improves upon the process and the prediction accuracy in general by aggregating (e.g. averaging) over a bunch of decisions trees (Mingers 1989). These decision trees are an outcome of a randomization aspect inserted into the machine learning algorithm by the ET method. Often, a random subset of the sample is chosen to develop the candidate decision tree models.

In the ET method, both the feature choice and the cut-off points are strongly randomized. In addition, the method does not bootstrap from the original sample – it uses the whole learning sample for developing all the individual decision trees. The features that appear towards the top of the tree contribute to the prediction decision for a larger portion of the sample. Thus, these features are more "important" than the features closer to (and including) the leaf nodes in a decision tree (Morris et al. 2001). This relative importance is measured by the expected fraction of learning samples whose prediction is a contribution of the feature in question.

In the implementation of Extra-Trees, a criterion function is a measure the quality of a split. There are two supported criteria: "gini" for the Gini impurity and "entropy" for the information gain. We utilized the default function of "gini". The best feature in each group obtained from the Extra-Trees method in decreasing order of importance (Abeel et al. 2009) is depicted in Table 2.

Table 2. Selection of best features

Best features	Data set	Feature importance
Visit duration	Site	0.158862
Groups	Groups	0.081802
Profile fields	User	0.091854
Friends	Friends	0.111291
Comments	Activity	0.111370

4.2   Support Vector Machines (SVM)

Machine learning consists of defining a model with parameters that are optimized using training data (referred to as a learning process) for prediction purposes. Machine learning algorithms are increasingly adopted in predicting user behaviors (Chong 2013). Classification is one of the many applications of machine learning, which involves categorizing a new observation in the presence of training data (supervised learning). Support vector machine (SVM) is one of the most robust methods in the process of supervised learning. SVM is a commonly used prediction algorithm that has been applied in IS research (Schwegmann et al. 2013).

SVM (Burges 1998) has been used in many domains for prediction (Nachev and Stoyanov 2012), particularly in computer security. SVM is one of the most stable and well-studied machine learning algorithms for binary predictions. SVM has been ranked as one of the top 10 algorithms in classification by prominent researchers (Wu et al. 2008). SVM is robust to distributions of the data and is accurate with the small size of training data (Pal and Foody 2012; Wu et al. 2008). SVM provides quick training performance and applies to different data types (Basnet 2017). Owing to these reasons, we choose SVM for the prediction model.

Using the best features from ET method, we ran the SVM model through its implementation. SVM classifies data into two or more classes using the concept of hyperplanes. A hyperplane, in general, is a set described by any scalar product equality. In the context of data with N dimensions, it represents all the points in a plane in the N − 1 dimensional space. SVM aims to find the maximum-margin hyperplanes to separate an observation into pre-defined classes based on training data (Auria and Moro 2008; Mountrakis et al. 2011).

In SVM, kernel functions help map that data to a high-dimensional feature-space where it is possible to draw a hyperplane between two support vectors (Schwegmann et al. 2013). These kernel functions can be linear, polynomial or radial basis (RB). In this paper, based on Joachims (1998), we have used RB function over the others. The key part of any classification model is to find parameters with good performance. We trained SVM model to estimate the best parameters (An et al. 2007). We estimated the best model over a range of values for various parameters of the classifier. The best value of the regularization parameter C was found to be 1000, and that of gamma was estimated at 1E−6. C determines how smooth or rough the decision surface is. Gamma suppresses the influence of a single training data point (Hastie et al. 2004).

5   Evaluation of the Prediction Model

In this section, first, we detail the standard practice of k-fold cross validation. Subsequent to that, we discuss the performance metrics used to validate the prediction model. Technology artifacts whose objectives are prediction-related functionalities are often evaluated on the basis of evaluation metrics in predicting "out-of-sample" data points (Shmueli and Koppius 2010). Since there are no comparable studies that predict privacy control, there are no comparable performance metrics to weigh the results against. Therefore, this is exploratory research that provides a benchmark for similar studies in future.

5.1   Cross Validation

Cross validation is a standard way to evaluate the performance of the prediction model. We resorted to the standard practice of k-fold cross validation (Kohavi 1995), where the dataset is divided into k-subsamples of equal size. From these k-subsamples, k − 1 subsamples are used to train the prediction model and the remaining sample is used to evaluate the performance of the prediction model. The process is repeated k-times with each of the subsample used only once as the training set and evaluation set. The performance metrics (discussed in the next sub-section) are averaged across the k-experiments to estimate the performance of the prediction model.

While there are many ways of choosing the subsamples (Arlot and Celisse 2010), we utilized a method whereby each subsample consisted of consecutive rows from the main dataset. We also chose k = 5 as it is more robust and popular (Nachev and Stoyanov 2012), which means the dataset was divided into 5 subsamples. Four subsamples were used for training, while the fifth subsample was used for evaluation. This process was repeated five times for estimating the performance metrics.

5.2   Performance Metrics

Performance metrics, used in evaluating the performance of a prediction model, are created from an error matrix (commonly referred to as confusion matrix (Stehman 1997)). Confusion matrix is widely used in the literature to evaluate prediction algorithms (Puniskis et al. 2006). Confusion matrix compares the predicted scores with actual scores and creates a measure of misclassification. The extent of misclassification is assessed by the number of Type I and Type II errors. Within confusion matrix, the lower the number of misclassifications, the better is the performance.

In evaluating the prediction model in this paper, we developed a confusion matrix to compare the objective/predicted privacy control from the prediction model to the perceived privacy control obtained based on the survey. The columns in the confusion matrix represent predicted privacy control, and the rows represent the actual privacy control. The confusion matrix allows us to determine the percentage of correctly classified and misclassified students based on their privacy control.

With the help of the confusion matrix, we define the various effectiveness measures. Following Powers (2011), we define accuracy as the proportion of the total number of students that were correctly classified. Precision is the proportion of the predicted high privacy control students that were correctly classified. Recall is the proportion of actual high privacy control students that were correctly classified. F-measure is the geometric mean of precision and recall.

5.3   Evaluation Results

Using the best features, we ran the SVM algorithms through its implementation. For the SVM model, the features set, consisting of site-, activity-, group-, user- and friends-level features were included in the model simultaneously, to determine how the prediction model performs overall. In this sub-section, we summarize the results of the evaluation process. Table 3 shows the mean AUC (Area under ROC Curve) for both

Table 3. Mean AUC (Area under ROC Curve)

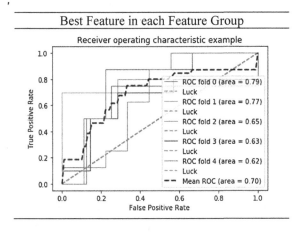

the prediction approaches. AUC is the ratio of true positive to false positive. AUC has often been recommended as a better measure of machine learning algorithms, especially in supervised learning when compared to overall accuracy (Bradley 1997).

The mean AUC for both the SVM prediction model with best feature in each group is 0.71. The AUC mean is above the random prediction score of 0.50 (Heumann 2011), which suggests that the SVM prediction model represents a reliable method of predicting privacy control based on users' interactions on HuddleUp. The performance metrics also suggest that the prediction model with best feature in each feature group is a reliable objective method for automating perceived privacy control (Accuracy = 71%; Precision = 71%; Recall = 71%; F-score = 71%).

6 Discussion and Conclusion

In the present study, we used CPM theory to investigate privacy control by adults who use SNSs. We have integrated technological, personal and social factors into privacy management framework that helps predict privacy control. Using Machine Learning model SVM, we predict privacy control through social, personal and technological factors. The results suggest that the SVM prediction model represents a reliable method of predicting privacy control based on users' actions on SNS. This is among first research to investigate privacy control from a behavioral/computational lens.

The privacy prediction model proposed in this paper can be useful for both social media companies as well as organizations that push for privacy-protecting regulations. Commercial entities can benefit from the prediction of privacy control. Accurate prediction of privacy control can also be helpful in proposing privacy-oriented legislation and promoting privacy-conscious practices in data-collecting environments. Organizations and legislations tend to generalize privacy for all human beings and do not take into account the aspect of personal choice. Prediction based on actions can help make the latter an important factor in shaping policies that would eventually be more positive towards business goals of organizations as well. In addition to more effective privacy protection, measurements based on human actions on social media may help companies add more value to their services more effectively instead of pushing it to everyone, thus risking erosion in trust amongst its users.

In this paper, inspired by the status of research on privacy in SNS, we have presented a novel approach to studying this phenomenon through the lens of privacy control. Research in information privacy in SNS has mostly studied using survey or other forms of data collection for empirical and behavioral objectives. We have not seen studies where the analysis stems from observations of actual behavior, a group of predictive modeling techniques, and where the data generated is an outcome of a full-fledged artifact development. This paper uses the principles of design science research for the study.

The privacy profiling model presented here bridges from a data source to a data analytics component with sufficient effort put into translating data from one end of the artifact to the other. This translation takes place through careful choice of features. The privacy profiling terminates with reliable predictions about privacy control based on users' actions on the SNS with the help of SVM method.

This study has of the following limitations: (a) While the variables that are selected for the purposes of predicting privacy decisions are specific to the behavior demonstrated by people on common SNSs, however, because we develop a custom-built SNS and mandate its use by students in a classroom setting, there may be limitations in its generalization to SNSs such as Facebook where users are not restrained by class-specific behavior. (b) The sample size is limited to the number of the students registered in the class.

In future studies, the privacy profiling model can be enhanced by introducing privacy-affecting intervention for the subjects. For example, the default sharing mode on both the activity and the groups of the website can be set to "Anyone" and hence public sharing can be changed from opt-in to opt-out. Our intention in the future study can be to test the accuracy of the prediction across different privacy paradigms within the same SNS.

Acknowledgements. This research has been funded in part by NSF under grants 1651475, 0916612 and 1227353. Usual disclaimer applies. The authors would also like to thank the reviewers whose comments have greatly improved the paper.

References

Abeel, T., Helleputte, T., Van de Peer, Y., Dupont, P., Saeys, Y.: Robust biomarker identification for cancer diagnosis with ensemble feature selection methods. Bioinformatics **26**(3), 392–398 (2009)

Acquisti, A., Grossklags, J.: Privacy attitudes and privacy behavior. In: Camp, L.J., Lewis, S. (eds.) Economics of Information Security. ADIS, vol. 12, pp. 165–178. Springer, Boston (2004). https://doi.org/10.1007/1-4020-8090-5_13

Altman, I.: The Environment and Social Behavior: Privacy, Personal Space, Territory, and Crowding, No. 156 A4 (1975)

An, S., Liu, W., Venkatesh, S.: Fast cross-validation algorithms for least squares support vector machine and kernel ridge regression. Pattern Recognit. **40**, 2154–2162 (2007)

Arlot, S., Celisse, A.: A survey of cross-validation procedures for model selection. Stat. Surv. **4**, 40–79 (2010)

Auria, L., Moro, R.A.: Support vector machines (SVM) as a technique for solvency analysis. DIW Discussion Papers, No. 811 (2008)

Basnet, R.: Automated Quality Assessment of Printed Objects Using Subjective and Objective Methods Based on Imaging and Machine Learning Techniques. Rochester Institute of Technology, Rochester (2017)

Bradley, A.P.: The use of the area under the ROC curve in the evaluation of machine learning algorithms. Pattern Recognit. **30**(7), 1145–1159 (1997)

Brandimarte, L., Acquisti, A., Loewenstein, G.: Misplaced confidences privacy and the control paradox. Soc. Psychol. Pers. Sci. **4**(3), 340–347 (2013)

Burges, C.J.: A tutorial on support vector machines for pattern recognition. Data Min. Knowl. Discov. **2**(2), 121–167 (1998)

Chong, A.Y.L.: Predicting m-commerce adoption determinants: a neural network approach. Expert Syst. Appl. **40**(2), 523–530 (2013)

Compano, R., Lusoli, W.: The policy maker's anguish: regulating personal data behavior between paradoxes and dilemmas. In: Moore, T., Pym, D. (eds.) Economics of Information Security and Privacy, pp. 169–185. Springer, Boston (2010). https://doi.org/10.1007/978-1-4419-6967-5_9

Culnan, M.J.: How did they get my name?: An exploratory investigation of consumer attitudes toward secondary information use. MIS Q. **17**, 341–363 (1993)

DiMicco, J.M., Geyer, W., Millen, D.R., Dugan, C., Brownholtz, B.: People sensemaking and relationship building on an enterprise social network site. In: 42nd Hawaii International Conference on System Sciences, pp. 1–10. IEEE (2009)

Dinev, T., Hart, P.: Internet privacy concerns and their antecedents-measurement validity and a regression model. Behav. Inf. Technol. **23**(6), 413–422 (2004)

Dong, C., Jin, H., Knijnenburg, B.P.: Predicting privacy behavior on online social networks. In: Ninth International AAAI Conference on Web and Social Media (2015)

Geurts, P., Ernst, D., Wehenkel, L.: Extremely randomized trees. Mach. Learn. **63**(1), 3–42 (2006)

Geyer, W., Dugan, C., DiMicco, J., Millen, D.R., Brownholtz, B., Muller, M.: Use and reuse of shared lists as a social content type. In: Proceedings of the SIGCHI Conference on Human Factors in Computing Systems, pp. 1545–1554 (2008)

Gregor, S., Hevner, A.R.: Positioning and presenting design science research for maximum impact. MIS Q. **37**(2), 337–355 (2013)

Gross, R., Acquisti, A.: Information revelation and privacy in online social networks. In: Proceedings of the 2005 ACM Workshop on Privacy in the Electronic Society, pp. 71–80. ACM (2005)

Hastie, T., Rosset, S., Tibshirani, R., Zhu, J.: The entire regularization path for the support vector machine. J. Mach. Learn. Res. **5**, 1391–1415 (2004)

Heumann, B.W.: An object-based classification of mangroves using a hybrid decision tree—Support vector machine approach. Remote Sens. **3**(11), 2440–2460 (2011)

Hevner, A., March, S.T., Park, J., Ram, S.: Design science in information systems research. MIS Q. **28**(1), 75–105 (2004)

Hoadley, C.M., Xu, H., Lee, J.J., Rosson, M.B.: Privacy as information access and illusory control: the case of the Facebook News Feed privacy outcry. Electron. Commer. Res. Appl. **9**(1), 50–60 (2010)

Joachims, T.: Text categorization with support vector machines: learning with many relevant features. In: Nédellec, C., Rouveirol, C. (eds.) ECML 1998. LNCS, vol. 1398, pp. 137–142. Springer, Heidelberg (1998). https://doi.org/10.1007/BFb0026683

Johnson, C.A.: Privacy as personal control. Man-Environ. Interact.: Eval. Appl.: Part 2, 83–100 (1974)

Kairam, S., Brzozowski, M., Huffaker, D., Chi, E.: Talking in circles: selective sharing in Google+. In: Proceedings of the SIGCHI Conference on Human Factors in Computing Systems, pp. 1065–1074. ACM (2012)

Kisekka, V., Bagchi-Sen, S., Rao, H.R.: Extent of private information disclosure on online social networks: an exploration of Facebook mobile phone users. Comput. Hum. Behav. 29(6), 2722–2729 (2013)

Koch, M., Schwabe, G., Briggs, R.O.: CSCW and social computing. Bus. Inf. Syst. Eng. 57(3), 149–153 (2015)

Kohavi, R.: A study of cross-validation and bootstrap for accuracy estimation and model selection. In: IJCAI, vol. 14, no. 2, pp. 1137–1145 (1995)

Kostakos, V., Venkatanathan, J., Reynolds, B., Sadeh, N., Toch, E., Shaikh, S.A., Jones, S.: Who's your best friend?: Targeted privacy attacks in location-sharing social networks. In: Proceedings of the 13th International Conference on Ubiquitous Computing, pp. 177–186. ACM (2011)

Laufer, R.S., Wolfe, M.: Privacy as a concept and a social issue: a multidimensional developmental theory. J. Soc. Issues 33(3), 22–42 (1977)

Malhotra, N.K., Kim, S.S., Agarwal, J.: Internet users' information privacy concerns (IUIPC): the construct, the scale, and a causal model. Inf. Syst. Res. 15(4), 336–355 (2004)

Margulis, S.T.: Conceptions of privacy: current status and next steps. J. Soc. Issues 33(3), 5–21 (1977)

Margulis, S.T.: On the status and contribution of Westin's and Altman's theories of privacy. J. Soc. Issues 59(2), 411–429 (2003a)

Margulis, S.T.: Privacy as a social issue and behavioral concept. J. Soc. Issues 59(2), 243–261 (2003b)

McLaren, T.S., Head, M.M., Yuan, Y., Chan, Y.E.: A multilevel model for measuring fit between a firm's competitive strategies and information systems capabilities. MIS Q. 35(4), 909–929 (2011)

Mingers, J.: An empirical comparison of selection measures for decision-tree induction. Mach. Learn. 3(4), 319–342 (1989)

Mohammadi, P., Ebrahimi-Moghadam, A., Shirani, S.: Subjective and objective quality assessment of image: a survey, pp. 1–50. arXiv Preprint https://arxiv.org/abs/1406.7799 (2014)

Morris, C.W., Autret, A., Boddy, L.: Support vector machines for identifying organisms—A comparison with strongly partitioned radial basis function networks. Ecol. Model. 146(1), 57–67 (2001)

Mountrakis, G., Im, J., Ogole, C.: Support vector machines in remote sensing: a review. ISPRS J. Photogramm. Remote Sens. 66(3), 247–259 (2011)

Mullen, C., Hamilton, N.F.: Adolescents' response to parental Facebook friend requests: the comparative influence of privacy management, parent-child relational quality, attitude and peer influence. Comput. Hum. Behav. 60, 165–172 (2016)

Nachev, A., Stoyanov, B.: Product quality analysis using support vector machines. Inf. Models Anal. 1, 179–192 (2012)

Pal, M., Foody, G.M.: Evaluation of SVM, RVM and SMLR for accurate image classification with limited ground data. IEEE J. Sel. Top. Appl. Earth Obs. Remote Sens. 5, 1344–1355 (2012)

Peffers, K., Tuunanen, T., Rothenberger, M.A., Chatterjee, S.: A design science research methodology for information systems research. J. Manag. Inf. Syst. **24**(3), 45–77 (2007)

Petronio, S.S.: Boundaries of Privacy: Dialectics of Disclosure. State University of New York Press, Albany (2002). xix, p. 268

Powers, D.M.W.: Evaluation: from precision, recall and F-measure to ROC, informedness, markedness and correlation. J. Mach. Learn. Technol. **2**(1), 37–63 (2011)

Puniskis, D., Laurutis, R., Dirmeikis, R.: An artificial neural nets for spam e-mail recognition. Electron. Electr. Eng. (2006). ISSN 1392-1215

Schwegmann, B., Matzner, M., Janiesch, C.: A method and tool for predictive event-driven process analytics. In: Wirtschaftsinformatik, p. 46 (2013)

Sheehan, K.B., Hoy, M.G.: Dimensions of privacy concern among online consumers. J. Public Policy Mark. **19**(1), 62–73 (2000)

Shmueli, G., Koppius, O.: Predictive analytics in information systems research. MIS Q. **35**(3), 553–572 (2010)

Skeels, M.M., Grudin, J.: When social networks cross boundaries. In: Proceedings of the ACM 2009 International Conference on Supporting Group Work, GROUP 2009. ACM, New York (2009)

Smith, H.J., Milberg, S.J., Burke, S.J.: Information privacy: measuring individuals' concerns about organizational practices. MIS Q. **20**(2), 167–196 (1996)

Staddon, J., Huffaker, D., Brown, L., Sedley, A.: Are privacy concerns a turn-off?: Engagement and privacy in social networks. In: Proceedings of the Eighth Symposium on Usable Privacy and Security, Washington, DC (2012)

Stehman, S.V.: Selecting and interpreting measures of thematic classification accuracy. Remote Sens. Environ. **62**(1), 77–89 (1997)

Tan, W.K., Nguyen, T.T.D., Tha, K.K.O., Yu, X.: Designing groupware that fosters social capital creation: can Facebook support global virtual team?. In: AMCIS 2009 Proceedings, p. 525 (2009)

Tuv, E., Borisov, A., Runger, G., Torkkola, K.: Feature selection with ensembles, artificial variables, and redundancy elimination. J. Mach. Learn. Res. **10**, 1341–1366 (2009)

Wang, Y., Norcie, G., Komanduri, S., Acquisti, A., Leon, P.G., Cranor, L.F.: I regretted the minute I pressed share: a qualitative study of regrets on Facebook. In: Proceedings of the Seventh Symposium on Usable Privacy and Security, p. 10. ACM, July 2011

Wehner, B., Ritter, C., Leist, S.: Enterprise social networks: a literature review and research agenda. Comput. Netw. **114**, 125–142 (2017)

Wellman, B., Wortley, S.: Different strokes from different folks: community ties and social support. Am. J. Sociol. **96**(3), 558–588 (1990)

Westin, A.F.: Privacy and Freedom. Atheneum, New York (1967)

Westin, A.F.: Social and political dimensions of privacy. J. Soc. Issues **59**(2), 431–453 (2003)

Wu, X., Kumar, V., Quinlan, J.R., Ghosh, J., Yang, Q., Motoda, H., McLachlan, G.J., Ng, A., Liu, B., Yu, P.S., Zhou, Z.-H., Steinbach, M., Hand, D.J., Steinberg, D.: Top 10 algorithms in data mining. Knowl. Inf. Syst. **14**(1), 1–37 (2008)

Xu, H.: The effects of self-construal and perceived control on privacy concerns. In: ICIS 2007 Proceedings, p. 125 (2007)

Xu, H., Dinev, T., Smith, J., Hart, P.: Information privacy concerns: linking individual perceptions with institutional privacy assurances. J. Assoc. Inf. Syst. **12**(12), 798 (2011)

A Knowledge Interface System for Information and Cyber Security Using Semantic Wiki

Riku Nykänen$^{(\boxtimes)}$ and Tommi Kärkkäinen

University of Jyväskylä, Jyväskylä, Finland
riku.t.nykanen@student.jyu.fi

Abstract. Resilience against information and cyber security threats has become an essential ability for organizations to maintain business continuity. As bullet-proof security is an unattainable goal, organizations need to concentrate to select optimal countermeasures against information and cyber security threats. Implementation of cyber risk management actions require special knowledge and resources, which especially small and medium-size enterprises often lack. Information and cyber security risk management establish knowledge intensive business processes, which can be assisted with a proper knowledge management system. This paper analyzes how Semantic MediaWiki could be used as a platform to assist organizations, especially small and medium-sized enterprises, in their information and cyber security risk management. The approach adopts design science research and service design methodologies in the derivation and evaluation of the system.

Keywords: Information security · Cyber security · Design science research
Knowledge management · Risk management

1 Introduction

In the recent decade, the importance of information security (IS) has constantly increased for all businesses. Proper management of IS provides competitive advantage, whereas shortcomings can constitute a serious source of risks. Hence, risk management activities are needed in all sized organizations, but small and medium-size enterprises (SMEs) are still struggling to manage their information security and implement basic security controls [33]. Information security management standards do exist, but the focus of the standards is the existence of policies and processes, and not how they can be accomplished in practice [38]. It has been also noted that existing standards do not take into account the special needs of SMEs [45].

Information security risk management is faced with multiple challenges, especially related to assets, security-cost trade-offs, and cost estimation in general [10]. Security knowledge management emphasizes the asset protection [32]. The asset availability, i.e., proper identification and organization of the competencies, processes, and technological resources for IS, was found to have the largest indirect effect on the organization performance [14].

Humans still provide the most significant risks related to information security [11]. Information security policies and procedures have an important role for SMEs, who

© Springer International Publishing AG, part of Springer Nature 2018
S. Chatterjee et al. (Eds.): DESRIST 2018, LNCS 10844, pp. 316–330, 2018.
https://doi.org/10.1007/978-3-319-91800-6_21

with limited resources typically just focus on keeping the necessary technology up and running in their everyday security management [4]. However, the technological choices might not be the most effective ones [13]. Even two thirds of the risk reducing controls in SMEs might not be designed properly or not operating as expected, mostly due to underestimating the risk level [34]. To conclude, especially SMEs need support in their IS risk management in order to select cost-effective countermeasures against increasing cyber and information security threats.

Information security management system (ISMS) has become common practice to define organizations' information security management goals and practices. ISO/IEC 27001 [18] is a widely adopted international standard, which defines requirements for ISMS and specifies security controls that an organization needs to implement. The controls are described in detail in the ISO/IEC 27002 standard [19]. There exist also other control catalogues, like NIST SP 800-53 [27] and BSI IT Grundschutz Catalogues [5]. All the three mentioned ISMS specifications establish risk-driven approach. ISO/IEC 27001 has been extended to support cyber security domain with the descriptive standard ISO/IEC 27032 [20].

In the cyber domain, risk management activities are similar to information security risk management (ISRM). One must identify assets; assess vulnerabilities and threats; evaluate risk; and select appropriate controls and implement them [9]. Where information security protects information assets, cyber security focuses protecting assets reachable via cyberspace [44]. As information is in the modern organizations stored in digital form, it is also reachable via cyberspace. Hence, information security and cyber security overlap, but there are also physical assets, which can be compromised via cyberspace, for example, devices that can be controlled and monitored using SCADA systems. Hence, it is more and more vital for SMEs to establish proper security risk management procedures to understand and mitigate both information and cyber security risks.

In the information security context, risk evaluation and control selection methodologies can be divided into three categories; quantitative, qualitative, and hybrid (semi-quantitative) [37]. In the quantitative methods, one derives a numeric estimate of the risk realization probability and cost and then selects optimal controls to mitigate the risk based on the return of the investment. Qualitative methods, on the other hand, are more knowledge-driven and the control selection is based on expertise of the stakeholders [37]. Hence, risk management processes are knowledge-driven, so they can be referred as knowledge intensive business processes (KIBP). Availability of expertise and knowledge is essential.

Our objective is to use design science research in developing an information and cyber security knowledge management artifact that provides operational support for organizations in the information and cyber risk management. To lower the adaptation barrier, the artifact should respond to the existing challenges of especially SMEs. These challenges include availability of resources, like money and knowledge. Hence, the artifact should especially tackle the knowledge gap of SMEs not utilizing the existing information and cyber security baselines to support their risk management activities. The solution should also be scalable and variable for different types of the organizations to avoid limiting the users of the artifact to a specific business domain or size. The artifact development encompasses an ongoing research activity, where all design science research cycles have been executed at least once. Here, the role of KIBP in relation to the rigor cycle [15, 16], as an existing knowledge-intensive process, is emphasized. It is taken into account in the design cycle, by utilizing challenges of KIBP as identified in [26] in the evaluation framework of the artifact.

2   Background

2.1   Information and Cyber Security Risk Management

There exists a number of reference models for information security risk management. Fenz and Ekelhart [9] have identified the common information security risk management phases from widely adopted models: *(i) System characterization*: identification of the scope of the risk management activities; *(ii) Threat and vulnerability assessment*: identification of possible scenarios how a risk could be realized; *(iii) Risk determination*: evaluation of the probability of the risk and impact of the realized risk; *(iv) Control identification*: identification of possible countermeasures to mitigate the risks; *(v) Control evaluation and implementation*: selection and implementation of the controls that mitigate a risk to an acceptable level.

As a process, organization shall, after setting the scope of the risk management activities, identify the assets that are needed in the operations. Asset is, by the definition, something that has value for the organization [18]. For the risk assessment, organization identifies possible threats targeting the assets. The risk determination focuses on the evaluation of the likelihood and impact of the risks, which also includes valuation of the assets for the organization. Also other properties can be evaluated to prioritize risks.

The control evaluation aims to select optimal controls to mitigate the one or more of the risks. In the control evaluation, there are four ways to address a particular risk: *(i) Accept*: Organization understands the risk and its consequences, but decides not to address it in other manner; *(ii) Avoid*: Activities exposing organization to a risk are avoided; *(iii) Transfer*: Consequences of the realized risk are transferred to other party; *(iv) Mitigate*: Countermeasures are implemented to reduce the risk to an acceptable level.

In general, the risk management may fail in all phases [9]. Fenz et al. [10] highlights that common failures are asset identification and valuation, risk prediction and control selection. Especially asset valuation and risk prediction are critical phases for quantitative methods. The quantitative methods require detailed information of the asset values and incident likelihood [37]. Qualitative approach relies on judgments and perceptions of the evaluated scenario and proposes suitable safeguards for it [40]. This highlights the need for knowledge management and sharing. Although, neither of the methods is superior to other, qualitative methods are less time consuming [40] and hence can be, in general, more suitable for SMEs with limited resources.

Although, users are often noted as the "weakest link" of the chain of security, they also have valuable information for security risk management process [39]. Collaboration can be also seen as one factor to engage employees to security and its enhancement. Vice versa, lack of knowledge sharing is one of the common challenges of the information security risk management [9]. Knowledge sharing also increases security awareness, which has direct impact on organizations capability to protect themselves against cyber-attacks [23]. Therefore, knowledge management, and knowledge management systems, hold an essential role in information and cyber security risk management processes.

2.2   On Knowledge-Intensive Business Services and Processes

The continuous increase of knowledge intensity in the digital economy was recognized in [1] and the importance of knowledge in information security risk management was pointed out in [7]. Knowledge-Intensive Business Services (KIBS) refer to a versatile set of both professional and technology-based services, which are characterized by high demands of professional knowledge and relevant information sources as the key ingredients of service design [24]. As usual, one separates the explicit and tacit knowledge. Note that in [1] it is noticed that KIBS are often developed and innovated by SMEs. KIBS are utilized in knowledge-intensive business processes (KIBP).

Belsis et al. [3] point out that security management of information systems is a knowledge-intensive activity that depends on professional knowledge. They also argue that the knowledge dimension of the security management, e.g., transformation of raw log or survey data into actionable knowledge, has been neglected. Hence, security management support requires KIBS. This is mostly addressed by the systems school of knowledge management whose primary focus is on information and knowledge-based systems [7], especially structure and usefulness of databases, repositories, and platforms containing codified and accessible explicit knowledge about the domain of interest [6].

A complex decision making is often not solved by a single user, but it is solved by the collaborative contributions of multiple participants [2]. Conduct and execution of knowledge-intensive business processes heavily dependent on knowledge workers performing various interconnected knowledge intensive decision making tasks [41]. As genuinely knowledge, information and data centric processes, IS risk management process meets definition of KIBP. Characteristics of knowledge-intensive business processes compared non-KIBP [17] are presented in Table 1.

Table 1. KIBP compared non-KIBP [17].

KIBP	Non-KIBP
Mostly complex	Simple or complex
Mostly hard to automate	Mostly easy to automate
Mostly repeatable	Highly repeatable
Predictable or unpredictable	Highly predictable
Need lots of creativity	Need less creativity
Structured or semi/unstructured	Structured

The challenges of information and cyber security risk management in [7, 10] emphasize the presence of KIBP characteristics compared to the non-KIBP characteristics. Mundbrod and Reichert [26] represent eight challenges of Knowledge-Intensive Business Processes:

- *Meta-model design*: design of the meta-model that supports required information and tasks.
- *Lifecycle support*: KIBPs require both design and runtime flexibility, which applies also tools used in the conduction of the processes.
- *Variability support*: KIBP results heavily depend on the knowledge used on the process, which requires high variability.
- *Context Support*: related to lifecycle and variability support, KIBPs can be very specific for certain context, which requires support for contextual parameters.
- *View support*: when amount of activities and knowledge required in processes conduction and execution is high, requirement for personal views emerges.
- *Authorization support*: KIBP execution includes variety of tasks and information, which include collaboration of people in various roles, authorization support is necessity from security perspective.
- *Synchronization support*: successful task execution requires that all the necessary information is available on the time. Therefore, synchronization of the information and documentation is required.
- *Integration support*: KIBP may directly correlate and initiate pre-specified and standardized business processes. Hence, integration is required to receive status updates and get outputs of the processes.

The presented KIBP challenges apply also to information and cyber security risk management and we adopt these challenges in the evaluation of the presented artifact.

2.3 Knowledge Management Systems

Knowledge management systems are utilized in KIBP to support the execution of the complex processes [17]. From risk management perspective, knowledge is considered as an important resource for organizations to ensure the business continuity. Experience and expertise of the employees will help organization to react in accurate manner when incidents occur as people understand the complexities of the organization and its operations. Knowledge sharing is also a necessity in information security risk management [10].

Wiki platforms are popular knowledge and information management tools especial for intra-organizational collaboration, and have been applied in variety of business processes [28]. Semantic additions, like Semantic MediaWiki (SMW), provide opportunity to define and manage structured information in the wiki platforms, which are by nature usually non-structured. Semantic wiki adds possibility to define properties for each wiki page. This means, for example, that for each page describing a city, the number of inhabitants can be defined. With semantic query, it is then possible to search cities with more than 100.000 inhabitants as the queries support comparison operators for semantic properties. With the non-semantic wiki, it is only possible to find pages by classification (categories) or matching text. The semantic search is one of the emphasized functions of semantic wikis and enables complex functions implemented with the wiki platform.

There is difference between managing security knowledge and securing knowledge management. Jennex and Zyngier [21] discusses aspects how to secure knowledge management and related processes, while this paper focuses on management of security information. Anyway, it is important to consider the security of the information security knowledge management system and its service delivery to avoid lack of confidence to system's security as an adaptation barrier.

3   Research Process

The research follows the Design Science Research (DSR) approach, which includes development of a set of artifacts to solve a wicked problem [15]. DSR is composed of the three related cycles: (i) the relevance cycle, (ii) the rigor cycle, and (iii) the design cycle. The relevance cycle ensures that technology-based solutions solve important and relevant business problems. The rigor cycle provides the prior scientific knowledge and theories as a foundation to the research [15, 16], but also ensures that rigorous methods are applied in the construction and evaluation of the design artifact [43]. The design cycle contributes as the construction and evaluation phase of the artifact. Note that Peffers et al. [30] presented more refined composition of DSR steps as follows: (i) identify problem, (ii) define solution objectives; (iii) design and development, (iv) demonstration, (v) evaluation, and (vi) communication.

Based on the DSR approach, the goal of this research is to develop and evaluate an artifact, the demonstrator consisting of multiple components, that provides a solution to information and cyber security risk management challenges of, especially, SME organizations. We apply the criteria defined by Venable [42] to assess DSR applicability for the research.

An overview of the methodologies for designing services is proposed by Morelli [25]. He advises one of the three main directions "definition of possible service scenarios, verifying use cases, and sequences of actions and actors' roles in order to define the requirements for the service and its logical and organizational structure". Also, Edvardsson [8] includes service system as part of the service design in addition to service concept and service processes. The service system includes resources and infrastructure enabling delivery of the service.

4   Artifact Description

4.1   Artifact Development

Development of a software system is newer confined to the successive steps [35]. Although we adopt an existing software platform, the development of the information security knowledge management system is a combination of software development and data migration. The development iterations follow the identified information and cyber security risk management use cases. During each development iteration, the meta-model for information security controls is extended as new wiki functions are introduced. The changes of the meta-model also affect to the import of the knowledge information from public data sources.

Hence, we apply iterative design process in the construction of the artifact, which is described in Fig. 1. The iterative approach also corresponds to DSR cycles, although there are multiple development cycles for a one design and evaluation DSR cycle. The relevance cycle is focused on identifying the problems within the information and cyber security risk management of the SMEs. Also common practices are evaluated and why SMEs fail to implement them. In the rigor cycle, the main developed asset is the meta-model, which is the basis for the system's demonstrator. The design cycle implements the actual functions on top of the SMW platform utilizing the meta-model. Also the evaluation of demonstrator is part of the design cycle.

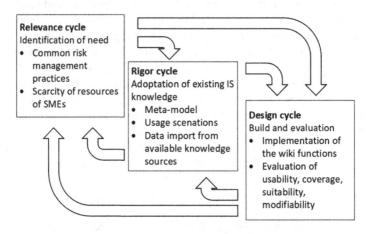

Fig. 1. Iterative design process presenting DSR cycles with outcomes of the cycles.

Iterative development is applied to three main artifacts that are developed in parallel; meta-model, data import and wiki functions. The meta-model is in the central position as both, data import and wiki functions depend on it. The meta-model will evolve during the development iterations as new functions are being introduced. Hence, the two iterative development loops both affect the meta-model as shown in Fig. 2. This is similar approach as the concept of reciprocal shaping of ADR presented in [36], where recursive cycles of decisions at finer levels of detail of the IT artifact and the organizational context.

Fig. 2. Development cycles of the demonstrator.

In the development process, the wiki functions refer to the additional risk management functionality implemented and added to the SMW platform. These functions are derived from the common risk management process tasks, which are part of the common risk management approaches. Such functions are, for example, asset identification, risk evaluation, and control selection. For example, if user recognizes assets of a certain type, the wiki queries can be used to propose security controls that mitigate risks for the asset type and in addition these control implementation order can be prioritized based on the priorities defined in NIST SP 800-53 specification. Common use cases are identified following the service design principles. Each use case adds new incrementally new functionality to demonstrator following the activities of demonstration and evaluation by Peffers et al. [30]. The main required functions (see Sects. 1 and 2) are asset identification, threat identification, risk evaluation, control identification, and control evaluation.

As a result of the asset identification, an organization should have recognized and valued at least all the business critical assets. Valuation of the assets is important as all assets don't have similar importance for the organization. Assets valuation is usually performed with numeric value in quantitative methods or with classification of assets in qualitative methods [37].

Treat identification can be assisted using a threat catalogue. ISO 27002 [19] or NIST SP 800-53 [27] include only control catalogues, but BSI IT Grundschutz Catalogues [5] includes also a threat catalogue in addition to control catalogue. The user should be assisted to identify the threats, for example, by the asset types an organization is having. This requires that threats are classified by the asset types. In this process, knowledge of the assets within the organization is a mandatory requirement to perform successful identification.

In the risk evaluation, the organization shall perform estimation on how a realized risk may be handled. The common four ways to address the risk are accepting, avoiding, transferring, or mitigating a particular risk (see Sect. 2.1). Regardless of the handling method, the organization should document the actions and explanation for the decision. The documentation of the rationale will increase knowledge sharing compared to the tacit knowledge of undocumented decisions.

Control identification can be helped with the control catalogue [5, 19, 27]. When controls are linked to threats they are preventing, the threat identification also generates a list of potential controls. The organization shall select and document control implementation status of the selected countermeasures. Based on the risk assessment, organization shall have a list of the prioritized list of controls to be implemented. The prioritization is based on the priorities of security controls defined in NIST SP 800-53 baseline. In the SMW platform queries are defined to provide views to list (i) controls that are implemented, (ii) controls that are selected to be implemented, but implementation is not completed and (iii) controls that are for the time being excluded.

4.2 Artifact Components

The research aims to create a knowledge-based system that helps especially SME organizations in their cyber risk management activities. As SMEs struggle with limited resources for cyber security risk management, at the same time there exists variety of publicly available information in multiple knowledge bases. Bringing this data with the viewpoints that adapt to organization's needs, is expected to help the organizations to manage their cyber risks.

The developed artifact consists of the following components:

• Model of security concepts relevant for SMEs to create a security knowledge base
• Demonstrator of the information and cyber security risk management system
• Data-gathering templates.

We adopt the roles of Knowledge Interface Systems (KIS) by Gregor et al. [12] in the following diagram (Fig. 3).

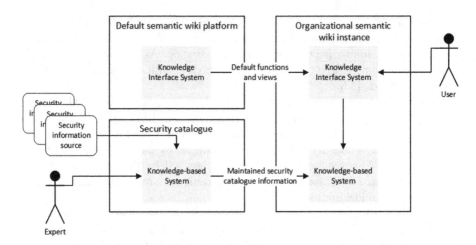

Fig. 3. Role of knowledge interface system and knowledge base.

The system shall use information and cyber security knowledge from public sources like NIST SP 800-53 control catalogue [27] as well as other control catalogues [5, 19, 20]. Each of the utilized control catalogues is mapped to the meta-model, which is developed as part of the system. Hence, organizations shall have publicly available information ready in the knowledge-based system.

The common knowledge base updates are delivered by the service, which will also maintain the platform itself. However, the SMW platform enables organizations to add new functions also by themselves utilizing new templates and queries, if the supported use cases don't include all functions required by the organization. As an individual organization operates with the separate wiki instance, the modifications are not disseminated to other organizations.

The knowledge itself is not a solution to successfully accomplish cyber risk management activities. Therefore, knowledge platform needs to be extended with the functions to enable to perform cyber risk management activities. The SMW enables adding template pages and use queries to evolve knowledge base to a system that implements functions of a risk management system. SMW also enables to extend the meta-model based on the organization's needs, unlike many other risk management tools. We have developed [28] a meta-model for security control catalogue with risk management functions. The meta-model has evolved from security control catalogue meta-model to contain also risk management elements. Further development iterations are required to support all the use cases identified in the rigor cycle.

4.3   Description of the Demonstrator

Demonstrator is based on the Semantic MediaWiki (SMW) platform. MediaWiki is a software mostly known by its use as the software platform of the Wikipedia. The SMW is an extension to MediaWiki, which enables semantic functions to be used. Such functions are structured pages and semantic queries.

Advantage of the MediaWiki is that users are familiar with the basic functions of the platform. The SMW enables using MediaWiki as a knowledge management platform [28]. With the forms, users can enter also new data, like assets and risk evaluations, in the structured form. In addition to the structured data, the traditional wikitext descriptions can also be used. Such semi-structured approach enables better variability for different purposes compared to a fixed data-model. More detailed description of the control catalogue and the basic risk management functions have been given in [28].

SMW Data Transfer plugin is used to import existing security controls specification data into SMW platform. In the first iteration, NIST SP 800-53 control specification [27], which is available in XML format, was transformed using XSLT to XML schema defined by the developed meta-model. After the transformation, Data Transfer plugin generates wiki-page for each control at the import.

Demonstrator is delivered for user organizations as own wiki instances. Each instance will be delivered as a service, but could also be set up by the organization as own in-premises instance of the wiki, if seen feasible, for example, for the security reasons. The deliverable consists of the SMW platform, added functionality and templates as well as imported data. When an organization takes the service into use, it shall define users and apply roles. After that, the organization can start performing cyber and risk management activities with the system.

5   Evaluation

5.1   Research Evaluation

Evaluation of the research is performed following the evaluation criteria for assessing DSR work defined by Venable [42]:

- Relevance of the problem to industry/society clearly established
- Significance of the problem to industry/society clearly established
- Depth of analysis and clarity of understanding of the problem and its causes
- Depth or profoundness of insight leading to the new design artefact
- Novelty of the new design artefact
- Size and complexity of the new design artefact
- Amount of effort that went into the development of the new design artefact(s)
- Elegance of the design of the new artefact(s)

- Simplicity of the design of the new artefact(s)
- Clear understanding of why the new artefact works.

The significance and "wickedness" of the problem has been identified in the number of the papers and reports [13, 14, 22, 45]. Also the causes of the problem have been identified in those papers, which consistently highlight the lack of resources and suitable methods and tools.

The profoundness of the artifact has been identified by following the common risk management process activities as identified by Fenz and Ekelhart [9]. The developed artifact must respond to activities in each phase of the process with appropriate manner.

The artifact approaches the information security risk management problem from knowledge management perspective. The wiki-based knowledge management systems have been utilized in multiple domains, as identified in [31], but in the domain of the information security there does not exist similar artifacts.

The design of the artifact aims to be simple as it reuses existing knowledge management platform, SMW, and extends its functionality. The simple approach provides users a familiar interface, but also the meta-model defining the data structure is modifiable, if organization has special needs or requirements. With this approach, the adaptation barrier should remain low as the artifact can respond to competence, usability and modifiability requirements.

The service delivery of the artifact has also been covered in the artifact design as proposed by [8]. The service delivery is especially important aspect in this research as SMEs don't have resources to take into use complex systems, only to support decision making. This is the weakness of SMW platform as it is intended to be used for knowledge sharing. Therefore, it lacks support to have multiple knowledge bases within one instance of platform. Although MediaWiki provides concept of namespaces, it does not sufficient functionality to separate confidential information of multiple organizations within one instance. There are multiple options to solve the lifecycle challenge as deployment of new instance could be automated using container technologies. As this is more technical issue, it is left outside of the scope of the research.

5.2 Response to KIBP Challenges

Table 2 contains responses to the challenges of KIBP identified in [26] as presented in Sect. 2.2.

As can be seen from the responses, the meta-model and SMW platform with additional functions are in essential position to overcome these common challenges. To avoid the challenges, the iterative research and development cycles are applied. The most weakest response to KIBP challenges is with the lifecycle support, which is already covered in the evaluation of the service delivery.

5.3 Validation Using Data-Gathering Templates

Survey-based empirical evaluation among SMEs shall be performed utilizing data-gathering templates. The evaluation shall include survey of SME users of the artifact. Survey should request response to following topics, which are seen to be advantage of the artefact.

Table 2. Response to KIBP challenges.

Challenge	Response
Meta-model design	Meta-model is an integral part of the developed artifact. It is utilized by the KIS when security information from the public knowledge bases is mapped to the meta-model
Lifecycle and variability support	SMW, as a platform, enables modification of the functions without platform modifications. Lifecycle and variability support shall be also considered in the meta-model. Deployment of the platform as a service can be considered as a weakness of the solution. Each user organization must have a separate instance of the SMW platform
Context support	Context support shall be considered in the meta-model, but can be also implemented as part of SMW page definitions
View support	View support can be implemented with the semantic queries and extendibility of the SMW platform. The platform enables users to create pages that meet the personal needs
Authorization support	SMW platform has built-in authorization functions. The built-in functions may be extended to meet more complex authorization scheme requirements
Synchronization and integration support	SMW platform has possibility to integrate other data sources as well as build functional integrations. Synchronization support must be taken into account in the meta-model design

- Did the artifact improve the resource usage and competence requirements in SMEs?
- Were the proposed functions comprehensive for organization's needs?
- Is a risk management system using SMW user interface easy to adopt in a SME context?
- Was organization able to find suitable security controls to implement based on the suggestions made by the platform?
- Did the organizations modify the SMW meta-model or wiki functions? If yes, what kind of modifications an organization made? The latter question should evaluate completeness of the artifact.

Other survey topics can be introduced, when identified during the DSR development cycle. Results of the evaluation shall be communicated as design science methods suggest.

6   Conclusions

Importance of information and cyber security risk management has become a necessity for all-sized organizations. Especially SMEs have not implemented all the required security measures to protect themselves. Often the reason for this is the lack of competence and other resources required to implement proper risk management processes.

This paper represented a research process adopting design science research to develop and evaluate novel knowledge based approach for information and cyber security risk management. The developed artifact is based on the SMW platform, which is extended with the additional functionality for risk management and incorporated with the information security information available in public specifications. The research is currently in progress. In the initial cycle, as described in [29], the initial meta-model with control inventory was implemented including import of the NIST SP 800-53 control inventory. During the next cycle, we extended the meta-model to support features critical for cyber resilience as well as basic risk management features in [28]. In the future, the artifact is enhanced with the meta-model and risk management functions supporting the common risk management process phases supporting all phases from asset identification to control implementation.

The research process involves characteristics of Action Design Research (ADR) [36], where the ongoing nature of the development of the semantic wiki based artifact has been depicted in the earlier publications [28, 29]. Moreover, the research problem arises from the information and cyber security practices of SMEs, incorporating both knowledge and risk management theories. Also, following the ADR principles, the research is practice inspired seeking solution to problems of information and cyber security risk management from intersection of IT and risk management domains.

Design science research provides an appropriate framework to identify relevant foundations of the artifact as well as to develop and evaluate the artifact, being both practice-inspired and theory-ingrained [36]. As described, there is practical need for a system assisting SMEs in their information and cyber risk management activities. We have argued the potential of the knowledge-based approach to meet these needs.

References

1. Bahrs, J., Müller, C.: Modelling and analysis of knowledge intensive business processes. In: Althoff, K.-D., Dengel, A., Bergmann, R., Nick, M., Roth-Berghofer, T. (eds.) WM 2005. LNCS, vol. 3782, pp. 243–247. Springer, Heidelberg (2005). https://doi.org/10.1007/11590019_28
2. Baumeister, J., Striffler, A.: Knowledge-driven systems for episodic decision support. Knowl.-Based Syst. 88, 45–56 (2015)
3. Belsis, P., Kokolakis, S., Kiountouzis, E.: Information systems security from a knowledge management perspective. Inf. Manag. Comput. Secur. 13(3), 189–202 (2005)
4. Bhattacharya, D.: Leadership styles and information security in small businesses. Inf. Manag. Comput. Secur. 19(5), 300–312 (2011)
5. Bundesamt für Sicherheit in der Informationstechnik: IT-Grundschutz Catalogues, 15th edn (2015)
6. Cox, L.A., Babayev, D., Huber, W.: Some limitations of qualitative risk rating systems. Risk Anal. 25(3), 651–662 (2005)
7. dos Santos França, J.B., Netto, J.M., Barradas, R.G., Santoro, F., Baião, F.A.: Towards knowledge-intensive processes representation. In: La Rosa, M., Soffer, P. (eds.) BPM 2012. LNBIP, vol. 132, pp. 126–136. Springer, Heidelberg (2013). https://doi.org/10.1007/978-3-642-36285-9_14
8. Edvardsson, B.: Quality in new service development: key concepts and a frame of reference. Int. J. Prod. Econ. 52(1), 31–46 (1997)

9. Fenz, S., Ekelhart, A.: Verification, validation, and evaluation in information security risk management. IEEE Secur. Priv. **9**(2), 58–65 (2011)
10. Fenz, S., Heurix, J., Neubauer, T., Pechstein, F.: Current challenges in information security risk management. Inf. Manag. Comput. Secur. **22**(5), 410–430 (2014)
11. Furnell, S.M., Clarke, N., Komatsu, A., Takagi, D., Takemura, T.: Human aspects of information security: an empirical study of intentional versus actual behavior. Inf. Manag. Comput. Secur. **21**(1), 5–15 (2013)
12. Gregor, S., Maedche, A., Morana, S., Schacht, S.: Designing knowledge interface systems: past, present, and future. In: Breakthroughs and Emerging Insights from Ongoing Design Science Projects: Research-in-Progress Papers and Poster Presentations from the 11th International Conference on Design Science Research in Information Systems and Technology, DESRIST (2016)
13. Gupta, A., Hammond, R.: Information systems security issues and decisions for small businesses: an empirical examination. Inf. Manag. Comput. Secur. **13**(4), 297–310 (2005)
14. Hall, J.H., Sarkani, S., Mazzuchi, T.A.: Impacts of organizational capabilities in information security. Inf. Manag. Comput. Secur. **19**(3), 155–176 (2011)
15. Hevner, A.R.: A three cycle view of design science research. Scand. J. Inf. Syst. **19**(2), 87–92 (2007)
16. Iivari, J.: A paradigmatic analysis of information systems as a design science. Scand. J. Inf. Syst. **19**(2), 39–64 (2007)
17. Işik, Ö., Mertens, W., Van den Bergh, J.: Practices of knowledge intensive process management: quantitative insights. Bus. Process Manag. J. **19**(3), 515–534 (2013)
18. ISO/IEC 27001:2013: Information technology – Security techniques – Information security management systems – Requirements. ISO copyright office, Geneva, Switzerland (2013)
19. ISO/IEC 27002:2013: Information technology – Security techniques – Information security management systems – Code of practice for information security management. ISO copyright office, Geneva, Switzerland (2013)
20. ISO/IEC 27032:2012: Information technology—Security techniques—Guidelines for cyber-security. ISO copyright office, Geneva, Switzerland (2012)
21. Jennex, M.E., Zyngier, S.: Security as a contributor to knowledge management success. Inf. Syst. Front. **9**(5), 493–504 (2007)
22. Mansfield-Devine, S.: Securing small and medium-size businesses. Netw. Secur. **2016**(7), 14–20 (2016)
23. Mejias, R.J.: An integrative model of information security awareness for assessing information systems security risk. In: Proceedings of 2012 45th Hawaii International Conference on System Sciences, pp. 3258–3267 (2012)
24. Miles, I., Kastrinos, N., Bilderbeek, R., Den Hertog, P., Flanagan, K., Huntink, W., Bouman, M.: Knowledge-intensive business services: users, carriers and sources of innovation. European Innovation Monitoring System (EIMS) Reports (1995)
25. Morelli, N.: Developing new product service systems (PSS): methodologies and operational tools. J. Clean. Prod. **14**(17), 1495–1501 (2006)
26. Mundbrod, N., Reichert, M.: Process-aware task management support for knowledge-intensive business processes: findings, challenges, requirements (2014)
27. NIST Special Publication 800-53: Recommended Security Controls for Federal Information Systems and Organizations Revision 3 (2009)
28. Nykänen, R., Kärkkäinen, T.: Supporting cyber resilience with semantic wiki. In: Proceedings of OpenSym, pp. 21:1–21:8. ACM, New York (2016)

29. Nykänen, R., Kärkkäinen, T.: Tailorable representation of security control catalog on semantic wiki. In: Lehto, M., Neittaanmäki, P. (eds.) Intelligent Systems, Control and Automation: Science and Engineering: Cyber Security: Power and Technology. Springer, Heidelberg (2018)

30. Peffers, K., Tuunanen, T., Rothenberger, M.A., Chatterjee, S.: A design science research methodology for information systems research. J. Manag. Inf. Syst. 24(3), 45–77 (2007)

31. Pei Lyn Grace, T.: Wikis as a knowledge management tool. J. Knowl. Manag. 13(4), 64–74 (2009)

32. Randeree, E.: Knowledge management: securing the future. J. Knowl. Manag. 10(4), 145–156 (2006)

33. Renaud, K.: How smaller businesses struggle with security advice. Comput. Fraud Secur. 2016(8), 10–18 (2016)

34. Rohn, E., Sabari, G., Leshem, G.: Explaining small business InfoSec posture using social theories. Inf. Comput. Secur. 24(5), 534–556 (2016)

35. Royce, W.W.: Managing the development of large software systems. In: Proceedings of IEEE WESCON, Los Angeles, vol. 26, pp. 328–338 (1970)

36. Sein, M.K., Henfridsson, O., Purao, S., Rossi, M., Lindgren, R.: Action design research. MIS Q. 35(1), 37–56 (2011)

37. Shameli-Sendi, A., Aghababaei-Barzegar, R., Cheriet, M.: Taxonomy of information security risk assessment (ISRA). Comput. Secur. 57, 14–30 (2016)

38. Siponen, M.: Information security standards focus on the existence of process, not its content. Commun. ACM 49(8), 97–100 (2006)

39. Spears, J.L., Barki, H.: User participation in information systems security risk management. MIS Q. 34(3), 503–522 (2010)

40. Tatar, Ü., Karabacak, B.: An hierarchical asset valuation method for information security risk analysis. In: 2012 International Conference on Information Society, i-Society (2012)

41. Vaculin, R., Hull, R., Heath, T., Cochran, C., Nigam, A., Sukaviriya, P.: Declarative business artifact centric modeling of decision and knowledge intensive business processes. In: 15th IEEE International IEEE Proceedings of Enterprise Distributed Object Computing Conference, EDOC, pp. 151–160 (2011)

42. Venable, J.R.: Design science research post Hevner et al.: criteria, standards, guidelines, and expectations. In: Winter, R., Zhao, J.L., Aier, S. (eds.) DESRIST 2010. LNCS, vol. 6105, pp. 109–123. Springer, Heidelberg (2010). https://doi.org/10.1007/978-3-642-13335-0_8

43. Venable, J.R.: Five and ten years on: have DSR standards changed? In: Donnellan, B., Helfert, M., Kenneally, J., VanderMeer, D., Rothenberger, M., Winter, R. (eds.) DESRIST 2015. LNCS, vol. 9073, pp. 264–279. Springer, Cham (2015). https://doi.org/10.1007/978-3-319-18714-3_17

44. von Solms, R., van Niekerk, J.: From information security to cyber security. Comput. Secur. 38, 97–102 (2013)

45. Yeniman, Y.E., Akalp, G., Aytac, S., Bayram, N.: Factors influencing information security management in small- and medium-sized enterprises: a case study from Turkey. Int. J. Inf. Manag. 31(4), 360–365 (2011)

Design Applications

Capturing User Generated Video Content in Online Social Networks

Clinton Daniel[(⊠)], Matthew Mullarkey, and Alan R. Hevner

Department of Information Systems Decision Sciences,
University of South Florida, Tampa, FL 33620, USA
{cedanie2,mmullarkey,ahevner}@usf.edu

Abstract. We build and evaluate an innovative artifact for the investigation of social content derived-platforms specifically to gain a unique understanding of the content shared and underlying behaviors of the contributors to these technology platforms. The artifact's innovation is derived from the solution's unique approach to converting and analyzing the multimedia – especially video - content to gain interesting insights into the social network connectivity of the actors on a given technology platform. The artifact directly addresses a practical need for industry practitioners to analyze social video network content using a rigorous and evidence-based DSR approach.

Keywords: User video content · Social network technology platforms
DSR · Elaborated ADR

1 Introduction

Social networking continues to grow through the generation and posting of user-generated multimedia content on social network technology platforms. These users post content in order to network and connect with others sharing similar interests. As the capacity for multiple media formats and the capabilites of these technology platforms continue to increase the resultant volume and variety of content increases exponentially. This media content has expanded from text to include images, videos, and animations. In this research, we use an elaborated action design research (eADR) approach [23] within the design science research (DSR) paradigm [17] to diagnose, design, implement, and evolve an innovative artifact for the investigation and mining of the multimedia spectrum of this growing content. The goodness of the digital artifact is evaluated in situ with practicing professionals and proposed as a unique IT solution for the class of problem.

Multimedia technology platforms, such as YouTube, exist to provide video content as the primary medium for sharing and connecting. Users post to these platforms as a means to communicate throughout a network with the understanding that the content can be consumed and easily accessed by other users with similar interests. Although the context of the medium, such as video, is easily viewed by other actors through either a visual or audible interpretation, it is not easily analyzed by those who want to gain an understanding of its semantic or latent meaning or by those seeking to understand the underlying social behaviors of the actors. The analysis of video content across a

© Springer International Publishing AG, part of Springer Nature 2018
S. Chatterjee et al. (Eds.): DESRIST 2018, LNCS 10844, pp. 333–347, 2018.
https://doi.org/10.1007/978-3-319-91800-6_22

multimedia platform presents researchers and practitioners with a rich contextual source of information on social networks, interpersonal norms and behaviors online, and interactions between platform users. Unfortunately, significant technical and algorithmic challenges exist for the analysis of multimedia content and this has tended to limit the ability of researchers and practitioners to make sense of this rich social content in context.

Our eADR approach was used to derive an innovative artifact for the search and analysis of multimedia content in a social content derived platform (YouTube) to gain a unique understanding of the content shared and underlying behaviors of the contributors to these technology platforms. The artifact's innovation is derived from the solution's unique approach to converting and analyzing the multimedia content to gain interesting insights into the behaviors of the actors active in the technology platform.

2 Motivation

Social networking data are analyzed and studied within academic research and industrial practice as a source for understanding social phenomena since its inception [25]. Typically the analysis takes the form of social network analysis of the connectivity between nodes and concentrates on edges, links, and ties that connects them. In some cases the nature of the interaction between nodes is analyzed by analyzing the text exchanged. In these cases, unstructured data generated by textual exchange in social networks involves the extraction of the text from a social networking source, transformation of the data into a workable data set, loading the data into a structure for further processing, constructing a text corpus, and finally using the results of the processed corpus to apply an algorithm that will execute the analytics [5].

The approach for text mining in these cases is generally well understood. Nonetheless, often in each of the phases throughout this process a developer is required to build a custom solution that will accommodate the corpus construction requirements attributable to a given social network, the nature of the content, and the type of connectivity involved. Inevitably, the data are then attributed to the network of nodes and act as a measure of their connectivity.

In our research, we find that online social networks create a collection of content (i.e. corpus) that result from the multimedia nature of many of these networks. In the metadata, these social networks use a variable set of media that can define the context of its communication. If we as researchers are to investigate more deeply than the graph structure of the network or the text exchanged between nodes, then we need a rich, variable, innovative digital design to analyze the composition of the multimedia information within any given social network.

This research proposes a methodical process for the artifact instantiations involving practicing experts from industry and academic researchers that combines the value of the corpus construction with the unique attributes defined by the multimedia metadata in a social video network. Due to the unique attributes that define the metadata generated by social networks which use video as its primary medium for content sharing, YouTube is used as a social network data source to investigate and develop an innovative artifact for the investigation and analysis of this third component of many social networks. We conduct our research using the paradigm of Design Science Research (DSR) [16] and focus on the abstraction of an innovtive artifact through a series of iterative interventions as detailed in the elaborated Action Design Research (eADR) [22, 23]. Specifically, this research will answer the question of "*How do we construct a metadata-enhanced corpus from social video networks?*" and "*How might an instantiated artifact help define a class of IT solution for analyzing multimedia in online social networks?*".

3   Literature Review

The principle goal of our literature review is to identify a specific social video network platform that has been consistently used within practice for the exchange of rich non-textual information between multiple nodes in a network. For the purpose of our literature review, a *social video network* is defined as a social network that uses video as its primary medium for content sharing. We searched for all articles that described a multimedia investigation and found 19 research articles published between 2007 and 2017 (see Table 1). In each case the investigators highlighted YouTube as a principle data source.

The research survey identifies YouTube as an interesting social network where video media defines the content and links to the connectivity of nodes. These studies contribute to knowledege of social network behavior in a variety of ways. For example, a study published in 2017 by Malik and Tian [20] cites the importance for researchers to data mine YouTube videos and their related metadata to support new knowledge discovery in domains such as STEM education and the medical sciences.

Additionally, the literature review reveals a significant overlap in methods used to collect data from YouTube in order to conduct research activities such as social network analysis, descriptive statistics, data characterization, data property assessment, content analysis, market analysis, trend analysis, consumer impact analysis, and effectiveness of automatic captioning as shown in Table 1.

In general, most research studies require the acquisition of YouTube's data to conduct some type of emperical analysis. In most cases, the researchers acquire YouTube's metadata for analysis which includes attributes such as the title, comments, channel, video category, video id, timestamps, like counts, and other aggregated statistics. Researchers extract the YouTube data using data collection methods such as implementing the YouTube Data API, web scraping, web crawling, custom scripting, and manual processing. The data are then extracted to files and/or relational database management systems for further processing and analysis. For instance, an article by Ahmad et al. [2] demonstrates an entire framework that is motivated to analyzing the content generated by the YouTube platform. Such sophisticated artifacts collect comments and other metadata using the YouTube Data API. Other sophisticated artifacts, such as the one architected in Chen et al. [9], acquire YouTube captions with the use of web crawling techniques.

In the collection of articles reviewed, we observe that no research reports the implementation of an artifact that is designed to collect both the YouTube captions and the metadata using the YouTube Data API. We found that there is a strong emphasis on

Table 1. Summary of literature using content generated by YouTube as a research data source

Author(s)	Research motivation	Data collection methods	Publication year
Cha et al. [6]	User-generated content linked to videos	Web crawler	2007
Gill et al. [13]	Traffic characterization	YouTube Data API	2007
Santos et al. [26]	Analyzed structural properties and social relationships	Custom web crawler and extractor	2007
Cheng et al. [10]	Video statistics	Web scraping, web crawling, YouTube Data API	2008
Lange [19]	Study how video sharing supports social networking	Manually viewed videos and reading of comments to recruit interviews	2008
Abhari et al. [1]	Understand YouTube traffic	Web scraping	2009
Chatzopoulou et al. [8]	Fundamental properties of video popularity	YouTube Data API	2010
Siersdorfer et al. [28]	Commenting and comment rating behavior	YouTube Data API	2010
Yuan et al. [31]	Concept-based video search	Manual collection using YouTube site	2011
Figueiredo et al. [12]	Characterized growth patterns of video popularity	Google Charts API	2011
Yoganarasimhan [30]	How network structure impacts diffusion of content	Custom Perl script to parse HTML, MySQL	2011
Miller [21]	Content analysis	Comments were manually coded	2015
Chen et al. [9]	Trend analysis	Web crawling, raw caption file	2015
Gupta et al. [14]	Framework for marketing/promotional strategies	Video content was manually coded	2016
Harrison et al. [15]	Evaluate the impact of consumer-targeted videos	Manual collection of video metadata	2016
Ahmad et al. [2]	Content analysis	YouTube Data API	2017
Smith et al. [29]	Effectiveness of the automatic captioning tool	Manually viewed video and automatic captions, then analyzed errors in spreadsheet	2017
Malik et al. [20]	Data collection and discovery	YouTube Data API, MySQL, Java	2017

the importance of collecting YouTube data to answer research questions in a variety of different domains. However, although the literature supports the implementation of more sophisticated techniques for analyzing social video networks such as YouTube, they are limited by their ability to automate the collection of captions and metadata using the YouTube Data API.

We shared our observations with practicing professional experts in the problem class of mining social network content and received confirmation that no existing IT artifact – tool or technique – exists to adequately mine the multimedia captions and metadata in context in social network sites for user generated content like YouTube. We identify this gap as the opportunity for the creation of an innovative artifact for the extraction and analysis of the full, rich YouTube multimedia content to mine the content in an automated, scalable manner that sheds new insights on the nature of the social behavior in multimedia social network platforms.

4   Method

The host platforms for social video networks, such as YouTube, offer complex application programming interfaces (APIs) to access their data structures for analysis. These APIs are complicated but offer unique access to metadata that is otherwise difficult or inaccessible to a consumer of the social content. In order to use these APIs for data analysis, an application programmer must develop a custom solution to construct a document corpus that will meet the requirements and address a specific research or business question within a specific context. Additionally, the programmer may require a technical solution that is capable of responding to changes with the question as intelligence is acquired through the supplement of metadata. This presents researchers and practitioners with what is called a *wicked problem* [16]. Design Science Research (DSR) offers a unique framework that is designed to address wicked problems and expose research entry points which can directly address a technical problem domain [16, 18].

One product of DSR can be an innovative IT artifact that can be abstracted and implemented as a generalized utility within a problem domain. The Design Science Research Methodology (DSRM) developed by Peffers et al. [24] can be used for the production and presentation of a DSR artifact that addresses a given problem and can be generalized to an abstracted innovative artifact that addresses a class of problems with a practice-inspired, research-ingrained instantiated system.

Each iteration of the DSR process offers an opportunity to inform research and practice through the build and evaluation of an artifact. Sein et al. [27] proposes the Action Design Research (ADR) methodology which can be used for the creation of an ensembled DSR artifact through building, intervention, and evaluation activities that occur in whole or in part during interventions with practitioners. The DSR artifact can then be instantiated within the context of *practice-inspired* requirements that have been influenced by an iterative and *theory-ingrained* process. The elaborated Action Design Research (eADR) methodology proposed by Mullarkey and Hevner [22, 23] offers both researcher and practitioner with an *ADR process continuum* that provides an expanded framework for iterative design cycles with multiple project entry points.

We use the eADR methodological approach to iteratively diagnosis, design and implement an innovative artifact to analyze social video network content (see Fig. 1). Each of these stages are informed by a continuum of ADR cycles that iterate until a state is reached which indicates a contribution toward one or more innovative artifacts.

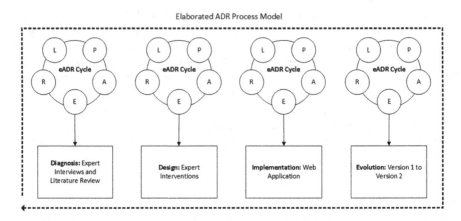

Fig. 1. Illustrates the nature of the interventions at each stage in the eADR method. Adapted from [23]. Note: in the eADR cycle: P = Problem Formulation/Planning, A = Artifact Creation, E = Evaluation, R = Reflection, and L = Learning.

For instance, as described in the Literature Review section above, several iterations of eADR cycles are implemented to inform the "*Diagnosis*" stage where we worked with experts at our host companies and the technical literature to gain a precise understanding of the existing solutions in this class of IT problems. Practical discovery of the problem domain was inspired by expert interviews from firms such as LeapDoctor.com and DIYCaptions.com. Upon further evaluation of the data collected by the expert interviews, the literature review was initiated to further refine an understanding of the class of IT solutions available and determine the state of the solution domain. Each time an iteration of the ADR cycles within a stage was satisfied, the process was advanced to another stage.

To re-enforce the "*practice-inspired*" principle of the eADR methodology, design attributes of the artifact were initially influenced by a practical problem exposed during an expert interview with LeapDoctor.com. This intervention had a direct impact in the initial design of the research artifact. Additional inspiration for the DSR artifact was derived from an expert evaluation and intervention with DIYCaptions.com of the initial version of the video media analysis artifact. These expert interventions acquired through multiple eADR iterations directly contributed to the overall definition of the "goodness", where "goodness" represents the measure to satisfy the problem domain, and practical utility of the desired ensemble artifact. The eADR Cycles make explicit the iterative, cyclical intervention activity at each stage that abstracts one or more artifacts for evaluation. This iterative approach helped us develop multiple innovative artifacts at each stage in the methodical movement towards an implementable social video content analysis solution.

The next section describes the continuation of the eADR approach as the team of practitioners and researchers moved into artifact design, implementation and evolution.

5 Artifact Description

The intial version of the artifact was evaluated by researchers and practioners for the purpose of informing design decisions. Once design decisions are made, the eADR cycles iterate to further refine the design of the artifact. For instance, during one of the first iterations within the *"Design"* stage, a topic model analysis is performed to analyze the YouTube transcript document corpus that includes all of the target video captions. Specifically, Latent Dirichlet Allocation (LDA) [4] is used to generate a probable distribution of topics that include a probable distribution of terms which are distributed throughout the document corpus. This algorithm is chosen to perform analysis on the social video network because it generates a generalized probable distribution of topics that could describe the conversations occurring within the corpus of captioned text documents.

During a subsequent Design iteration, we plan, abstract, and evaluate a summative task required to measure the topics generated by LDA. We follow this iteration with a topic intrusion evaluation task. Chang et al. [7] developed topic intrusion evaluation tasks as a means of identifying topics that are generated by the LDA algorithm which may not fit well with the others. In other words, topic intrusion tasks help to identify an *intruder* topic among a distribution of topics generated by the LDA algorithm. This iterative evaluation of possible solutions lead to the generation of two potentially viable designs for consideration and evaluation prior to implementation.

5.1 DSR Artifact Version 1

The first version of the implementated DSR artifact consists of a five phase process to construct the text corpus required to peform social video network analysis. These five phases (as seen in Fig. 2) collectively define the artifact in the form of a process and can be summarized as follows:

1. *Extract caption data from YouTube using API and* Downsub.com. *Webscrape YouTube metadata using Python.* This phase of the design is motivated and informed by the results of the comprehensive literature review. The literature review reveals a constistent use of the YouTube Data API, web scraping, and custom scripting to create a collection of files (a corpus) for analysis.
2. *Generate .TXT and .SRT files for store on local file system using Python.* Because the initial phase in this artifact requires the extraction of data from a source, a collection of files must be stored in a file system for further processing at a later phase.
3. *SQL Workflow loads and processes files into RDBMS.* A Microsoft SQL Server Integration Services (SSIS) custom workflow is developed to extract, transform, and load the .TXT and .SRT files into a set of Microsoft SQL Server relational tables.

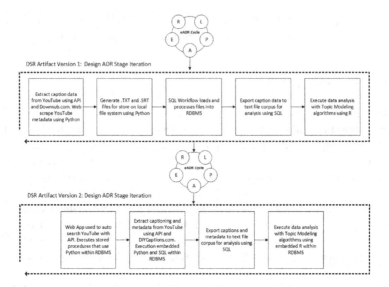

Fig. 2. Illustrated summary of the two ensemble artifact designs after iteration through diagnosis and design stages of the eADR method.

These tables are constructed in schemas which support staging, processing, and permanent storage.

4. *Export Caption data to text file corpus for analysis using SQL.* Once the data has been structured for permanent storage in the relational database, a custom SQL script is written to extract the captions from the relational database to a text corpus for analysis. The SQL script includes a query of the collected metadata to produce a targeted set of text files.

5. *Execute data analysis with Topic Modeling algorithms using R.* Once the targeted text corpus has been constructed, social video network analysis is performed using R. The topic modeling algorithm, Latent Dirichlet Allocation (LDA), is used to generate a distribution of topics.

The first version of the DSR artifact is consistent with the work of other researchers as observed within the literature review. The new contribution of the artifact is the methodology in which it was constructed and the use of a third-party (Downsub.com) tool combined with the YouTube Data API to extract the actual captions of a YouTube video. Our research is motivated to acquire the YouTube captions for the purpose of using machine learning algorithms, such as LDA, to generate a distribution of topics. These topics are used to generalize the conversations that are occuring within the social video network based off of a search term such as "emerging technologies 2016".

The use of Downsub.com is incoorporated into the version 1 design because we quickly realized that the YouTube Data API could only extract video captions using the "captions.download" method if third-party contributions are enabled for the specific caption. The API would return a 403 error on many of the captions we attempted to download using the "caption.download" method. The YouTube Data API documentation reports this 403 (forbidden) error response to be: *"The permissions associated with the request are not sufficient to download the caption track. The request might not be properly authorized, or the video order might not have enabled third-party contributions for this caption.".* Third party applications, such as *Downsub.com*, have the ability to download captions that are forbidden and otherwise unaccessible via the API. This led us to question how it is possible that third party applications are able to acquire these data based on the constraints of the API. Thus, we needed to find a new, innovative approach to achieve our goals of understanding video content on social networks.

5.2   Digital Innovation

In late 2017 we started investigating third party applications to determine how they are able to extract these data. At that time, we hypothesized that the lack of scalable access to the caption data may have been a major contributor to the limited use of these data found in current research. We discovered a third party web-based tool at diycaptions.com that would accept a YouTube videoID as a search term to generate automatic captions. The videoID is used by YouTube to identify a unique video posted to its platform and can be found within a YouTube URL. We tested the videoIDs that were forbidden for download by the API and they all returned captions for download. We contacted the site developer and asked him if he would be willing to evaluate our artifact and perhaps provide expert consultation on how we could improve upon our current design. His response to our e-mail was, *"I'm using an API that Google uses internally but which isn't documented for public use. I'd be happy to talk to you about it."* We then injected the helpful DIYCaptions.com developer into our eADR process so that he could evaluate and intervene with our design.

Working with the expert we identified that YouTube has an undocumented API method called "get_video_info" that can be called from a URL. An example of this URL is: https://youtube.com/get_video_info?&video_id={videoid}.

The {videoid} portion of the URL would be substituted with a specific videoid associated with the video we are targeting for a caption extraction. The URL then exposes a very long (can be up to 16 pages in a document) and complex encoded string. We had to decode the string to expose a JSON data structure buried within the file that contains important fields needed to extract the targeted caption. The two most important fields found within the encoded JSON string are baseURL and languageCode (see Table 2). We found that the baseURL field provides a direct link to an XML document which contains the caption data for the specific videoid. Additionally, the languageCode field identifies which language the captions are available for translation. For instance, in the example included in Table 2 there are two baseUrl entries in two different languages. The languageCode "nl" will take the user to a caption translated in Dutch while the languageCode "en" will take the user to a caption translated in English. Another valuable discovery we made with these URLs is that they will expire within a short period of time. So, it was important that we extract the XML data from the URL that includes the captions translated to English before the accessible URL expires.

Table 2. Example of encoded URLs found within the JSON string fields baseURL and languageCode. This JSON string is encoded within the get_video_info data.

baseUrl	languageCode
https://www.youtube.com/api/timedtext?caps=asr&hl=en_US&sparams= asr_langs,caps,v,xorp,expire&expire=1516448002&xorp=True&signature= C136764856DB2D4997A522236FBA65079B44D5BF.9044FB3AB0E434 90946A9C4E450F6789A4832591&key=yttt1&asr_langs=nl,pt,es,ru,en,ja, fr,de,ko,it&v=6MBaFL7sCb8&lang=nl	nl
https://www.youtube.com/api/timedtext?caps=asr&hl=en_US&sparams= asr_langs,caps,v,xorp,expire&expire=1516448002&xorp=True&signature= C136764856DB2D4997A522236FBA65079B44D5BF.9044FB3AB0E434 90946A9C4E450F6789A4832591&key=yttt1&asr_langs=nl,pt,es,ru%2Cen, ja,fr,de,ko,it&v=6MBaFL7sCb8&lang=en	en

5.3   DSR Artifact Version 2

Capitalizing on the digital innovation that we achieved during the eADR cycle evaluating the limits to the goodness of DSR artifact version 1, we were able to proceed with improvements and construct version 2. Version 2 of the DSR artifact consists of four phases (see Fig. 2) to include:

1. *Web App used to auto search YouTube with API.* This feature executes stored procedures that use Python within the Relational Database Management System (RDBMS). SQL Server 2017 is used as the RDBMS to write Python embedded scripts within SQL statements. These scripts are then executed as stored procedures and permanently stored in a database residing within the SQL 2017 instance. The stored procedures would then receive parameters that are passed as arguments through the web front end application in the form of a search term. The search term received from the web app would then be passed through to the YouTube Data API and retrieve a list of relevant video ids. A partial screen shot of the web app, we call "TUBE TOPIC", is illustrated below in Fig. 3.

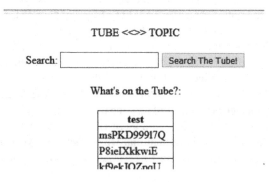

Fig. 3. Illustration of the DSR artifact version 2 web app called "TUBE TOPIC"

2. *Extract captioning and metadata from YouTube using API and* DIYCaptions.com. *Execution embedded Python and SQL within RDBMS.* Some of the YouTube captions are extracted using the YouTube Data API. However, after collaboration with the developer of DIYCaptions.com we decided to leverage their technology and extract some of the captions using their web application. Collectively, we are able to store all necessary captions and metadata within the SQL Server 2017 instance that were required to perform social video network analysis.

3. *Export captions and metadata to corpus for analysis using SQL.* With a scalable and data rich version 2 of the DSR artifact, we are able to extract the captions from the SQL server instance, similar to version 1, and construct the text corpus for social video network analysis. However, in version 2 we are able to construct each text file to include both the caption data and the metadata into a single file. This is what we term a *metadata-enhanced corpus.*

4. *Execute data analysis with Topic Modeling algorithms using embedded R within RDBMS.* The metadata-enhanced corpus is then used by topic modeling algorithms, LDA, to generate a distribution of topics for analysis. The advancement of this process in version 2 is that it includes scripts within SQL Server 2017 that allow R code to be embedded within the SQL code. This allows the system to execute a single script in a single service environment without the movement of files from one location to another.

6 Evaluation

As seen in Fig. 1, evaluation of each abstraction of a DSR artifact occurs within each iteration of the eADR cycles. The first opportunity for evaluation occured within the eADR cycles as they informed the *Diagnose* stage. An expert interview was conducted with LeapDoctor.com that resulted in the practical inspiration to develop the initial version of the DSR artifact. For instance, during the interview a question was asked about how LeapDoctor.com would make a decision once they recognized they had a technical problem. Part of the response was: *"If we are going to start from scratch – we have a lot of options. There are a 1000 ways to do the same thing. So we asked ourselves, what kind of technology do we want to use? Who had the technical expertise to work on the new technology? If we were to use the old technology, what kind of sense does this make if we are not using new technology?"*

We recognized that there is a need for a practical utility that any firm could use to easily discover what people are "talking about" within the context of a domain of interest. In early 2017, the development of version 1 of the DSR artifact was initiated using YouTube's social video network data to meet the practical requirements of the artifact inspired by LeapDoctor.com. Evaluation of the version 1 artifact was performed via user reviews [11]. Additionally, an expert interview and evaluation of the version 1 artifact was conducted with the lead developer of DIYCaptions.com in late 2017. The evaluation and intervention tasks conducted within each eADR cycle were critical to establishing the requirements for version 2 of the artifact.

Early on in the development of the version 2 artifact, a *Reflection* phase of an eADR cycle revealed that we needed an algorithm that would generalize a conversation that a user could use to evaluate the output of the artifact. A topic modeling algorithm, LDA, was selected because it resulted in a distribution of topics that consist of a distribution of words which could be used provide a probabilistic implicit view into a group of conversations discovered within YouTube. Topic intrusion tasks, as described by Chang et al. [7] and reproduced within the medical domain by Arnold et al. [3], were conducted to evaluate the results of the topics generated by the DSR artifact (see Fig. 4).

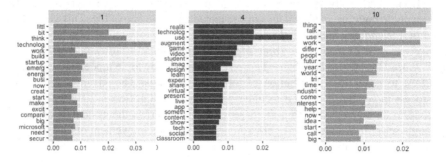

Fig. 4. Topic Intrusion task example. Example of topics generated by the artifact using LDA on a text corpus. The probability distribution of topics generated by the LDA algorithm that are associated with the text corpus are as follows: Topic 1: .382, Topic 4: .025, and Topic 10: .189 In this case, the highest probable intruder is Topic 4.

Ultimately, each iterative cycle of artifact planning, abstraction, evaluation, and reflection leads to learnings that inspire the next cyle within or between a stage in the eADR method. Once we had implemented an ensemble artifact, our evaluation of its goodness in situ with practitioners demonstrated a number of limitations on its utility. A second iteration through the Design stage yielded a breakthrough in our options for solving the problem. The resultant digital innovation has been implemented and its evaluation, in situ, resulted in a consensus among the practitioners and researchers that a unique ensemble artifact has been constructed to meet the unique needs of this problem class.

7   Discussion and Conclusion

The DSR artifact constructed in this research contributes toward a novel artifact that could add value to industry practicioners and scholarly researchers. The artifact directly addresses a practical need for industry practicioners to analyze social video network content using a rigorous and evidence based approach. Additionally, the artifact presents researchers and practitioners with a technical and algorithmic solution to detect topics of information being shared between the social video network nodes.

This research proposes an analytical process design that combines the importance of the corpus construction requirement with the unique attributes defined by the metadata of a social video network. Specifically, this research addresses the questions of *"How do we construct a metadata-enhanced corpus from social video networks?"* and *"How might an instantiated artifact help define a class of IT solution for analyzing multimedia in online social networks?"*. To accomplish this, a methodical, iterative eADR method in situ is deployed. The iterations within the Diagnosis, Design, Implementation, and Evolution eADR stages lead to the construction of the novel DSR artifact. The eADR methodology consistently informs the various iterations. Each iteration offers an opportunity to abstract, evaluate, reflect, and learn as the researchers and practitioners plan the next iteration. Overall, the methodology approaches used in this research contributes to the practical utility and rigorous quality of the DSR artifact.

This research will contribute to the existing body of knowledge for the IT solution class of social video network analysis with the implementation of an artifact that is designed to collect both the YouTube captions and the metadata using the YouTube Data API. Future research directions will apply the artifact in data analytic studies involving YouTube. A clear limitation of the current research is the exclusive focus of the artifact on YouTube video content. Moving beyond YouTube, we will adapt the artifact for use in other social network platforms where video content is prevalent. We plan to observe how the artifact can be used to analyze social video network behavior through utilities such as network search activities.

References

1. Abhari, A., Soraya, M.: Workload generation for YouTube. Multimed. Tools Appl. **46**, 91–118 (2009). https://doi.org/10.1007/s11042-009-0309-5
2. Ahmad, U., Zahid, A., Shoaib, M., AlAmri, A.: HarVis: an integrated social media content analysis framework for YouTube platform. Inf. Syst. **69**, 25–39 (2017)
3. Arnold, C.W., Oh, A., Chen, S., Speier, W.: Evaluating topic model interpretability from a primary care physician perspective. Comput. Methods Program. Biomed. **24**, 67–75 (2016)
4. Blei, D., Ng, A., Jordan, M.: Latent dirichlet allocation. J. Mach. Learn. Res. **3**, 993–1022 (2003)
5. Borgatti, S.P., Everett, M.G., Johnson, J.C.: Analyzing Social Networks. SAGE, Los Angeles (2013)
6. Cha, M., Kwak, H., Rodriguez, P., Moon, S.: I tube, you tube, everybody tubes: analyzing the world's largest user generated content video system. In: Proceedings of the 7th ACM SIGCOMM Conference on Internet Measurement, pp. 1–14. ACM, San Diego (2007)
7. Chang, J., Boyd-Graber, J., Gerrish, S., Wang, C., Blei, D.M.: Reading tea leaves: how humans interpret topic models. In: Proceedings of the 22nd International Conference on Neural Information Processing Systems, NIPS 2009, pp. 288–296. Proceedings of the 2009 Conference, Vancouver (2009)
8. Chatzopoulou, G., Sheng, C., Faloutsos, M.: A first step towards understanding popularity in YouTube. In: INFOCOMM IEEE Conference on Computer Communications Workshops, pp. 1–6. IEEE, San Diego (2010). https://doi.org/10.1109/infcomw.2010.5466701

9. Chen, L.-C., Tesng, H.-H., Liao, I.-E.: Information and communication technology trend analysis using. In: Recent Researches in Applied Informatics: Proceedings of the 6th International Conference on Applied Informatics and Computing Theory (AICT 2015), pp. 158–166. WSEAS Press, Salerno (2015)
10. Cheng, X., Dale, C., Liu, J.: Statistics and social network of youtube videos. In: 16th International Workshop, IQQos 2008, pp. 229–238. IEEE, Enschede (2008)
11. Daniel, C., Dutta, K.: Automated generation of latent topics on emerging technologies from YouTube Video content. In: Proceedings of the 51st Hawaii International Conference on System Sciences 2018, pp. 1762–1770 (2018). http://hdl.handle.net/10125/50109
12. Figueiredo, F., Benevenuto, F., Almeida, J.: The tube over time: characterizing popularity growth of youtube videos. Retrieved from Fabricio Benevenuto, Computer Science Department, Federal University of Minas Gerais (2011). http://homepages.dcc.ufmg.br/~fabricio/download/wsdm11.pdf
13. Gill, P., Arlitt, M., Li, Z., Mahanti, A.: Youtube traffic characterization: a view from the edge. In: Proceedings of the 7th ACM SIGCOMM Conference on Internet Measurement, pp. 15–28. ACM, Dan Diego (2007)
14. Gupta, H., Singh, S., Sinha, P.: Multimedia tool as a predictor for social media advertising- a YouTube way. Multimed. Tools Appl. **76**(18), 18557–18568 (2017)
15. Harrison, D., Wilding, J., Bowman, A., Fuller, A., Nicholls, S.G., Pound, C.M., Sampson, M.: Using YouTube to disseminate effective vaccination pain treatment for babies. PLoS ONE **11**(10), 1–10 (2016)
16. Hevner, A.R.: Design science research. In: Tucker, A., Topi, H. (eds.) Computing Handbook, 3rd edn, pp. 22-1–22-23. Chapman and Hall/CRC, New York (2014)
17. Hevner, A.R., March, S.T., Park, J., Ram, S.: Design science in information systems. MIS Q. **28**(1), 75–105 (2004)
18. Hevner, A., Chatterjee, S.: Design research in information systems. Springer, New York (2010). https://doi.org/10.1007/978-1-4419-5653-8. Eds. by R. Sharda and S. Vob
19. Lange, P.G.: Publicly private and privately public: social networking on YouTube. J. Comput. Mediat. Commun. **13**, 361–380 (2008)
20. Malik, H., Tian, Z.: A Framework for collecting YouTube meta-data. In: The 8th International Conference on Emerging Ubiquitous Systems and Pervasive Networks (EUSPN 2017), vol. 113, pp. 194–201. Procedia Computer Science (2017)
21. Miller, E.D.: Content analysis of select YouTube postings: comparisons of reactions to the sandy hook and aurora shootings and hurricant sandy. Cyberpsychol. Behav. Soc. Netw. **18**(11), 635–640 (2015)
22. Mullarkey, M.T., Hevner, A.R.: Entering action design research. In: Donnellan, B., Helfert, M., Kenneally, J., VanderMeer, D., Rothenberger, M., Winter, R. (eds.) DESRIST 2015. LNCS, vol. 9073, pp. 121–134. Springer, Cham (2015). https://doi.org/10.1007/978-3-319-18714-3_8
23. Mullarkey, M.T., Hevner, A.R.: An elaborated action design research process model. Eur. J. Inf. Syst. (2018). https://doi.org/10.1080/0960085X.2018.1451811
24. Peffers, K., Tuunanen, T., Rothenberger, M., Chatterjee, S.: A design science research methodology for information systems research. J. MIS **24**(3), 45–77 (2008)
25. Robins, G.: Doing Social Network Research. SAGE, Los Angeles (2015)
26. Santos, R., Rocha, B., Rezende, C.G., Loureiro, A.: Characterizing the YouTube video-sharing community. Retrieved from Rodrygo Santos: Department of Computer Science, Federal University of Minas Gerais (2007). http://homepages.dcc.ufmg.br/~rodrygo/wp-content/papercite-data/pdf/santos2007report.pdf
27. Sein, M.K., Henfridsson, O., Purao, S., Rossi, M., Lindgren, R.: Action design research. MIS Q. **35**(1), 37–56 (2011)

28. Siersdorfer, S., Nejdl, W., Chelaru, S., San Pedro, J.: How useful are your comments?: analyzing and predicting youtube comments and comment ratings. In: Proceedings of the 19th International Conference on World Wide Web, WWW 2010, pp. 891–900. ACM, Raleigh (2010)

29. Smith, C., Allman, T., Crocker, S.: Reading between the lines: accessing information via YouTube's automatic captioning. Online Learn. **21**(1), 115–131 (2017)

30. Yoganarasimhan, H.: Impact of social network structure on content propagation: a study using YouTube data. Quant. Mark. Econ. **10**, 111–150 (2009). https://doi.org/10.1007/s11129-011-9105-4

31. Yuan, J., Zheng-Jun, Z., Zheng, Y.-T., Wang, M., Zhou, X., Chua, T.-S.: Utilizing related samples to enhance interactive concept-based video search. IEEE Trans. Multimed. **13**(6), 1343–1355 (2011)

Software-Embedded Evaluation Support
in Design Science Research

Jonas Sjöström[1]([⊠]), Leona Chandra Kruse[2], Amir Haj-Bolouri[3],
and Per Flensburg[3]

[1] Department of Informatics and Media, Uppsala University, Uppsala, Sweden
jonas.sjostrom@im.uu.se
[2] Institute of Information Systems, University of Liechtenstein, Vaduz,
Liechtenstein
leona.chandra@uni.li
[3] Division of Informatics, University West, Trollhättan, Sweden
{amir.haj-bolouri,per.flensburg}@hv.se

Abstract. Even though the practice of integrating evaluative features into software has long been applied in commercially available software, it is still underrepresented in the Information Systems (IS) community. This paper presents a framework for embedded evaluation support. We are aware of the challenges of evaluation of socio-technical systems and take this issue into consideration in our framework. Our framework is the result of conceptualizations drawing from the evaluation discourse discussion on the topics of artifact evaluation in DSR. We also demonstrate our ideas through two examples of embedded evaluation support mechanisms designed and used in a DSR project in the Swedish healthcare sector.

Keywords: Embedded evaluation · Design science research
Design guidelines

1 Introduction

Information system design (ISD) includes the process of defining, designing, implementing and evaluating architecture, components, and features of an information system. During the process, designers and stakeholders articulate the desired features and characteristics of the software. In ISD, evaluation is also a core activity [1].

Design Science Research (DSR) in its various forms is the prevailing research paradigm in information systems when it comes to addressing design as an integrated part of a research process. In this paper, we focus on evaluation as a core activity in DSR. Design science researchers need to demonstrate the efficacy and utility of their designed artifacts [1, 2], where artifact quality implicitly signals the value of the knowledge accumulated in the artifact [1]. There has been a vivid discourse about evaluation in the context of DSR in IS. Evaluation frameworks have emerged and been recommended for conducting an adequate DSR. Venable et al. [1] present a comprehensive overview and synthesis of the DSR evaluation discourse. Evaluation frameworks provide thorough guidelines for planning and executing evaluation, and for interpreting evaluation results. The researchers' choice of evaluation method(s) depends on the characteristics of the artifact under consideration, its use context, and the evaluation objectives.

Designing an appropriate and insightful evaluation is challenging, and its execution can be time-consuming and is prone to human error. Previous research has paid little attention to software support for DSR evaluation. Potentially, digital tools may mitigate some of the evaluation challenges. For instance, through minimizing human error, reducing resources for data collection and data analysis, and by improved collaboration between stakeholders in the evaluation process. Our starting point is that software-supported evaluation can occur through either an 'external' evaluation mechanism that is independent of the artifact or through evaluation features embedded in the software artifact itself. In this paper, we focus the latter: Embedding evaluation features into software.

The idea of integrated evaluation mechanisms in the software artifact is not novel. It is intuitively appealing to design an artifact and at the same time employ it as a means for its self-evaluation. Software engineering research has addressed the idea of self-evaluating software, e.g., through developing the concept of self-repairing software [3–5]. Commercial software vendors also apply increasingly sophisticated techniques, such as the crash reports submitted to operation systems and application vendors when a malfunction is detected. We are all familiar with the pop-up window that automatically appears when our word processor experiences problem and needs to be closed. Through the pop-up window, we are asked whether we want to send error reports to the software developers by clicking a dedicated button. In some cases, there is an option to provide a free-text description of the problem. We suggest that DSR researchers pay more attention to how a software artifact in its practical use context can be used to support the collection of data for its evaluation.

Researchers in other fields have elaborated on the idea of embedded evaluation support. It was introduced in the field of education in the 1980's [6]. Further, it is part of the Design for Testability (DFT) and Built-In Self-Test (BIST) for industrial and electronic artifacts [7, 8], to name a few. The rationale behind BIST is related to, among others, the effort to reduce dependability on external testers as well as to increase efficiency, speed, and the possibility for hierarchical testing through an integration of test infrastructure into the artifact [9, 10].

One example of embedded evaluation in human-computer interaction, is the prototyping of CLASP – a digital artifact that supports adults with Autistic Spectrum Disorder [11]. Another example is the power-on-self-test (POST) in almost all operating systems. The POST routine executes when the device is turned on to detect any system error. Even in large-scale online systems integrated evaluation tools are not unusual, as reflected in the availability of various rating features, open-ended comment boxes, automatic error reporting, and other features to encourage stakeholders to contributing feedback about technology. Other examples include the use of standard web technologies for logging [12] and the use of log data in eHealth research [13].

Interestingly, the DSR community has not paid much attention to the possibility to adopt embedded evaluation support in their evaluation strategies. The existing DSR evaluation discourse does not provide guidance to researchers on how to embed evaluation support into their software artifacts. The fact that evaluation support is underrepresented, if not underexplored, in DSR is indeed unfortunate. With regards to this identified tension, we pose the following questions:

How can evaluation support be embedded into an artifact in the context of DSR?

We synthesize various elements of the DSR evaluation discourse into a framework for software-embedded evaluation support (SEES) with focus on the typology of SEES. Finally, we provide an expository instantiation of the framework within a DSR project and discuss implications for both practice and research. Our contribution is the exploration and conceptualization of an underexplored dimension of evaluation in DSR: the integration of evaluation mechanisms into artifact instantiations. We hope that our work – addressing a theme that has long been intuitively and implicitly applied in other fields – initiates a continued discussion about how to best use technology to support the DSR process.

The paper proceeds as follows. In Sect. 2, we provide a general overview of approaches to evaluation in IS and proceed to some examples of self-evaluation healthcare information systems. In Sect. 3, we account for our proposed framework of embedded evaluation support. In Sect. 4, we provide two examples of software embedded evaluation support, followed by concluding remarks in Sect. 5.

2 Information Systems Evaluation

In this section, we provide an overview on previous work on information system – the starting point for our work on embedded evaluation support in IS artifacts.

2.1 Types of Evaluation

There are several purposes for evaluation in DSR, as well as a variety of different methods, strategies, and activities for conducting an evaluation. In this section, we provide a rough overview of the DSR evaluation discourse and later focus on topics relevant to the purpose of building evaluation support into the artifact.

There are different approaches to artifact evaluation [1, 14]. A regular feature is that evaluation approaches use temporality to distinguish between types of evaluation: We can evaluate a situation in a predictive (ex-ante) manner, where the potential impact of an artifact is assessed speculatively before the implementation. In contrast, a post-implementation (ex-post) evaluation seeks to measure the actual impact of an implemented artifact. Since the result of ex-ante evaluation is expected to feedback to the improvement of the artifact design, this type of evaluation is also termed as being formative. On the other hand, an ex-post evaluation sums up the efficiency and usefulness of an artifact, thus also called as being summative. The conceptual difference is the focus shift between evaluation temporality (ex-ante/ex-post) to functional evaluation purpose (formative/summate).

Such distinction has been extended in the Framework for Evaluation in Design Science (FEDS) [1]. The authors formed their classification by addressing underlying questions as to when, why, and how to evaluate an artifact. FEDS distinguish between the functional purpose and evaluation paradigm of evaluation. The functional purpose dimension addresses both when and why question, and views evaluation as either formative or summative. On the other hand, the evaluation paradigm dimension addresses the how question, and distinguishes naturalistic evaluation from artificial evaluation. In a naturalistic evaluation, the artifact is evaluated in its real use setting, while an artificial evaluation measures the artifact's impact in an artificial or unnatural setting, such as a laboratory environment. In addition to the classification of evaluation, FEDS also specifies four steps in conducting evaluation, based on an analysis and synthesis of work on evaluation in DSR and other domains of IS [14–16].

The formative perspective of FEDS captures the possibility to reduce risks by evaluating early, before undergoing the effort of building and strictly evaluating an instantiation of a design. The summative perspective offers a possibility for evaluating the instantiated artifact in reality, and not just in theory. In contrast to the formative and summative perspectives, naturalistic evaluation methods offer the possibility to evaluate the real artifact in use by involving real users solving real problems. Artificial evaluation methods offer the possibility to control potential variables more carefully and prove or disprove testable hypotheses, design theories, and the utilization of design artifacts [1].

The FEDS framework with evaluation strategies highlights the idea of choosing an existing or building an own DSR evaluation strategy that maps specific criteria for evaluation. For instance, the DSR researcher needs to identify whether the evaluation shall be conducted in a realistic environment together with real users, or in an artificial environment together with prospective users.

Other DSR evaluation methods such as the ones presented by Peffers et al. [17] emphasize the distribution of evaluation method types, based on the artifact type (e.g., method, instantiation, construct). They guide how to conduct DSR evaluation, based on the purpose of artifact use and utility. FEDS incorporates a similar notion of evaluation guidance. Thus we find the FEDS approach to be a suitable source of inspiration for a framework for embedded evaluation support.

2.2 Support Evaluation Through Automation

Let us clarify the scope of our evaluation support by relating it to evaluation dimensions derived from the DSR evaluation discourse. In the attempt to automate evaluation, we mainly deal with naturalistic ex-post evaluation (Pries-Heje et al. [30]; Venable et al. [1]), which has the character of real users, real problems, and real systems. While such evaluation is considered to be the best evaluation of effectiveness and identification of side effects, it also comes with the highest cost and a potential risk for participants (Venable et al. [1]). Naturalistic ex-post evaluation can be carried using various methods, including (but not limited to) methods such as action research, case study, focus group, participant observation, ethnography, phenomenology, and qualitative or quantitative surveys. We thus position our discussion within the practice approach to DSR (Iivari [29]), where we focus on the effects an artifact has in its use context, and the meaning that stakeholders ascribe to artifacts.

We propose automated data collection during the lifetime of an artifact. Thus it may be used in a formative manner, e.g., as part of an action design research cycle of building-intervening-evaluating [18], or for summative purposes to demonstrate the qualities of an artifact after a period of use. However, despite the idea that the artifact embeds evaluation mechanisms, the evaluation does not necessarily concern the artifact as such [19] in the sense of a software instantiation. Software-embedded evaluation features may, for instance, support the collection of data to evaluate the use of the software.

Despite the focus on evaluation of a software instantiation, we recognize the high-order goal of DSR evaluation to demonstrate the value of abstracted design knowledge, e.g., in the form of design theories, design principles, or technological rules (Baskerville et al. [31]). Artifact-centric evaluation is a means to demonstrate qualities of abstracted concepts. We subscribe to the view of [17] that "when an artifact is evaluated for its utility in achieving its purpose, one is also evaluating a design theory that the design artifact has utility to achieve that purpose. From the point of view of design theory, a second purpose of evaluation in DSR is to confirm or disprove (or enhance) the design theory."

In a similar vein, the discussion on the nature of artifact to be evaluated becomes indispensable. The idea of supporting evaluation in DSR primarily concerns socio-technical artifacts, even though – to some extent – it can be applied to software qualities per se. While a socio-technical system indeed involves human actors, there are many examples of artifacts that do not include a human actor, for instance, algorithms used as part of a software system. What differentiates such agents from human agents is the process underlying their task execution. These so-called automata execute operations depending on pre-determined and well-defined conditions. Therefore the entire system is algorithmic. In fact, a similar distinction has been pointed out by Bunge [20], between human and what he called *automata*, that is the non-human agent:

> "Although automata can store 'theories', as well as clear-cut instructions to use them, they lack two abilities: (1) they have no judgment or flair to apply them, i.e. to choose the more promising theories or to make additional simplifying assumptions, (2) they can't invent new theories to cope with new situations, unpredicted by the designer and to which the stored theories are relevant" (p. 160).

We show implications of this definition of scope in the section that follows, where we derive the methods to support evaluation in DSR and describe them using socio-technical vocabularies and identify the justificatory knowledge drawn from both a social and a technical foundation.

3   SEES: A Framework for Software-Embedded Evaluation Support

This section presents our framework for software-embedded evaluation support (SEES).

3.1   Embedded Evaluation Data Collection

Our proposition about design for software-embedded evaluation support concerns two dimensions derived from the core activities in an evaluation, namely *data collection* and *data analysis*. About data collection, the crucial issue is to identify the type of data to be collected that fits into the purpose of evaluation – i.e., to address what data to collect. Following Cronholm and Goldkuhl [19], we distinguish between three types of data to be collected for evaluation: (1) criteria-based, (2) goal-based and (3) goal-free (open-ended). The choice of data type naturally depends on the context and purpose of evaluation and will be explicated in the next subsections.

Once we have identified the appropriate type of data, the next step is to address the question of how to collect the data. We draw from [21] to distinguish between (a) fully automated data collection conducted by the system and (b) self-reported data from users or external testers. A fully automated data collection corresponds to logging mechanisms of software use. In contrast, self-reported data collection refers to software features that permit and promote users to provide feedback to developers and DSR researchers. Combining these two categories produces a data collection method matrix as shown in Table 1.

Table 1. Six categories of software features for embedded data collection

	Auto-collected data	Self-reported data
Criteria-based evaluation	Automated collection of data to support evaluation based on pre-defined generic criteria, e.g. usability guidelines	Criteria-based questionnaires filled out by users, artifact-in-use observation
Goal-based evaluation	Automated collection of data to support evaluation based on goals derived from the business context, e.g. number of logins, returning clients, sales, performance times, et cetera	Goal-based instruments filled out by users, financial indicators, other quantitative indicators
Goal-free evaluation	Extensive logging to enable rich retrospective analysis of business action conducted through the software	Open-ended questions to users asked via the software

Note that we place emphasis on supporting evaluation of socio-technical artifacts, even though SEES may to some extent also apply to the evaluation of pure technical artifacts. Observe the mélange of social or business goals (e.g., employee's satisfaction and financial indicators) and technical goals (e.g., automatic forwarding of technical failure messages with time stamp) that reflect the sociotechnical nature of information systems.

Criteria-Based SEES. This type of evaluation requires a set of pre-defined criteria that do not necessarily reflect the goal of designing the system. These criteria may be related to particular features or material properties of the systems in particular, or certain generic quality criteria for the functionality of artifact in general (Cronholm and Goldkuhl [19]). The generic quality criteria may include utility/effectiveness, efficiency, efficacy, and ethicality of the designed system [1]. These generic criteria cover chiefly the evaluation of what Cronholm and Goldkuhl termed *"IT-systems as such"* [19].

Evaluation based on pre-defined criteria requires users to fill out a questionnaire (that could also free-text answers as well as questions with options) with criteria-related domains or items. Another possibility is through observation of how users work with the IS artifact or how they make use of the artifact – what Cronholm and Goldkuhl termed "IT-systems in use" [19]. The behavioral checklist contains items related to the pre-defined criteria and is filled out by the ones who are in charge of the evaluation.

We propose an embedded or automated manner of this kind of evaluation through a software-enabled automatic collection of usage data related to the pre-defined criteria. This way, the collected data is less exposed to the subjectivity of users' self-report and can be completed more efficiently.

Goal-Based SEES. Goal-based evaluation is conducted based on pre-defined goals of designing the system [19]. These pre-defined goals may be related to business or organizational goals that represent financial and social objectives. While financial objectives are usually clear-cut and well defined, social objectives need further definition, e.g., as employees' satisfaction with their work procedures or even in a much broader term, such as public perception of the company image. Well-defined constructs and corresponding measures facilitate quantitative analysis of goal fulfillment.

Similar to the non-automated criteria-based evaluation, self-reported goal-based evaluation relies on users' and external testers' account on the extent to which the goals of designing the system have been fulfilled. When involving quantitative indicators that can be generated post-implementation, such reliance is even stronger. In addition to quantitative indicators, qualitative data (e.g., customer opinions and goal-based questions to staff and customers) may be self-reported by people using the system.

What we propose is, however, an automatic or embedded mechanism of collecting data that reflect the fulfillment of specific goals. Goals can include internal organization variables, e.g., number of logins, the amount and frequency of returning clients, performance speed, and sales levels, or externally projected goals such as median rating on review websites.

Goal-Free SEES. Cronholm and Goldkuhl define goal-free evaluation as "gathering data on a broad array of actual effects and evaluating the importance of these effects in meeting demonstrated needs." Without any pre-defined goal or criterion, goal-free evaluation has the potential to enable a broader understanding of the function and effects of IS artifact – even to the extent that we can discover unintended positive or negative impacts.

Goal-free evaluation that relies on users' self-report or external testers' report requires these parties to keep an open mind to take into account various possibilities of the effects resulting from both IT-systems as such and IT-systems in use. It poses a challenge to ensure that researchers collect relevant data that can also account for unforeseeable or unintended effects. Goal-free self-reported data would also include qualitative data from (e.g.) a user-group discussion forum where they can speak about the software in general.

Automated data collection can promote the richness of data, e.g., through generalized logging mechanisms. A wide range of logging creates a rich data set that may prove useful to retrospectively analyze various aspects of the impact of the IS artifact. Therefore, we propose adopting generic logging framework to enable rich retrospective analysis of business action conducted through the software.

4 Two Examples of Software-Embedded Evaluation Support

In this section, we two provide examples of software-embedded evaluation support in the context of U-CARE, a strategic research program in the Swedish health care sector [22, 23]. The research group developed web-based software to provide online cognitive behavioral therapy. The overarching goal of the research was to determine treatment efficacy and health economic aspects of online psychosocial care for individuals who suffer from a physical disease. In total, 11 trials have been conducted using the software, including more than 2000 participants.

The U-CARE software has evolved into a medium-sized software product, consisting of three subsystems, $\sim 40,000$ lines of code and ~ 100 database tables.

In the U-CARE software, online surveys are integrated into the software, allowing the researchers to not only provide treatment online but also to collect survey data using instruments for data collection such as the hospital anxiety and depression scale (HADS; ref). In addition to the research objectives defined in each study, the design of software to support treatment and research leads to an increased understanding of the problem domain, which in turn causes new knowledge interests to emerge. Such knowledge interests may include an interest in the design process as such, but may also concern design challenges that we did not expect at the inception of the research process. In the case of U-CARE, design issues arose relating to, among other things, privacy and accountability [24], crowd translation [25], decision support for therapists [26], principles for data export [27], and online survey evaluation techniques [28]. In essence, there is a need to reflect on the 'umbrella process' as well as sub-projects of the overall process focusing specific design issues. In this section, we provide an account of two such sub-projects and show how self-evaluation support were integrated into the IS artifact design.

4.1 Formative Evaluation Through Self-Reported Stakeholder Feedback

Case Outline. At an early stage in the U-CARE design process, it turned out to be problematic to manage the continual feedback from stakeholders. Therefore, a feature was built in the web portal to allow any user of the software to provide direct feedback about their user experience. Similar features exist in backlog management and bug-reporting software, and the reporting concept is also commonly used on commercial websites to collect input from customers about website and service quality. When a user submitted feedback, contextual information was also stored, including a screenshot of the user's current view, user name, the study the user was in, *et cetera*. The rich context description was intended to facilitate sensemaking of the user's comment.

The user can also select a category for the comment. A rephrasing of usability criteria, a simple 'I found a bug' category, and a pre-selected category named 'I've got this great idea' comprises the categories. The basic design idea is that it should be as easy as possible to provide feedback on the design of the software from the current context of use, and the feedback should be easily interpretable for both software developers and DSR researchers. The reported ideas were factored into the product backlog in the development process. All stakeholders also had access to the product backlog, where they could discuss ideas, and see the status of development work addressing their idea. The rationale for the design was to provide transparency, to motivate people to submit new ideas continually. The feature was available for patients, due to ethical concerns and that it might take their focus away from the treatment protocol.

The stakeholder comments were part of the agile design process, serving as a product backlog. Any comment in the backlog was shown as 'unprioritized' in the product owner view of the system, who prioritized the incoming ideas as either 'really cool', 'market advantage' or 'must have'. In each sprint meeting, new comments were discussed by a group consisting of researchers from each research group using the software, the research coordinator, information systems researchers and developers. Comments were discussed, and possibly priorities were re-estimated. At the end of the meeting, the research coordinator and the developers remained in the room to discuss how to translate stakeholder feedback into software development tasks. Task complexity was estimated by developers, followed by a sprint planning discussion. During the sprint work, once the tasks associated with a stakeholder feedback comments were completed, the stakeholder automatically received an internal message in the software with information that their idea has been implemented in the software. At that point, it would be available on the beta testing server, and in the production server in the next software release. The response mechanism from developers to actors providing feedback was deemed important to motivate all involved parties to keep providing feedback. The extensive use of the feedback mechanism signals the mechanism for stakeholder feedback has worked well.

Lessons Learned. The feedback feature generated open-ended self-reported data (users only categorized their ideas on a few occasions). It rendered ~ 1000 comments from users during 2013–2015. The stakeholder comments represent a variety of ideas, including but not limited to:

- New ideas about how the software should support interaction between psychologists and patients (written by psychologists)
- New ideas about how to design a 'helicopter view' for researchers to monitor ongoing research activity (written by researchers)
- Suggestions on how to revise existing features, e.g. usability and user experience related design ideas (written by various stakeholders)
- Bug reports (written by various stakeholders)
- Technical issues and software refactoring ideas (from developers).

The characteristics of the ideas thus concern social aspects (process support and interaction between stakeholders in the practice), user experience aspects, and purely technical aspects (internal software design issues). One important lesson learned is thus that an open-ended communication channel, conveniently accessible for a broad group of stakeholders, may provide qualitative data regarding the practice context in which the artifact is used – not only data regarding the technology as such.

The idea backlog as such is a comprehensive repository with various stakeholder impressions of qualities of the artifact at hand and the embedding workpractice. Clearly, such a repository is a rich source for artifact evaluation in DSR research as well as retrospective analysis of the DSR process.

A final reflection is that the feature was originally intended to be a 'criteria-based' evaluation mechanism as discussed above. The vast majority of feedback posts did not actively do so – instead, they passively selected the default value ("I just want to express something") instead of actively choosing a category. A lesson learned is that a mechanism for criteria-based self-reported evaluation needs to find a more suitable way to interact with the user to make them select a category.

4.2 Summative Evaluation and Identification of Stakeholders Using Log Data

Case Outline. This case illustrates the use of log data in the DSR evaluation process. We account for the evaluation of a crowd-translation mechanism called 'Babbler' built into the software [25]. In SEES terms, we classify this example as an example of goal-free autocollected data.

The conceptual solution for the Babbler translation mechanism is to allow users to translate text in the software as simple as possible (one-click to translate) in the user's current view. Further, it should be possible to make local translations in the current view as well as global translations affecting all views. Additionally, whenever a user translates, s/he should get decision support including existing translations in other languages and previous translations of the current text in the same language. A complicating factor in the web context is that any type of text element, independent of how it is embedded in the web page, should be possible to make translate. Another complicating factor is that web pages can be either fully loaded once, or consist of parts that are loaded through asynchronous requests.

A trivial conceptual model for storing translations is shown in Fig. 1. A phrase key (created by the software developers) can have several translations ('babbles') provided by different users. This is the core model – in the software instantiation, additional contextual information is available, such as user roles and.

A 'babble' is a translation of a phrase key into a particular language. When a new translation is stored for a phrase key, the old translation is marked as deleted, and the time of the deletion is stored. This model allows us to keep track of all translations for a phrase key for different languages. Note that the static model includes time stamps of translations, as well as information about who made the translation. The translations are never deleted from the database, only marked as deleted by a Boolean attribute. Therefore, the static model in Fig. 1 also serves as a rich log to study the process of creating and changing translations over time.

The dynamics of the translation tool (Fig. 2) is a bit more complex, due to the architecture of web pages that may require translation services in numerous situations.

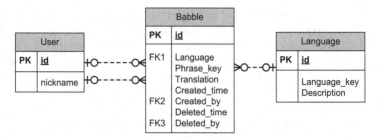

Fig. 1. Static conceptual model for babbler translations

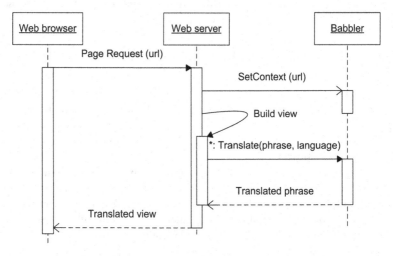

Fig. 2. Babbler translation dynamics

There is a need to handle both page load-translation and asynchronous translation. The latter situation is common due to the increased popularity of asynchronous web requests, i.e. scripted code on the client side that makes requests to the web server without reloading the entire web page. A web browser requests a page from the web server. The web server analyses the URL to set the translation context. This mechanism is necessary to allow for situated translations (on that page) or generic translations (translating into the same result across all pages). The code that produces the view that is returned to the browser utilizes Babbler functions to translate phrases. The developers are thus required to utilize the Babbler application programming interface (API) when presenting any piece of information in a view, to ensure that the view is fully translatable. They also need to decide if the translation of that text should be valid only in the current page, or across pages. In addition to the page request flow, a browser may also make asynchronous requests (e.g. loading a part of a page using Ajax). Therefore, there is a simplified flow, which basically consists of a request for a translation of a particular phrase, and a response (the translation). The server, therefore, needs to store the page context in the user session state to properly translate asynchronous translation requests. In addition, the server keeps track of the logged in user, and the user's preferred language.

Due to the multiple ways to build web pages, e.g. divergent implementations of standards such as JavaScript and HTML, the implementation of the Babbler feature was quite complicated and needed multiple iterations of development and beta testing to work satisfactory. Our evaluation interests thus concerned both (i) technical proof-of-concept (a working instantiation of the Babbler concept) and (ii) proof-of-value (that the translation mechanism was working satisfactory to support the translation practice in the organization).

Lessons Learned. Babbler was introduced to the users of the U-CARE software in a development sprint. Domain experts – who were also future users of the portal – were informed about the translation tool basics. Developers were instructed how to make text elements translatable by using the Babbler API. Minimal instructions were given, and the stakeholders were expected to self-organize the translation work. Evaluation of the babble translation feature started with a log analysis. Based on database queries into the log we identified users who contributed substantially to the translation work (Table 2).

Table 2. Top 10 translators and their translation count

User	Count	User role
Donald	1744	Lead developer
Claire	226	Research coordinator
Peter	186	Account used by Donald to translate participants' views
Thomas	98	Therapist
Paula	97	Used by Claire to translate participants' views
Audrey	81	Research assistant
Phil	81	Used by Thomas to translate participants' views
David	59	Developer
Pagona	55	Used by a therapist to translate participants' views
Penelope	49	Used by a therapist to translate participants' views

The log files show the quick adoption of the translation feature, which signals ease-of-learning and ease-of-use. Log data reveals that the users started to organize themselves and took responsibility to translate the views that were most related to their specific interests in the software. Knowledge about the user roles a-lows us to make further interpretations based on the log. Claire did translations due to her role as a coordinator between different work groups, making her assume responsibility for the overall translation progress. Donald, lead developer, did the initial re-factoring of the software to support Babbler (evident through searches in the source code repository, another tool for automated data collection). While doing this he also added a lot of initial translations. At one point – as revealed by a large number of 'babbles' with an identical time stamp – translations from one language (Swedish for adults) were copied into another language (Swedish for teens) in order to facilitate language adaptations for each target group. The implication is that Donald's translation count was doubled. The other developer in the list, David, is not Swedish speaking, which explains his low translation count.

The identification of translators who contributed substantially was also useful to identify individuals to approach to conduct interviews. The interviews were used to do a qualitative analysis of people's perceptions of the translation process. Furthermore, the idea backlog in the first case example contained a large set of improvement ideas for the Babbler feature, serving as an additional frame of reference to assess the qualities of the babbler concept and its software instantiation. Thus, the Babbler log data as such was not sufficient to assess the implications of the translation features for practice, but it was clearly an integrated part in the assessment.

In summary, the automated data collection in the Babbler context supported the overall evaluation process as follows:

- In determining the scale and frequency of translations, i.e. use of the artifact
- In identifying users that contributed substantially to the translation process
- In inferring that the babbler artifact is easy to learn and easy to use (which was supported by the subsequent qualitative study)
- In supporting planning of additional evaluation (identifying users to interview).

5 Conclusions

In this paper, we have highlighted that the DSR evaluation discourse has not adequately addressed the role of information technology to support evaluation. To answer our research question, we have conceptualized software-embedded evaluation support (SEES) to support evaluation in DSR, and potentially in a broader scope of information systems design. SEES shows six categories of support for naturalistic ex-post evaluation, i.e., evaluation of software with real people in a production setting. We have provided examples of two cases where such evaluation support was built into software and used in DSR. Through the cases, we illustrate that embedded features for data collection may provide valuable insights into various stakeholders' use of software as well as their impressions of its design. Further, the Babbler artifact provided valuable information about how to conduct continued evaluation through interviews.

SEES covers various methods of data collection. Such evaluation support can not only serve and support the end-users while making use of the artifact but also generate input for DSR researchers throughout their cycles of DSR. Current frameworks and methods for DSR evaluation [1, 17] could benefit from adopting the general idea of SEES, which emphasize a notion of continuously improving artifact quality and utility. SEES may enhance the prescriptive nature of designing sufficient and efficient artifacts in DSR [2], by offering *in situ* features that captures evaluation data.

In summary, the main contribution of this paper is the SEES framework and its guidance for DS researchers or IS designers who are interested in embedding formative or summative evaluation support in software artifacts. We hope that our work inspires other researchers to engage with software-embedded evaluation support in their work, and contribute to further developing the idea.

References

1. Venable, J., Pries-Heje, J., Baskerville, R.: FEDS: a framework for evaluation in design science research. Eur. J. Inf. Syst. **25**, 77–89 (2016)
2. Hevner, A.R., March, S.T., Park, J., Ram, S.: Design science in information systems research. MIS Q. **28**, 75–105 (2004)
3. Le Goues, C., Nguyen, T., Forrest, S., Weimer, W.: GenProg: a generic method for automatic software repair. IEEE Trans. Softw. Eng. **38**, 54–72 (2012)
4. Le Goues, C., Forrest, S., Weimer, W.: Current challenges in automatic software repair. Softw. Qual. J. **21**, 421–443 (2013)
5. Sidiroglou, S., Laadan, O., Perez, C., Viennot, N., Nieh, J., Keromytis, A.D.: ASSURE: automatic software self-healing using rescue points. ACM SIGARCH Comput. Archit. News. **37**, 37–48 (2009)
6. Dave, R.H.: A built-in system of evaluation for reform projects and programmes in education. Int. Rev. Educ. **26**, 475–482 (1980)
7. Jervan, G., Peng, Z., Ubar, R., Kruus, H.: A hybrid BIST architecture and its optimization for SoC testing. In: Proceedings of the International Symposium on Quality Electronic Design 2002, pp. 273–279 (2002)
8. Nagle, H.T., Roy, S.C., Hawkins, C.F., McNamer, M.G., Fritzemeier, R.R.: Design for testability and built-in self test: a review. IEEE Trans. Ind. Electron. **36**, 129–140 (1989)
9. Agrawal, V.D., Kime, C.R., Saluja, K.K.: A tutorial on built-in self-test. I. Principles. IEEE Des. Test Comput. **10**, 73–82 (1993)
10. Agrawal, V.D., Kime, C.R., Saluja, K.K.: A tutorial on built-in self-test. 2. Applications. IEEE Des. Test Comput. **10**, 69–77 (1993)
11. Simm, W., Ferrario, M.A., Gradinar, A., Whittle, J.: Prototyping 'clasp': implications for designing digital technology for and with adults with autism. In: Proceedings of the 2014 Conference on Designing Interactive Systems, pp. 345–354 (2014)
12. Atterer, R., Wnuk, M., Schmidt, A.: Knowing the user's every move: user activity tracking for website usability evaluation and implicit interaction. In: Proceedings of the 15th International Conference on World Wide Web, pp. 203–212 (2006)
13. Van Gemert-Pijnen, J.E.W.C., Kelders, S.M., Bohlmeijer, E.T.: Understanding the usage of content in a mental health intervention for depression: an analysis of log data. J. Med. Internet Res. **16** (2014)
14. Remenyi, D., Sherwood-Smith, M.: Maximise information systems value by continuous participative evaluation. Logist. Inf. Manag. **12**, 14–31 (1999)
15. Stufflebeam, D.L.: The CIPP model for evaluation. In: Kellaghan, T., Stufflebeam, D.L. (eds.) International Handbook of Educational Evaluation. Kluwer International Handbooks of Education, vol. 9, pp. 31–62. Springer, Heidelberg (2003). https://doi.org/10.1007/978-94-010-0309-4_4
16. Smithson, S., Hirschheim, R.: Analysing information systems evaluation: another look at an old problem. Eur. J. Inf. Syst. **7**, 158–174 (1998)
17. Venable, J., Pries-Heje, J., Baskerville, R.: A comprehensive framework for evaluation in design science research. In: Peffers, K., Rothenberger, M., Kuechler, B. (eds.) DESRIST 2012. LNCS, vol. 7286, pp. 423–438. Springer, Heidelberg (2012). https://doi.org/10.1007/978-3-642-29863-9_31
18. Sein, M., Henfridsson, O., Purao, S., Rossi, M., Lindgren, R.: Action design research. MIS Q. **35**, 37–56 (2011)
19. Cronholm, S., Goldkuhl, G.: Strategies for information systems evaluation-six generic types. Electron. J. Inf. Syst. Eval. **6**, 65–74 (2003)

20. Bunge, M.: Philosophy of Science: From Explanation to Justification, vol. 2. Transaction Publishers, New Brunswick (1998)

21. Ågerfalk, P.J., Sjöström, J.: Sowing the seeds of self: a socio-pragmatic penetration of the web artefact. In: ACM International Conference Proceeding Series (2007)

22. Grönqvist, H., Olsson, E.M.G., Johansson, B., Held, C., Sjöström, J., Norberg, A.L., Hovén, E., Sanderman, R., van Achterberg, T., von Essen, L.: Fifteen challenges in establishing a multidisciplinary research program on eHealth research in a university setting: a case study. J. Med. Internet Res. **19**, e173 (2017)

23. Sjöström, J., von Essen, L., Grönqvist, H.: The origin and impact of ideals in eHealth research: experiences from the U-CARE research environment. JMIR Res. Protoc. **3** (2014)

24. Sjöström, J., Ågerfalk, P.J., Hevner, A.R.: Scrutinizing privacy and accountability in online psychosocial care. IT Prof. **19**, 45–51 (2017)

25. Sjöström, J., Hermelin, M.: In-place translation in information systems development. In: Helfert, M., Donnellan, B. (eds.) EDSS 2012. CCIS, vol. 388, pp. 88–98. Springer, Cham (2013). https://doi.org/10.1007/978-3-319-04090-5_9

26. Sjöström, J., Alfonsson, S.: Supporting the therapist in online therapy. In: ECIS 2012 Proceedings, Barcelona, Spain (2012)

27. Mustafa, M.I., Sjöström, J.: Design principles for research data export: lessons learned in e-health design research. In: vom Brocke, J., Hekkala, R., Ram, S., Rossi, M. (eds.) DESRIST 2013. LNCS, vol. 7939, pp. 34–49. Springer, Heidelberg (2013). https://doi.org/10.1007/978-3-642-38827-9_3

28. Sjöström, J., Rahman, M.H., Rafiq, A., Lochan, R., Ågerfalk, P.J.: Respondent behavior logging: an opportunity for online survey design. In: vom Brocke, J., Hekkala, R., Ram, S., Rossi, M. (eds.) DESRIST 2013. LNCS, vol. 7939, pp. 511–518. Springer, Heidelberg (2013). https://doi.org/10.1007/978-3-642-38827-9_44

29. Iivari, J.: Distinguishing and contrasting two strategies for design science research. Eur. J. Inf. Syst. **24**(1), 107–115 (2015). Nature Publishing Group

30. Purao, S., Baldwin, C.I., Hevner, A.R., Storey, V.C., Pries-Heje, J., Smith, B., Zhu, Y.: The Sciences of Design: Observations on an Emerging Field. Working Paper 09-056. Harvard Business School (2008)

31. Baskerville, R.L., Kaul, M., Storey, V.C.: Genres of inquiry in design science research: justification and evaluation of knowledge production. MIS Quart. **39**(3), 541–564 (2015)

Towards a Collaborative, Interactive Web Services Composition Approach Based on an Intentional Group Recommender System

Meriem Kasmi[1(✉)], Yassine Jamoussi[1,2],
and Henda Hajjami Ben Ghézala[1]

[1] Riadi Lab, ENSI, University of Manouba, Manouba, Tunisia
{meriem.kasmi,yassine.jamoussi,
henda.benghezala}@ensi.rnu.tn
[2] Department of Computer Science, College of Science,
Sultan Qaboos University, 36 Al-Khoudh 123, Muscat, Oman

Abstract. Nowadays, organizations are integrating human-computer interaction (HCI) into their information systems. This trend resulted in gathering developers and end-users in different tasks, particularly, the interactive Web services composition (WSC) task. Indeed, to search for solutions that go beyond their individual limited views, an increasing demand of collaboration among users has emerged. However, they are still facing uncomfortable situations especially when they are invited to select the appropriate Web service among functionally similar ones. More support is then needed to provide an effective composition. In this regard, a group recommender system providing the required functionality while considering the users' preferences, might be highly useful. In this paper, we present a holistic process spanning from capturing users requirements, constructing a global goal model "ColMAP" reflecting their intentions to performing a collaborative, interactive WSC. A step-by-step example illustrates the proposed process. We expect that this approach will pave the way for interactively, collaboratively engineered information systems.

Keywords: Interactive Web services composition · Collaboration
Group recommendation · MAP formalism

1 Introduction and Motivation

With the focus on improving the interaction between humans and computers, the human-computer interaction (HCI) has become one of the most thriving fields in nowadays' computing era. It has become even an integral part of information systems with the aim of helping their users (e.g. developers, project managers, customers, partners, or investors) to be more productive [23]. In fact, HCI growth has brought an unprecedented momentum to information systems by giving non-professional users the opportunity to interact with the different components. This interaction takes place on the basis of a service-oriented architecture (SOA) since it is considered as a reference architecture of information systems. SOA promises to achieve high agility of businesses as well as rich interoperability between distributed and heterogeneous applications.

© Springer International Publishing AG, part of Springer Nature 2018
S. Chatterjee et al. (Eds.): DESRIST 2018, LNCS 10844, pp. 363–377, 2018.
https://doi.org/10.1007/978-3-319-91800-6_24

Thus, different actors have henceforth the luxury of interacting with, information systems' components, mainly Web services by composing them in an interactive way. This process is called the interactive Web services composition (WSC) and builds upon an appealing investigation of approaches from HCI and SOA [4].

Unlike the manual WSC which is restricted to experts, the interactive WSC that belongs also to the end-user programming approaches, involves tech-novice users which lowers the cognitive barrier on all types of users [27]. But, one can notice that even an automatic composition is quite suitable for users with no technical background. Such concern is entirely appropriate. Still, it is also clear that full automation would miss the chance for users' to be productive and to break new ground by fine-tuning services to their needs [6]. Overall, the interactive WSC com-bines the advantages of manual and automatic modes and resolves their particular issues.

Yet, to search for solutions that go beyond their individual limited views, an increasing demand of collaboration among users has emerged. Consequently, these latter often operate in groups to accomplish tasks which are not feasible individually because of lack of expertise or time. Collaboration is then a necessity in organizations, as no one can possess all the required competences. Our research stresses then the interactive WSC performed in collaborative situations. Thereby, the involved stakeholders will be able to explore the differences constructively and perform an effective composition.

However, because of the abundance of available Web services, users are facing various uncomfortable situations even when collaborating with each other. To February 2018, the largest Web services repository, ProgrammableWeb.com[1], has registered 19,163 Web services. Within this wealth, many are functionally equivalent. This hampers the composition process and leads to users' frustration as they find it notoriously difficult to select the appropriate Web service. More support is then required to manage such an abundance of choices, as well as to guide users with no technical background to perform the most relevant alternative. Traditional Web service discovery approaches tried to solve this problem by relying on UDDI (Universal Description, Discovery and Integration) registries. Unfortunately, UDDI is no longer the choice, since the shutdown of public UDDI registries held by IBM, Microsoft, and SAP [15]. Consequently, Web service discovery approaches have moved toward using Web services search engines and public Web services repositories such as ProgrammableWeb.com. These alternatives turned out to be also ineffective as they are heavily dependent on correct queries from users [25]. Moreover, personalization in terms of mapping content to users' interests and preferences is absent. This raised new challenges for information systems engineers to find a solution that handles the problem of information overload, filters and efficiently delivers the most relevant Web services. It would be even desirable if this solution recommends Web services that align with users' interests without requiring the users to explicitly specify queries. In this regard, a group recommender system (GRS) providing the required functionality while considering the users' preferences, might be highly useful. In fact, recommender systems have become a widely adopted means to tackle the problem of information

---

[1] https://www.programmableweb.com/.

overload, e.g. products on Amazon [9] and movies on Netflix [10]. They were primarily developed to support individuals, but, with the growing need of group work, more elaborate recommender systems targeting groups came into the picture under the name of GRSs. Today, GRSs are used in real-world applications as well as in different research fields. To the best of our knowledge, there is no existing work in the literature which has exploited the opportunity of joining the group recommendation with the interactive WSC. While it is true that the work of Rong et al. [24] has exploited the idea of user group in the context of WSC, it has not provided group recommendations. It has rather identified similar users to apply the association rule mining technique in a *"collaborative-filtering fashion"* in order to rank the discovered Web services.

Hence, given the highlighted need for collaboration in interactive WSC and inspired by the high relevance of recommender systems, we intend in this paper to embrace the benefits of group recommendation in a collaborative, interactive WSC performed by information systems' users. To address this challenge, we propose a new collaborative, interactive WSC approach based on an intentional GRS. We believe that this solution will create new opportunities to develop smart and personalized information systems. The suggested GRS capitalizes on a synergy between the functional needs deducted from a global intentional model "ColMAP" that we introduce and build in this paper, as well as the stakeholders' preferences in order to discover relevant Web services. Our approach reflects a holistic process spanning from capturing users requirements, constructing a global goal-oriented model reflecting their intentions to performing a collaborative, interactive WSC assisted by a GRS.

The contributions of this paper include:

(i) The consideration of multiple stakeholders and capturing their goals from their queries;
(ii) The construction of a global goal-oriented model ColMAP aggregating individual retrieved goals and based on the MAP formalism [2];
(iii) The automation of the Web services discovery step by a GRS in order to find the most relevant Web services;

The next section presents foundations for the WSC modeling adopted for this work and reviews existing modeling approaches. In Sect. 3, we expose our approach with an overview of its general phases then we detail these steps with a running example. Finally, we present conclusions and directions for future work in Sect. 4.

2 Web Services Composition Modeling

Diverse approaches to modeling WSC have been suggested in the literature. The work done in [12] provides a classification of these approaches into four main groups: industrial approaches (e.g., ones using WSBPEL[2] or BPEL for short), semantic approaches based on ontologies notably OWL-S[3] to describe Web services,

---

[2] https://www.oasis-open.org/committees/tc_home.php?wg_abbrev=wsbpel.
[3] http://www.ai.sri.com/daml/services/owl-s/.

quality-oriented approaches focusing on improving the quality of services and formal approaches using mathematic formalisms and models. These formal approaches include operational approaches such as Petri nets and intentional or goal-oriented approaches which are based on a representation of the WSC according to the service consumers' intentions. The first three groups focus on expressing Web services in a low-level manner through technical details (e.g., input/output parameters). Obviously, these latter are far from being understandable by end-users which represent an important category of actors in information systems. Moreover, in the analysis of complex organizations, it is more relevant to study first goals instead of functions. Business goals will be then realized by business processes which in turn will be implemented in the information system. Modeling business goals constitutes thus, a central activity of the business process as well as of information systems. Such recognition has led to a whole stream of research called Goal-Oriented Requirements Engineering (GORE). It is a subarea of Requirement Engineering, addressing the use of goals for requirements elicitation, specification, verification/validation and negotiation [11].

For these reasons, a high-level modeling of the WSC centered on goals appears to be the most suitable to our context. In this paper, we adopt an intentional modeling of WSC. Given that the intended WSC is performed in a collaborative way, we tried to find a collaborative intentional model to represent it. However much we searched in literature, we did not find any goal model that copes with our work. At the first glance, the work elaborated in [17] seemed to be suitable for modeling our collaborative composition in an intentional level. This work introduces a collaborative intentional model called CSRML (Collaborative Systems Requirements Modelling Language). It is in fact an extension of the i* goal model [18] and aims at dealing with collaborative systems in which the awareness of the presence of other users as well as their actions are crucial. But, a closer look has revealed that we cannot choose such a model. In fact, collaborative plans evolve, and systems must be able to cope with any evolution e.g., involvement of a new actor, exclusion of an existing actor, change in actor's business process, etc. In CSRML, supporting such an evolutive, dynamic aspect is absent and can be done only manually by rebuilding the whole model.

Consequently, in this work, we argue for the idea of modeling individual intentions with a relevant goal model then aggregating these individual models into a collaborative one. In this way, any change that might occur can be easily embodied in individual model. Regarding the collaborative model, it will be automatically generated again by aggregation. Various goal models have been provided by the GORE community. The most popular ones are i* [18], TROPOS [19], KAOS [20], the Goal-oriented Requirement Language (GRL) [21] and the MAP formalism [2]. These models share interesting features such as expressiveness and understandability but regarding the variability support, MAP outperforms all other goal models [26]. In fact, MAP gives a multitude of paths between two intentions. Each path corresponds to a strategy to achieve the target goal from the source one. This explicit representation of variability offered by MAP is missing in other goal models. MAP has been also successfully used in previous works on modeling Web services-based applications [13, 14]. We give in the following an overview of the MAP formalism, on which our intentional global model, ColMAP, is based.

2.1 MAP Overview

MAP was proposed by Rolland et al. [2]. Its main objective is to describe processes in an intentional level. Graphically, it is represented as a labeled directed graph. The nodes correspond to intentions or goals and edges are labeled with strategies. A strategy refers to the manner a target goal is achieved from the source one. This explains why this graph should and labeled with the name of the strategy. MAP offers the possibility to follow different strategies to achieve intentions. Figure 1 shows the metamodel of MAP. As depicted in Fig. 1, the fundamental elements of MAP are Intentions, Strategies and Sections. Each section is a triplet <Ii, Ij, Sij> formed by one source intention Ii, one target intention Ij and only one edge Sij linking them. A MAP model is then based on a multitude of sections. Three types of relationships exist between sections namely bundle, multi-thread and path. Figure 2 illustrates these three relationships.

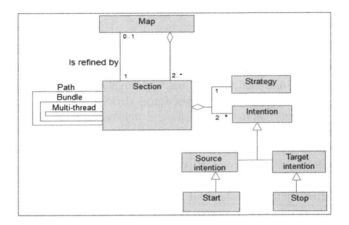

Fig. 1. The MAP metamodel

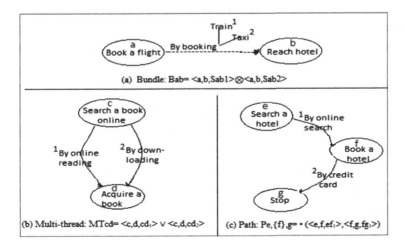

Fig. 2. Relationships between sections in MAP

In both bundle and multi-thread relationships, sections share the same source and target intentions. But in a bundle, only one strategy can be used to accomplish the target intention. Sections are then mutually exclusive in a bundle related by the logic function XOR using the operator «⊗». Graphically, a bundle is evinced by a dotted arrow. As for a multi-thread relationship, the target intention can be achieved from a source in many different ways. So, sections in a multi-thread can be executed simultaneously. They are related by the logic function AND/OR and represented by the operator «∨». Finally, a path relationship relies on a precedence/succession relationship. In this relationship, a target intention in a section, is a source one in another. It is represented by the operator "•". We note that it is possible to refine a section at level i into another MAP model at level i+1. The MAP model of level i+1 corresponds to a complex assembly of sections viewed as a unique section at level i.

In this paper, we adopt an intentional WSC modeling based on MAP. We specify each section within the MAP model by an Intentional Service Model (ISM) detailed in the following.

2.2   ISM Overview

Figure 3 was suggested by Rolland in [5] to abstract software Web services into intentional services. Since then, the ISM has been highly investigated. An intentional service corresponds to the intentional descriptors derived from users' queries. ISM focuses then on the intention to accomplish rather than on the functionality to perform. As shown in Fig. 3, there are three different aspects to consider in the description of an intentional service, namely the intentional service interface, behavior and composition. First aspect reflects that an intentional service satisfies an intention, given an initial situation and terminating in a final situation. Intention corresponds to the intentional service id, whereas Initial Situation and Final Situation are the IN/OUT parameters. Second, the behavioral aspect is specified through pre and post conditions. They are initial and final states respectively describing the required state to start accomplishing an intentional and the resulting state after achieving it. Finally, the composition part defines intentional services as aggregate or atomic services. An Atomic service corresponds to an operationalized section i.e. it cannot be refined. An Aggregate service is associated with a high level section that should be refined to the lowest possible level.

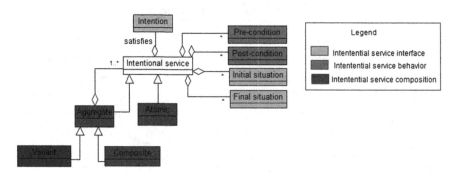

Fig. 3. The intentional service model

Aggregate services can be either Composite or Variant. Composite services can be generated according to a sequential, parallel, or iterative arrangement. As for Variant services, they express variability with alternatives and multi-choice.

3 The Proposed Approach

3.1 Approach Overview

In this paper, we propose a new interactive, collaborative WSC approach based on an intentional group recommender system. An overview of the proposed approach is shown in Fig. 4. It covers the four common WSC phases: the Planning phase, the Service Discovery phase, the Service Selection phase, and the Execution phase [8].

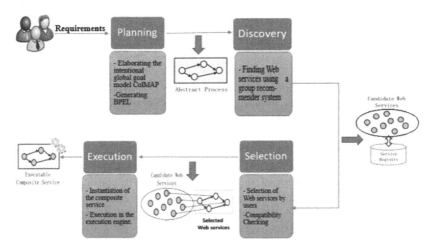

Fig. 4. Overview of the proposed approach

The planning phase determines the execution order of activities. In our approach, we opted for an intentional modeling of the WSC. Thus, to determine and coordinate activities, planning starts with a goal-oriented analysis of the stakeholders' requirements. This results in a set of partial individual intentions/strategies graphs for each stakeholder using the MAP formalism. Intentional services are then identified and specified for each section according to the ISM. Next, individual graphs are com- posed in a global goal model "ColMAP". Finally, a transformational operation from the intentional level to the operational level is carried out through the technique of model transformation. A BPEL abstract process model is produced.

The discovery phase finds the candidate services for each activity. In other words, it finds concrete components (Web services) that match the activities of the abstract process produced by the previous phase. Suitable Web services are located by searching the service registry. In our approach, this phase will be carried out by a GRS that considers two dimensions. On the one hand, it recommends Web services that match users' intentions derived from the intentional specification provided by ISM.

That is why, we call this GRS, an intentional GRS. On the other hand, this GRS recommends Web services according to each group preferences. Thus, recommended Web services will not only match their goals but also their interests inferred from their profiles which include explicit and implicit feedback (i.e. the provided ratings as well as the Web services invocation rates). It is noteworthy that GRSs have never been exploited in the SOC field.

During the third phase, users are invited to choose one Web service for each activity from the set of the recommended Web services. These latter will be provided in a clear and organized view to enable users to easily pick relevant Web services. The compatibility between selected Web services will be checked by a module for compatibility checking.

Finally, after all the required Web services are identified and bound to the corresponding activities, the composite service instance will be created and executed by the execution engine.

3.2   Detailed Process

We present details of the intended composition process spanning from capturing users requirements, constructing a global goal-oriented model leveraging all users' intentions to performing a collaborative, interactive WSC. The proposed process is illustrated with a step-by-step example from a clinical information system. In fact, with the move towards computerization, concepts such as "paperless hospitals" and "digital hospitals" are becoming widespread. Consequently, in hospitals, departments are increasingly using IT tools. We focus on the emergency department and give an example of a simplified patient care process in this department. Before, considerable time was wasted transmitting documents, namely patients' records from one stakeholder to another. In addition, some activities are distributed between departments which raised a data heterogeneity problem. Moreover, patients' records are written collaboratively by different stokeholds. It would be therefore useful to set up a collaborative solution in such a department. Applying our approach in such an environment is then quite appropriate.

Step 1. Pre-generating ColMAP. Every software development process starts with the phase of requirements analysis. This step results in a software requirements specification including functional and non-functional requirements. We note that non-functional requirements are out of the scope of this paper and that we focus mainly on functional requirements which are nothing else than users' intentions. Thus, unclear users' queries will result in improperly translating their intentions. However, we cannot expect from non-expert users to be always able to clearly express their intentions. Hence, we intend to provide them with a convenient interface showing intentions ranged by domain-specific categories e.g. travel, education, healthcare, etc. After successfully logging, users select intentions and the associated partial MAP models will be loaded. We note that MAP models should be already drawn by domain experts using an appropriate tool such as MetaEdit+[4].

---

[4] https://www.metacase.com/mep/ .

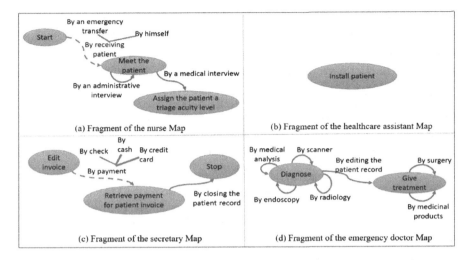

Fig. 5. Partial MAP models for a patient care scenario in a hospital emergency department

Figure 5 represents fragments of the partial MAP models of stakeholders involved in a scenario of patient care in an emergency department. This scenario gathers four roles: the Emergency doctor role, the nurse role, the secretary role and the assistant healthcare role. Once a patient arrives, a nurse will meet him/her to assess his/her triage acuity level. A healthcare assistant will then install him/her then the emergency doctor diagnoses and decides what treatment(s) to give. Finally, the patient will pay the cost for medical examinations he/she had.

Next, to elicit intentional services associated to each section of partial MAP models, we follow three rules [5]:

- R1. Associating every non-refined section to an atomic service. In the context of our example, we can associate 15 atomic services in total to the four individual MAP models of Fig. 5. For instance: The section <Edit invoice, Retrieve payment for patient invoice, By payment: By credit card> $\rightarrow$ $S_{\text{pay: By credit card}}$
- R2. Identifying paths of the partial MAP models by applying an adaptation of the Mc Naughton and Yamada's algorithm [3].
- R3. Determining aggregate services by establishing the following guidelines:

• Associate to sections in a bundle section an alternative intentional service. For example: $S_{\text{Meet the patient}} \rightarrow S_{\text{Meet the patient:: By himself}} \otimes S_{\text{Meet the patient: By an emergency transfer}}$
• Associate to sections in a multi-thread relationship, a multi-choice intentional ser-vices.
• Associate to sections in a path relationship, a sequential intentional service.

Step 2. Generating ColMAP. We define ColMAP as an extension of the MAP model in order to support collaboration. It is generated by composing partial MAP models through their potential dependencies. In the following, we give insight about the dependency concept and detail the ColMAP generation task.

Definition 1 MAP Models Dependency. Two MAP models are dependent if it exists at least one intention from the first which is dependent on one intention of the other.

Definition 2 Intentions Dependency. Let a section <x, i, S_{xi}> associated to an intentional service $Serv_{xi}$ from a MAP model m1 and a section <j, y, S_{jy}> associated to an intentional service $Serv_{jy}$ from a MAP model m2. i and j are dependent if it exists at least one intentional service $Serv_{ij}$ where: (i) $Serv_{ij}$.Pre-condition.value = $Serv_{xi}$. Post-condition.value and (ii) $Serv_{ij}$.Post-condition.value = $Serv_{jy}$.Pre-condition.value. In a MAP model, all intentions forming a section are dependent.

The ColMAP generation task starts by determining dependencies between two MAP models then arranges these dependencies.

Dependencies Determination. This task takes as input two partial MAP models as well as their elicited intentional descriptors (intentional services). These descriptors are contained in .xmi files obtained by instantiating the ISM using Kermeta[5]. For instance, the .xmi file of the intentional service $S_{pay:\ By\ credit\ card}$ is defined as:

```
<?xml version="1.0" encoding="ASCII"?>
<ism:Map xmi:version="2.0"
xmlns:xmi="http://www.omg.org/XMI"
xmlns:xsi="http://www.w3.org/2001/XMLSchema-instance"
xmlns:ism="http://ism/1.0"
xsi:schemaLocation="http://ism/1.0 ISM.ecore">
<service xsi:type="ism:Atomic"
intention="//@Intention.0"
pre_condition="//@Pre-Condition.0"
post_condition="//@Post-Condition.0"
initial_situation="//@Initial Situation.0"
final_situation="//@Final Situation.0"
id="Pay: By credit card "/>
<Intention description="Payment by credit card"/>
<Pre-Condition value="Invoice.Edit=true"/>
<Post-Condition value="Payment.State=true"/>
<resource name="Invoice"/>
<resource name="Payment"/>
<resource name="Card"/>
<Initial Situation input="//@resource.0 //@resource.2"/>
<Final Situation output="//@resource.1"/>
</ism:Map>
```

Dependencies are determined by mining the .xmi files of the different intentional services of the two MAP models. If any intentions dependency is found then these two MAP models are considered dependent. If exactly one intentional service is found for

---

[5] https://marketplace.eclipse.org/content/kermeta.

this dependency, then a section joining the two dependent intentions is formed. Otherwise, a dependencies arrangement task must be carried out.

Dependencies Arrangement Let n: the number of intentional services found for the dependency determination task between the intentions i and j. Thus, n sections must be formed between i and j. These sections can be: (i) All in a bundle relationship, (ii) All in a multi-thread relationship or (iii) some of them in a bundle and others in a multi-thread relationship. To resolve this, we argue for a naming convention regarding intentional services in a bundle relationship. These latter must have exactly the same words before the ":" symbol for their ids. In the context of our example, the id of $S_{pay:By\ credit\ card}$ must be "Pay:ByCreditCard" and the id of $S_{pay:By\ cash}$ must be "Pay:ByCash".

Thus, the intentional services for which this convention is validated are arranged in a bundle relationship while others join a multi-thread relationship. Figure 6 represents the generated ColMAP associated to the studied example.

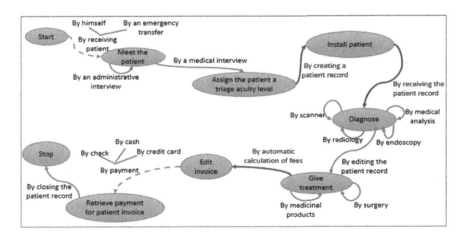

Fig. 6. The generated ColMAP model

Step 3. Generating BPEL. BPEL is a reliable standard in modeling and executing business processes. It is the most used language for orchestration in industry. With the advent of SOA, services are henceforth exploited to implement process tasks. Therefore, this justifies our choice for BPEL. Inspired by [7], we opt for a model transformation from the ISM to BPEL following the transformation rules reported in Table 1. The generated BPEL model is not executable. It is called an abstract BPEL model.

Step 4. Discovering Web Services Now that the planning phase is achieved, the Web services that operationalize intentional services must be discovered. However, a variety of potentially interesting Web services can match the required functionality. Therefore, the discovered set of Web services must be reduced. For this reason, we designed an intentional GRS. In fact, GRSs have proved to deal effectively with a large datasets and to retrieve useful items that are estimated to be collectively convenient for groups of users.

Table 1. Transformation rules from ISM to BPEL.

ISM Element	BPEL element
Atomic service	Invoke
Initial situation	Receive
Final situation	Reply
Pre-condition; Post-condition	Assign
Sequential composition	Sequence
Parallel composition	Flow
Iterative composition	while
Alternative variation	Switch, if, else
Multi-choice variation	Pick

To start, the system queries the Web services registry using keywords extracted from the .xmi files of the intentional services. These keywords are determined using the TF/IDF metric. Readers may refer to [1] for further details about this metric. TF/IDF allows us to filter out stop and low frequency words. Thereby, only meaningful words (i.e., keywords) having a high TF/IDF weight are maintained. As a result, a set of Web services will be returned. It is likely that a large number of candidate services will meet the requirements. Therefore, the GRS intervenes to reduce this number. It operates a two-level filtration.

In the first level, based on a semantic matchmaking between the .xmi files of the intentional services and the WSDL files of the returned Web services. This first filtration level generates a new reduced set to filter in a second filtration level according to users' preferences. To do so, the recommendation strategy as well as the approach to generating recommendations must be specified.

Current GRSs mainly falls into two categories based on the way recommendations are generated. The first category consists in aggregating individual models into group models. It merges individual user models into a group model and then generates recommendations using the aggregated group model. The second one aggregates individual recommendations already generated user, into group recommendation. Motivated by results of Berkovsky and Freyne [16] about comparing these two methods, we opt for the individual models aggregation method in this work. Individual models refer to rating matrices containing the users' ratings to the Web services they used. Obviously, such matrices are sparse due to the huge number of Web services compared to users. Thus, for pre-processing, we need to conduct rating matrix completion in order to estimate the individuals' preferences on the unseen items. For this, we adopt for matrix completion [22]. Next, the preferences (ratings and predictions) are aggregated with a specific aggregation strategy such as the average. We note that the aggregation strategy is not defined yet in this work. We intend to choose it during an experimentation phase.

Recommendations will be generated for each group of users performing the same role. In our example, given that we have four roles, we will have naturally four groups including different numbers of individuals performing the same role. The proposed GRS relies on a hybrid recommendation approach combining collaborative filtering and content-based recommendation. In the former, users are recommended items that like-minded users preferred in the past whilst in the latter, they are recommended items similar to the ones they liked before. We adopt a hybrid approach since it helps to avoid shortcomings of both content-based and collaborative approaches and incorporates the advantages of these two methods. Therefore, the final set of discovered Web services is produced after this filtration according to preferences.

Step 5. Selecting Web Services. In a context of an interactive WSC, this step is done by the users through a dedicated interface presenting possible alternatives (Web services) for each elementary goal. Users are then invited to pick one Web service per goal. However, the Web services incompatibility is amongst the common issues that may emerge in the design and implementation of WSC. The WSC process is a coordinated and collaborative service invocation task including several multi-service workflows. These interacting workflows can be constructed using various emerging standards to manage the Web services compatibility. If two services are not compatible, a warning message will be displayed informing users of the problem and suggesting other compatible service(s) for the predecessor service.

Step 6. Execution of the WSC. Once the Web services are fully selected, an executable BPEL model will implement at the abstract BPEL model with the selected services. It will be deployed in a composition engine and the composition will be executed. Finally, users will be invited to rate the composition process. This explicit feed- back helps to refine the future recommendations.

4   Conclusion

In this work, we explored how an interactive WSC can be effectively combined with a GRS in collaborative scenarios. This kind of composition is receiving a lot of attention in recent years, as it enables end-users to perform an active role in the composition process. As for group recommendation, it has never been exploited before for suggesting Web services. Therefore, we offer a unique approach for collaborative, interactive WSC where the composed Web services do not only satisfy the business needs but also the collective "taste" of the group. Moreover, in this paper, we set the goal of bridging the gap between intentional and operational level by generating a global goal model from individual MAP models and matching intentional services with their software equivalent ones.

We are currently working on a prototype to validate it. Afterwards, we intend to conduct a user study which compares in a qualitative and quantitative way how the proposed solution improves the service composition process. We are planning also to extend to support a conflict resolution process when users of the same group do not pick the same Web service. Thus, we are considering the use of a module that resolves this conflict and promotes more successful collaboration between stakeholders.

References

1. Salton, G., Buckley, C.: Term-weighting approaches in automatic text retrieval. Inf. Process. Manag. **24**(5), 513–523 (1988)
2. Rolland, C., Loucopoulos, P., Kavakli, V., Nurcan, S.: Intention based modelling of organisational change: an experience report. In: Proceedings of the 4th CAISE/IFIP 8.1 International Workshop on Evaluation of Modeling Methods in Systems Analysis and Design, Heidelberg, pp. 1–36 (1999)
3. McNaughton, R., Yamada, H.: Regular expressions and state graphs for automata. IRE Trans. Electron. Comput. **EC-9**(1), 39–47 (1960)
4. Liang, Q., Bharadwaj, A., Lee, B.S.: Interactive and iterative service-composition-based approach to flexible information system development. Int. J. Web Serv. Res. **8**(4), 81–107 (2011). https://doi.org/10.4018/jwsr.2011100104
5. Rolland, C., Kaabi, R-S.: An intentional perspective to service modeling and discovery. In: Proceedings of the 31st International Computer Software and Applications Conference (COMPSAC), Beijing, pp. 455–460 (2007)
6. Mehandjiev, N., Lécué, F., Wajid, U., Namoun, A.: Assisted service composition for end users. In: Proceedings of the 8th IEEE European Conference on Web Services (ECOWS), Ayia Napa, pp. 131–138 (2010)
7. Driss, M., Jamoussi, Y., Moha, N., Jézéquel, J.M., Ghézala, H.H.B.: Une approche centrée exigences pour la composition de services web. Revue des Sciences et Technologies de l'Information-Série ISI: Ingénierie des Systèmes d'Information **16**(2), 97–125 (2011)
8. Claro, D.B., Albers, P., Hao, J.-K.: Web services composition. In: Cardoso, J., Sheth, A. P. (eds.) Semantic Web Services, Processes and Applications, pp. 195–225. Springer, New York (2006)
9. Smith, B., Linden, G.: Two decades of recommender systems at Amazon.com. IEEE Internet Comput. **21**(3), 12–18 (2017)
10. Gomez-Uribe, C.A., Hunt, N.: The netflix recommender system: algorithms, business value, and innovation. ACM Trans. Manag. Inf. Syst. **6**(4), Article no. 13, 19 p. (2015). https://doi. org/10.1145/2843948
11. van Lamsweerde, A.: Goal-oriented requirements engineering: a guided tour. In: Proceedings of the 5th International Symposium on Requirements Engineering (RE), pp. 249–263. IEEE, Toronto (2001)
12. Ben Messaoud, W., Ghedira, K., Ben Halima, Y., Ben Ghezala, H.: Survey of web service composition. In: Proceedings of the 5th International Conference on Information & Communication Technology and Accessibility (ICTA), pp. 1–7 (2015)
13. Aljoumaa, K., Assar, S., Souveyet, C.: Publishing intentional services using extended semantic annotation. In: Proceedings of the 5th International Conference on Research Challenges in Information Science (RCIS), pp. 1–9. IEEE, Gosier (2011)
14. Rolland, C., Kirsch-Pinheiro, M., Souveyet, C.: An intentional approach to service engineering. IEEE Trans. Serv. Comput. **3**(4), 292–305 (2010)
15. Krill, P.: Microsoft, IBM, SAP Discontinue UDDI Registry Effort (2005). https://www. infoworld.com/article/2673442/application-development/microsoft–ibm–sap-discontinue-uddi-registry-effort.html. Accessed 22 Feb 2018
16. Berkovsky, S., Freyne, J.: Group-based recipe recommendations: analysis of data aggregation strategies. In: Proceedings of the 4th ACM conference on Recommender systems (RecSys), pp. 111–118. ACM, New York (2010). https://doi.org/10.1145/1864708. 1864732

17. Teruel, M.A., Navarro, E., López-Jaquero, V., Montero, F.: CSRML: a goal-oriented approach to model requirements for collaborative systems. In: Jeusfeld, M., Delcambre, L., Ling, T.W. (eds.) Conceptual Modeling (ER) 2011. LNCS, vol. 6998, pp. 33–46. Springer, Heidelberg (2011)

18. Castro, J., Kolp, M., Mylopoulo, J.: A requirements-driven development methodology. In: Dittrich, K.R., Geppert, A., Norrie, M.C. (eds.) Advanced Information Systems Engineering (CAISE) 2001, pp. 108–123. Springer, London (2001). https://doi.org/10.1007/3-540-45341-5_8

19. Bresciani, P., Perini, A., Giorgini, P., Giunchiglia, F., Mylopoulos, J.: Tropos: an agent-oriented software development methodology. Auton. Agents Multi-Agent Syst. **8**(3), 203–236 (2004)

20. van Lamsweerde, A., Letier, E.: Handling obstacles in goal oriented requirements engineering. IEEE Trans. Softw. Eng. **26**(10), 978–1005 (2000)

21. University of Toronto, Canada; GRL-Goal-oriented Requirement Language. http://www.cs.toronto.edu/km/GRL/. Accessed 21 Nov 2017

22. Kang, Z., Peng, C., Cheng, Q.: Top-N recommender system via matrix completion. In: Proceedings of the 30th AAAI Conference on Artificial Intelligence (AAAI), pp. 179–185 (2016)

23. Carey, J., Galletta, D.F., Kim, Y., Te'eni, D., Wildemuth, B., Zhang, P.: The role of human computer interaction in management information systems curricula: a call to action. Commun. Assoc. Inf. Syst. **13**(1), 357–379 (2004)

24. Rong, W., Liu, K., Liang, L.: Personalized web service ranking via user group combining association rule. In: Proceedings of the 7th IEEE International Conference on Web Services (ICWS), pp. 445–452 (2009)

25. Yao, L., Sheng, Q.Z., Ngu, A.H., Yu, J., Segev, A.: Unified collaborative and content-based web service recommendation. IEEE Trans. Serv. Comput. **8**(3), 453–466 (2015)

26. Driss, M., Moha, N., Jamoussi, Y., Jézéquel, J.-M., Ben Ghézala, H.H.: A requirement-centric approach to web service modeling, discovery, and selection. In: Maglio, P.P., Weske, M., Yang, J., Fantinato, M. (eds.) ICSOC 2010. LNCS, vol. 6470, pp. 258–272. Springer, Heidelberg (2010). https://doi.org/10.1007/978-3-642-17358-5_18

27. Cao, J., Fleming, S. D., Burnett, M.: An exploration of design opportunities for "gardening" end-user programmers' ideas. In: Proceedings of IEEE Symposium on Visual Languages and Human-Centric Computing (VL/HCC), pp. 35–42. IEEE (2011)

Author Index

Printed in the United States
By Bookmasters